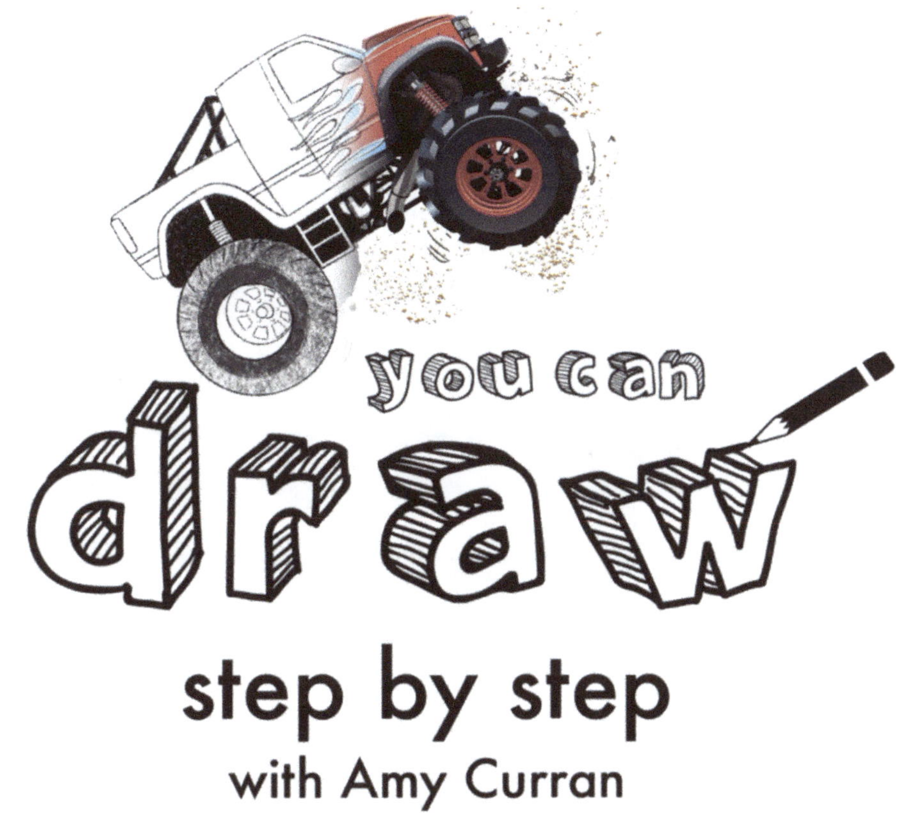


# step by step

## with Amy Curran

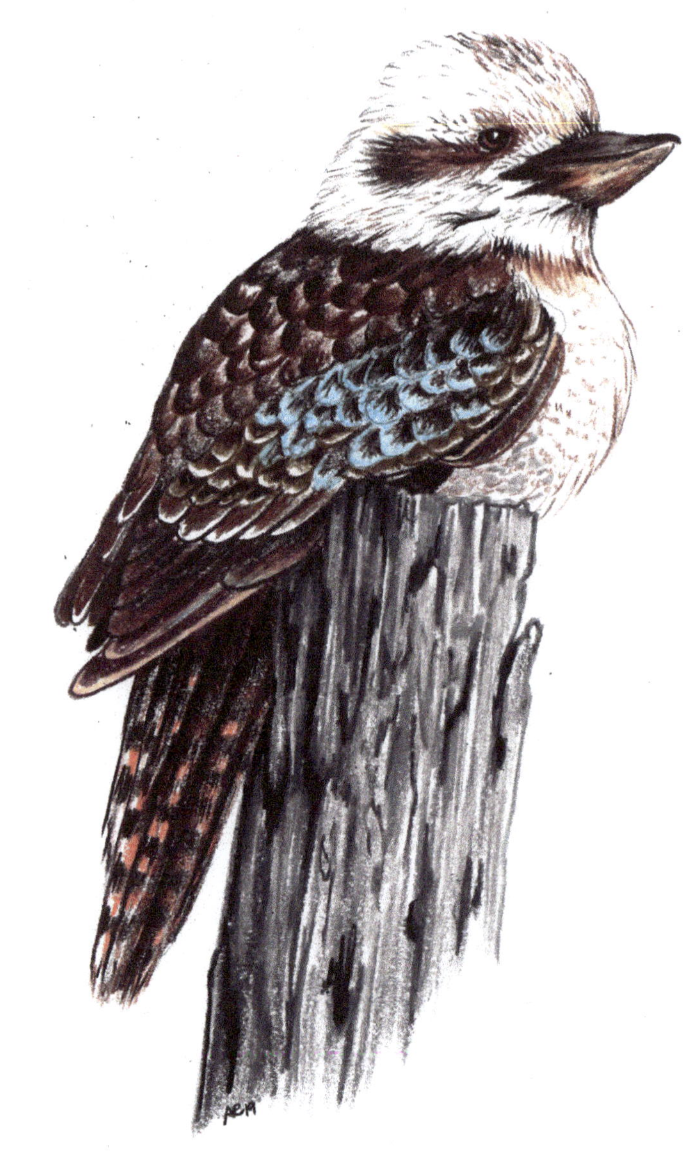

***Kookaburra - Coloured Pencil - Amy Curran***

YOU CAN DRAW: STEP BY STEP WITH AMY CURRAN
ISBN: 978-0-6484496-9-0

Published in Australia by
PINK COFFEE PUBLISHING
PO Box 483, Oberon NSW 2787



National Library of Australia Cataloguing-in-Publication entry information can be found at www.nla.gov.au

# Introduction

Hey! If you're reading this book, chances are you like to draw, whether it's doodling away on random pieces of paper, or sketching out more detailed ideas and subjects.

You may be a complete beginner to drawing techniques, or you may have already attended art classes. Wherever you are at, this book is sure to provide some valuable information.

This book is not targeted at a specific age group, rather it is developed on skill level, meaning children and adults alike can enjoy the process.

Start at the beginning of this book, and work your way through. As you progress, the drawings get more complex.

A common misconception is that drawing is a talent given to a select few. The truth is that anyone can learn to draw. All you have to do is get started, gain some knowledge about the basic skills needed, and practice, practice, practice.

Drawing is fun, relaxing and when you are able to put onto paper something that has been in your head you will feel a tremendous sense of satisfaction and achievement.

Amy 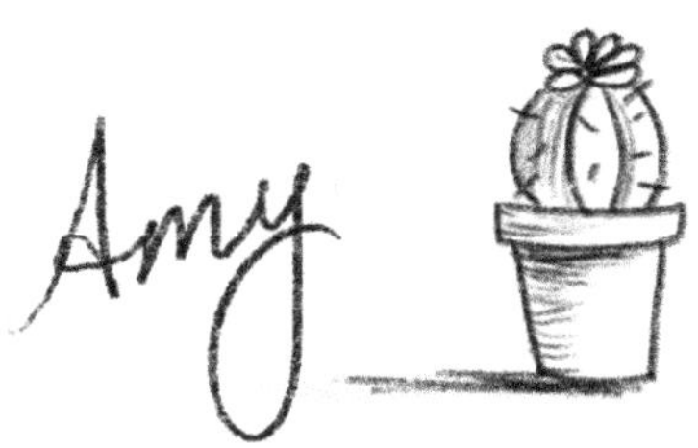

# Dedication

This book is for anyone who has the urge to put pencil to paper. Drawing is a learned skill, I truly believe anyone can draw when given the right tools.

I need to thank my after school class students and my own children for their help with this book. Trying out the tutorials, telling me which steps to take out or when more were needed and being my biggest encouragement.

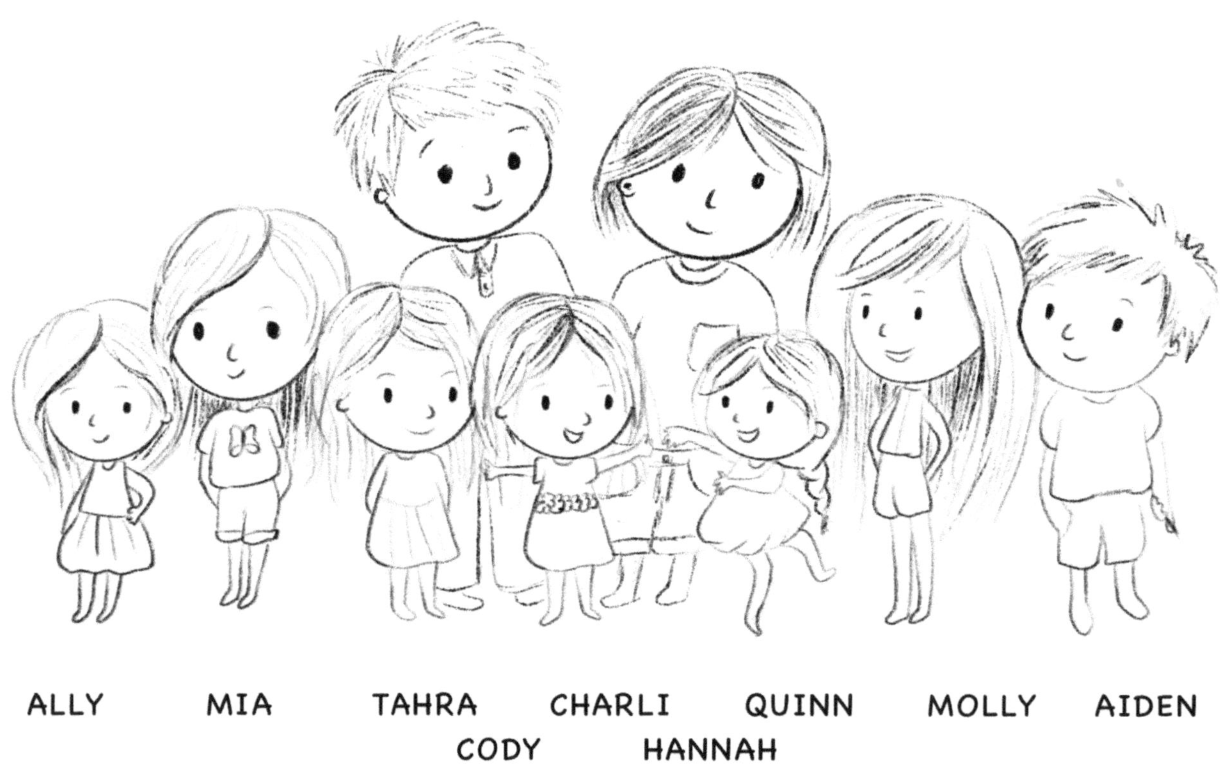

ALLY      MIA      TAHRA      CHARLI      QUINN      MOLLY      AIDEN
CODY      HANNAH

Term 4 After School group, Oberon 2020

# Contents

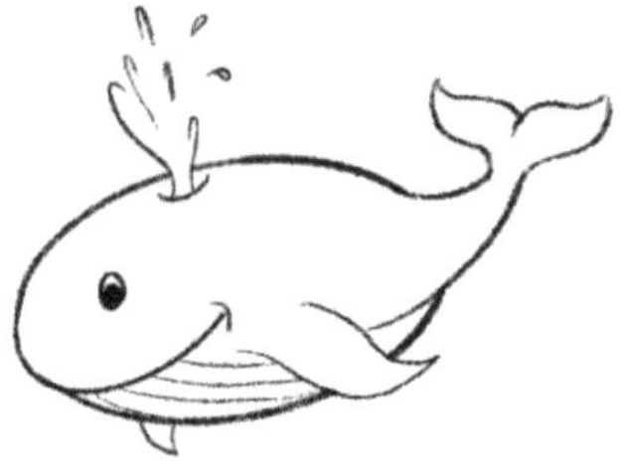

DRAWING TUTORIALS - Level 2

DRAWING TUTORIALS - Level 3



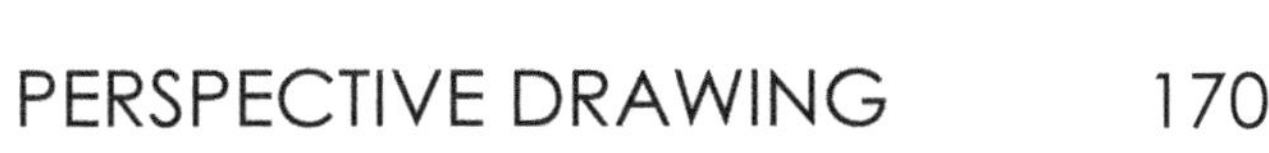

# About the Artist

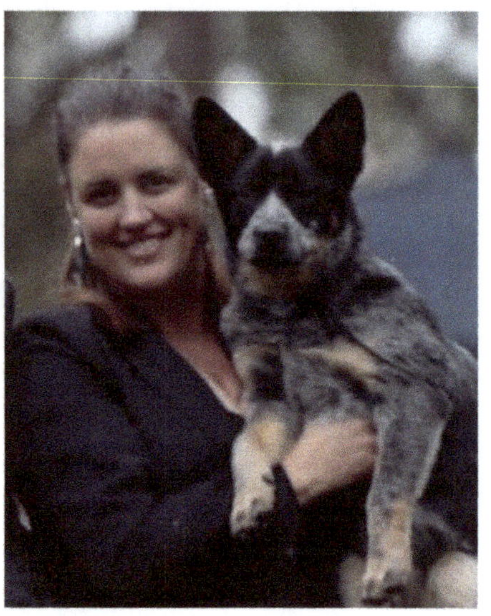

Amy Curran is an Australian Artist who to date has illustrated eighteen children's books. She graduated with a Distinction in the Diploma in Children's Book Illustration from the London Art College.

Amy teaches after school art classes each term in her local area as well as online classes for students all over Australia.

Amy's methods are simple and easy to follow, and her students regularly enjoy success in art competitions.

Amy's favourite things to draw and paint are dogs, horses, cats and Australian fauna.

Website: www.amycurran.com.au

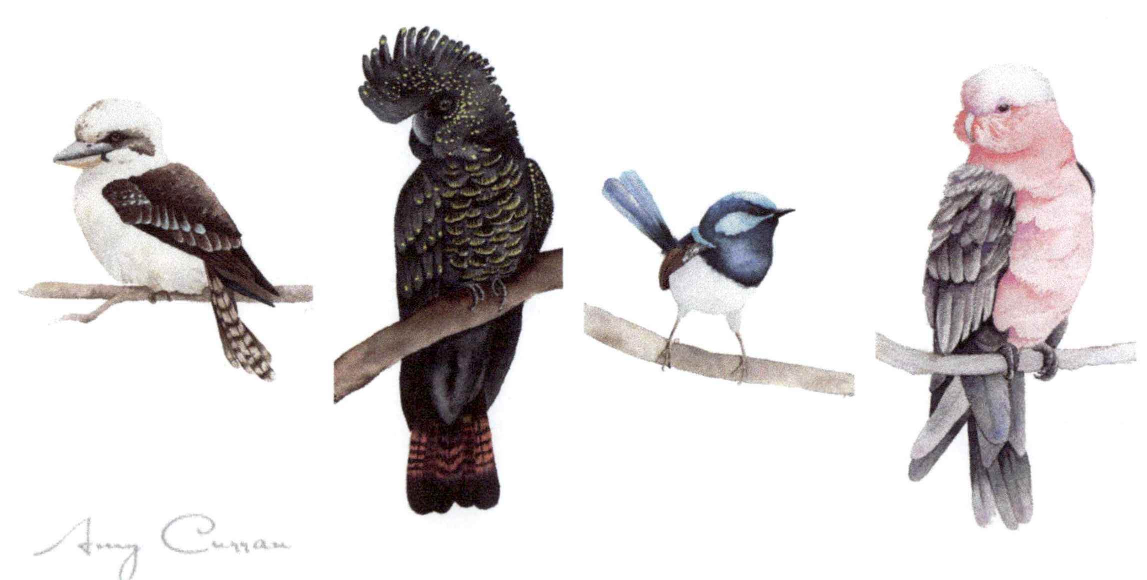

# What you will need

All of the activities in the book require only a lead pencil, an eraser and some plain paper. You should also have a pencil sharpener.

I recommend that you draw the guidelines lightly so they can be easily erased and then the final drawing can be defined with darker pencil lines.

As you progress to shading your drawings I suggest the following grades of pencils; 4H, 2H, HB, 2B, 4B and 6B.

Most importantly, enjoy the process and your journey.

Let's get started!

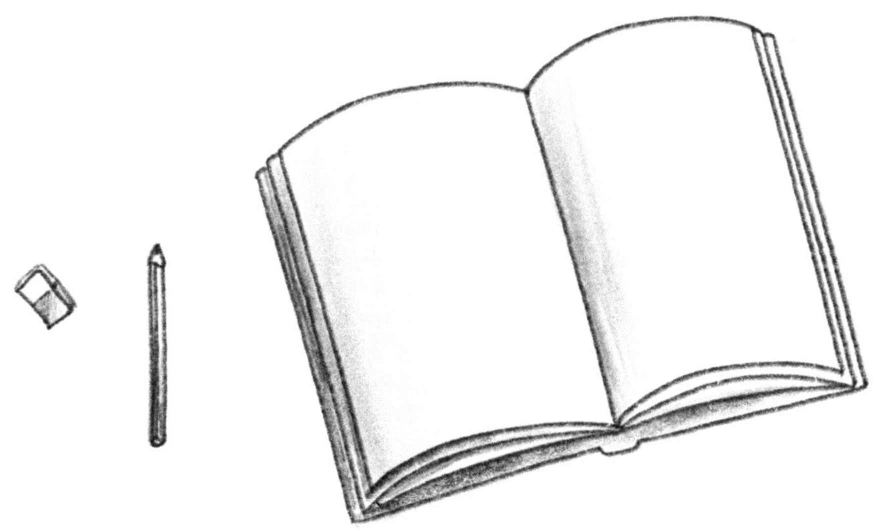

# Basic principles

Every drawing is made up of two things... **shapes** and **lines.** That's it!

You don't believe me do you? You will by the end of this book. To begin though, we need to practice basic shapes and lines. Grab your pencil and paper and let's begin. Have a look at the different lines below and draw a full page of them, all directions!

Straight lines ————————

Dotted lines  — — — ...... — — —

Squiggly lines ∿

Jagged lines ∧∧∧∧∧∧∧

Now, let's do some shapes. Draw a full page of the shapes below, all sizes and all directions.

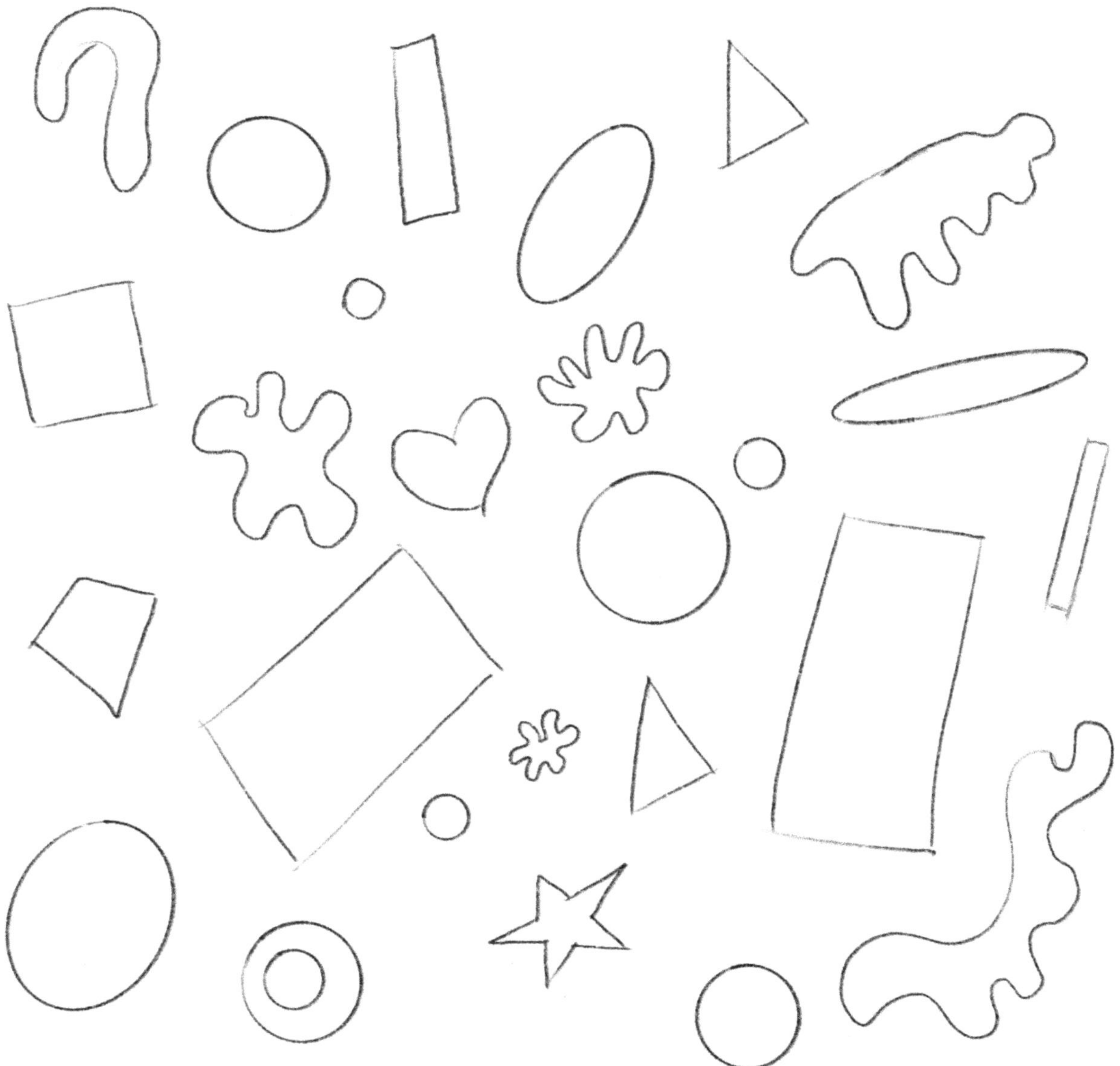

Practice whenever you can, the more you practice the smoother your lines will become and the more even your shapes will be.

# See the World as an Artist

Every thing you can see can be broken down into basic shapes and lines.

Have a look around you at the simple objects in your house first.

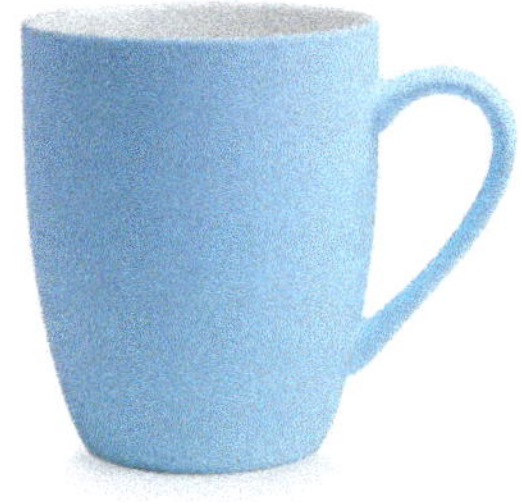 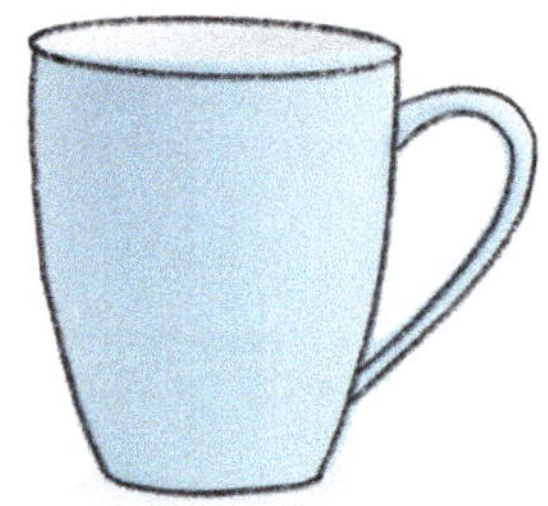 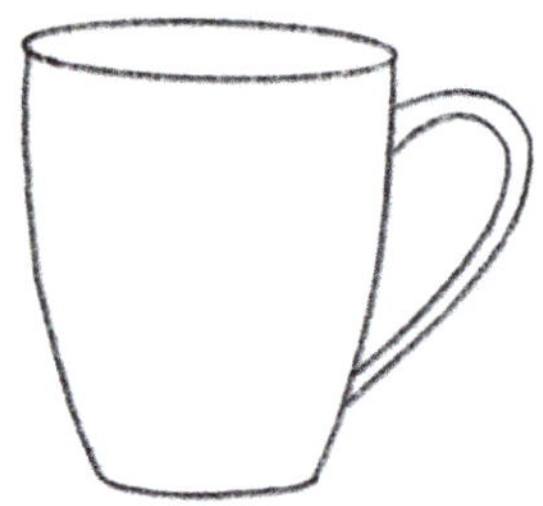

Look at the mug. Can you see it can be broken down into an oval and some lines?

 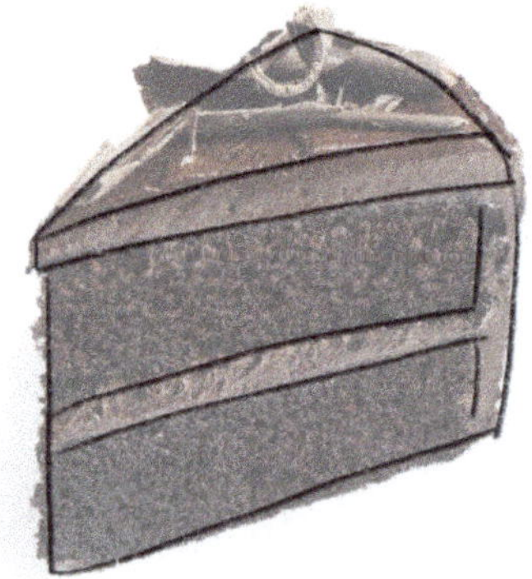 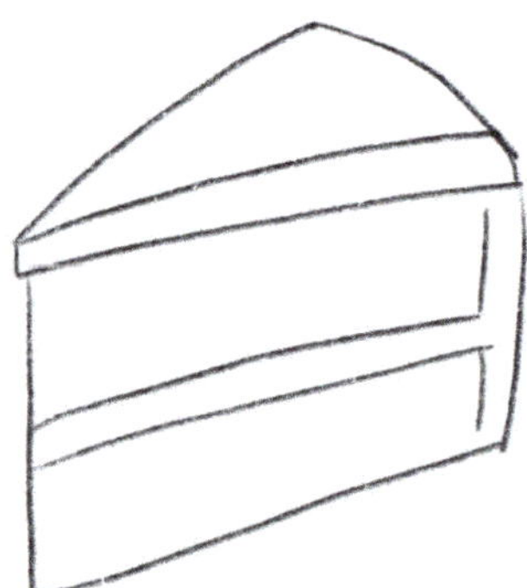

What about this piece of chocolate cake? Just triangles really!

# Drawing tutorials

Let's start the tutorials! Grab a lead pencil, an eraser and some plain paper. You should also have a pencil sharpener.

Each tutorial is step by step, draw the lines lightly though so you can erase them when you define the final picture.

As you progress through the book, the tutorials increase in detail and difficulty.

Start with basic shapes and lines

Let go of perfection

Connect the shapes

Add the detail

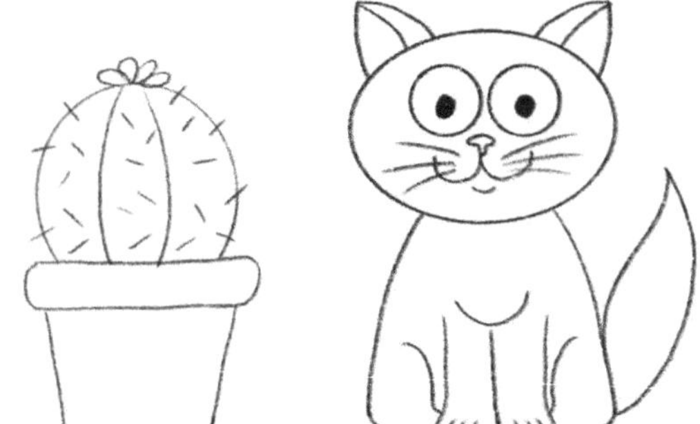

# Level One

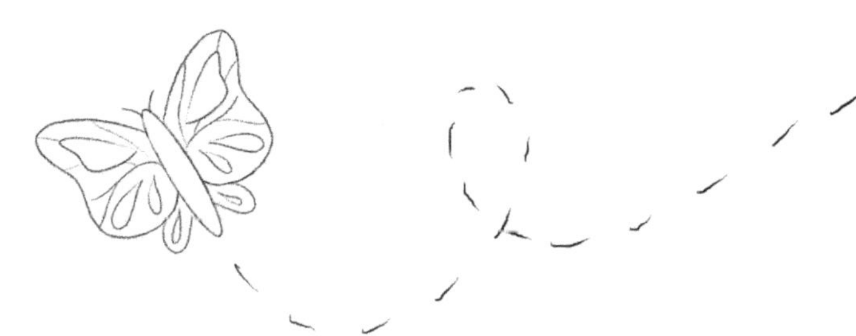

# Bee

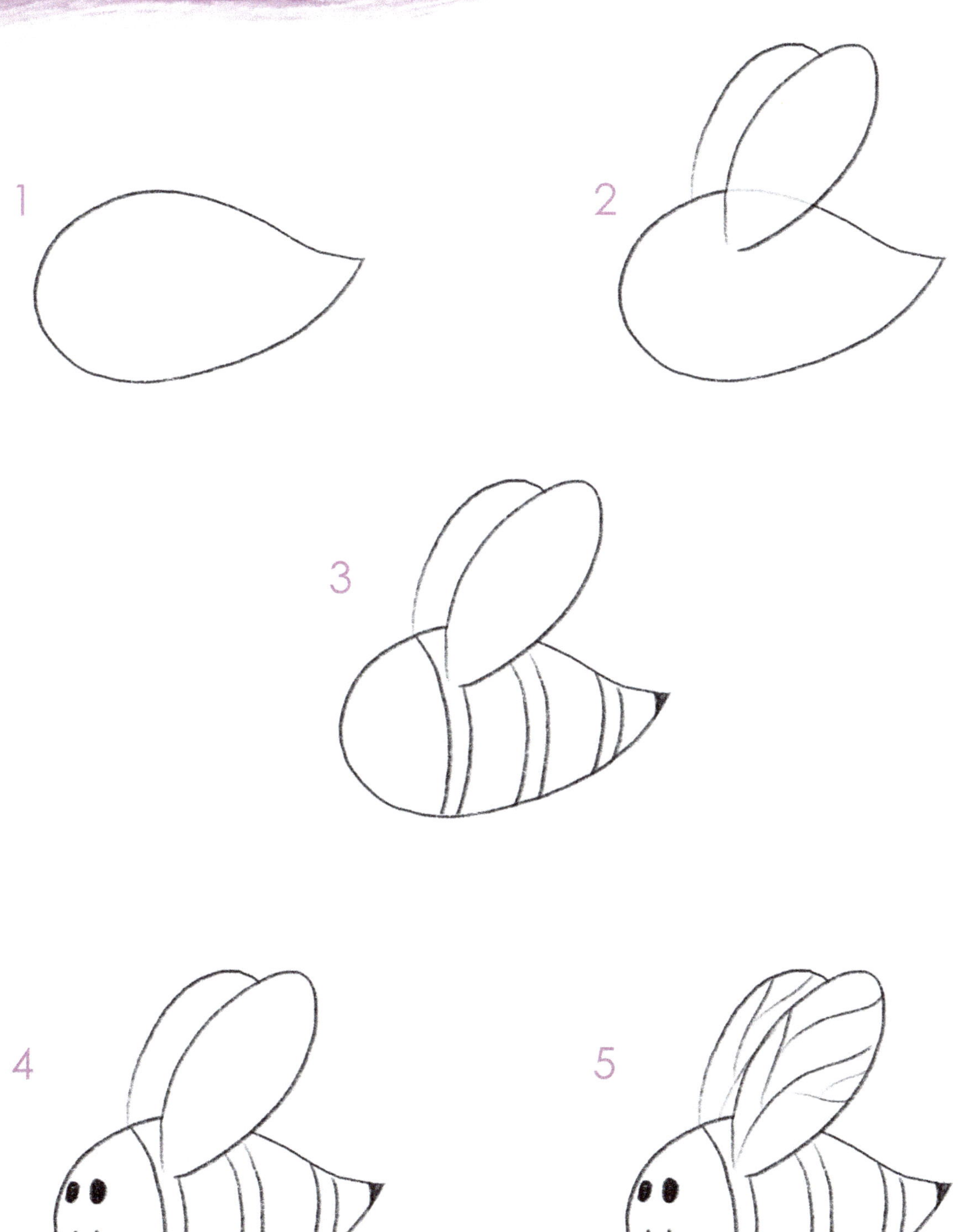

# Botanicals

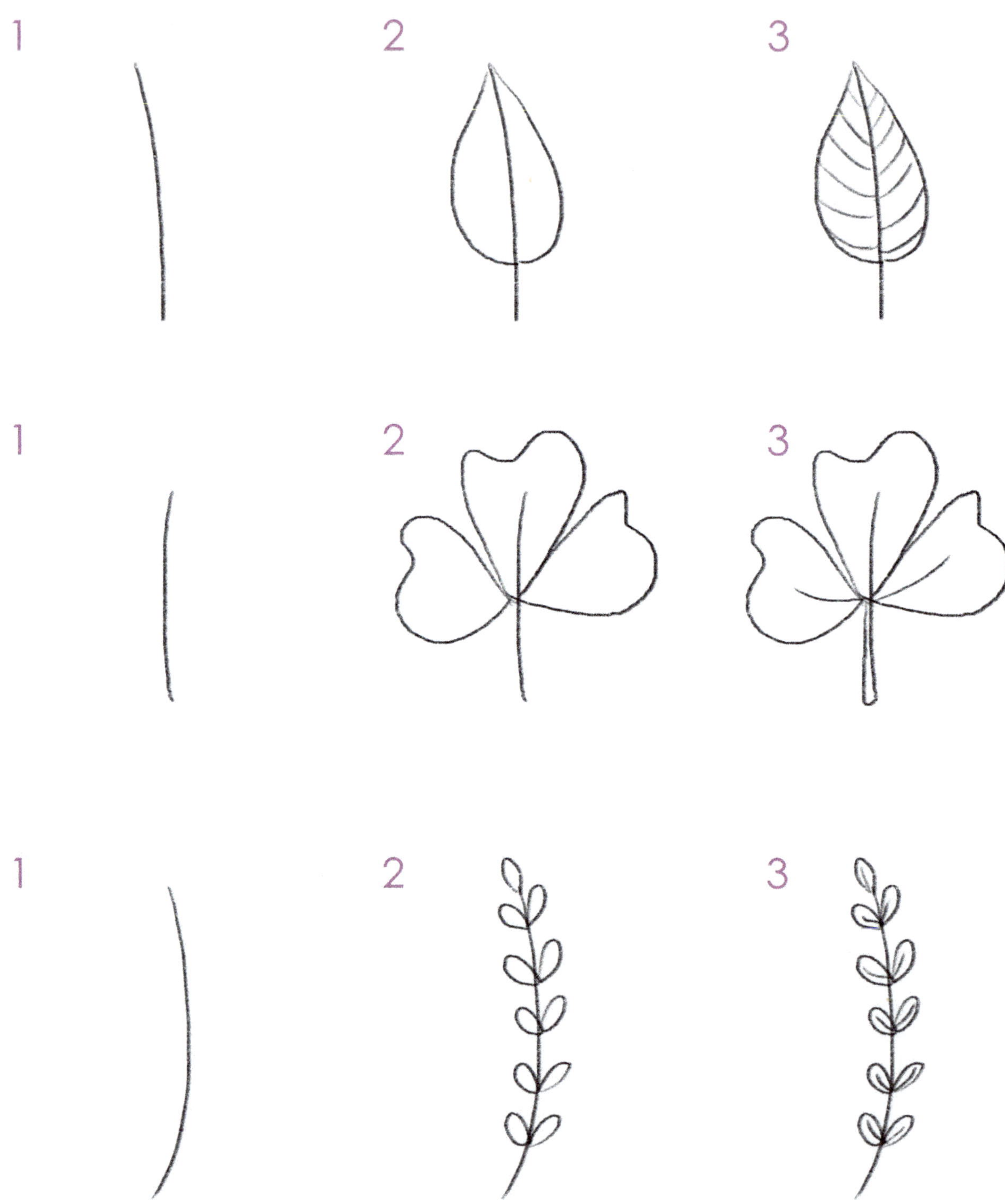

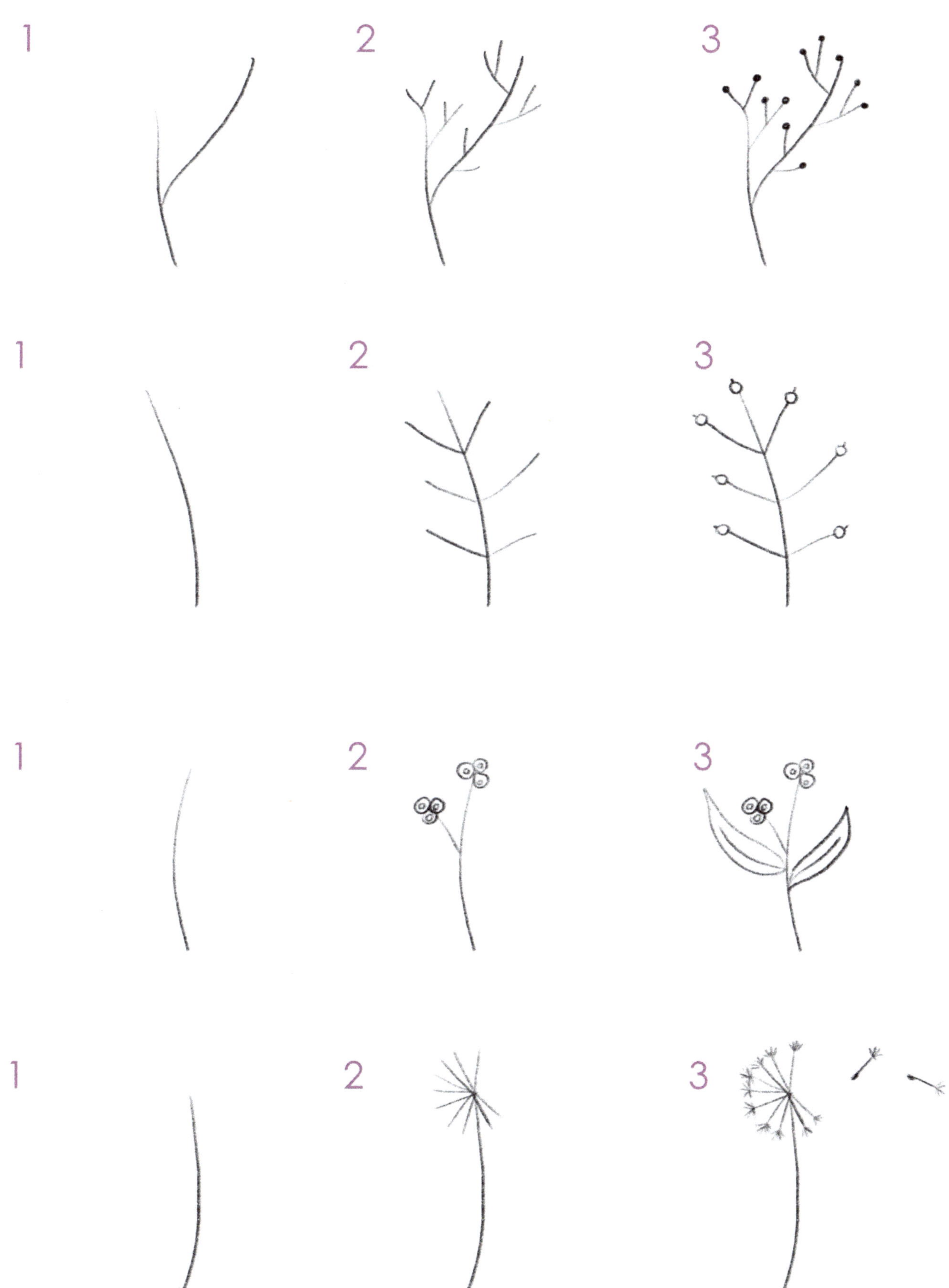

1     2     3

1     2     3

1     2     3

1     2     3

# Butterfly

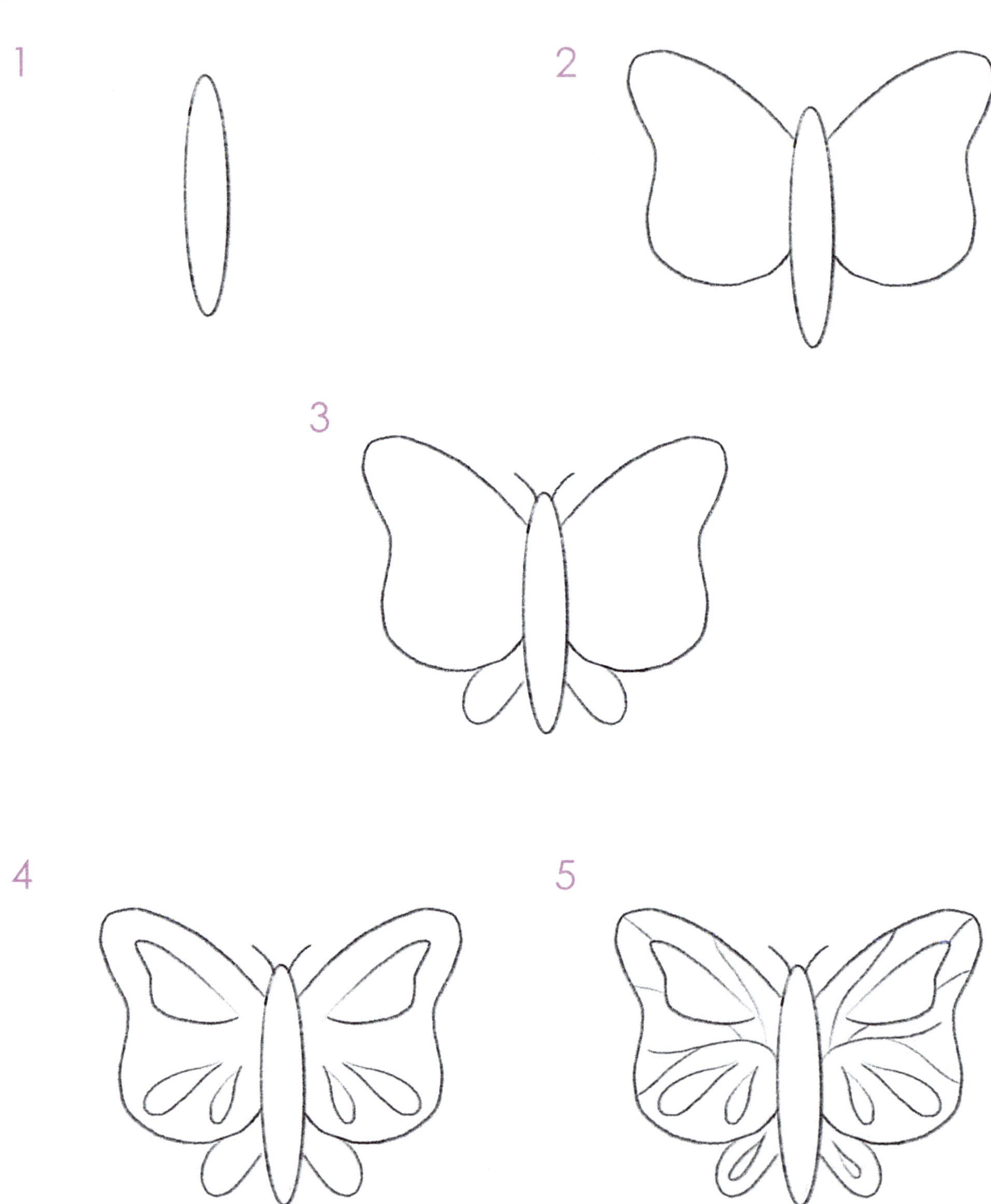

1

2

3

4

5

# Cactus

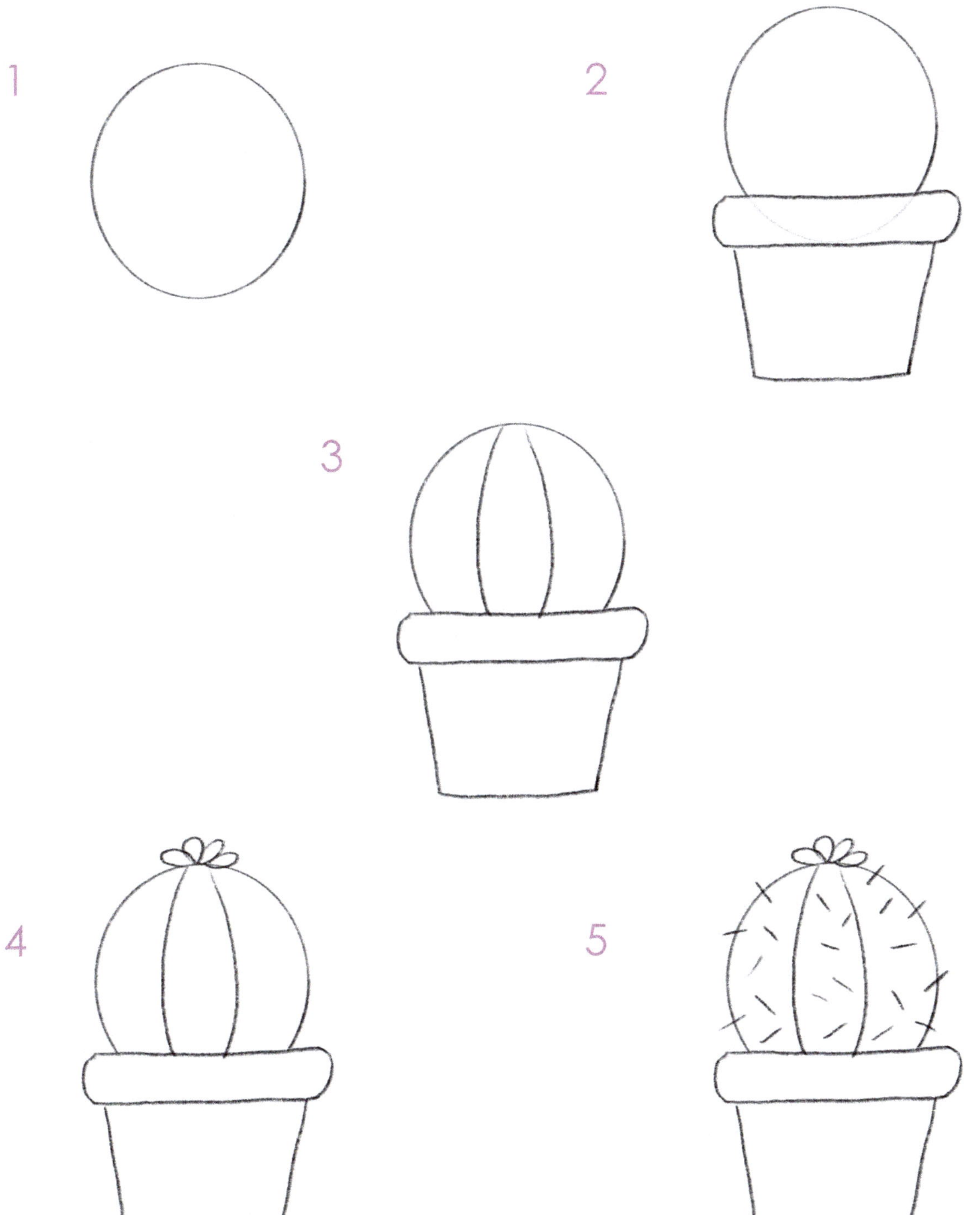

# Cat

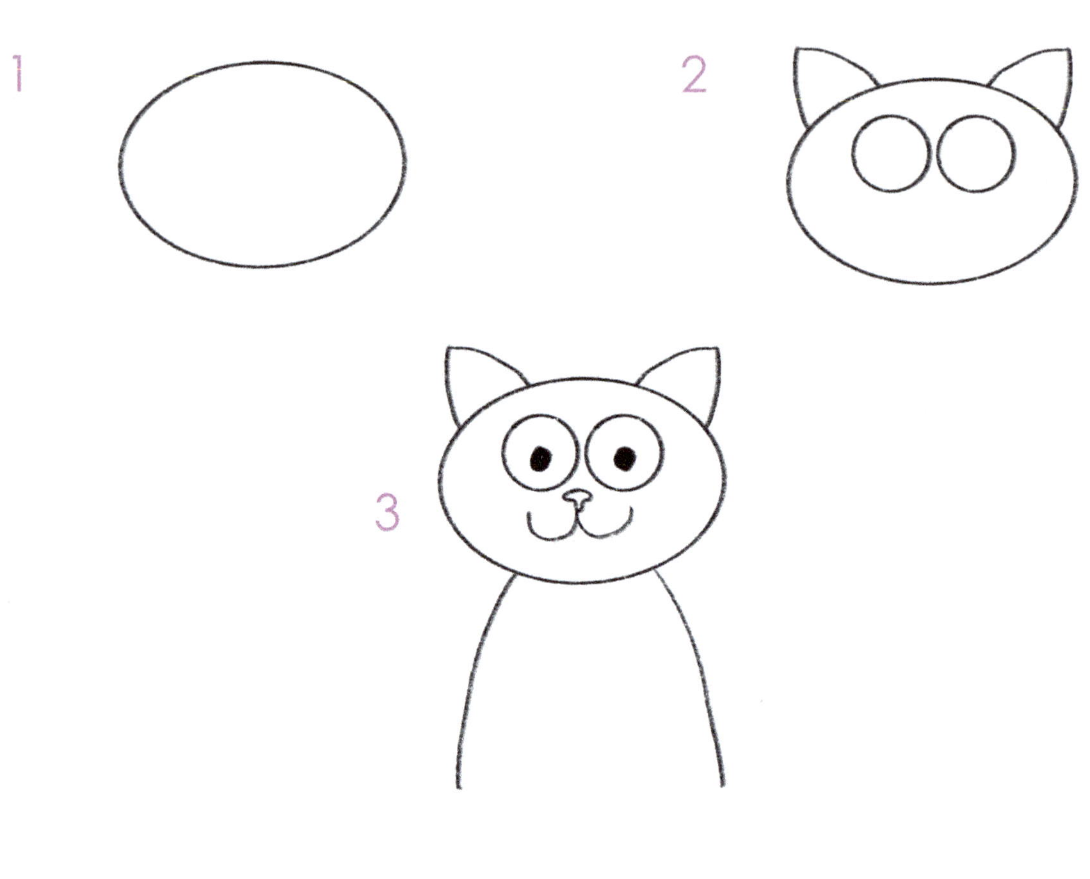

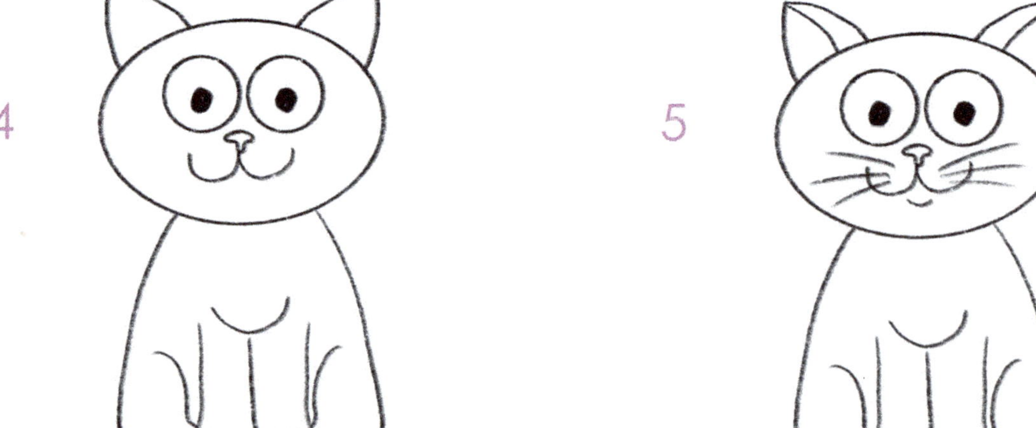

# Dog

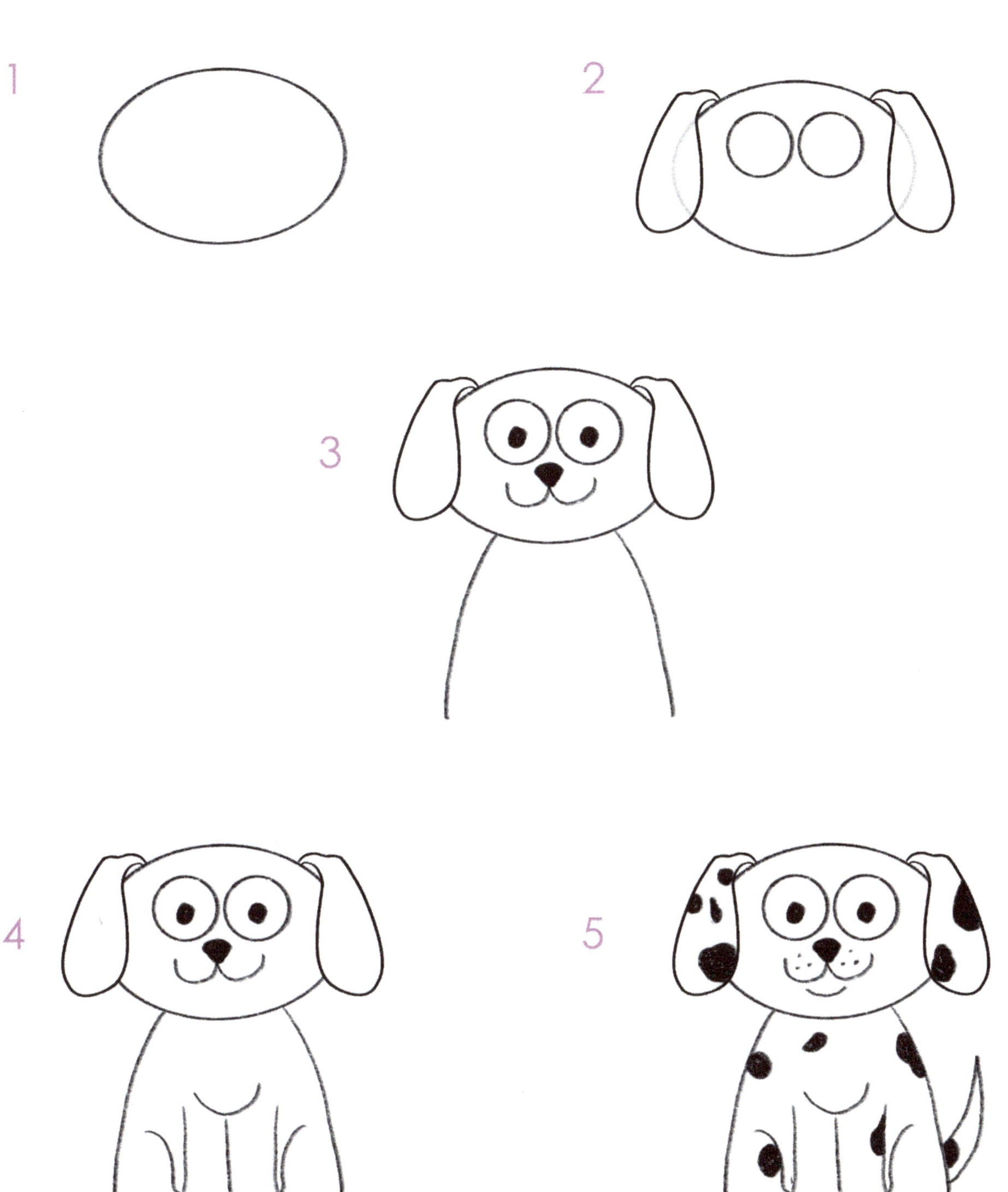

# Duck

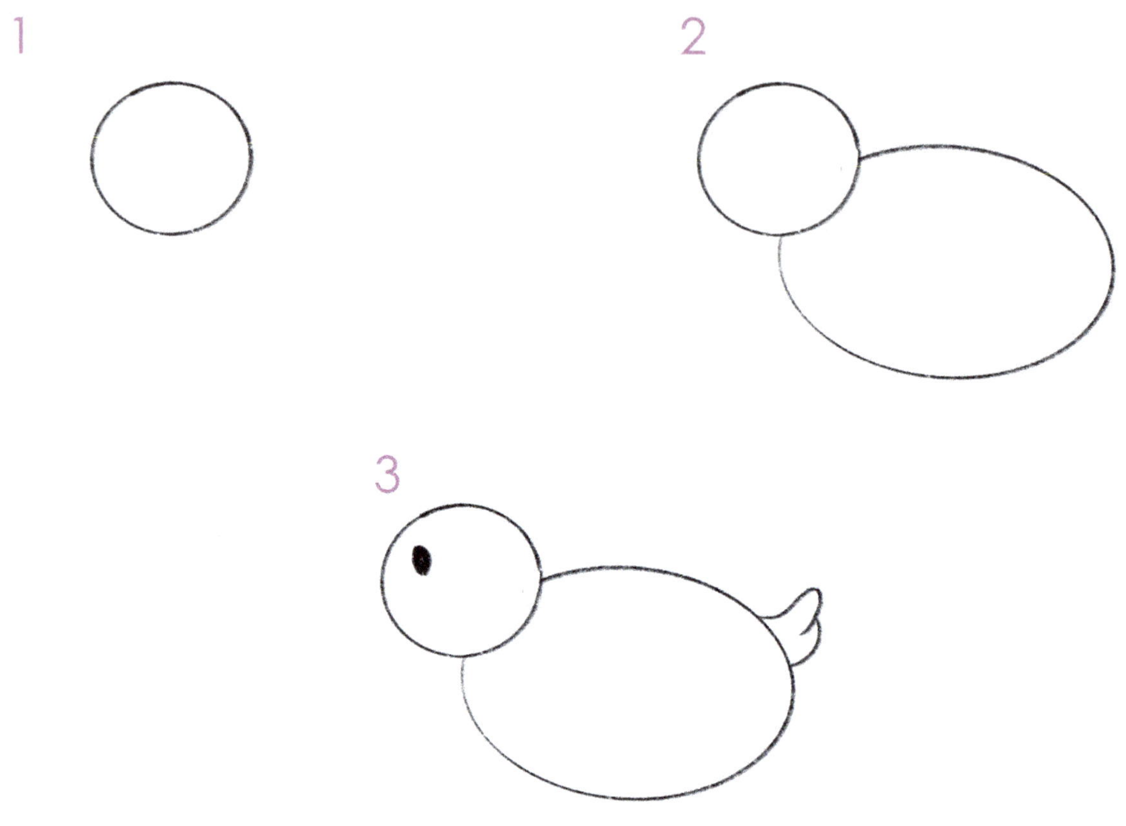

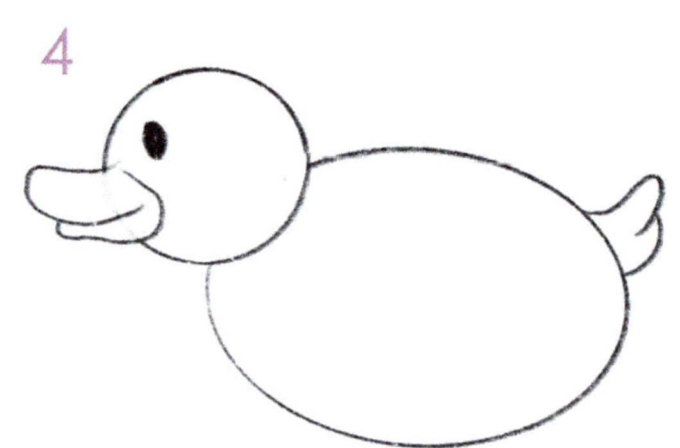

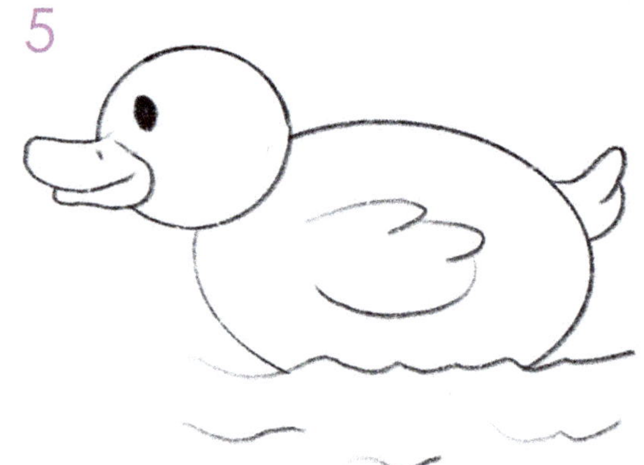

# Flower

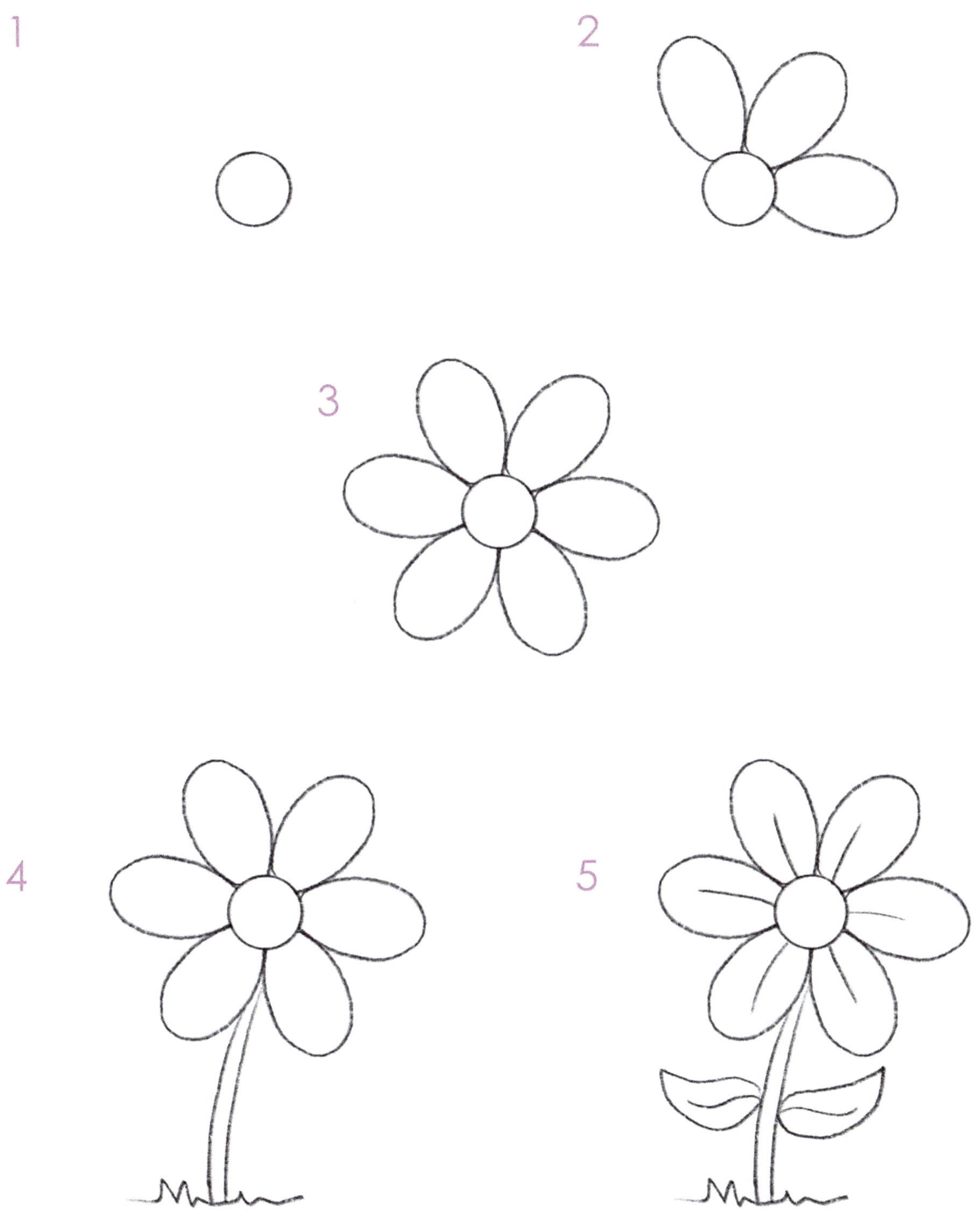

# Frog

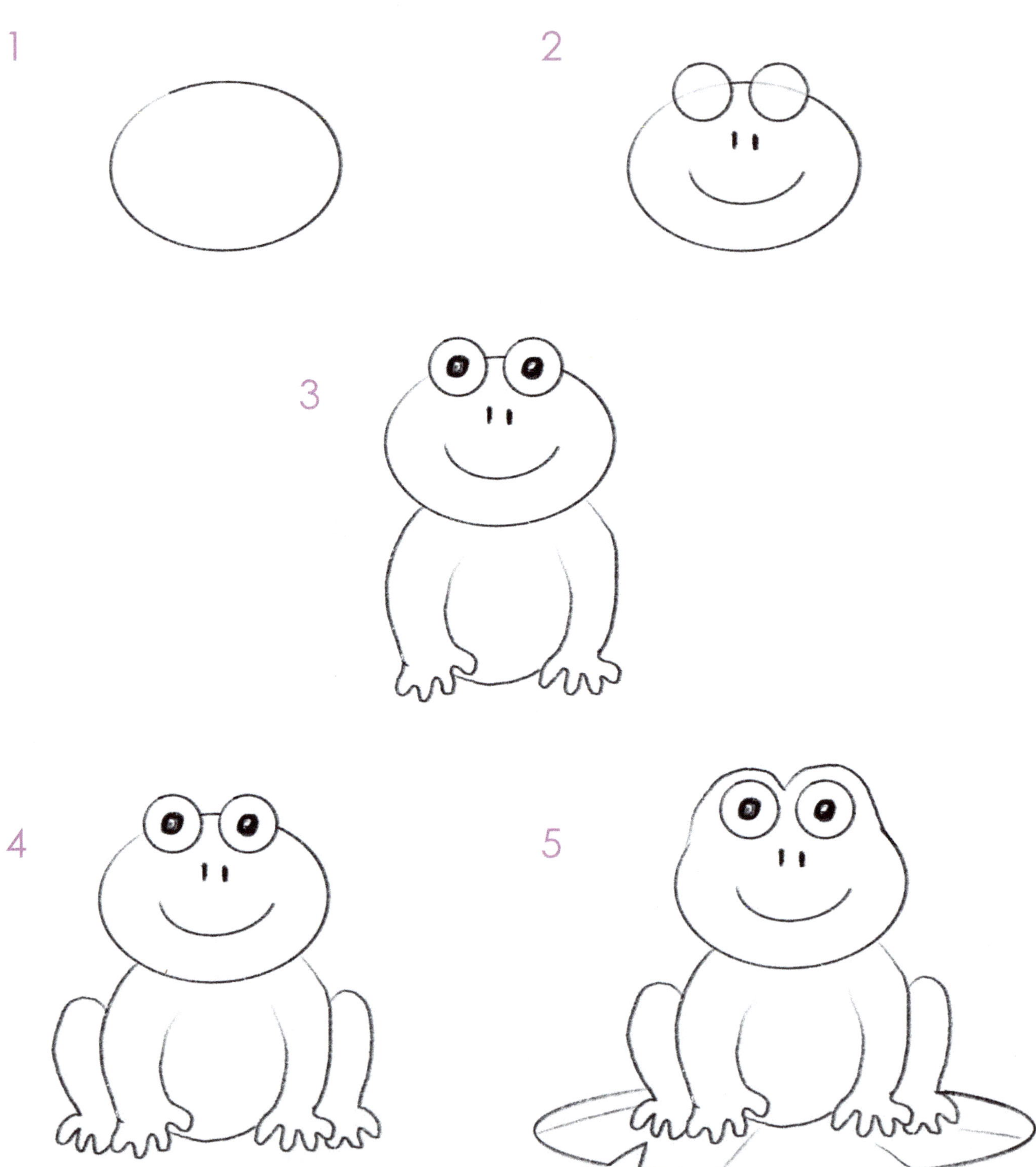

# Ice Cream

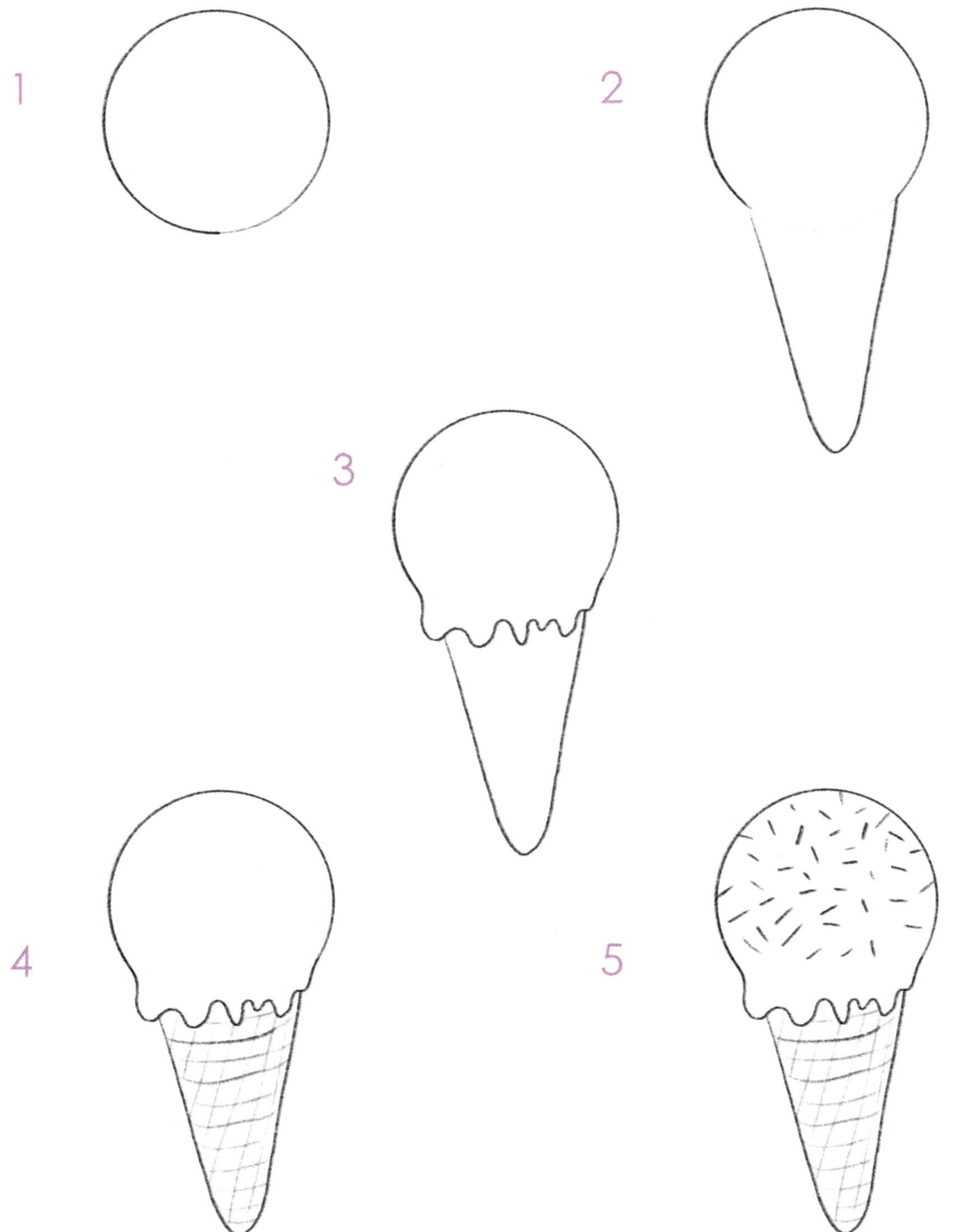

# Penguin

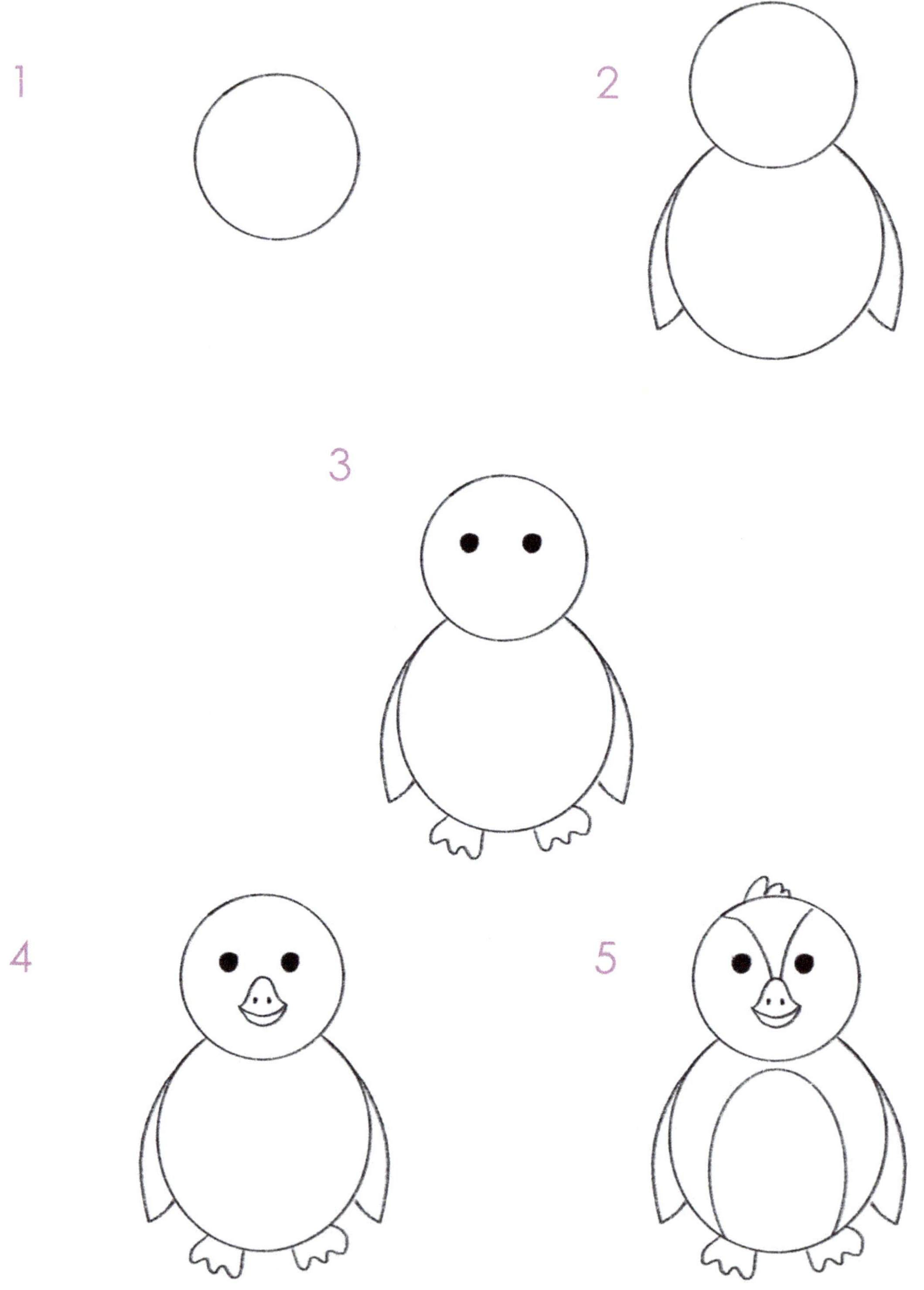

# Present

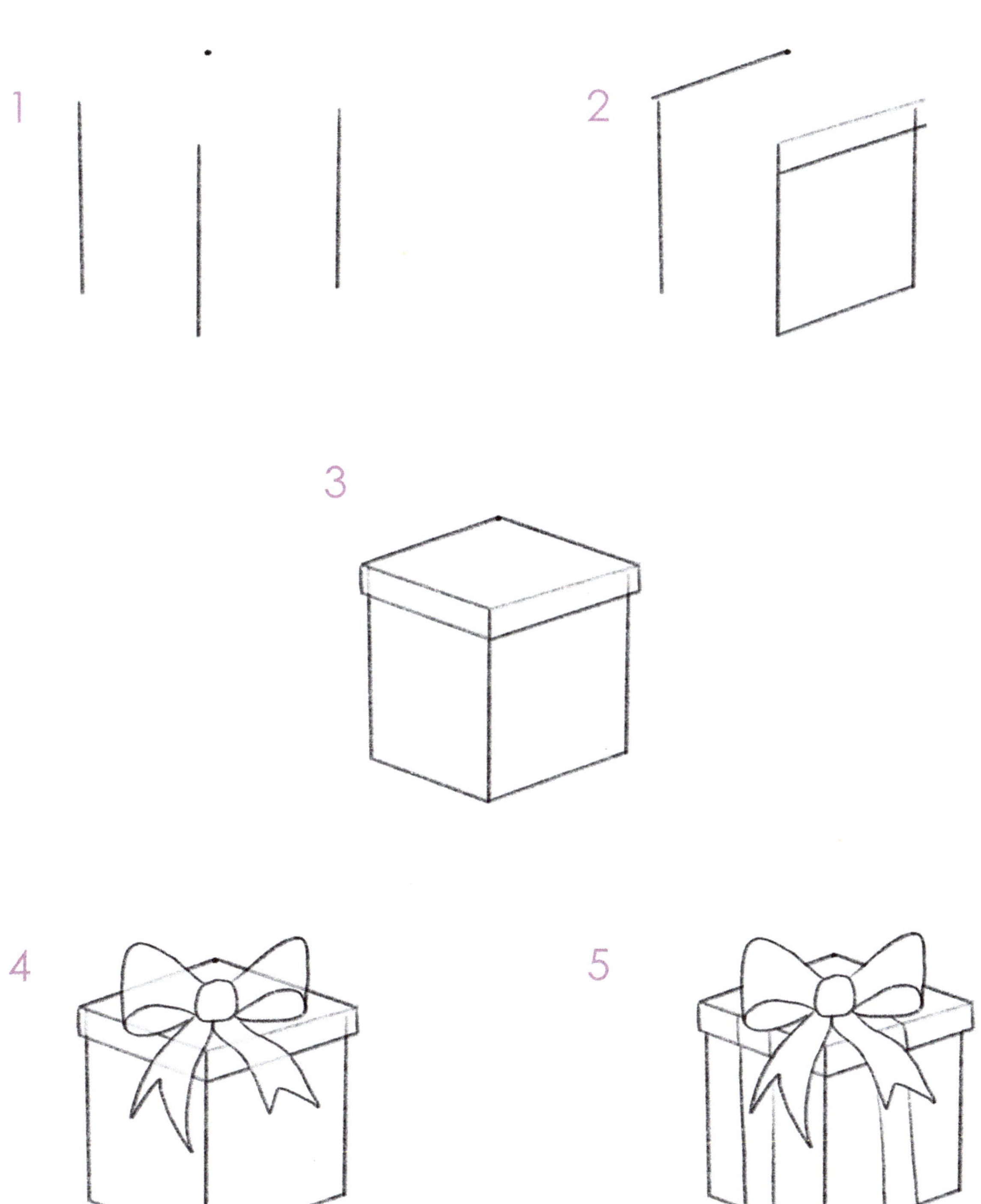

Congratulations on making it through to the
next level of tutorials!

The tutorials now have more steps than before,
but still all start with basic shapes.

Practice makes perfect! You're doing so well.

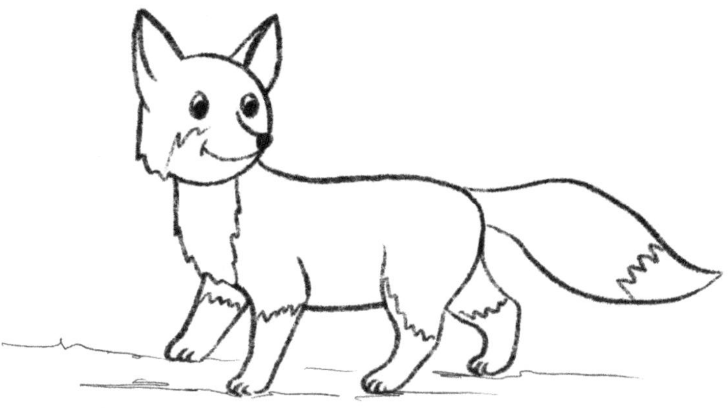

# Level Two

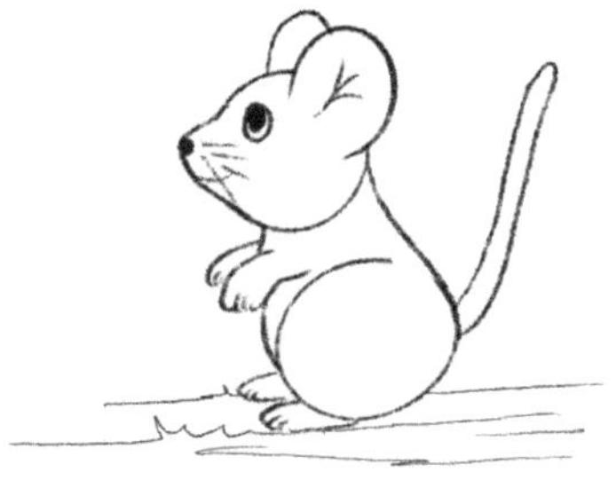

# Birthday Cake

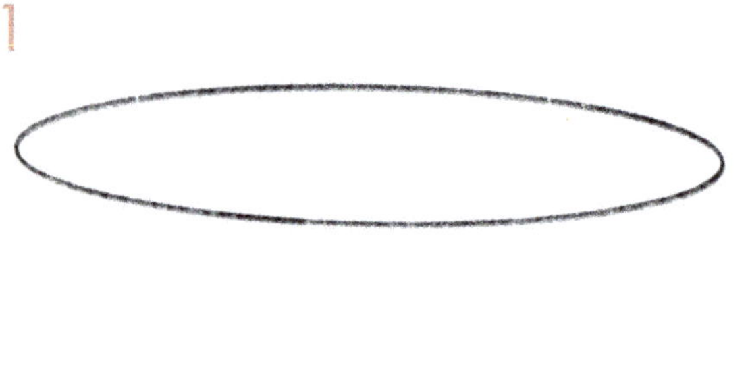

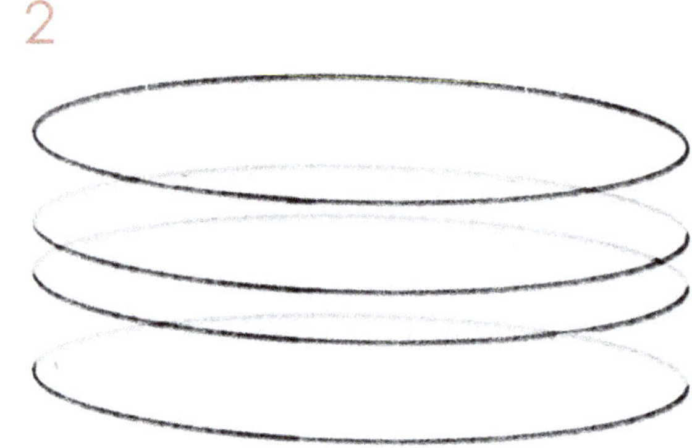

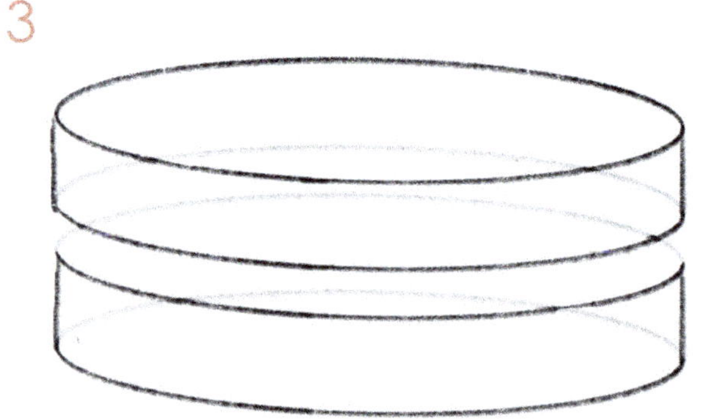

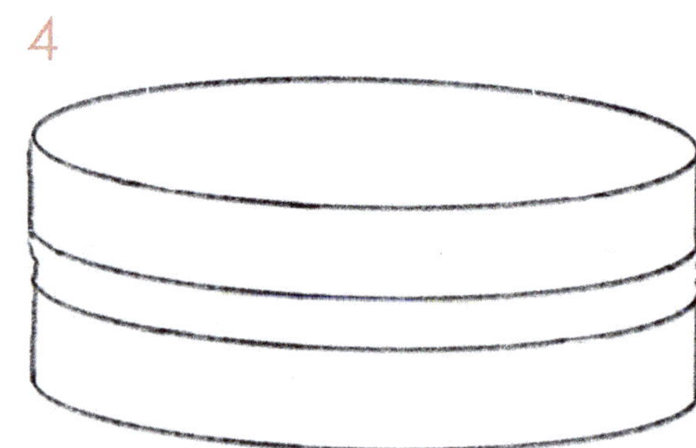

5

6

7

8

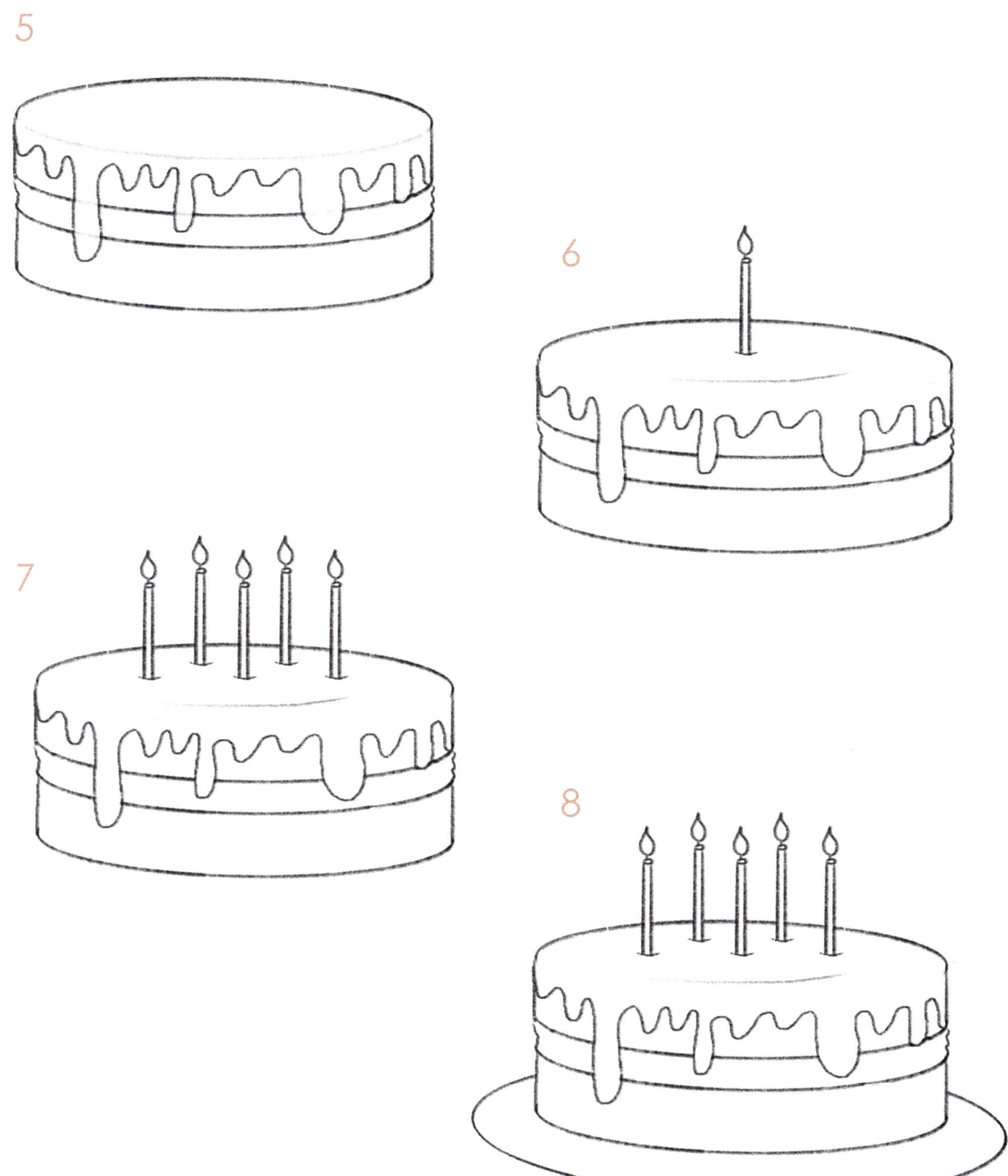

# Daffodil

1

2  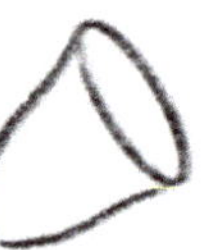

3  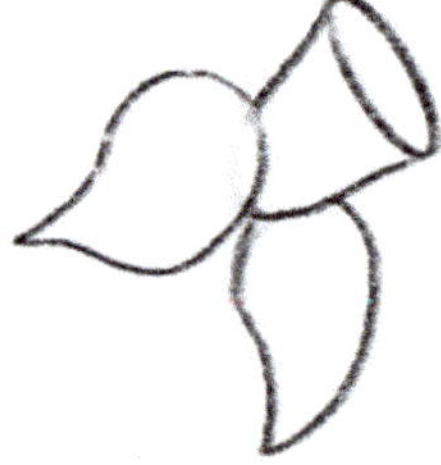

4  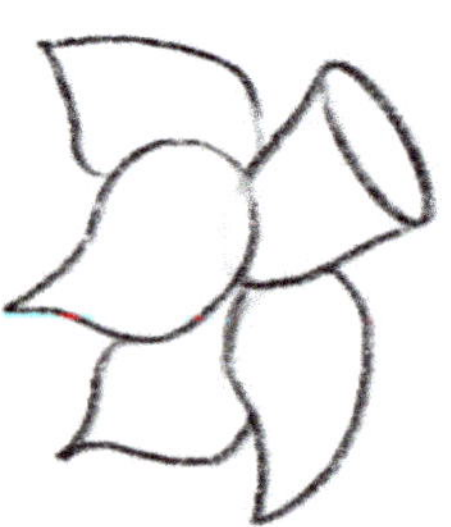

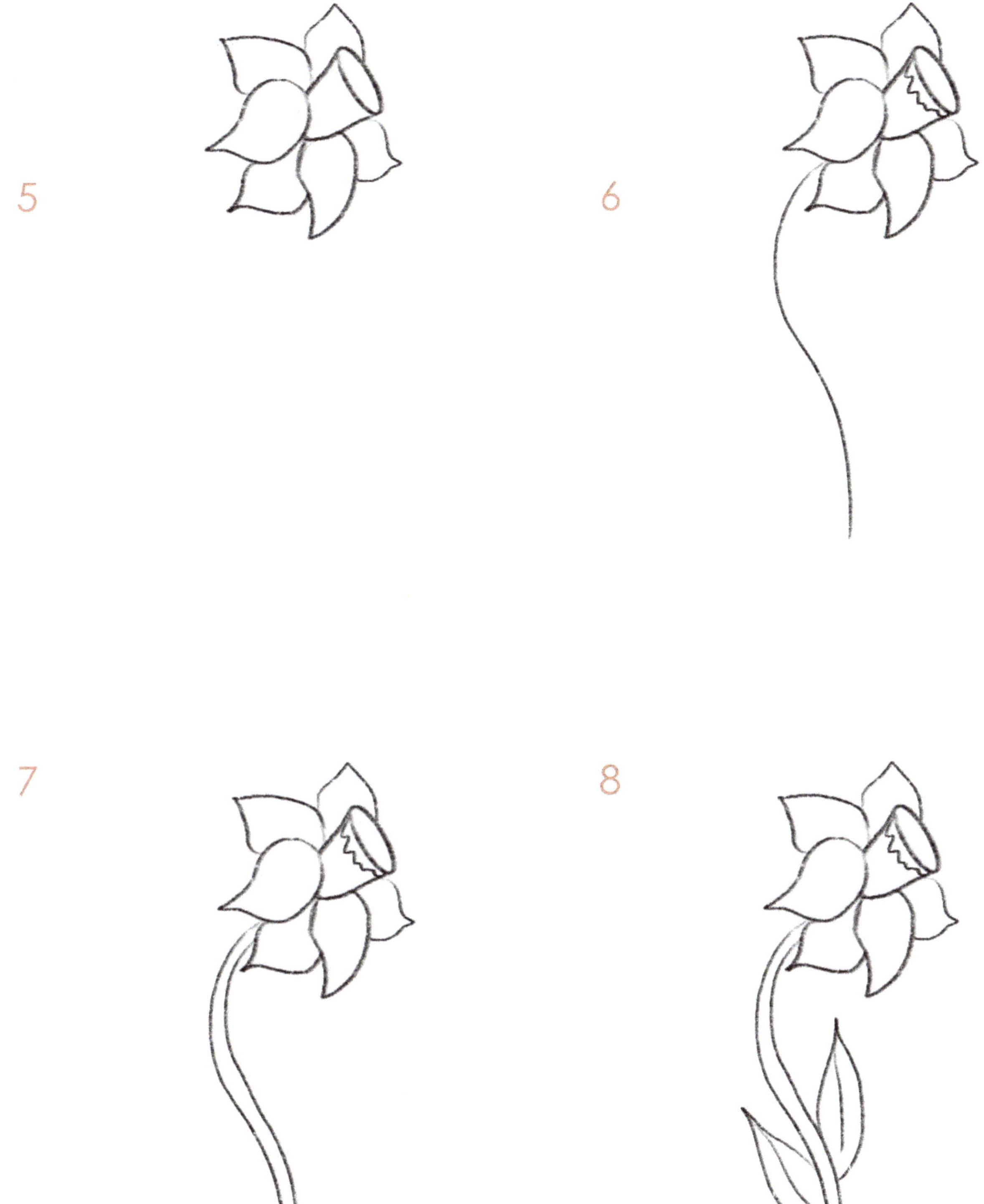
5
6
7
8

# Daisy

1

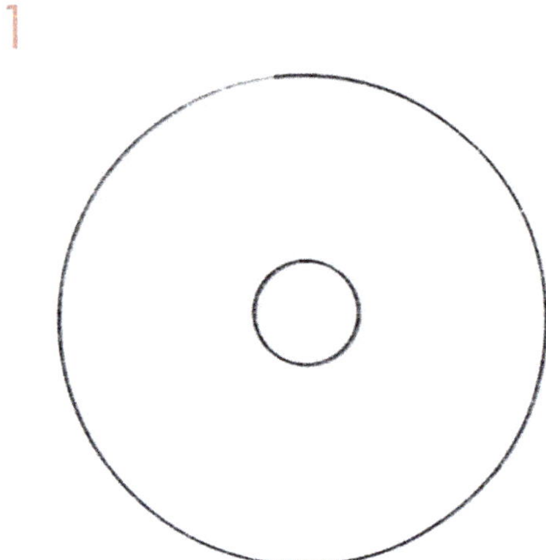

2

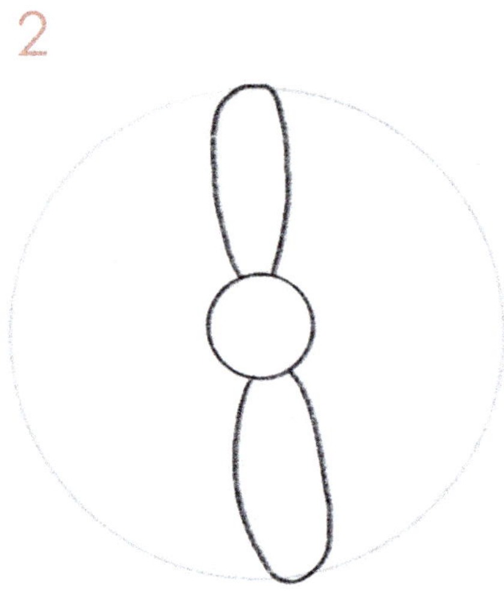

3

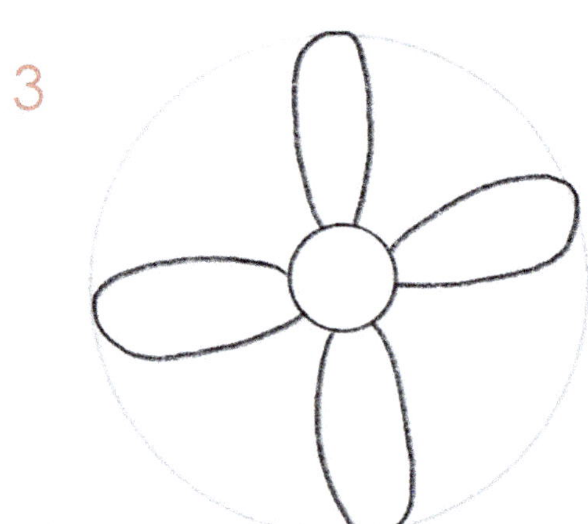

4

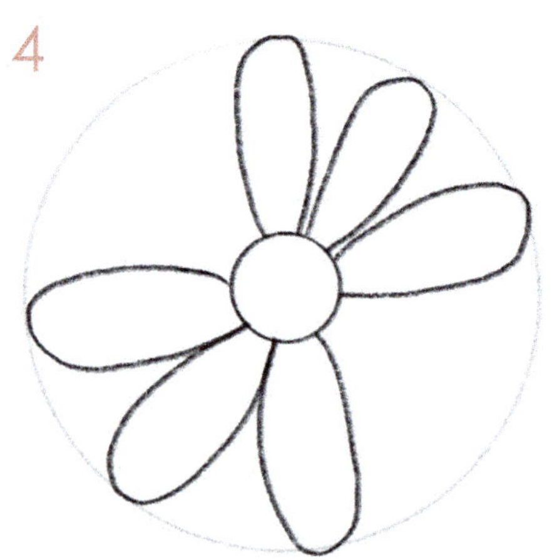

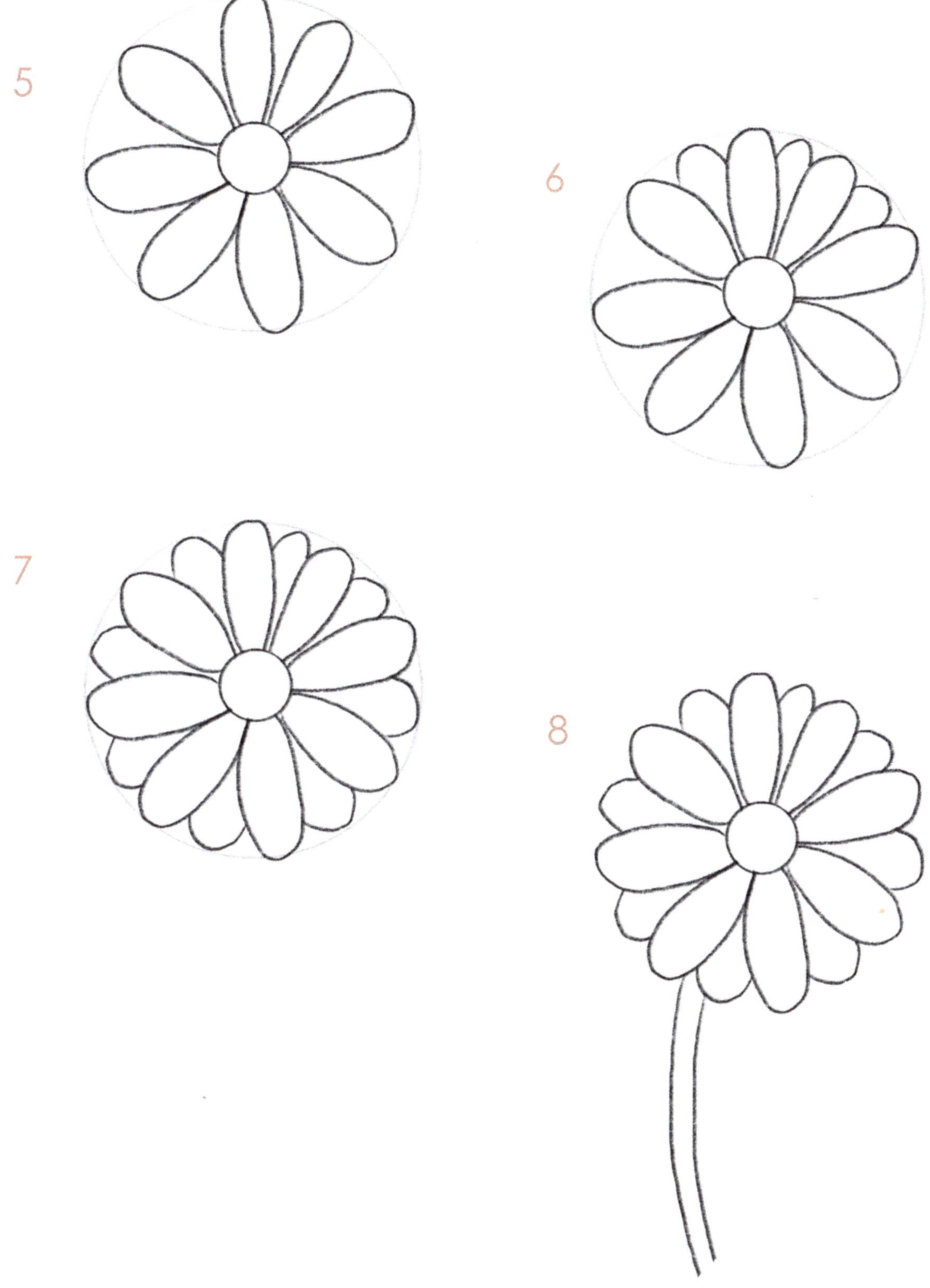

5

6

7

8

# Elephant

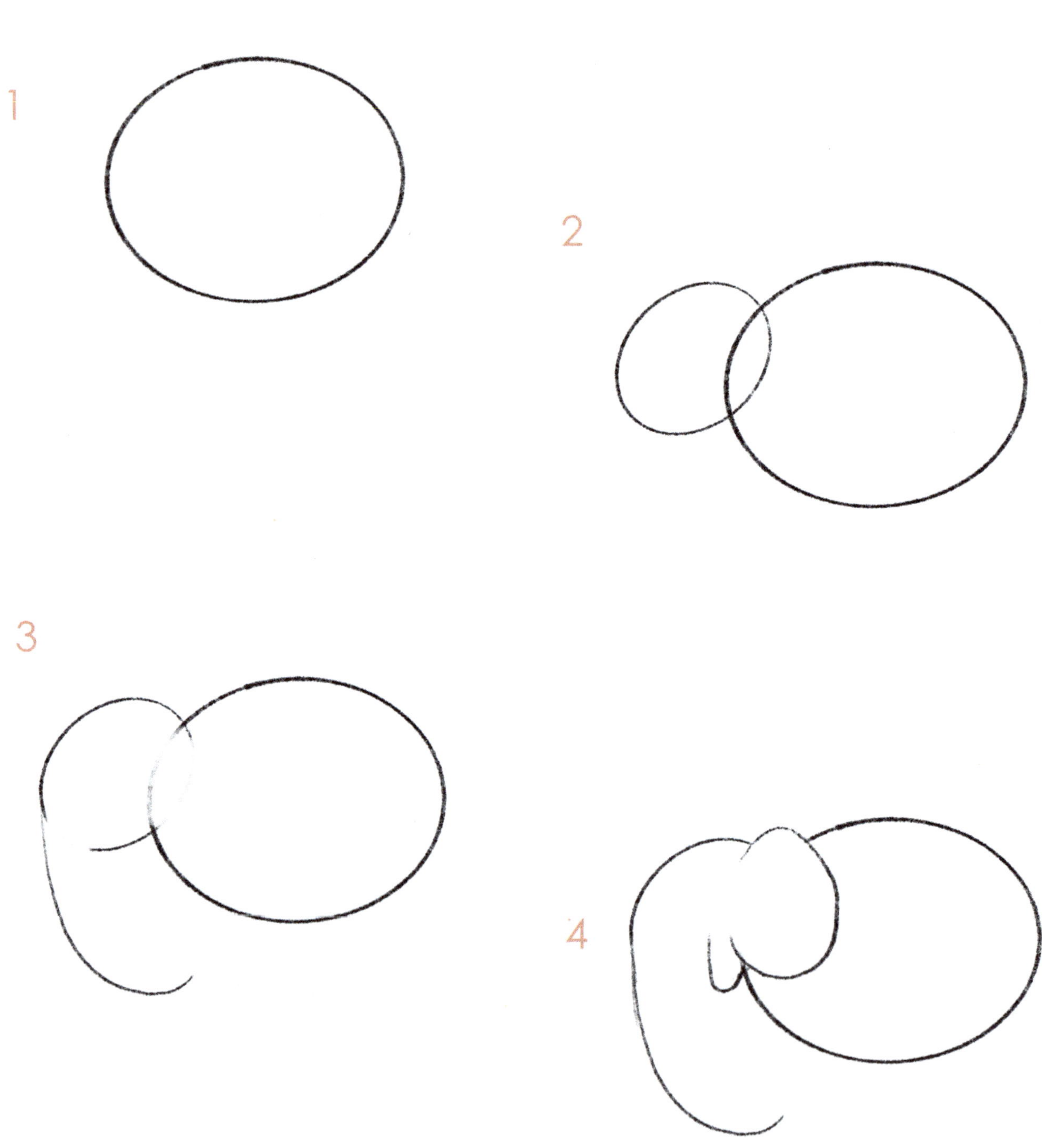

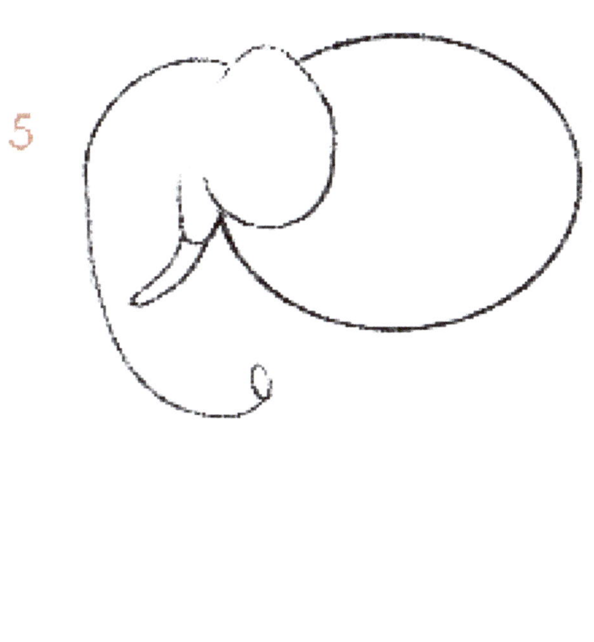

5

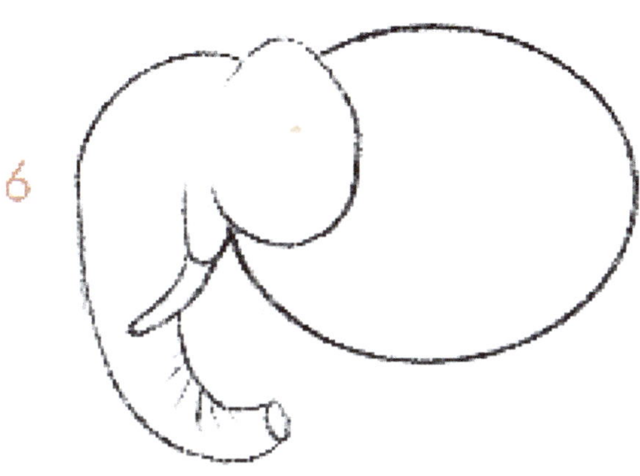

6

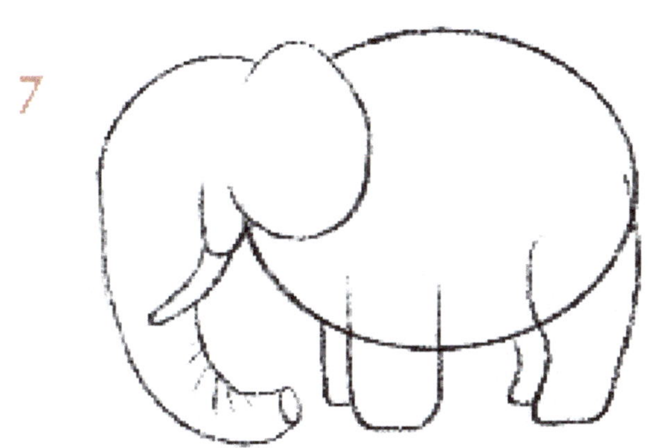

7

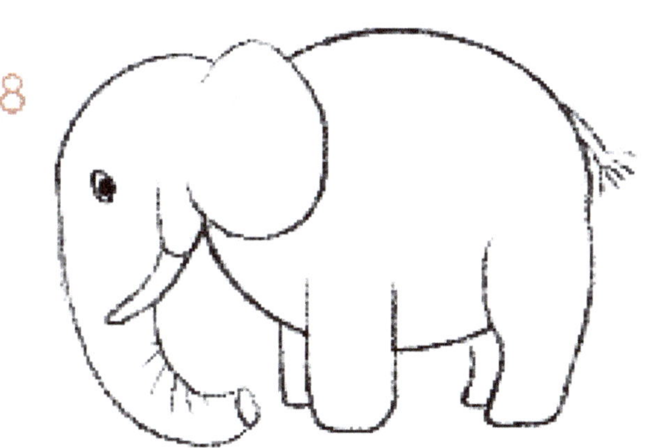

8

# Feather

5

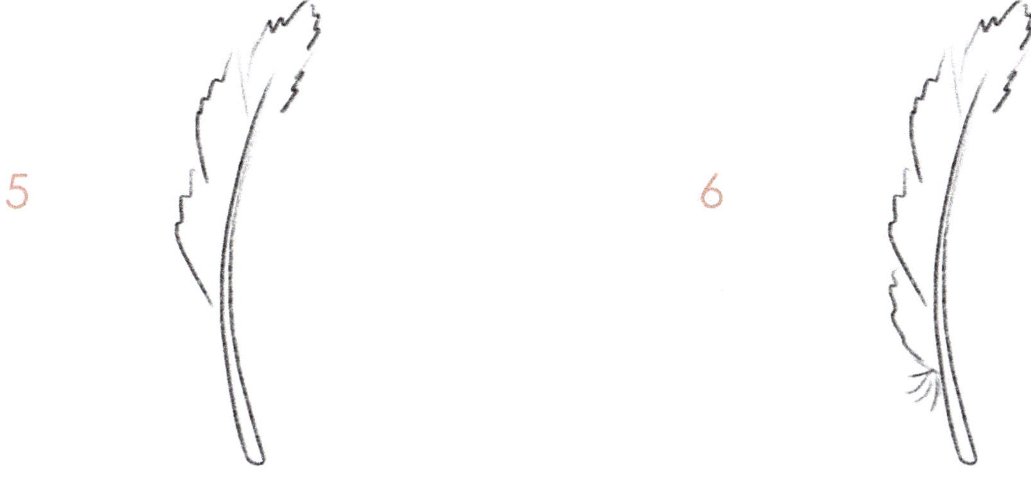

6

7

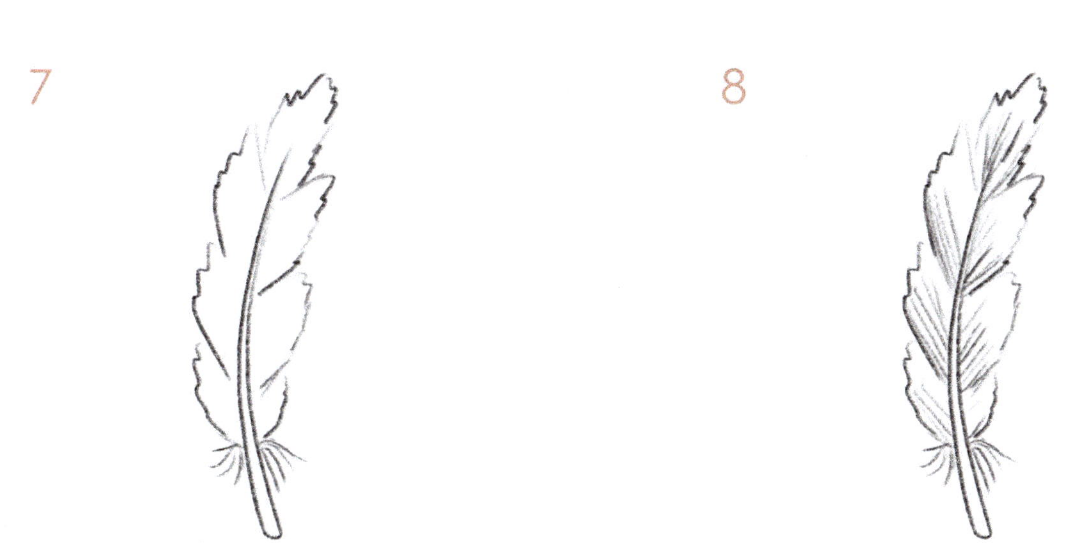

8

# Flamingo

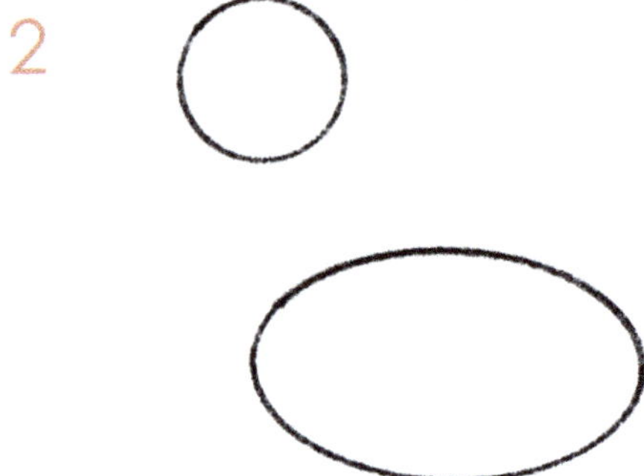

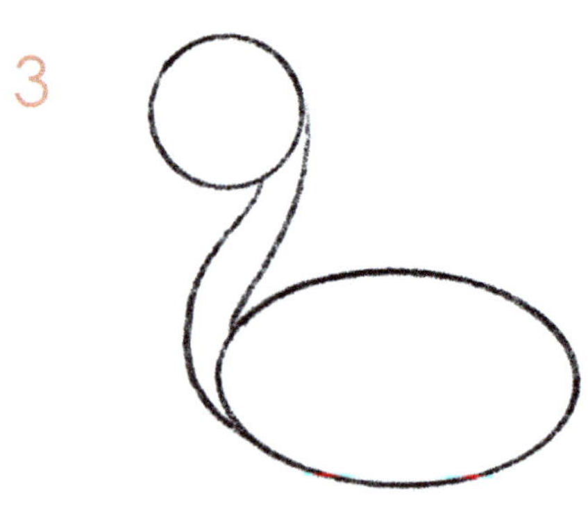

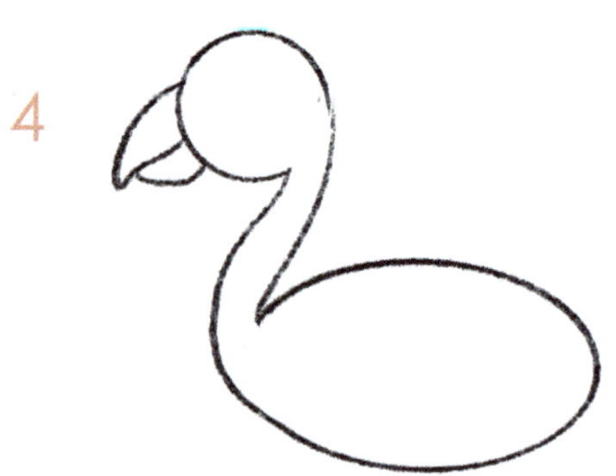

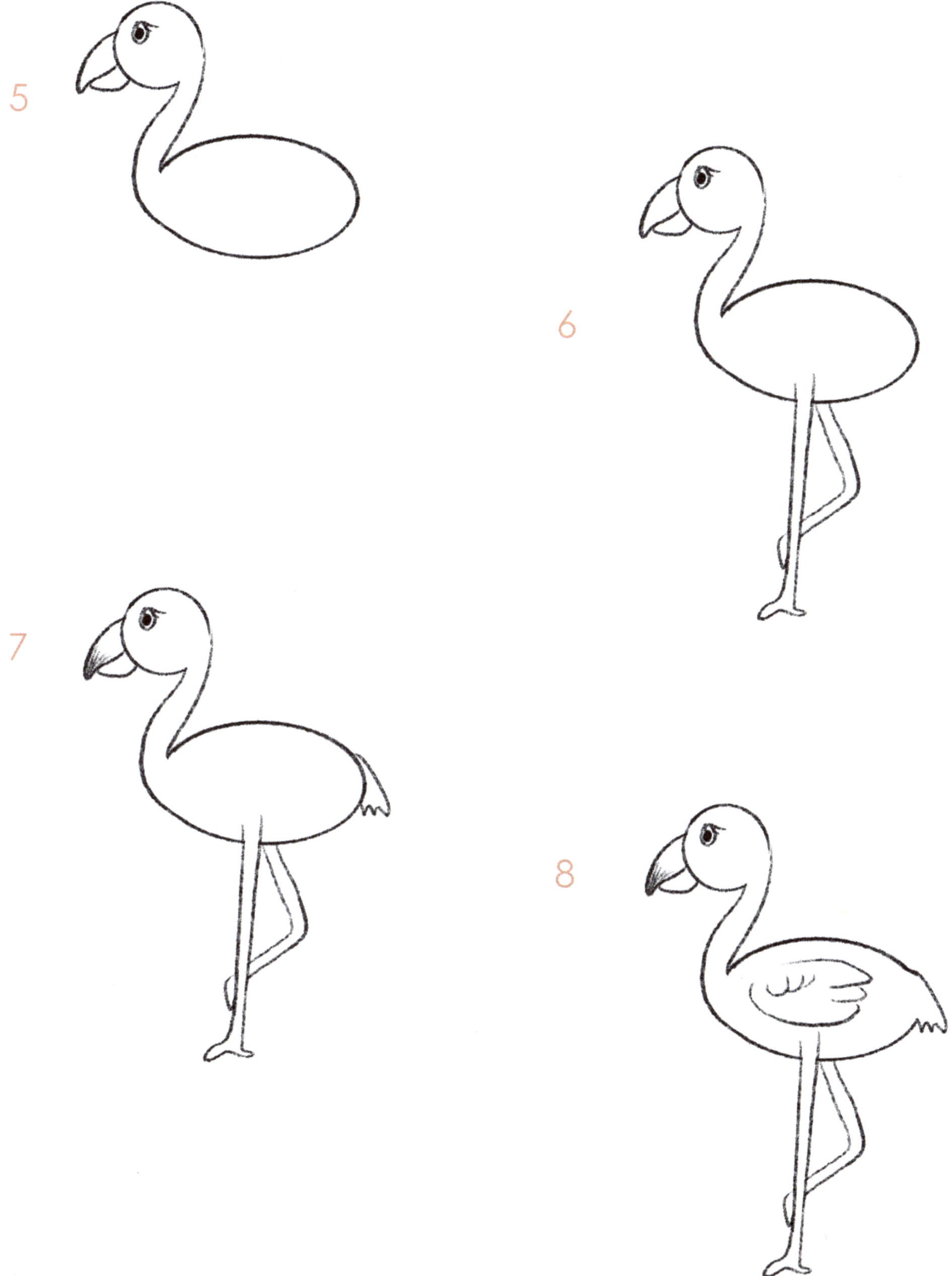

5
6
7
8

# Fox

1 

2 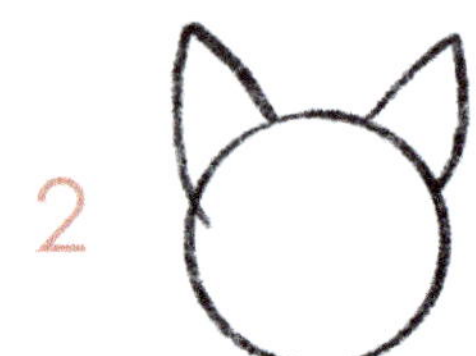

3 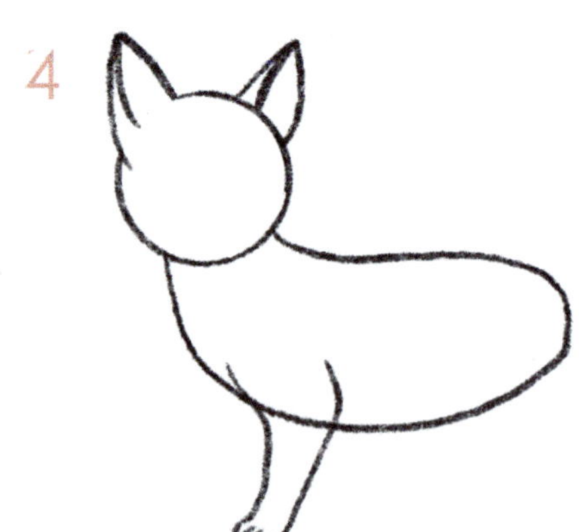

4

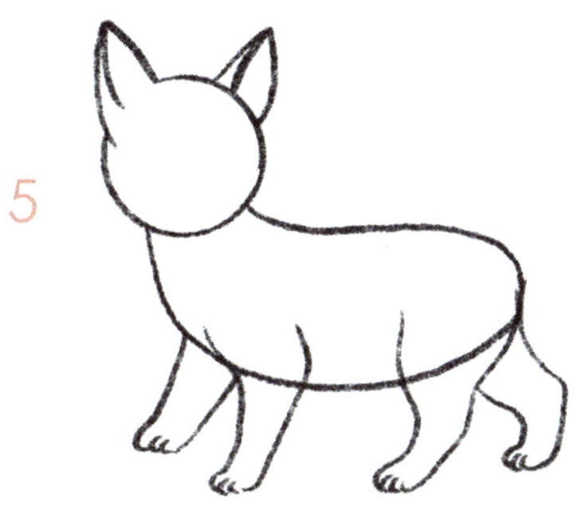

5

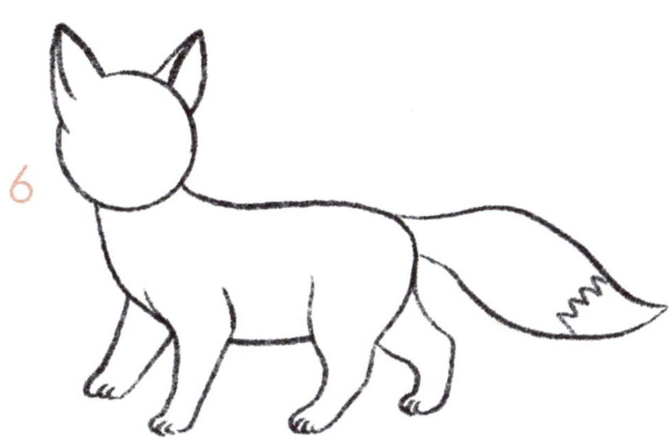

6

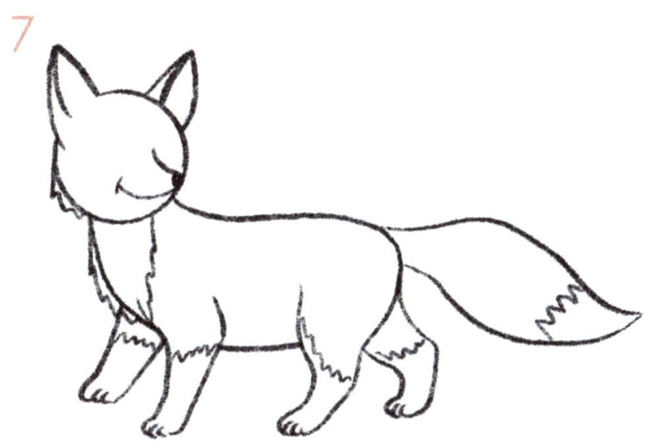

7

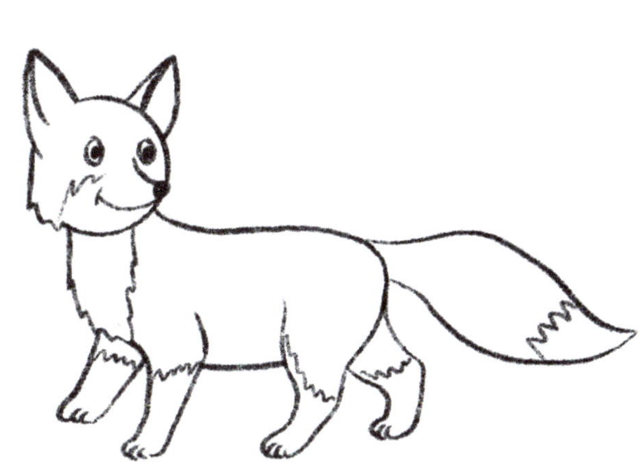

8

# Giraffe

1

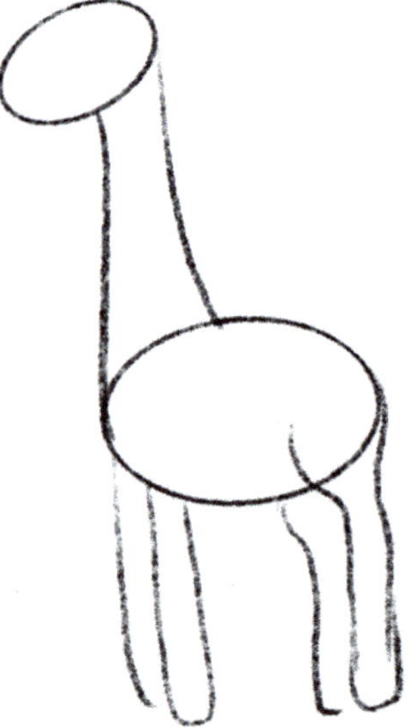

2

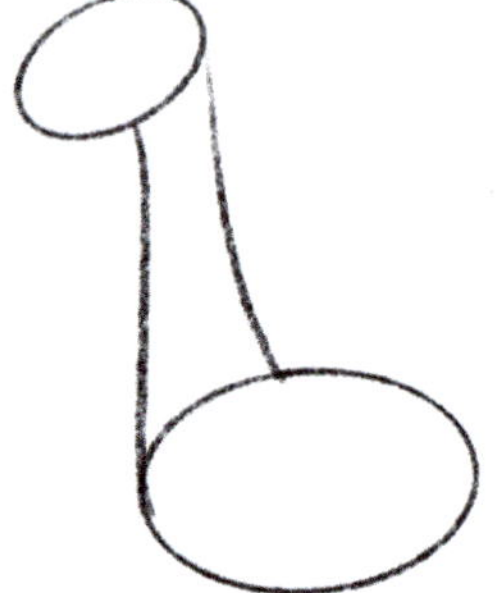

3

4

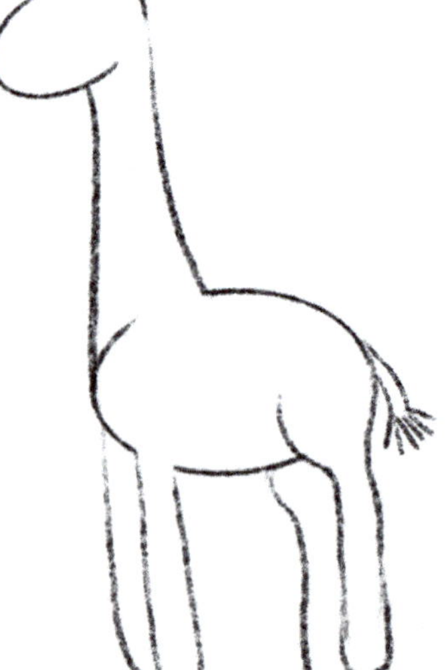

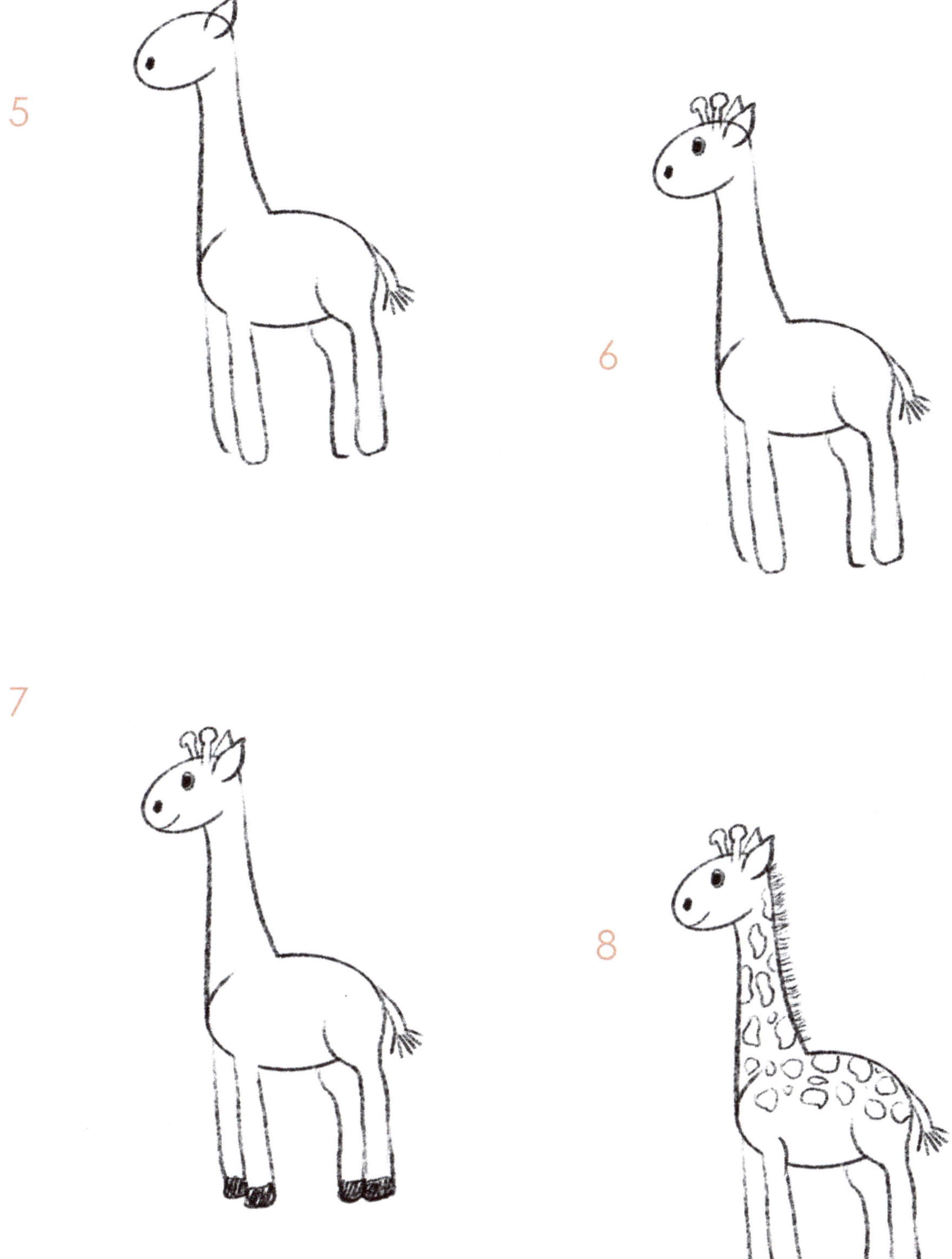


5
6
7
8

# Goldfish

1

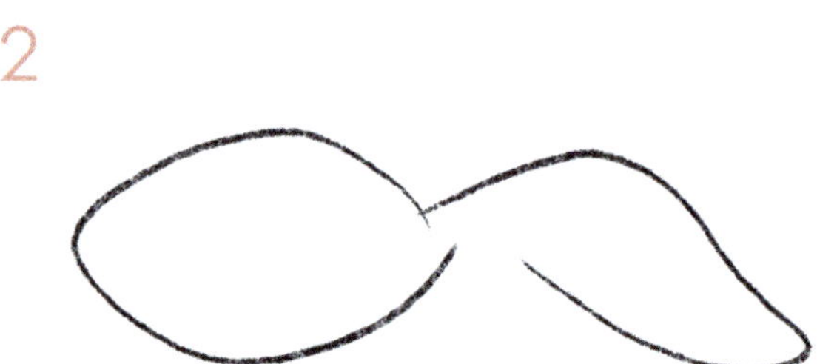

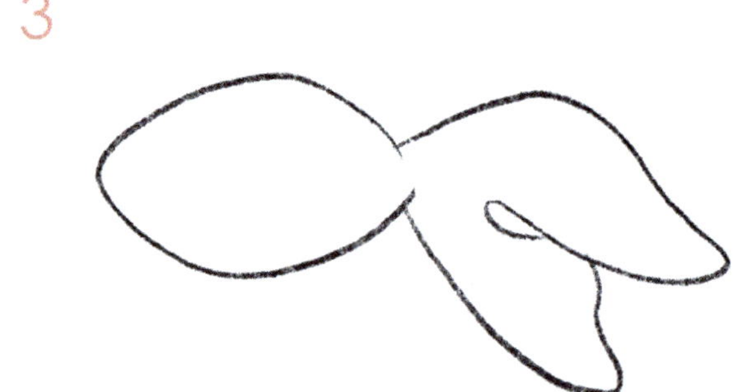

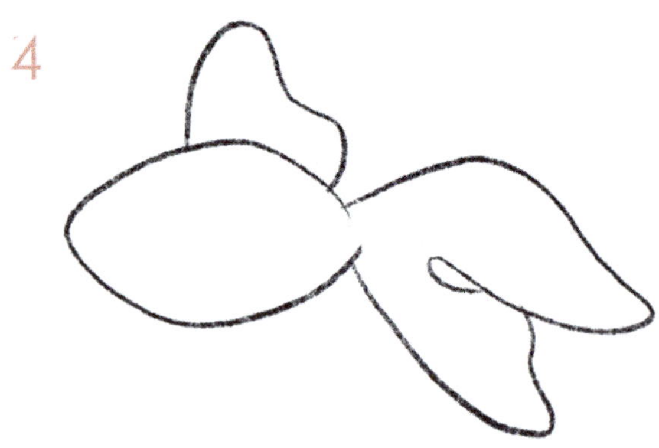

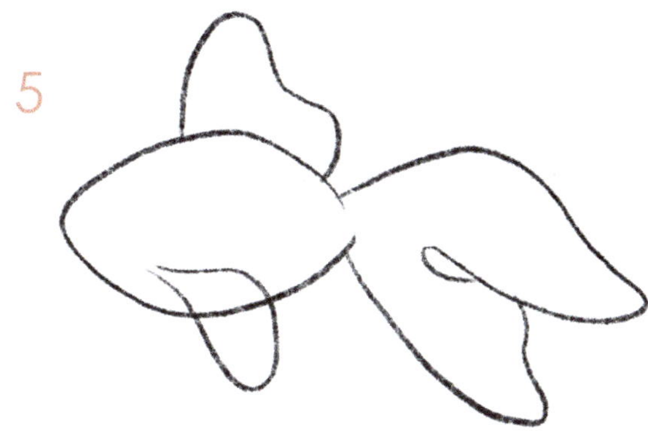

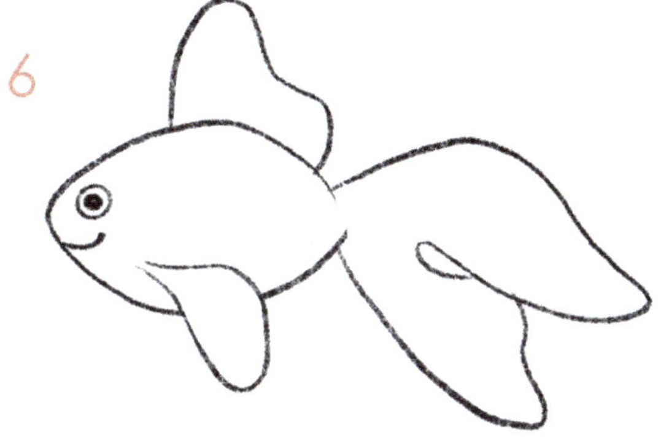

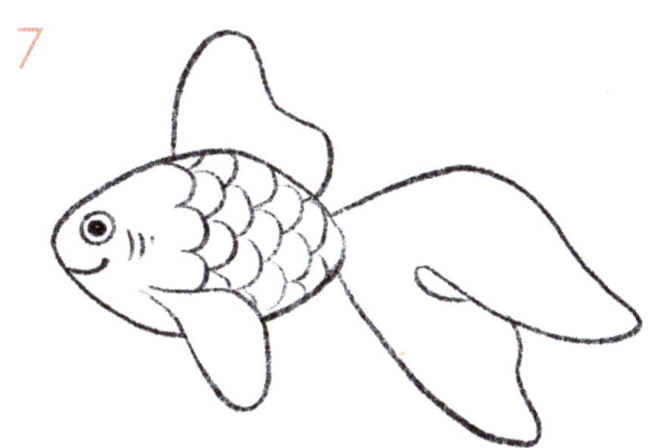

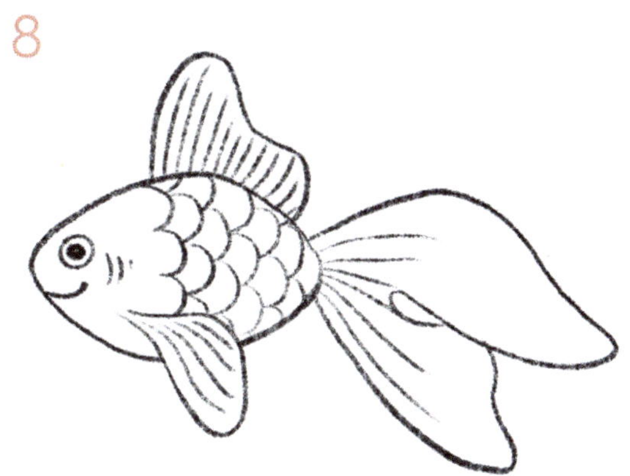

# Horse head

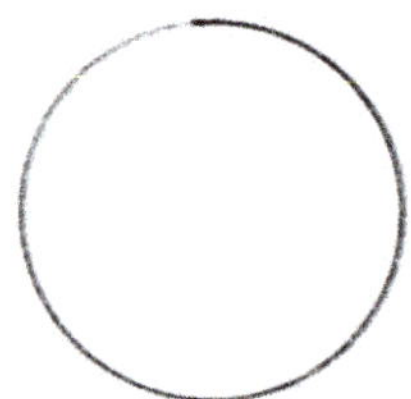

1

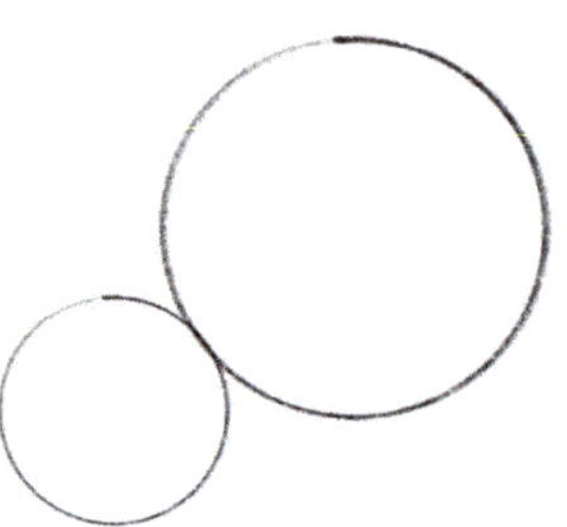

2

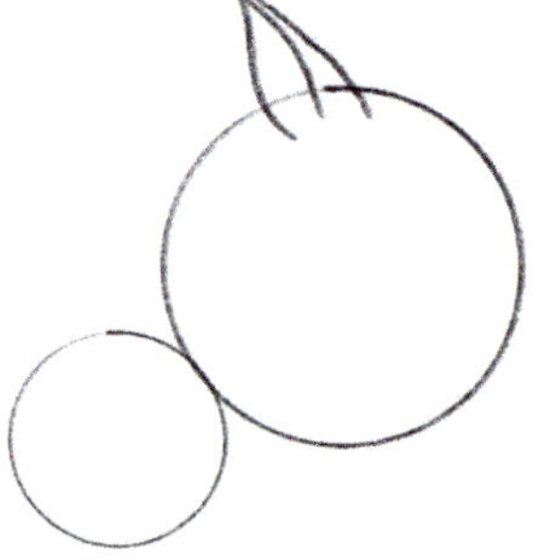

3

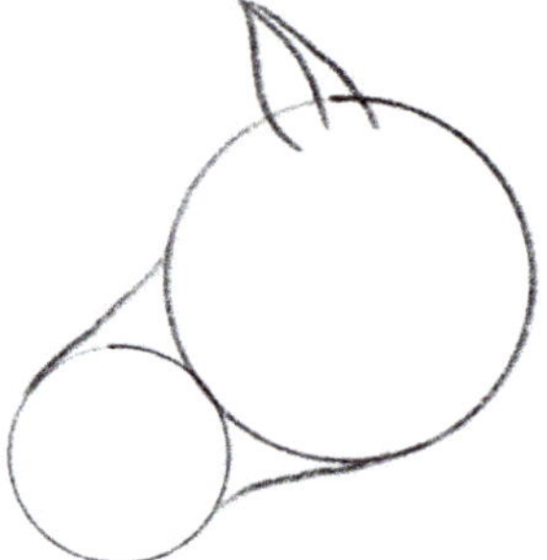

4

5

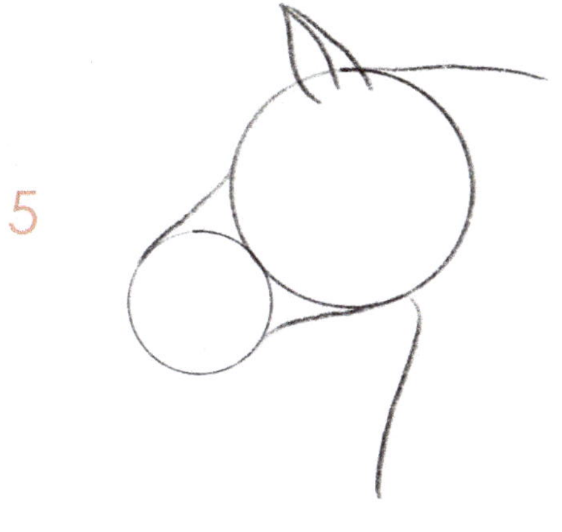

6

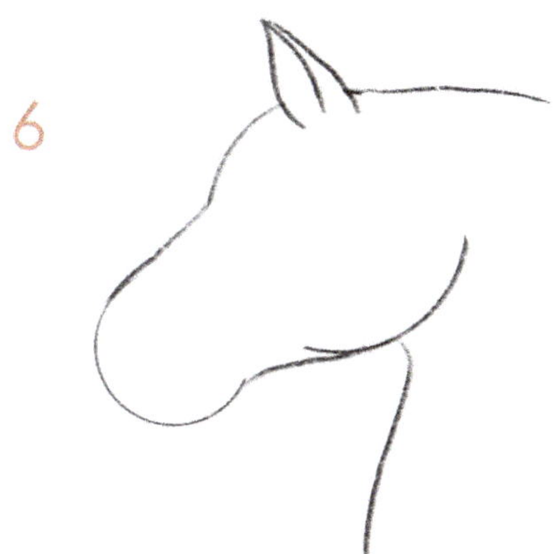

7

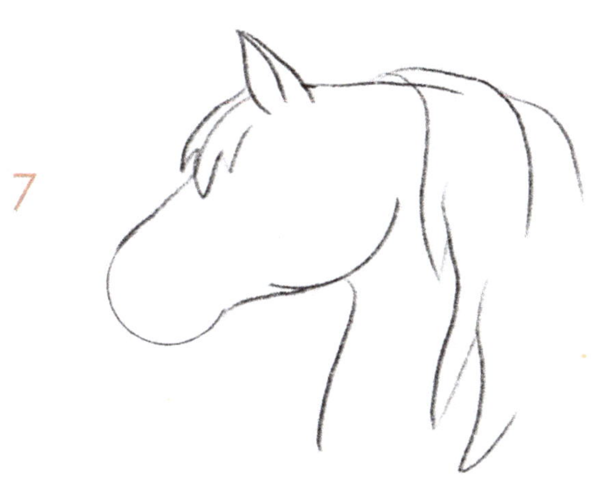

8

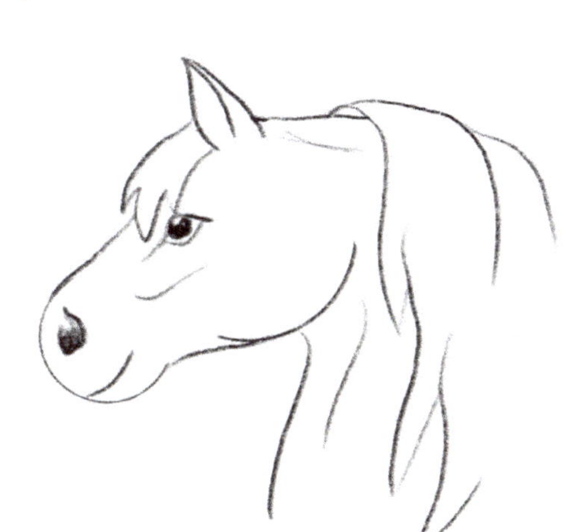

# Iced Chocolate

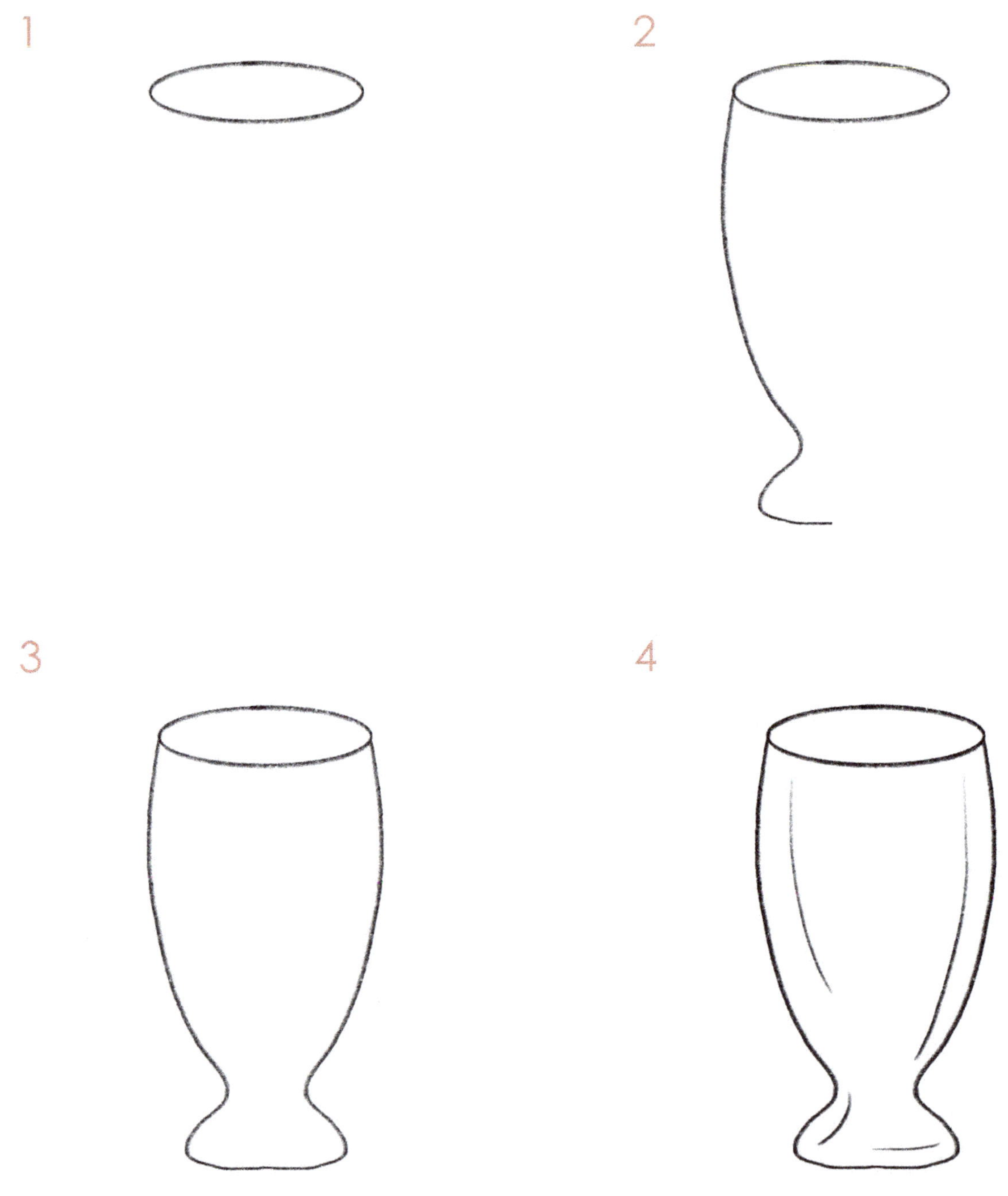

5

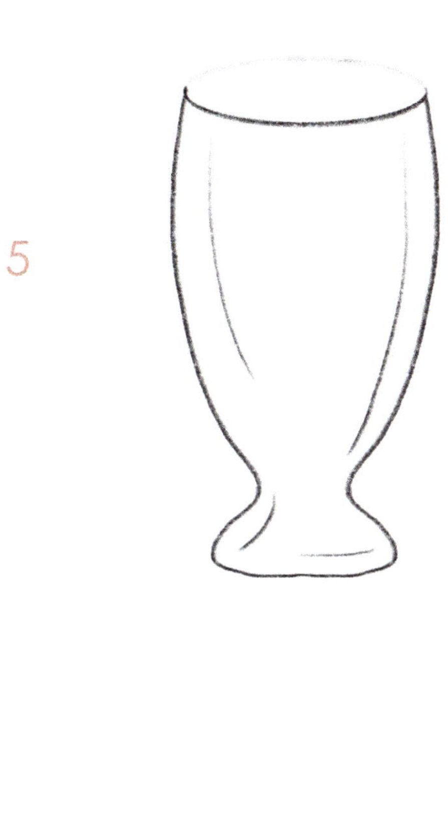

6

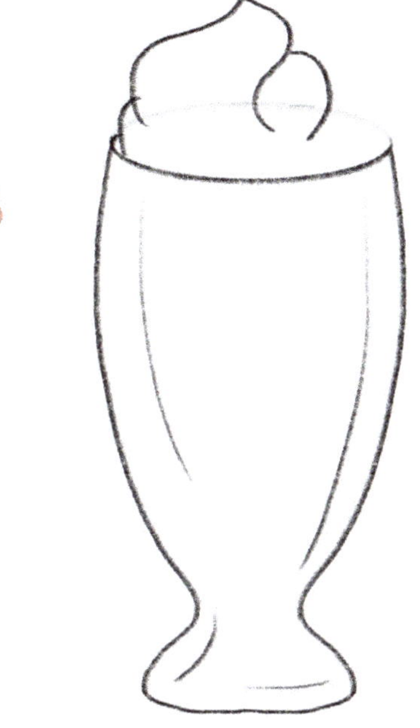

7

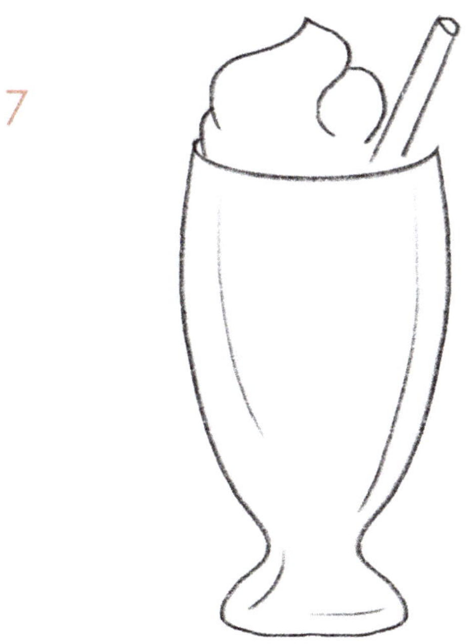

8

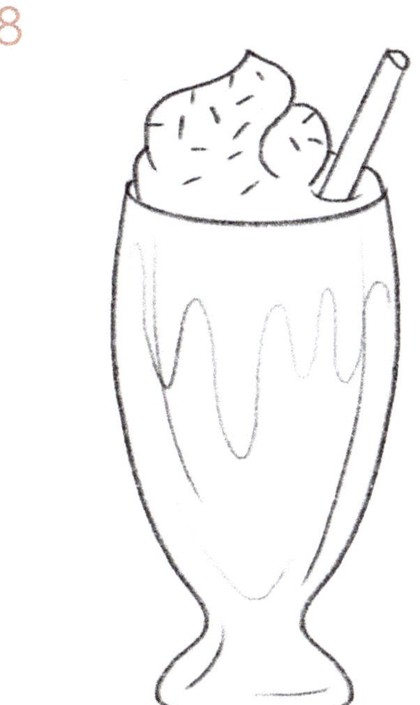

# Kangaroo

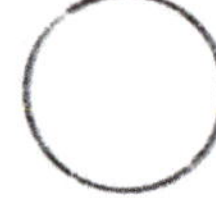

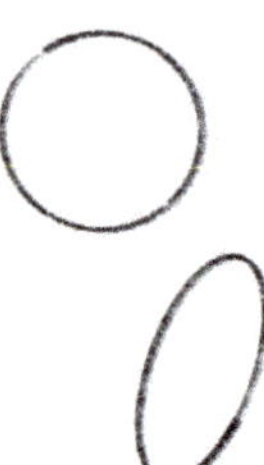

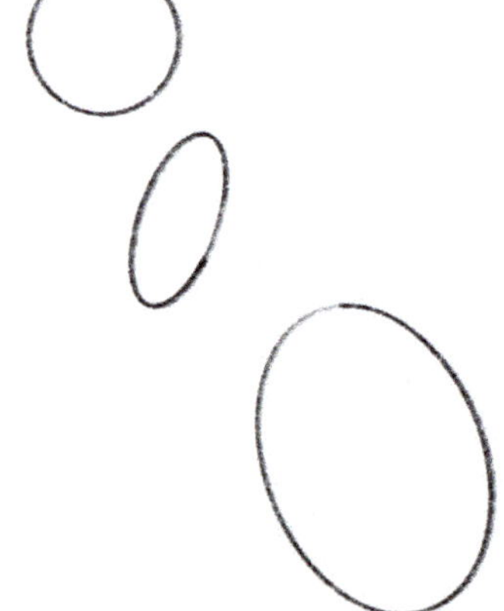

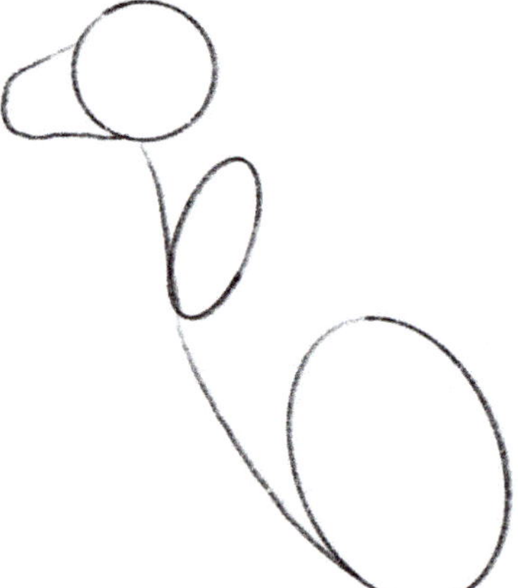

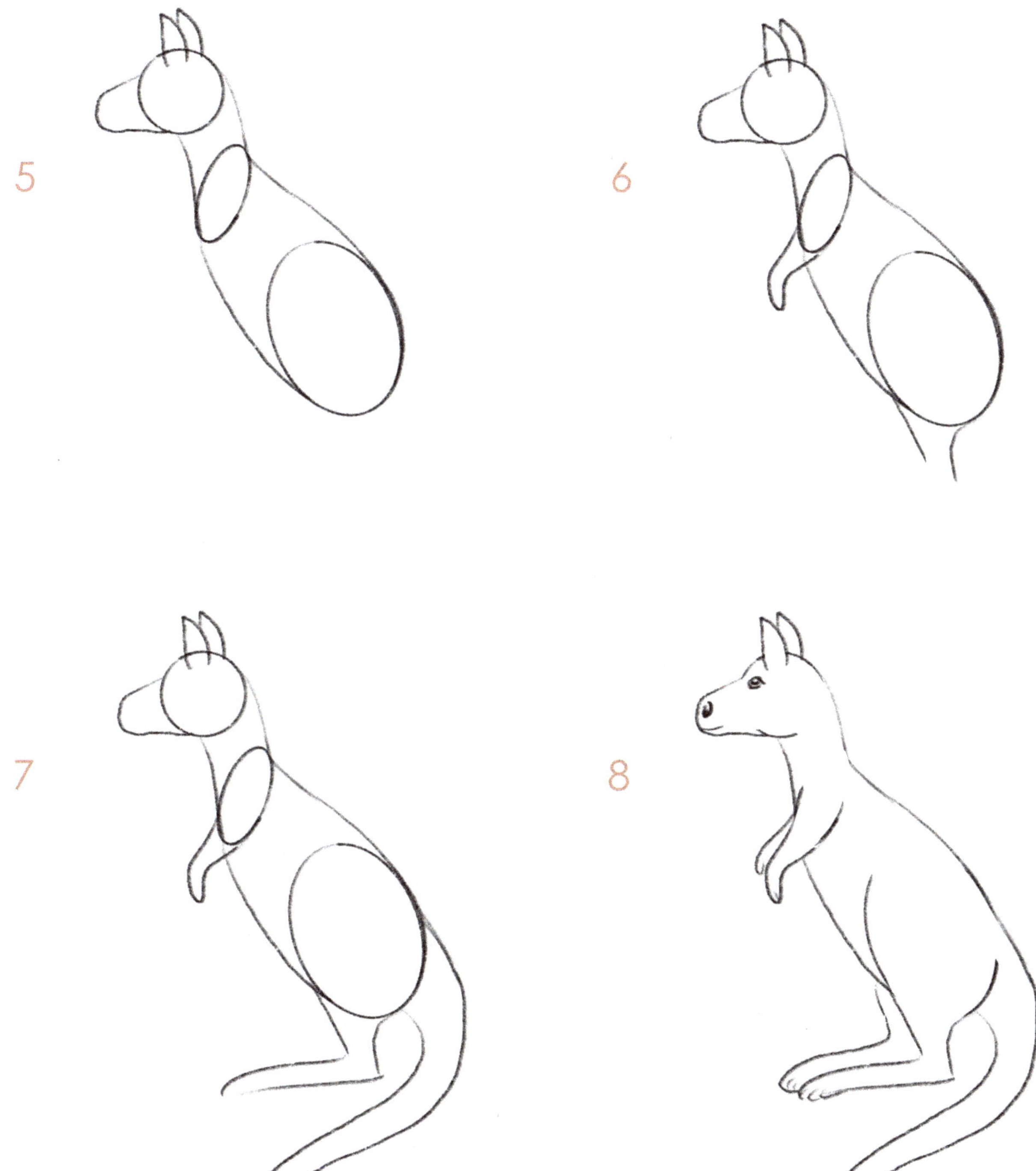

# Lily pad

1

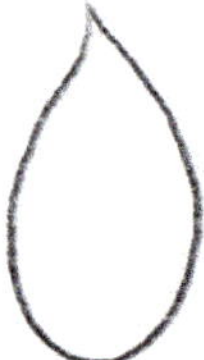

2

3

4

5

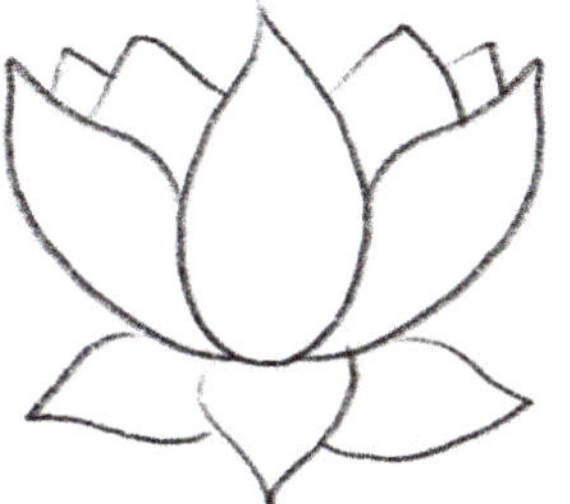

6

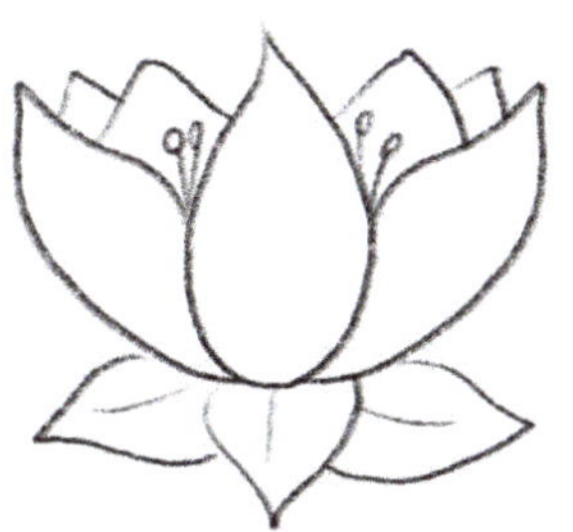

7

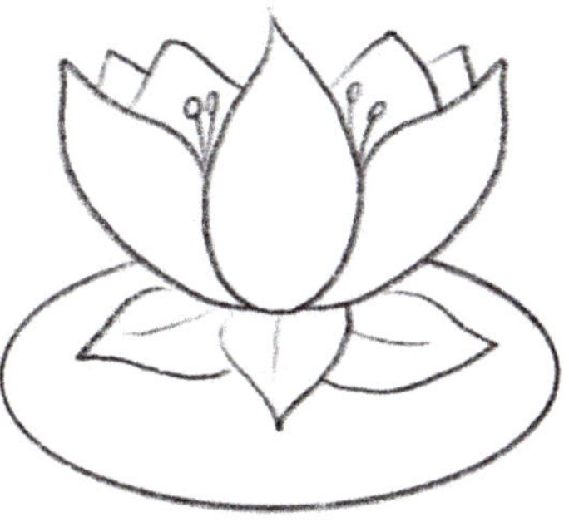

8

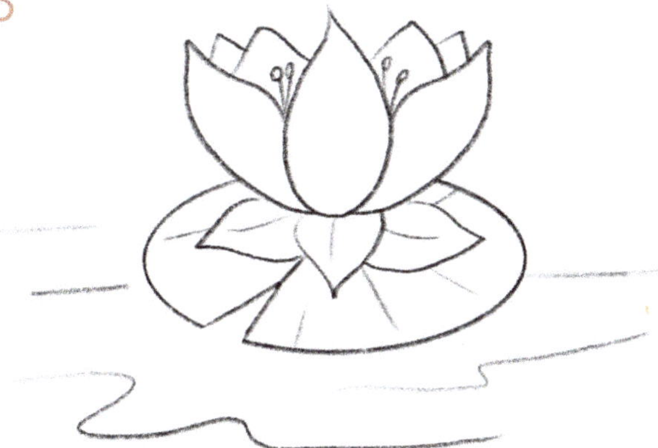

# Monkey

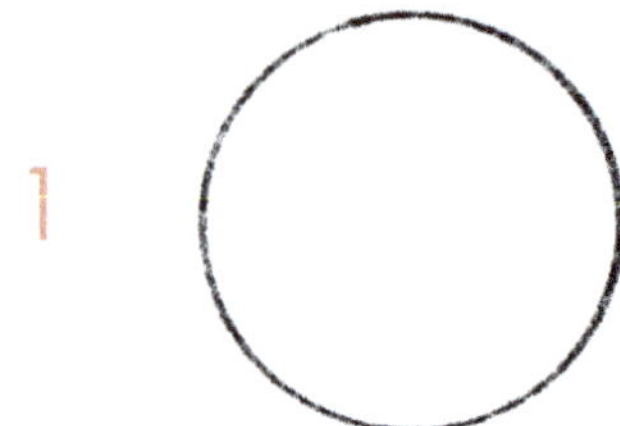

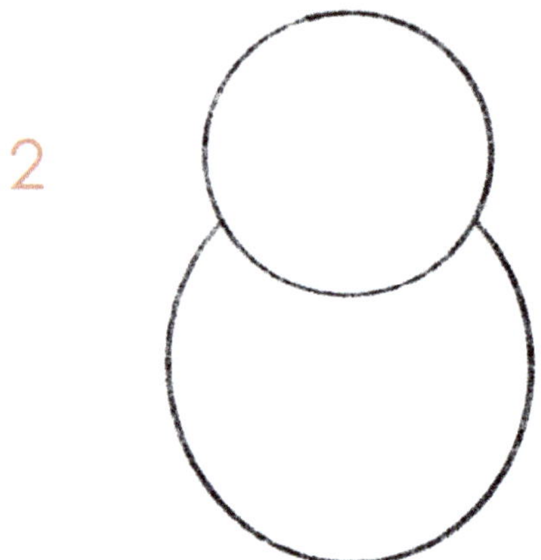

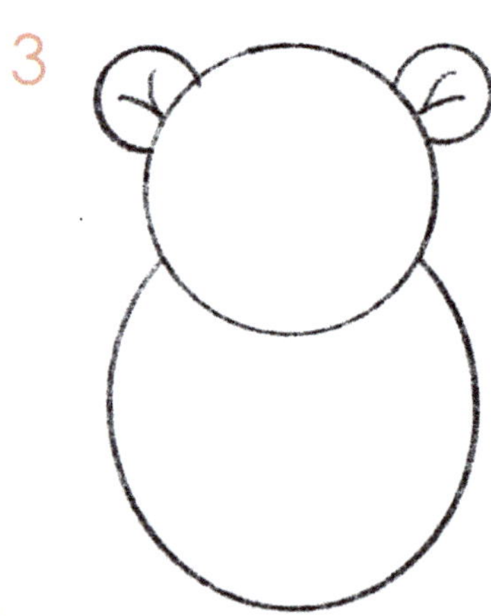

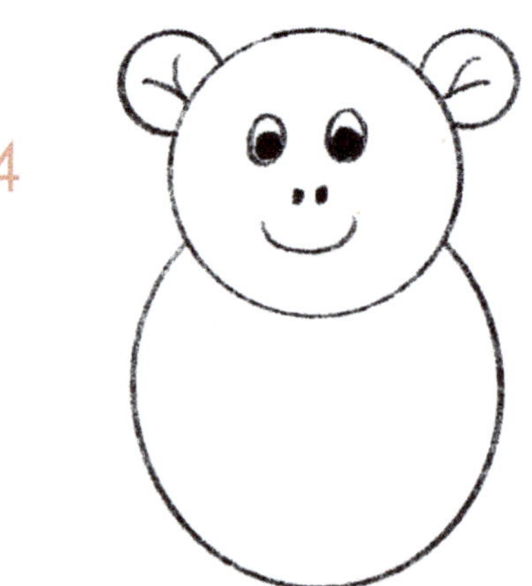

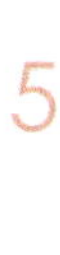 5

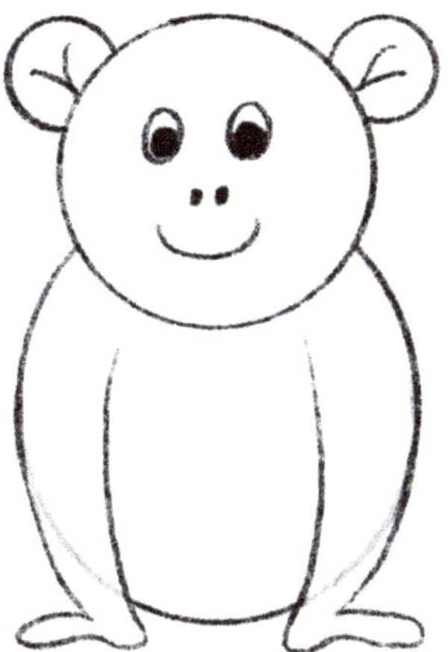

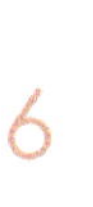 6

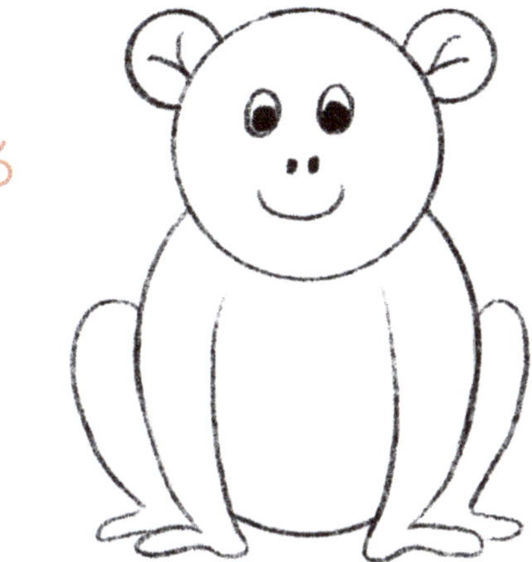

7

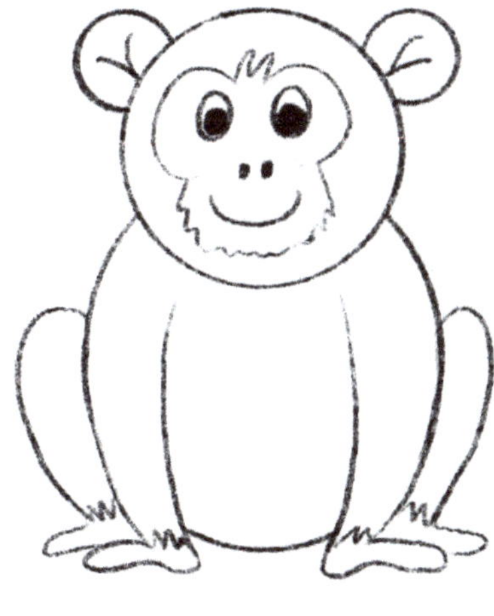

8

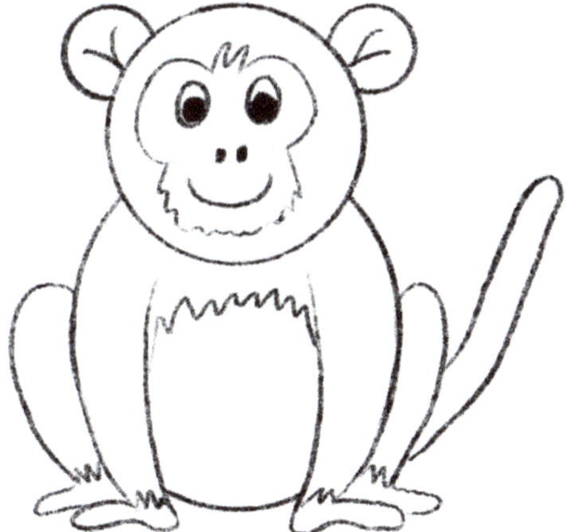

# Mouse

1

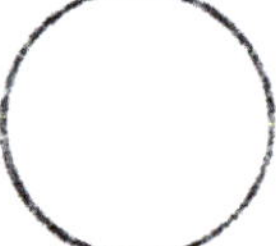

2

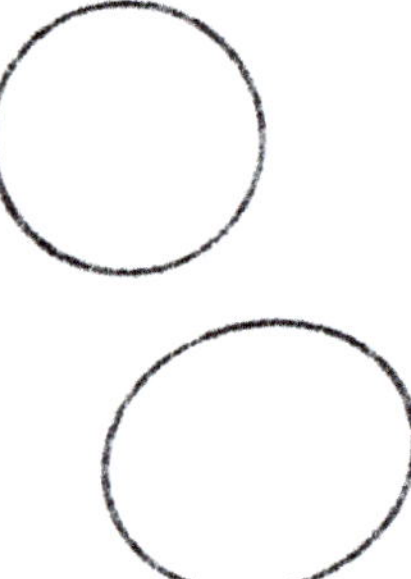

3

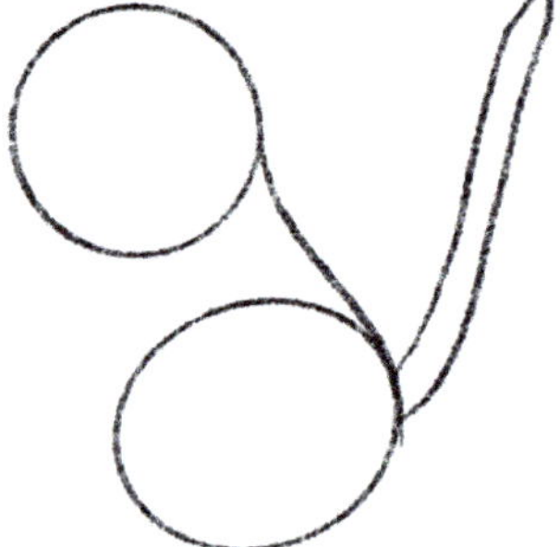

4

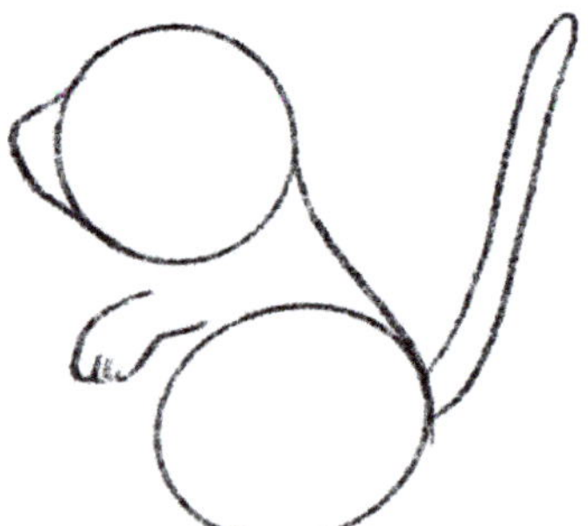

5

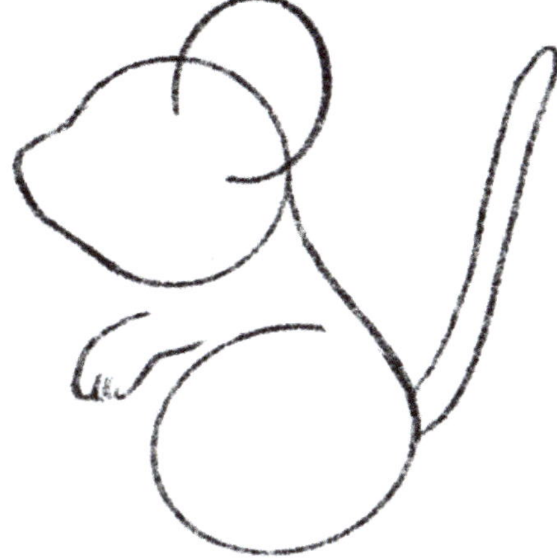

6

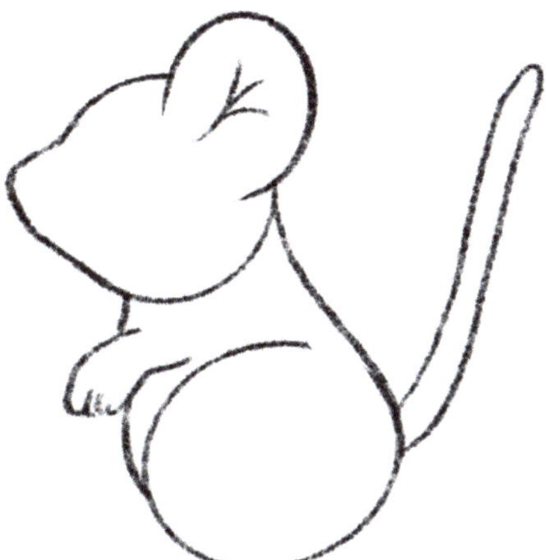

7

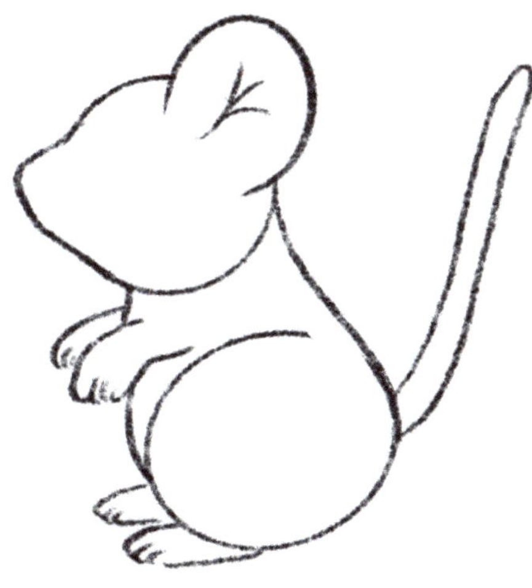

8

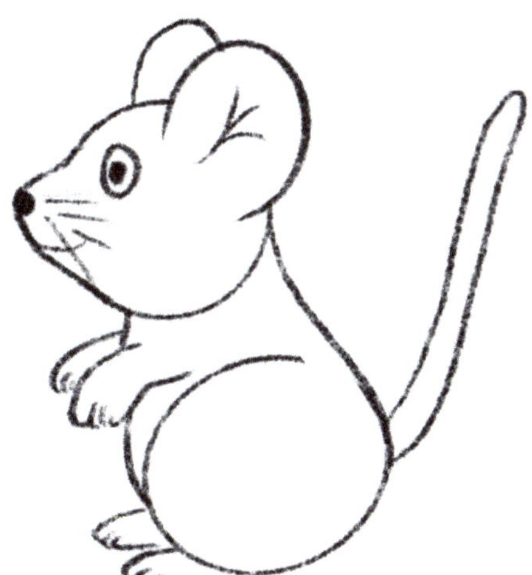

# Mushroom

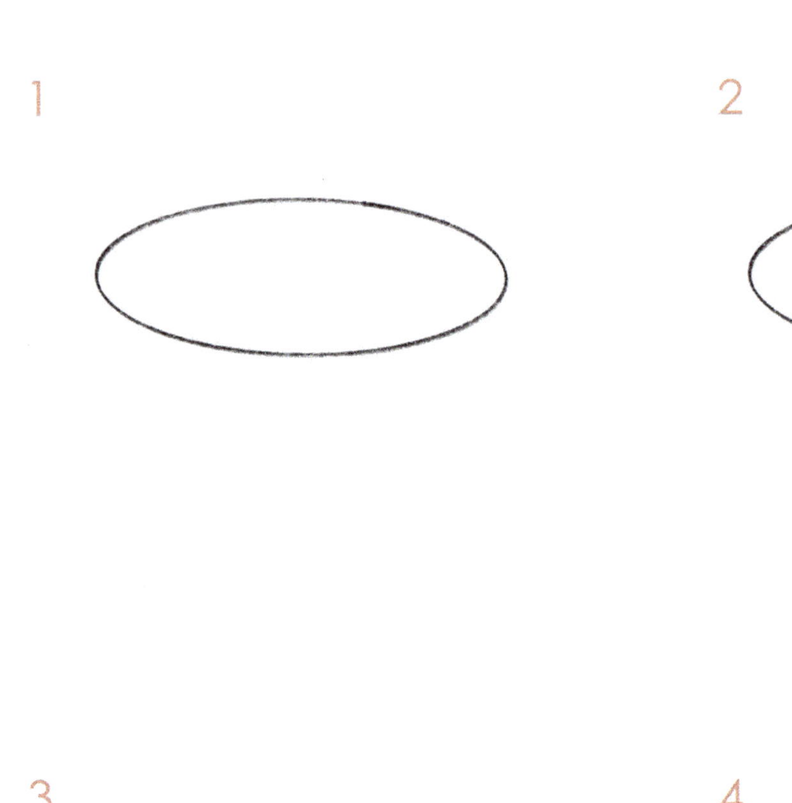

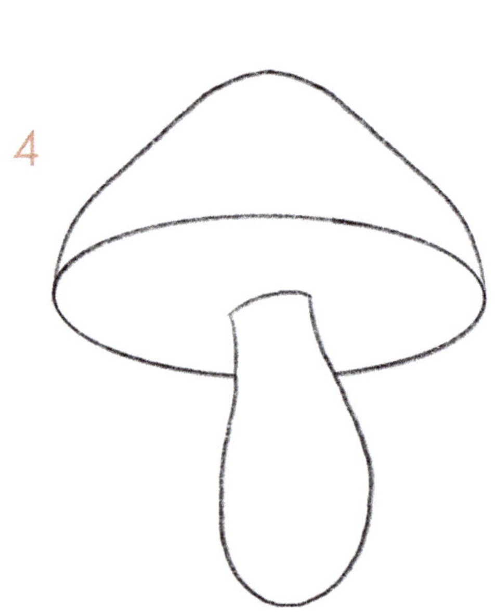

5

6

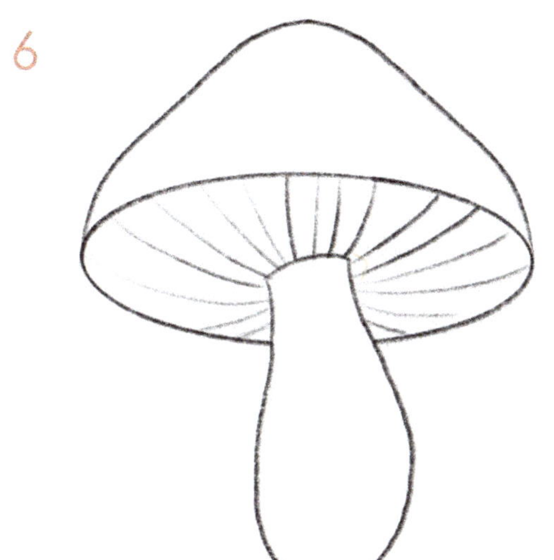

7

8

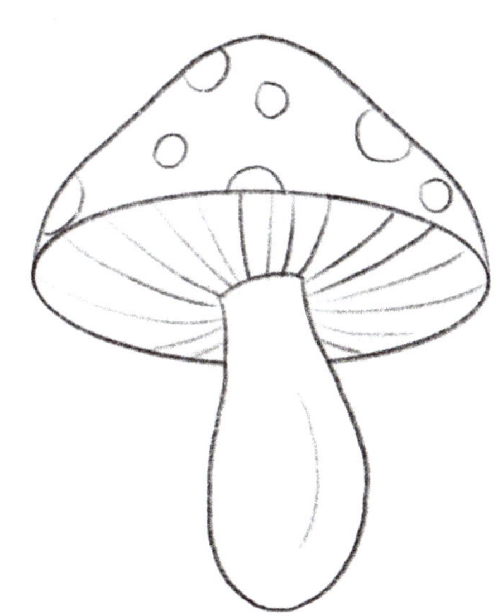

# Octopus

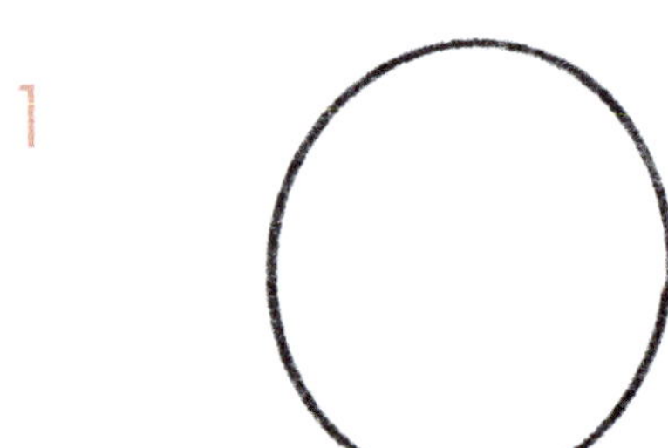

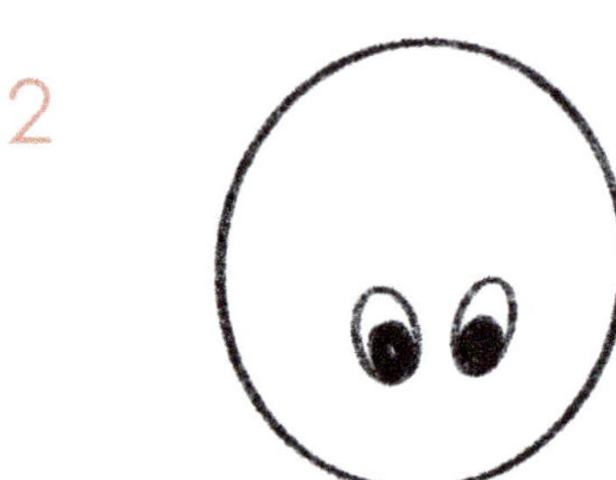

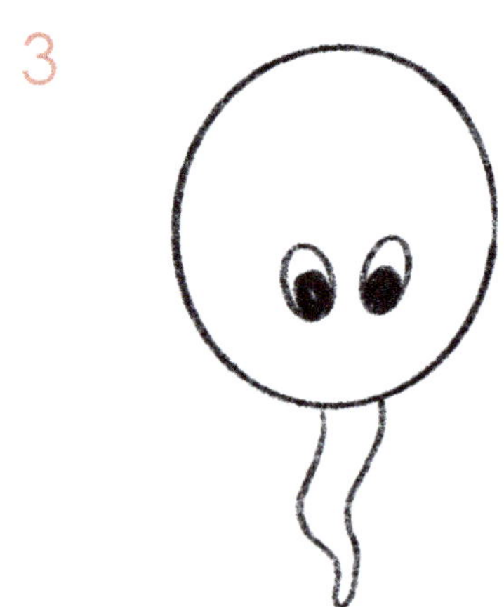

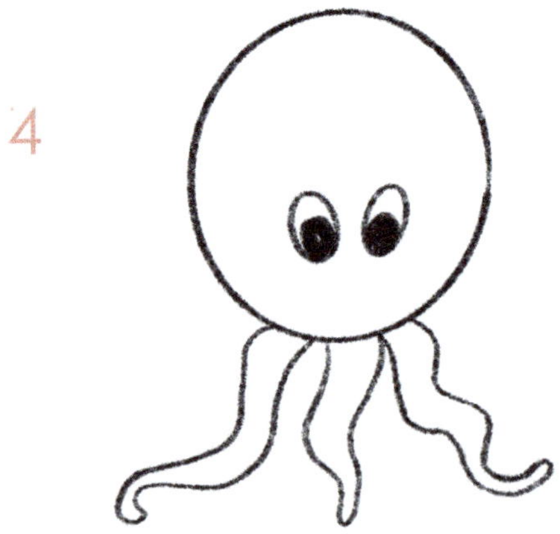

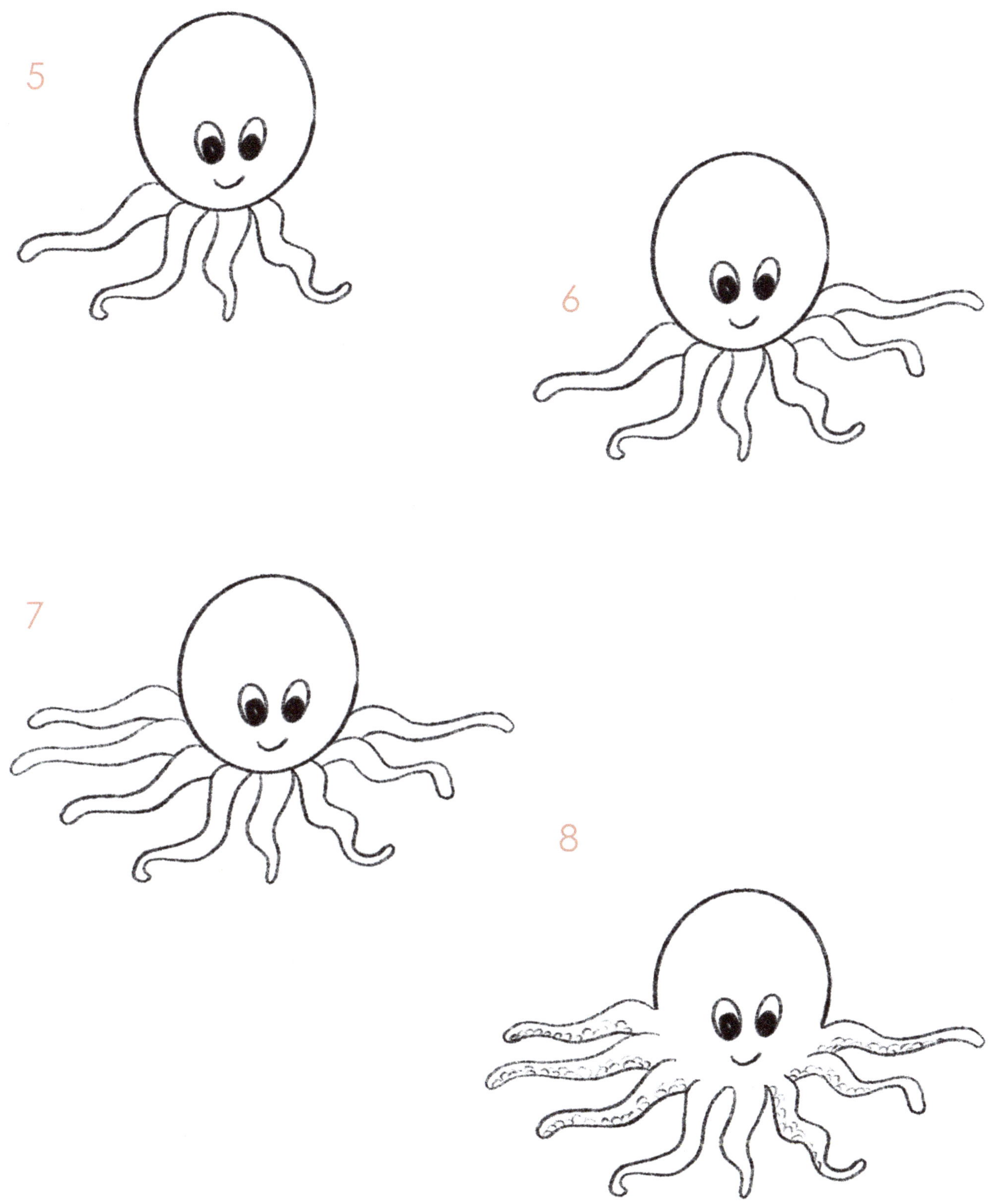


5
6
7
8

# Panda

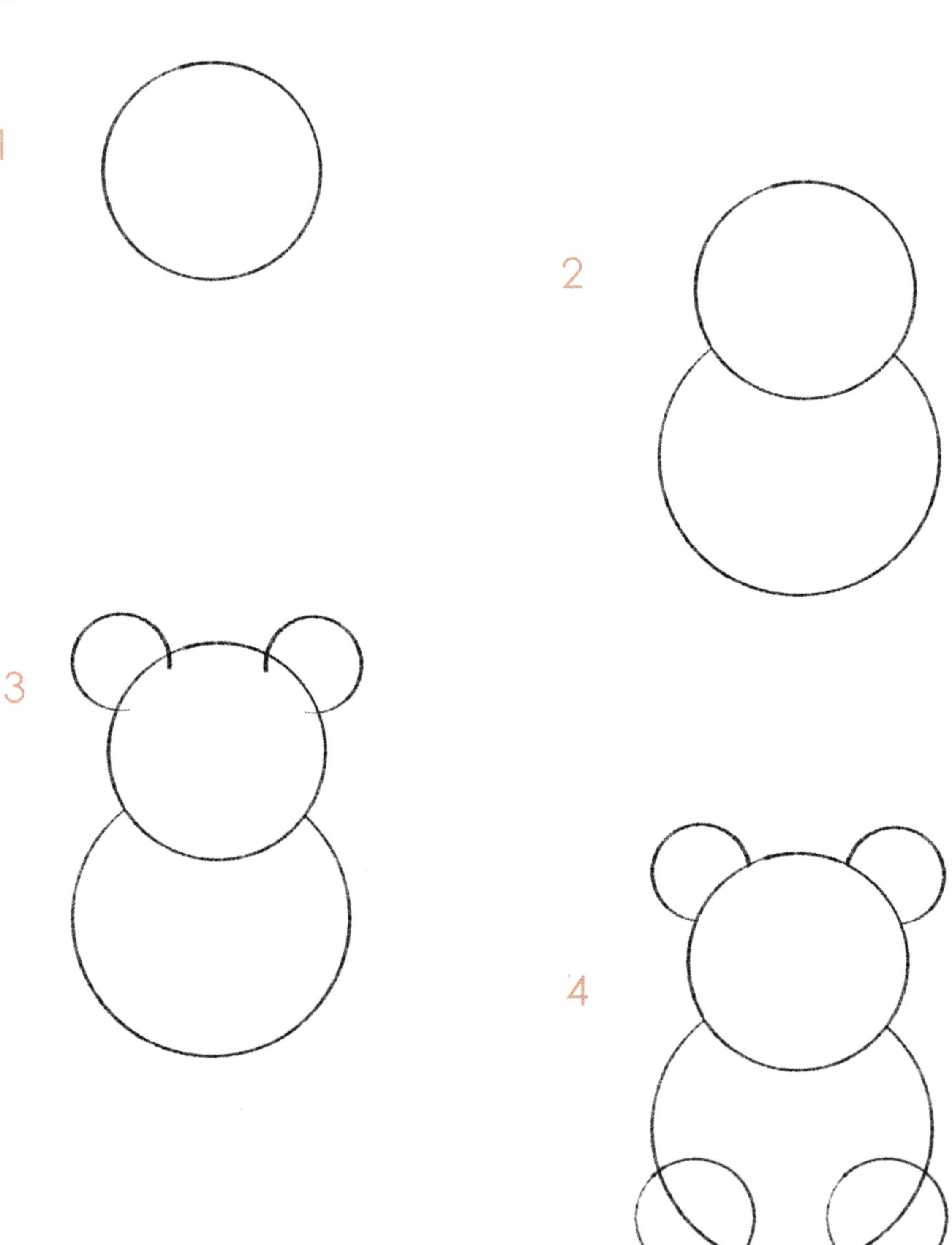

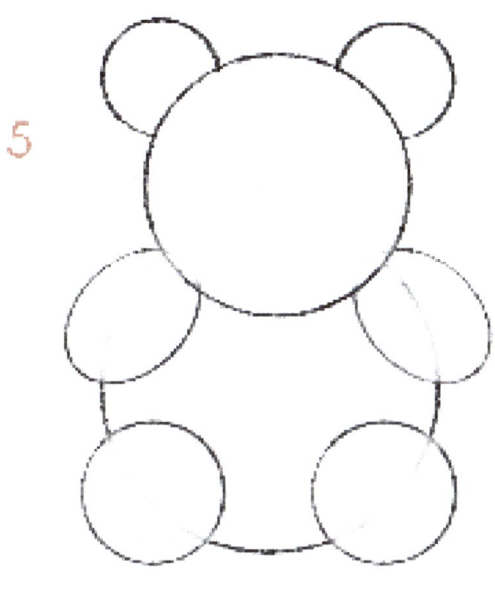

5

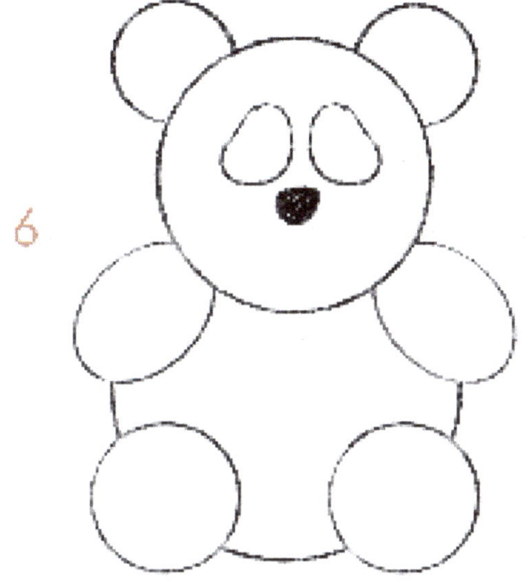

6

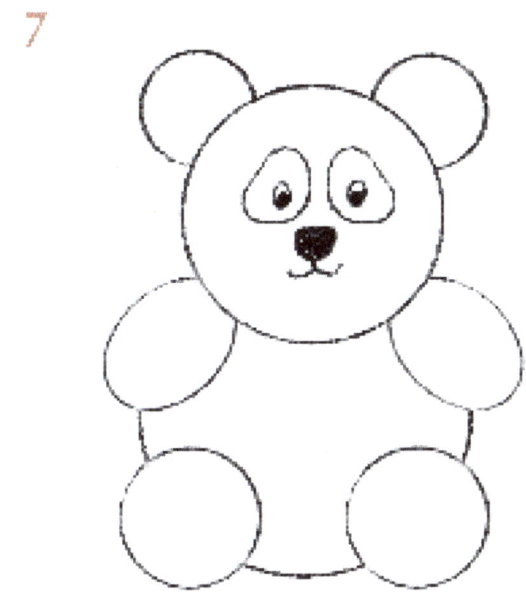

7

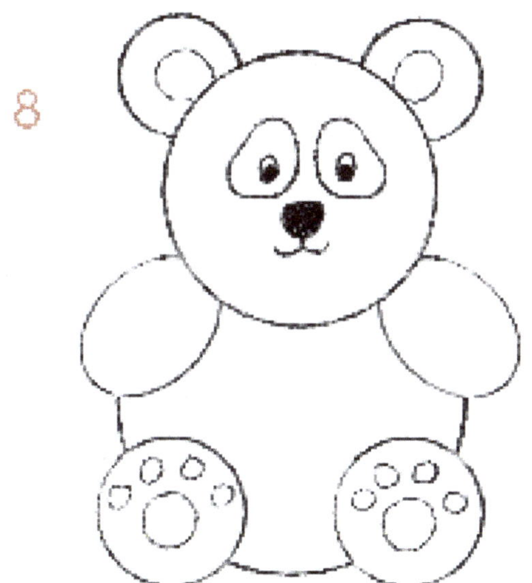

8

# Pig

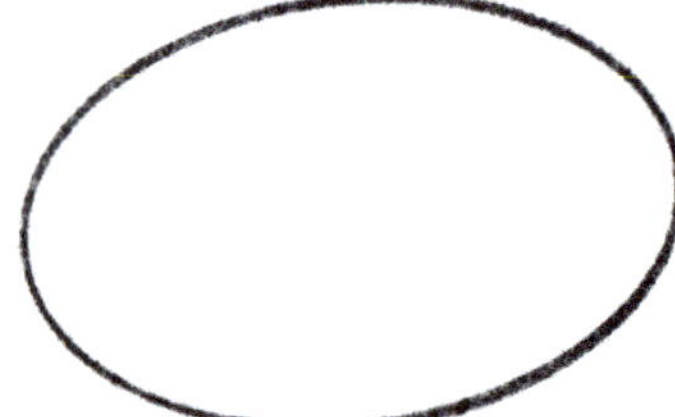

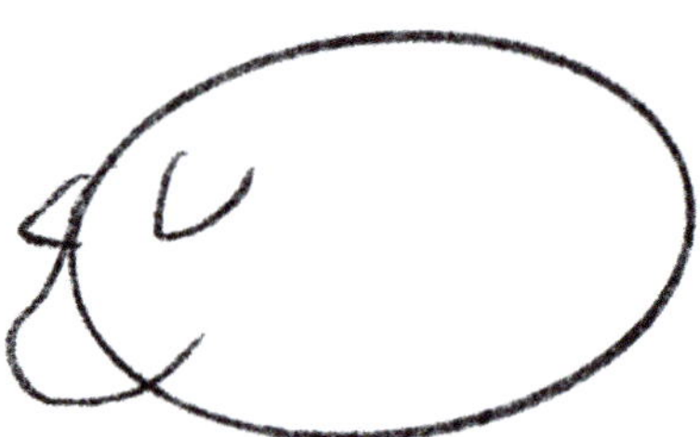

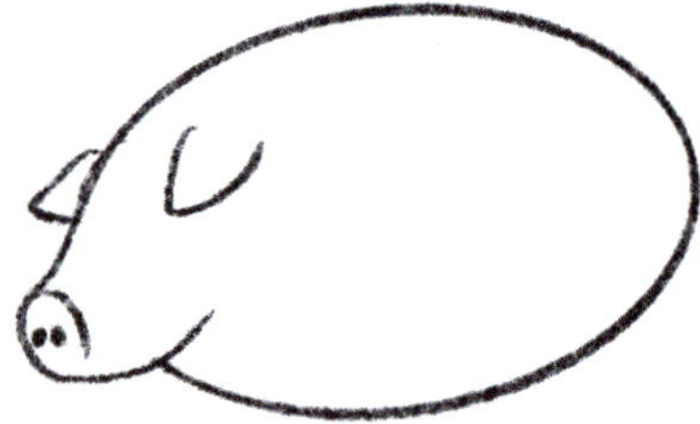

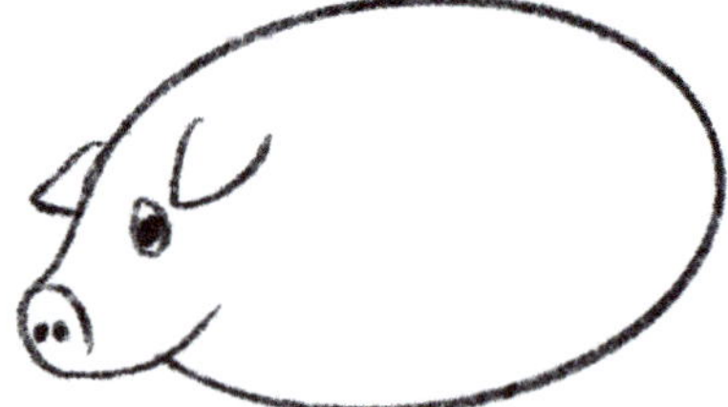

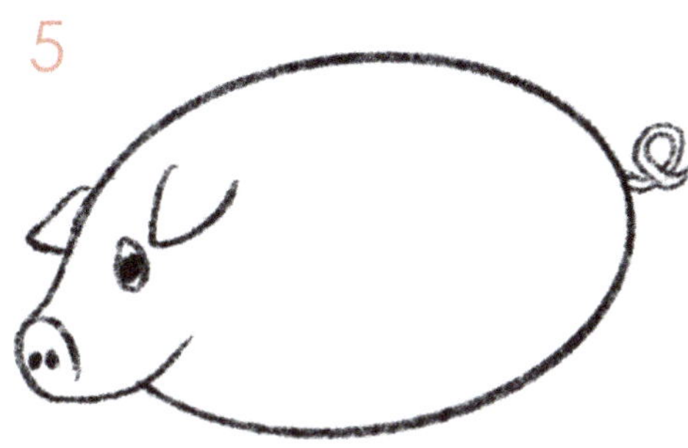

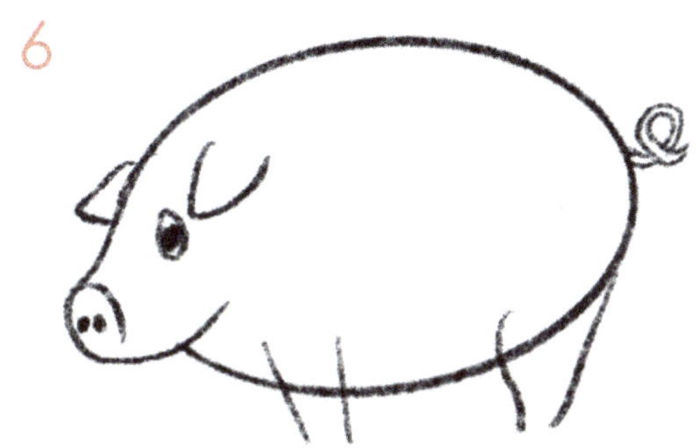

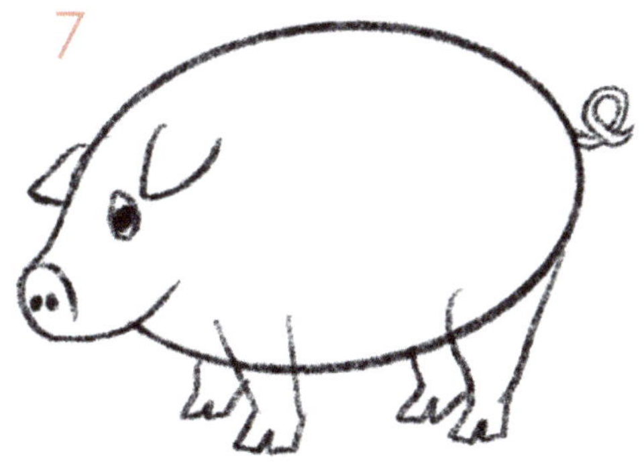

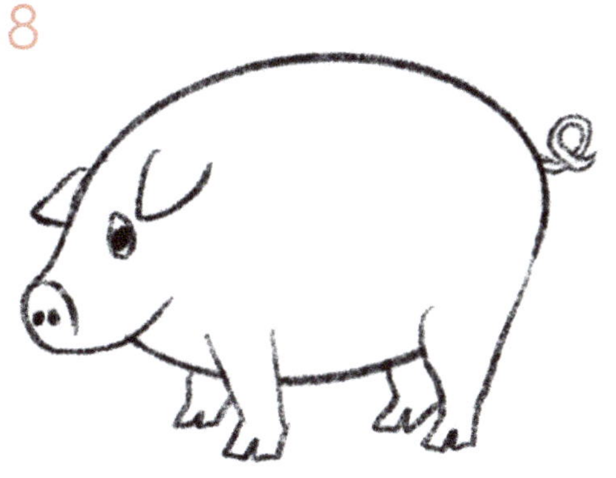

# Platypus

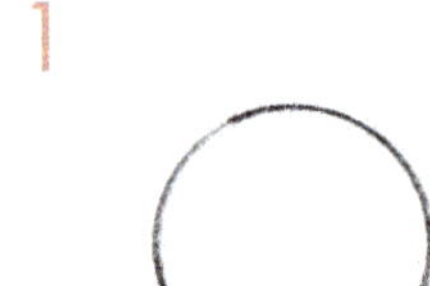

1

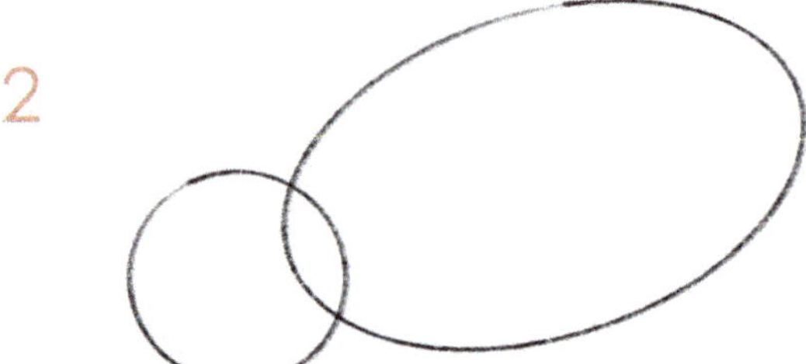

2

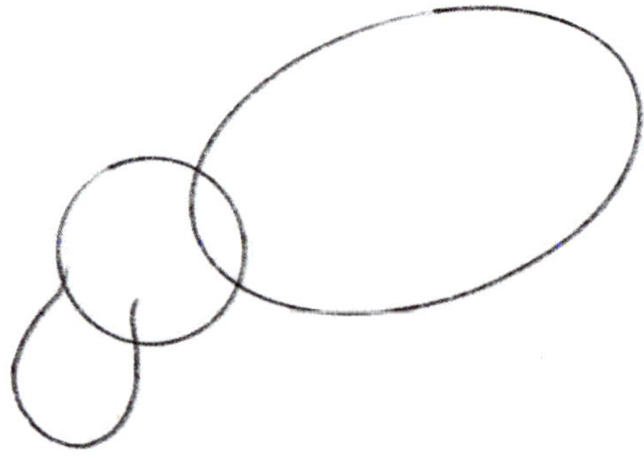

3

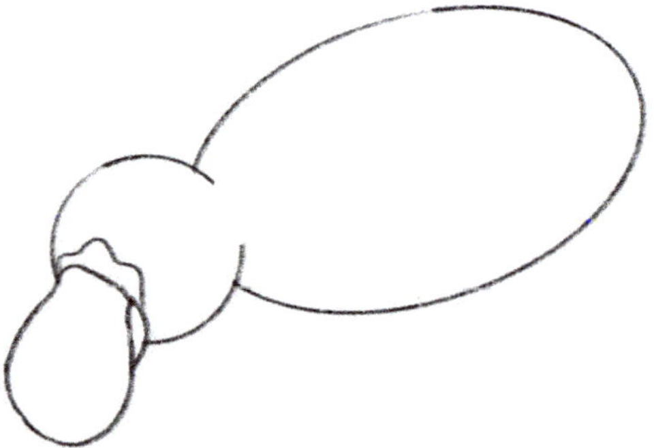

4

5

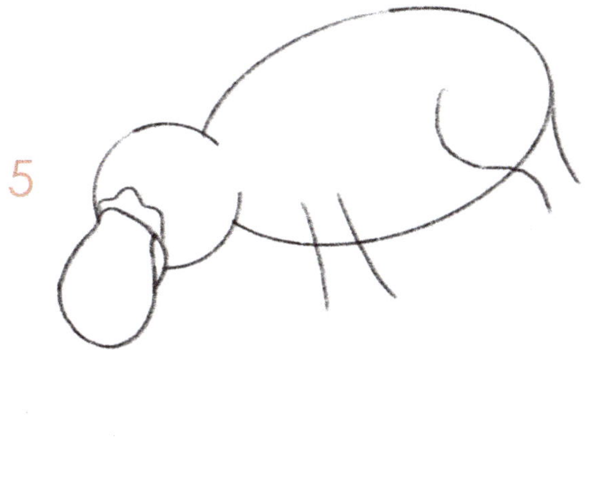

6

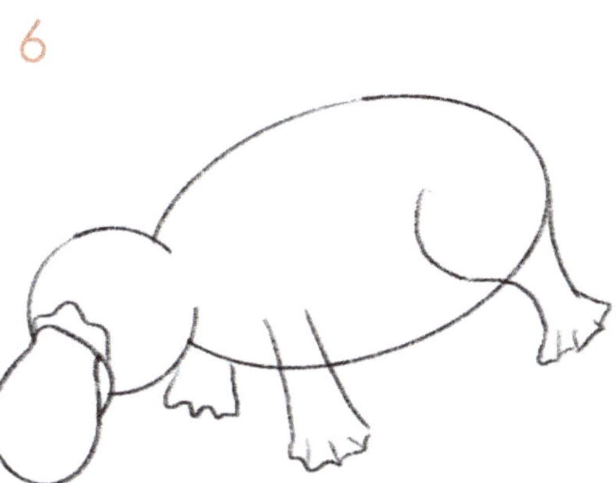

7

8

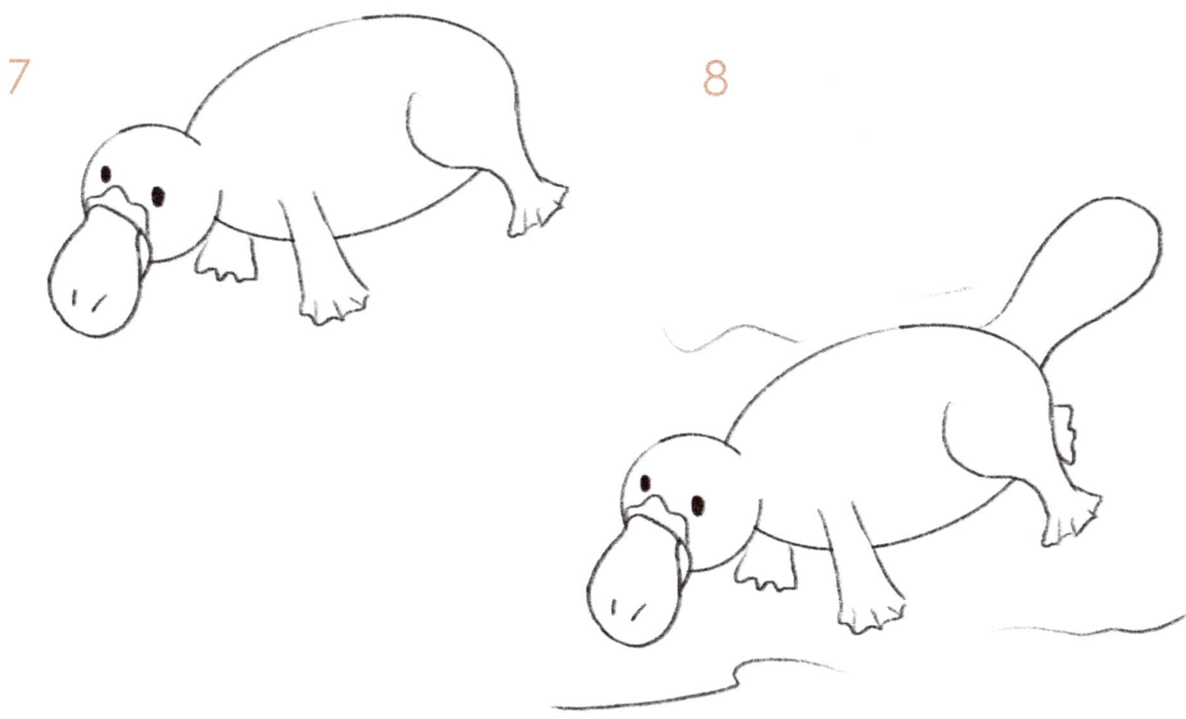

# Rabbit

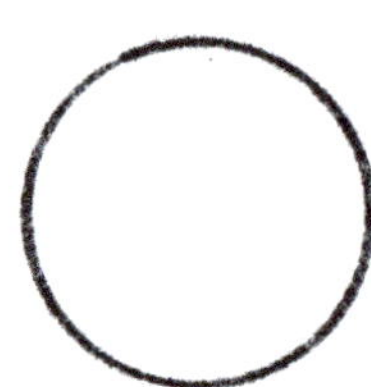

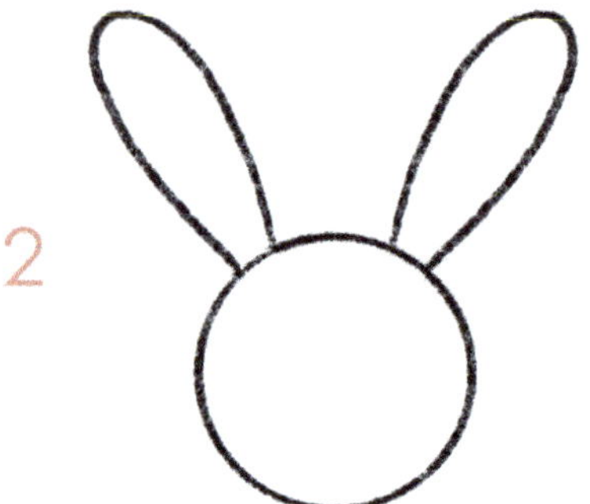

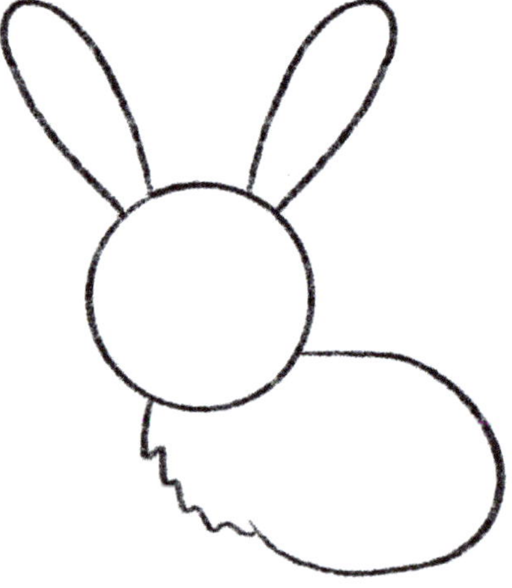

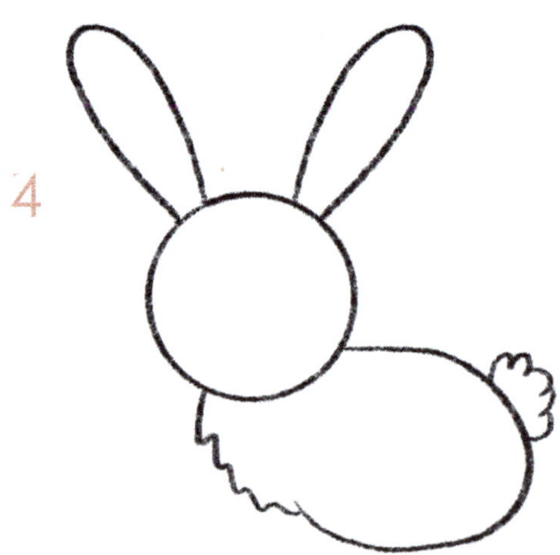

5

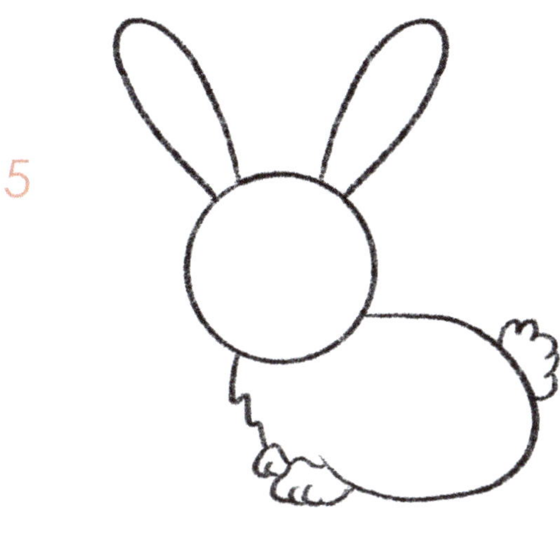

6

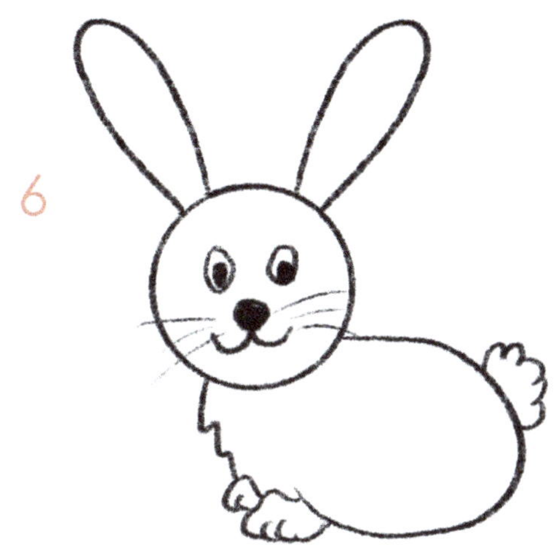

7

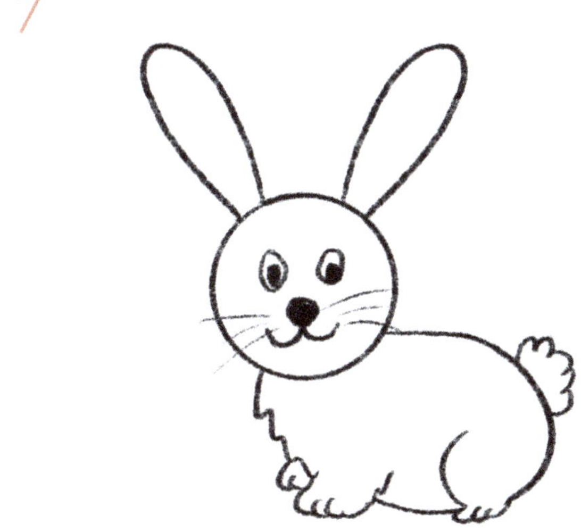

8

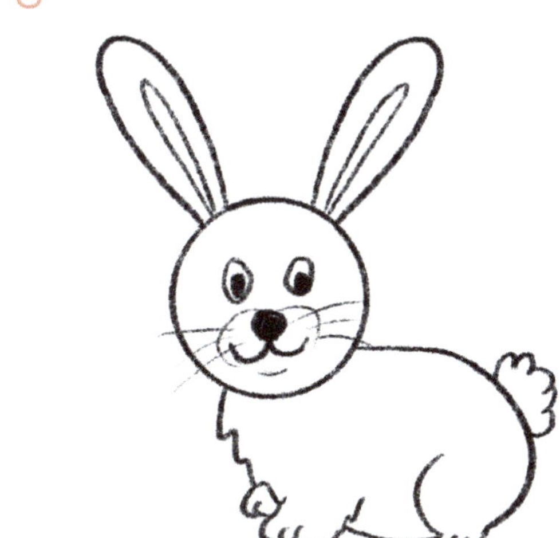

# Rose

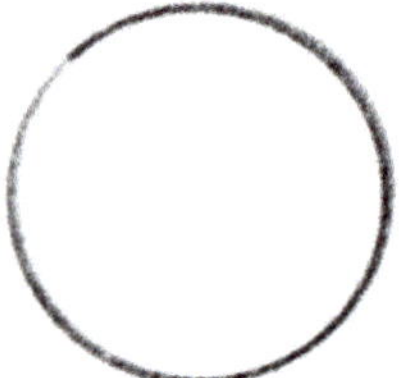

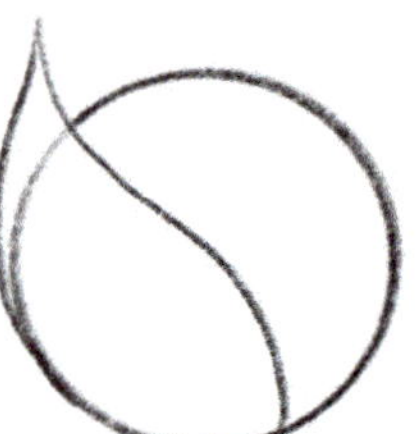

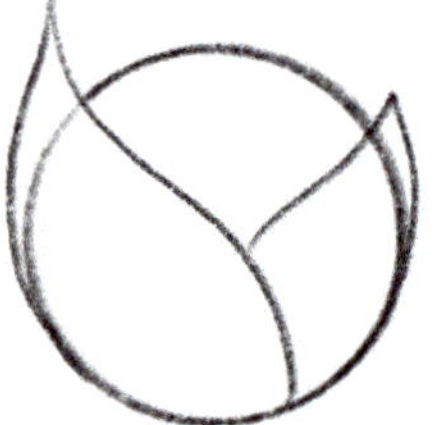

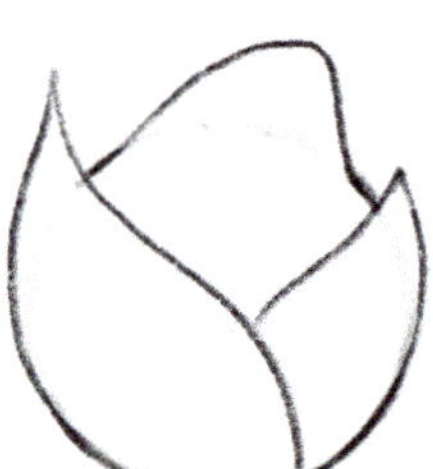

5 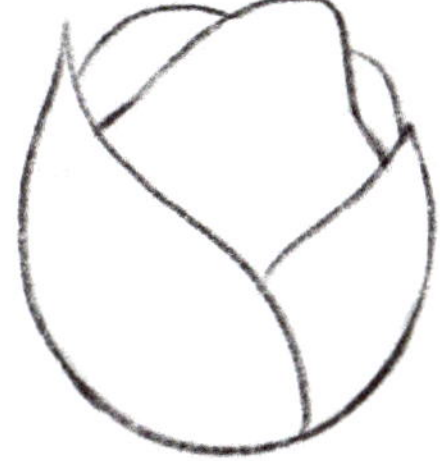

6 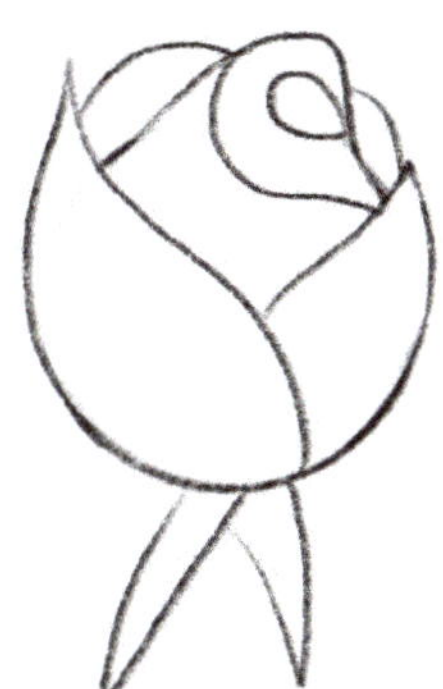

7 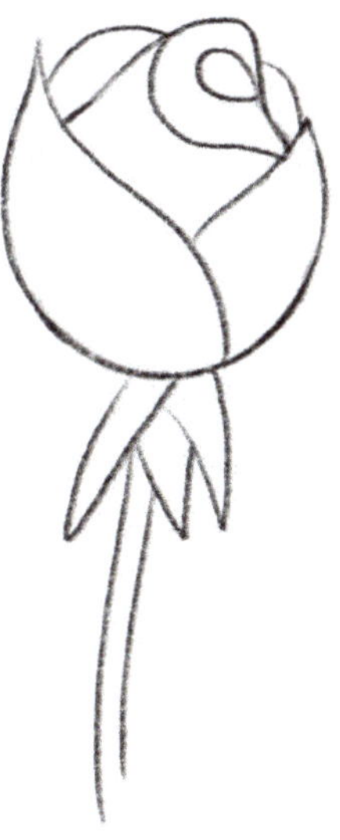

8 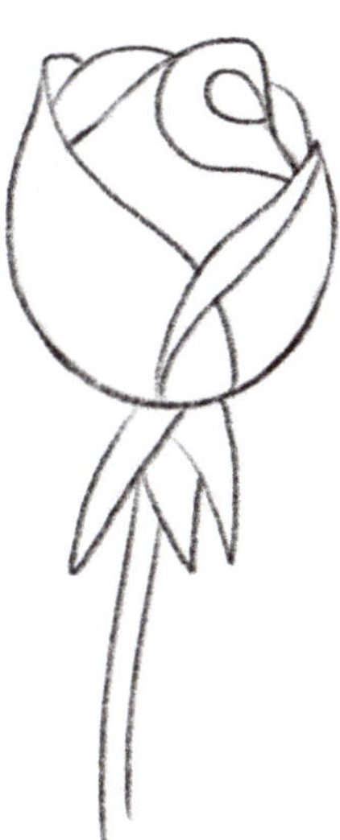

# Seahorse

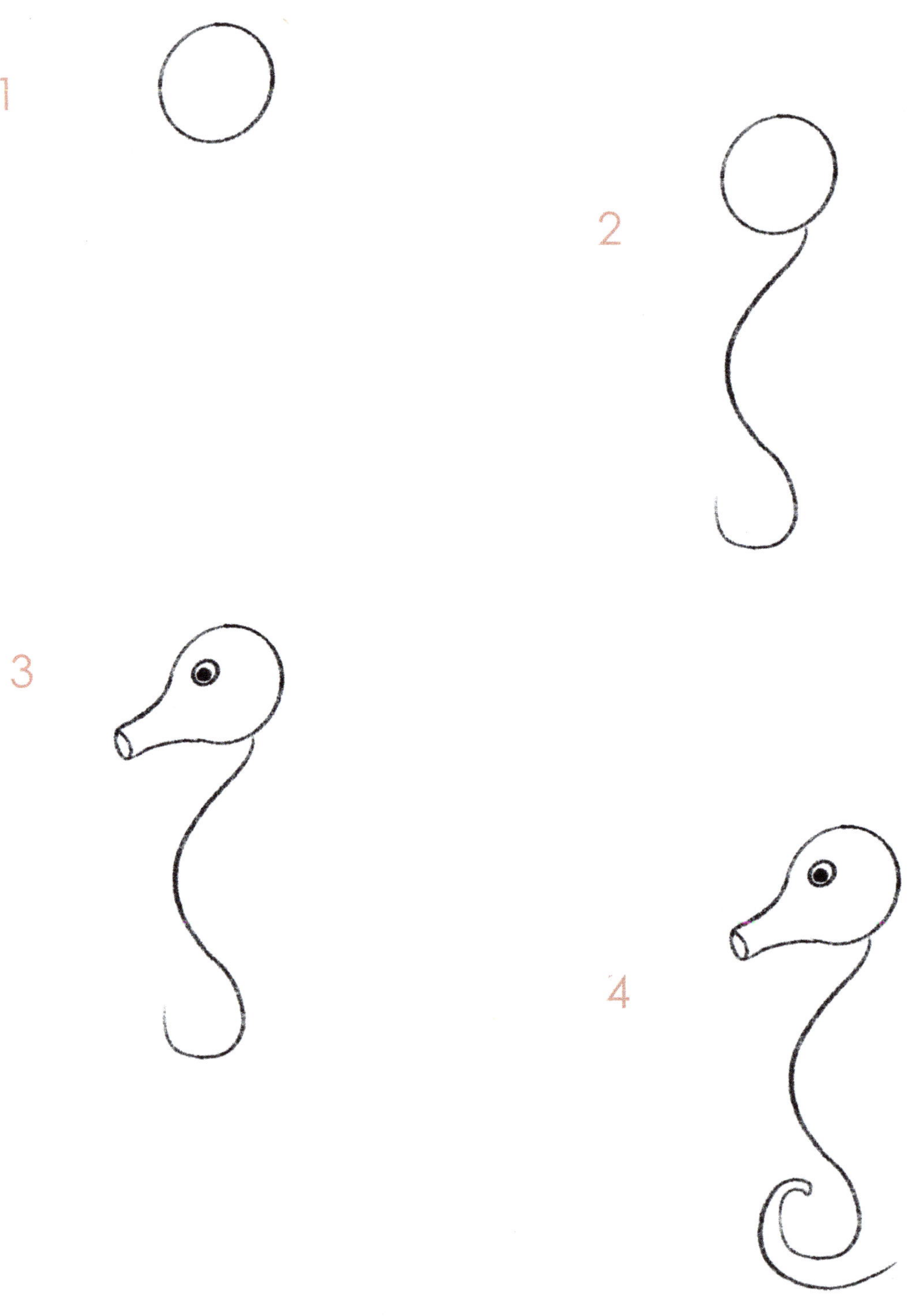

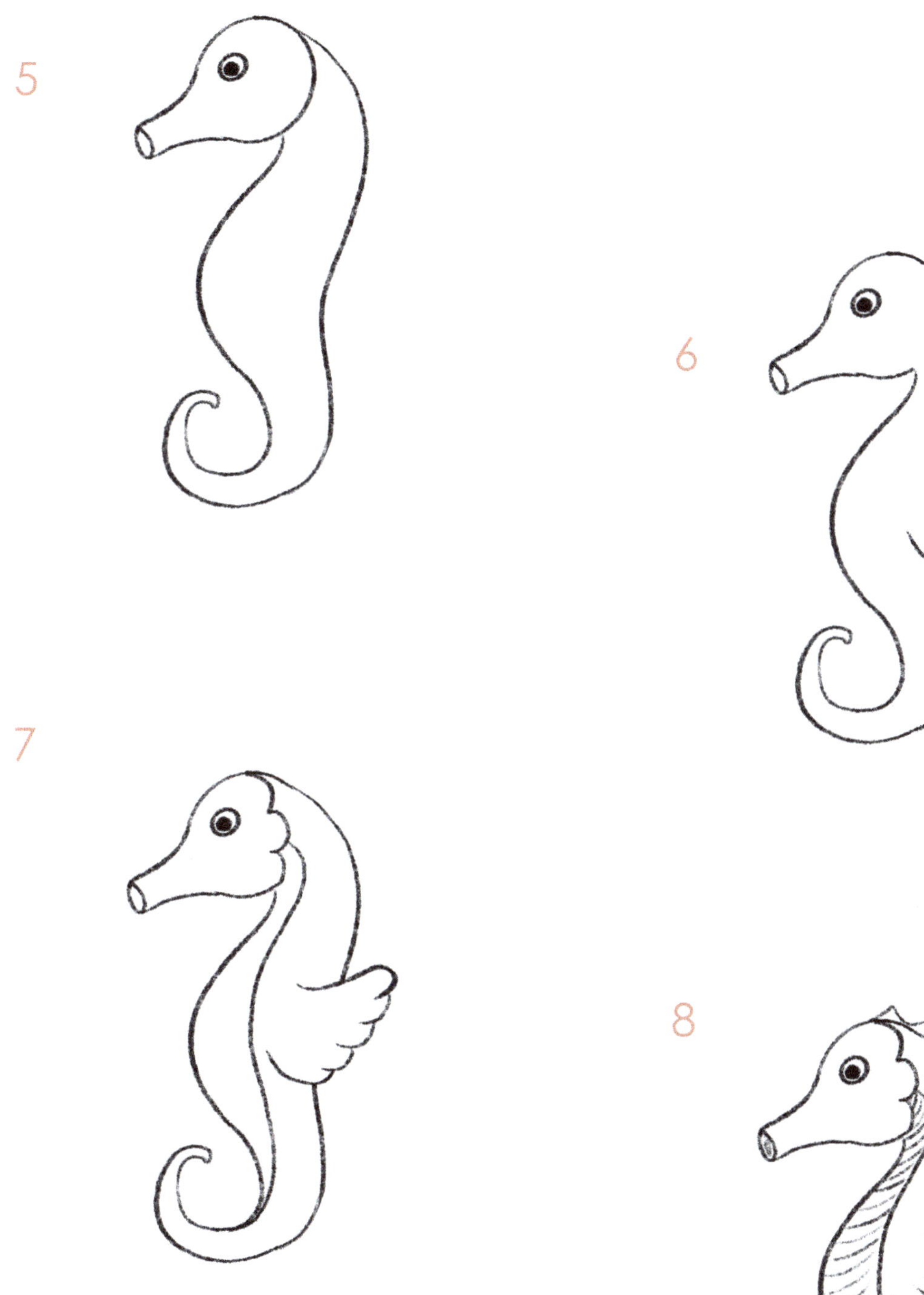


5
6
7
8

# Shark

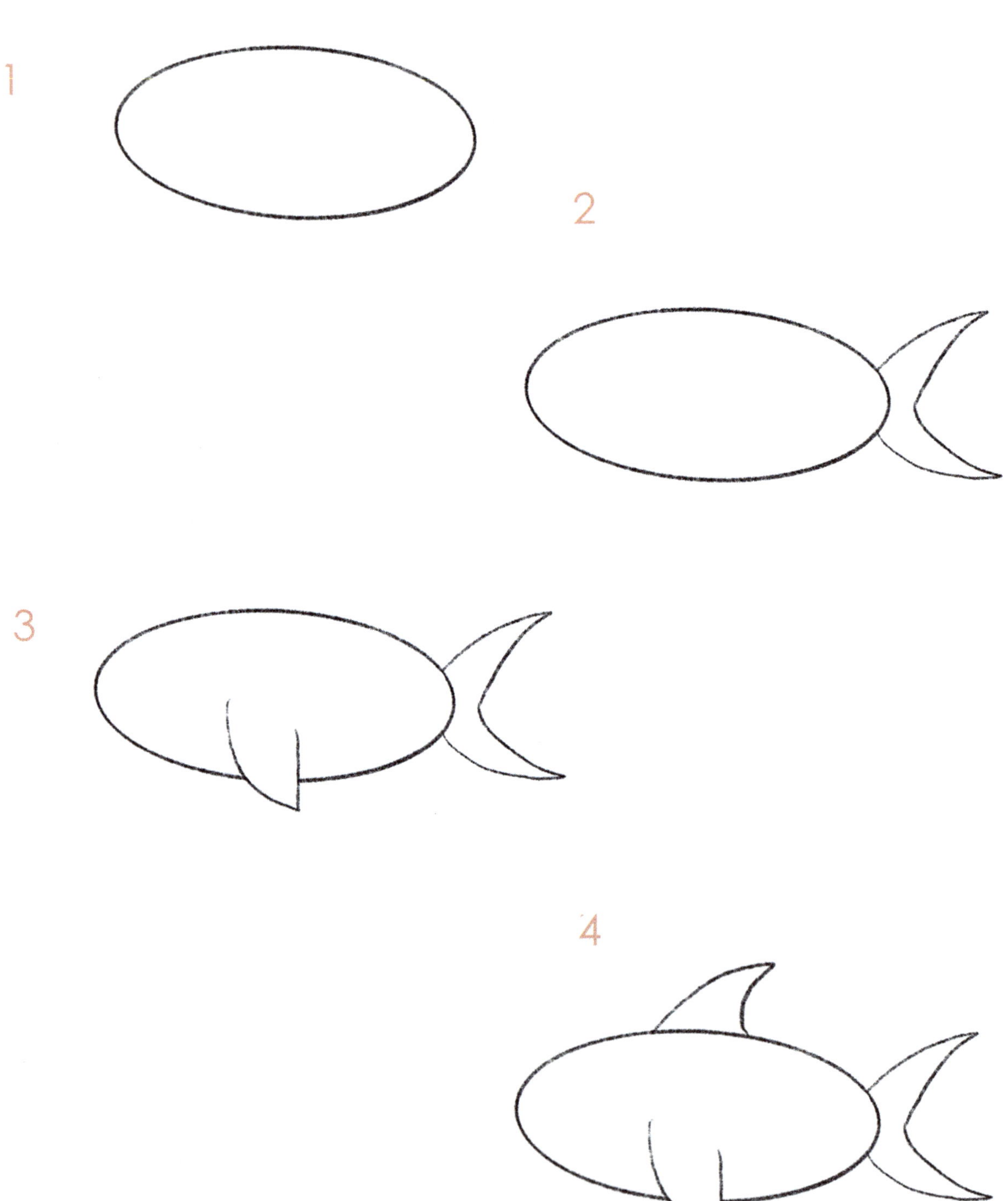

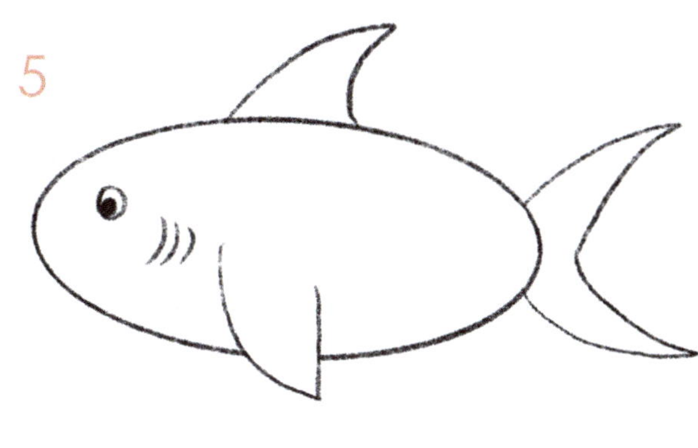

6

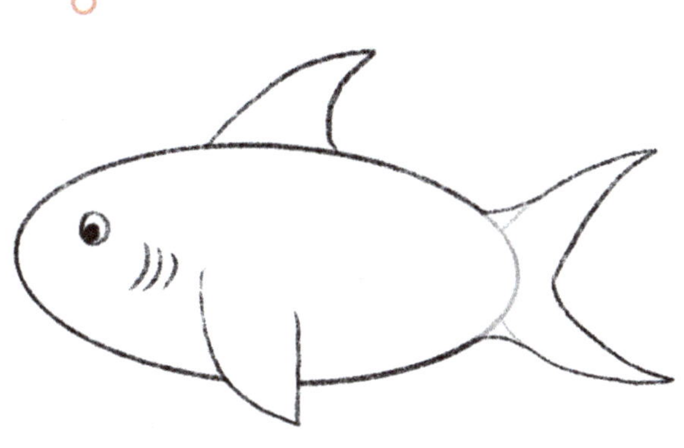

7

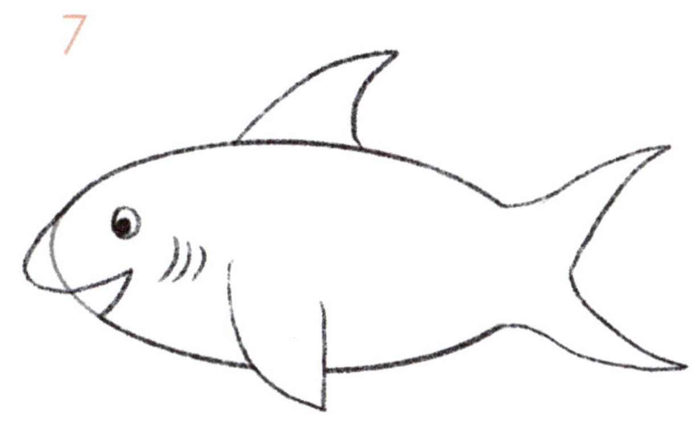

8

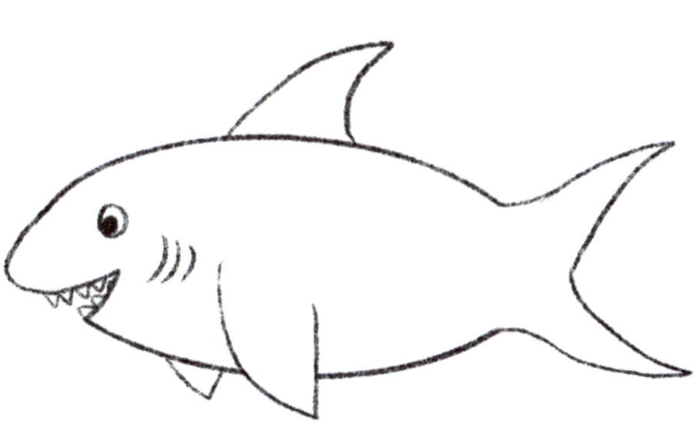

# Snake

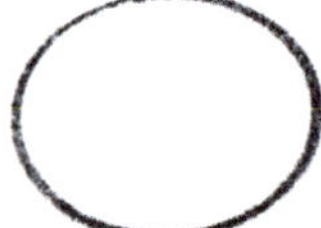

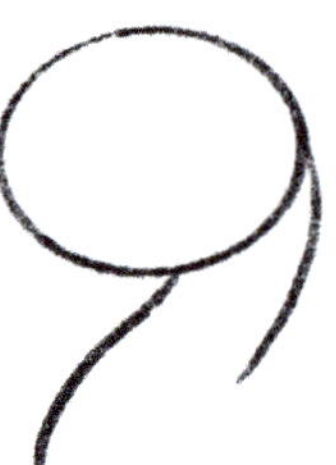

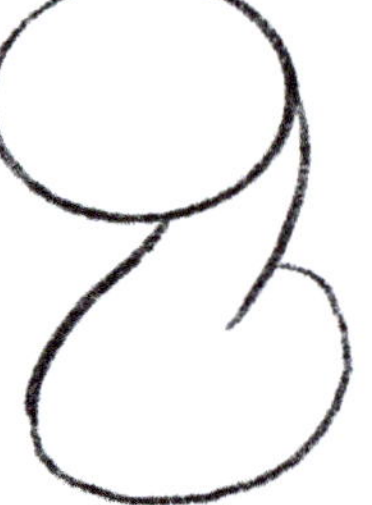

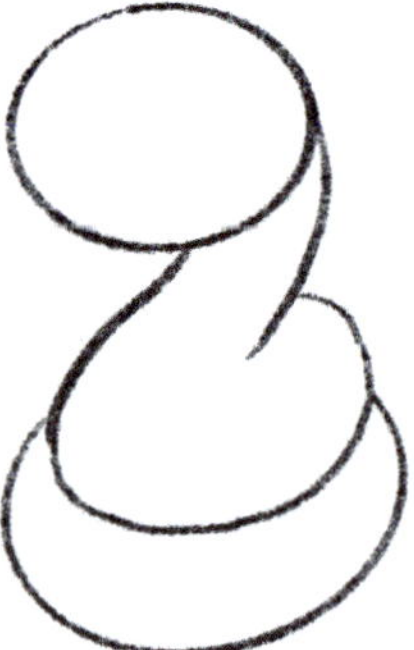

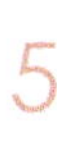

5

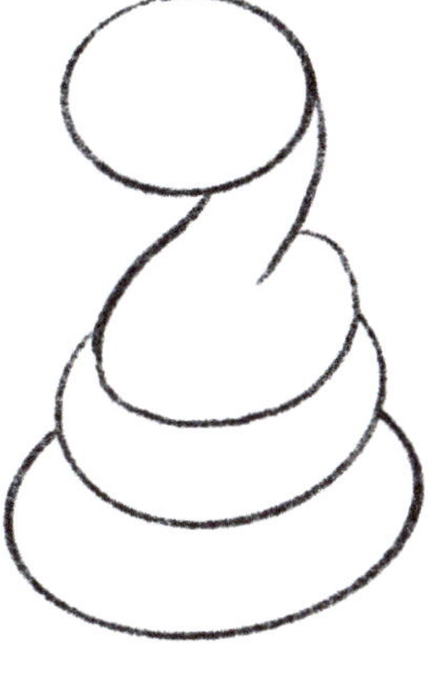

6

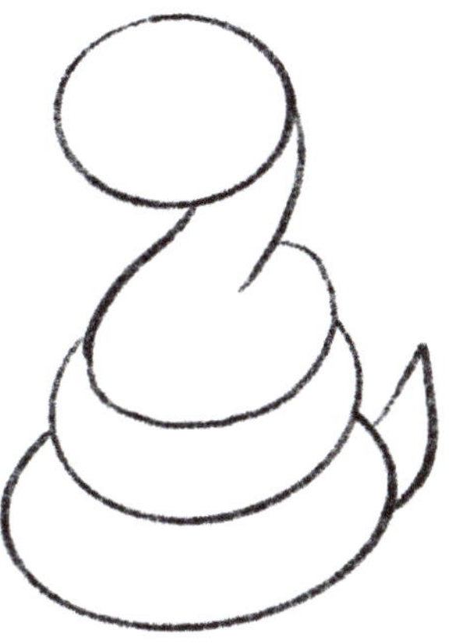

7

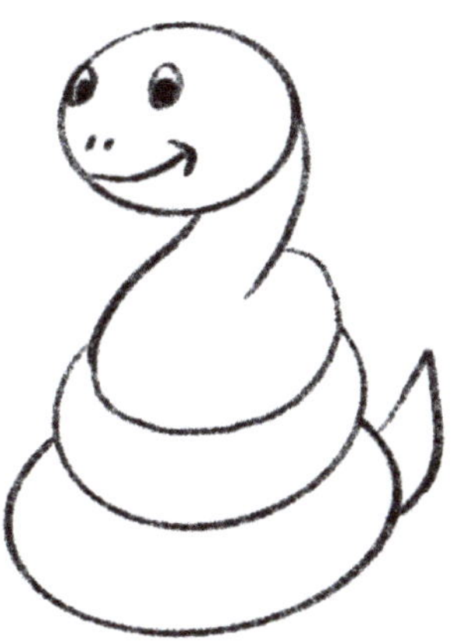

8

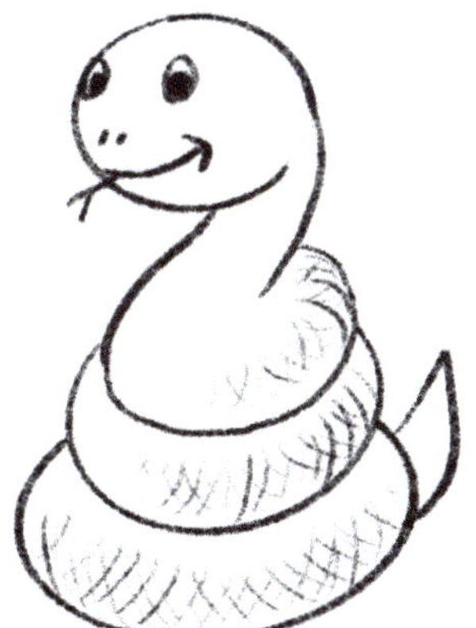

# Swan

1

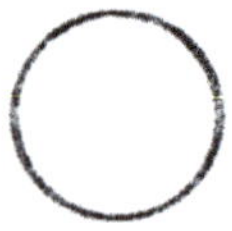

2

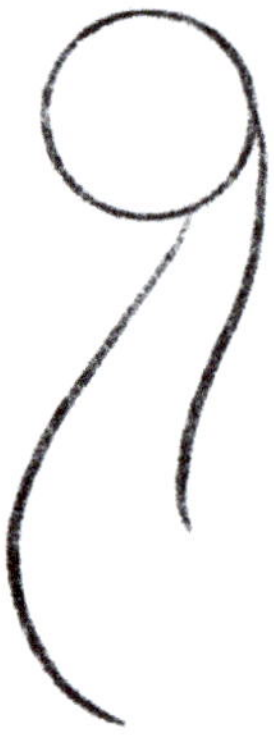

3

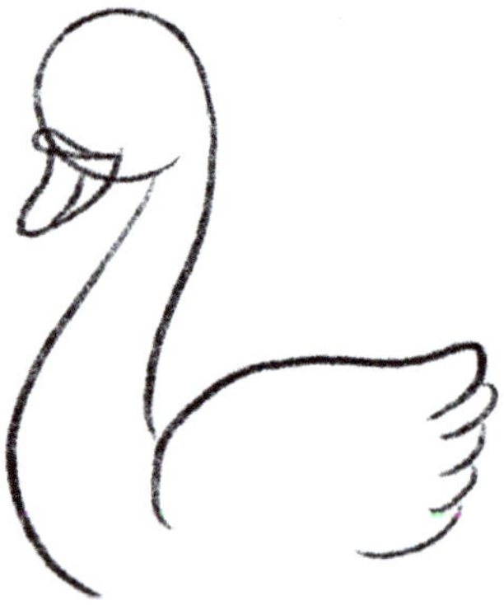

4

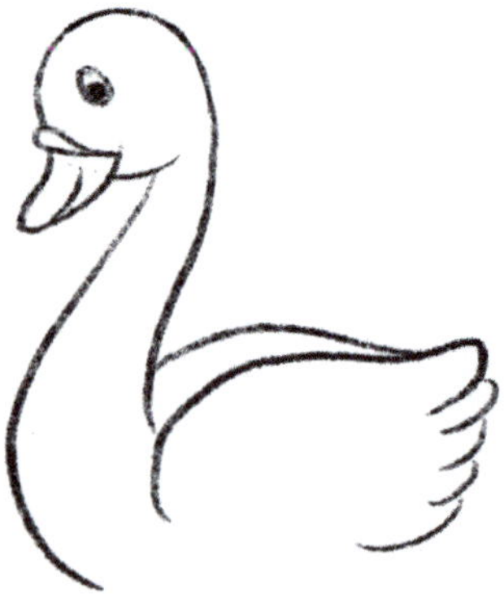

5

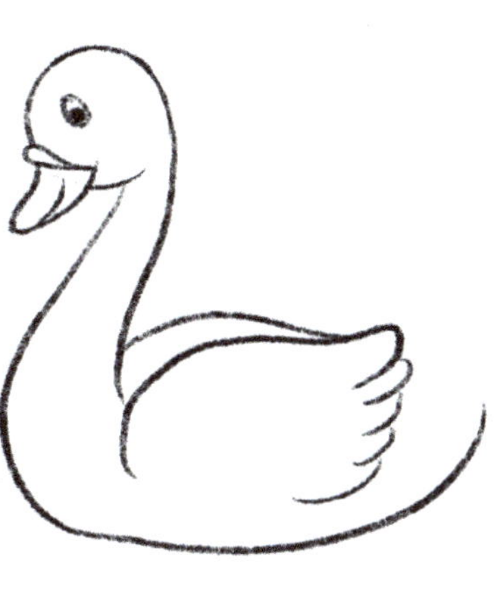

6

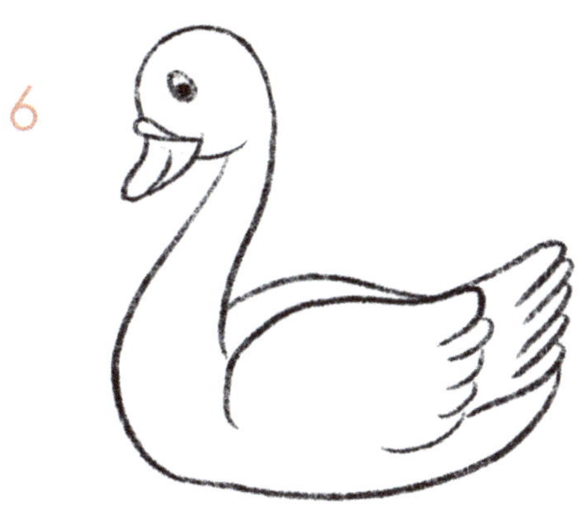

7

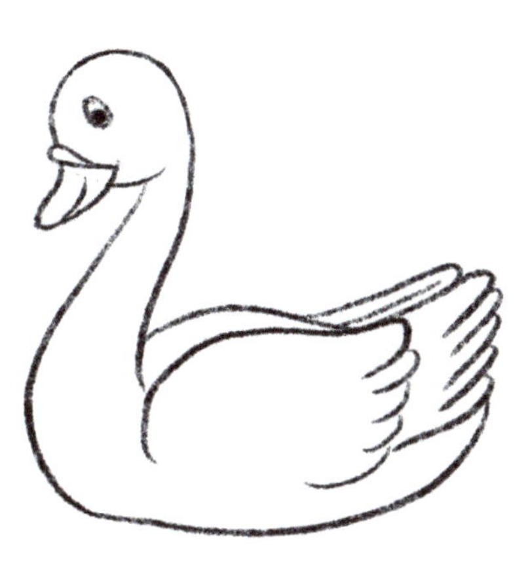

8

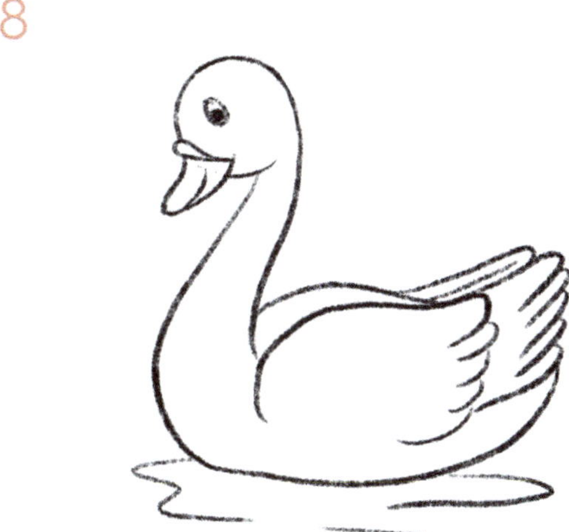

# Turtle

1 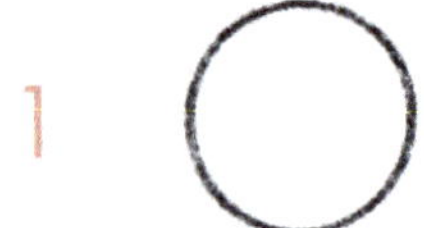

2 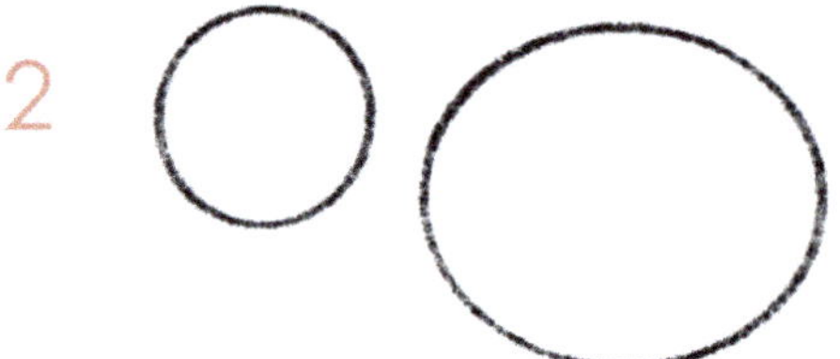

3 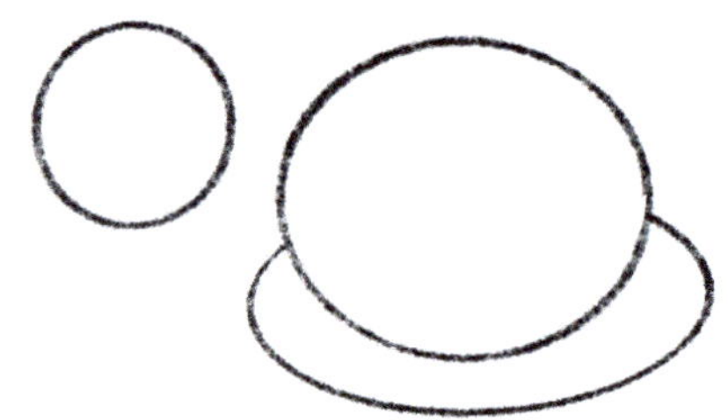

4 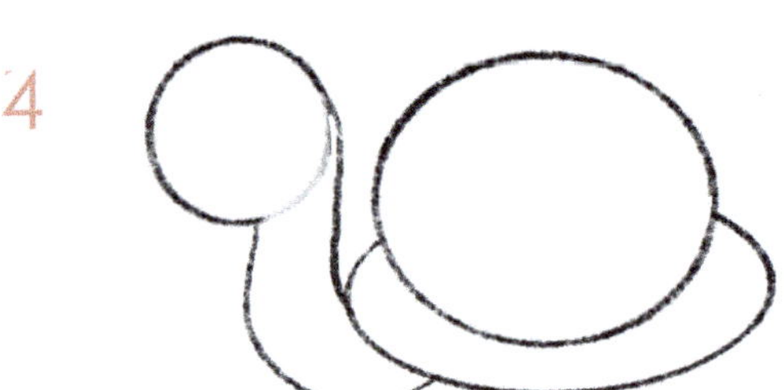

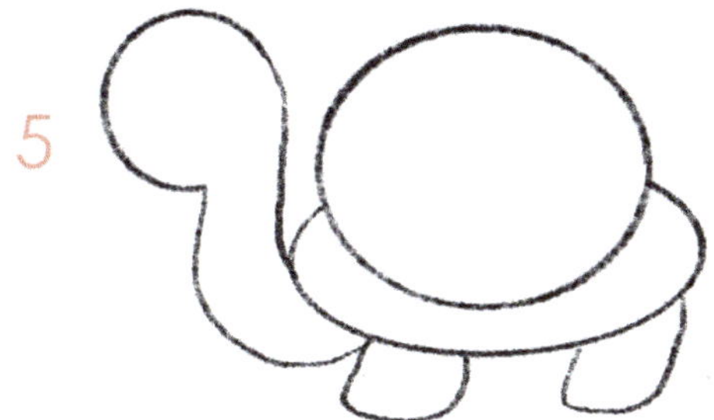

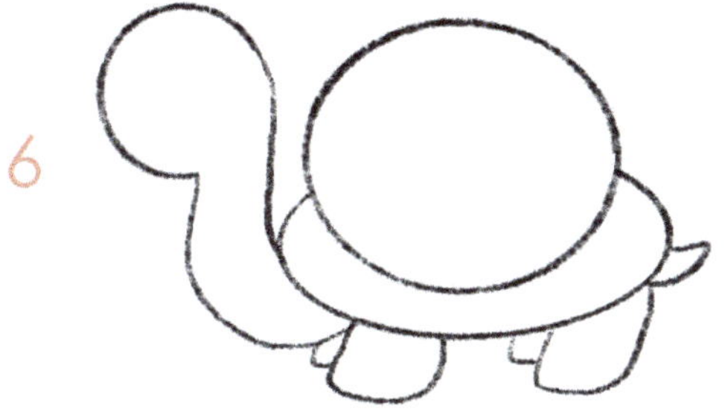

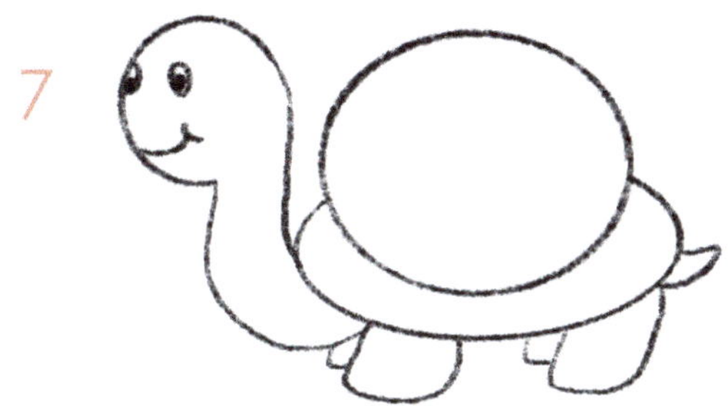

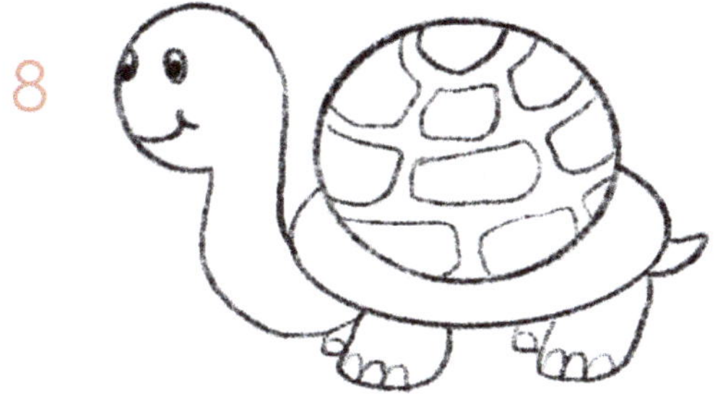

# Whale

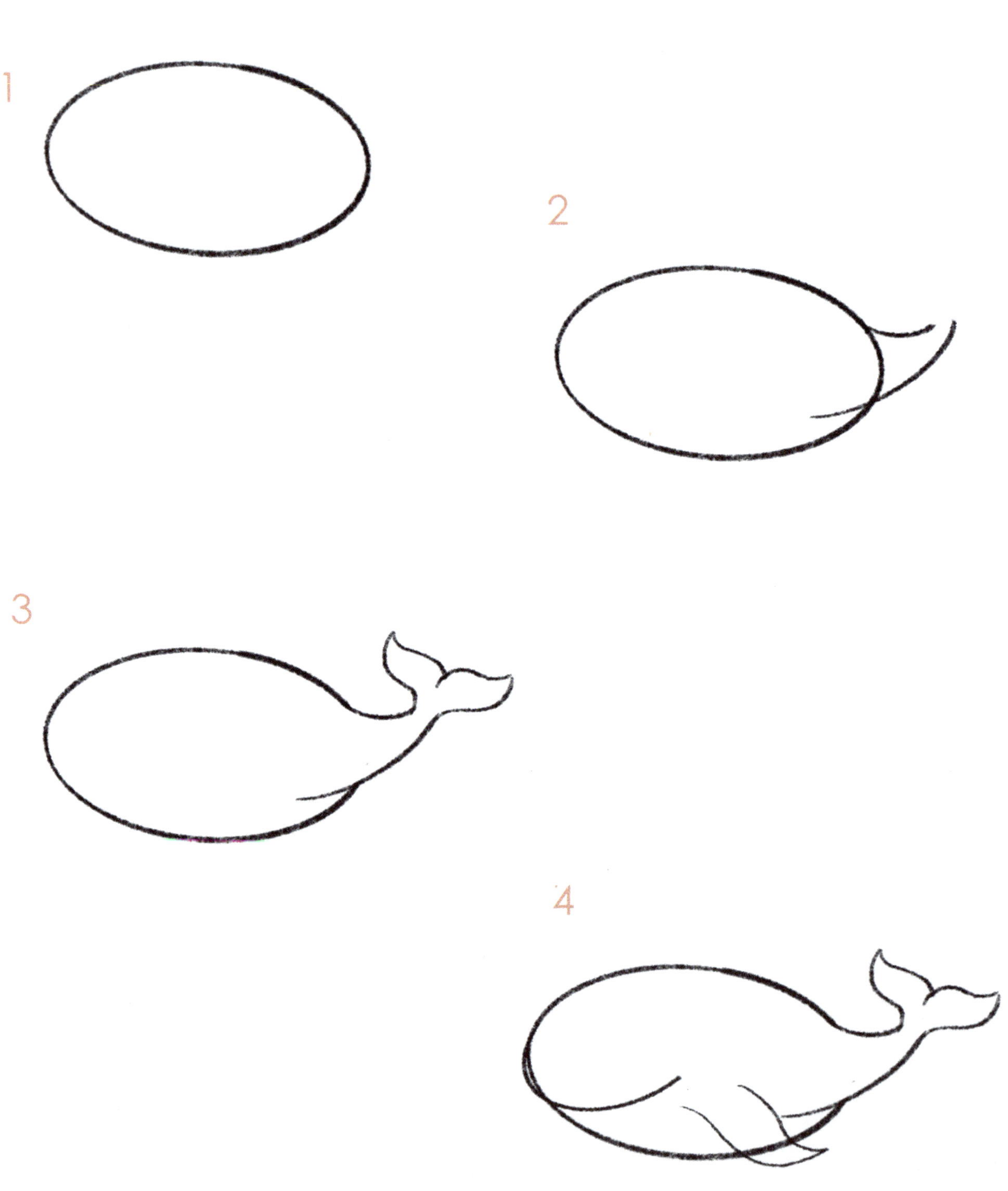

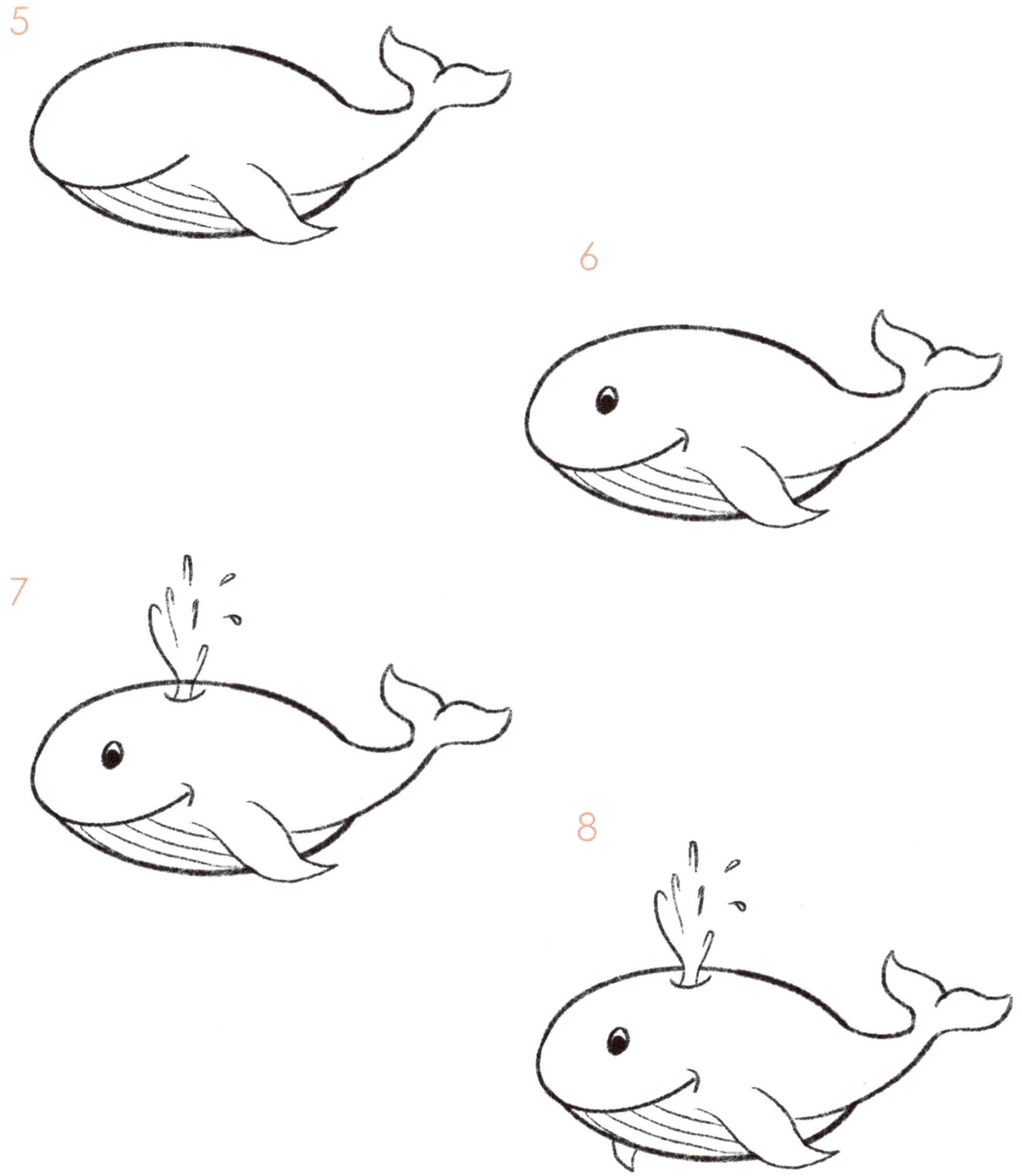


5
6
7
8

Congratulations on making it through to the
level three drawings!

As you proceed through the rest of the book
you will build on the skills you have learnt so far.
Each drawing still starts with basic shapes,
however have your eraser handy and press
lightly with your pencil, as you will erase more of
these starting shapes than before.
Remember they are guides.

You've done so well! Enjoy these next tutorials.

# Level Three

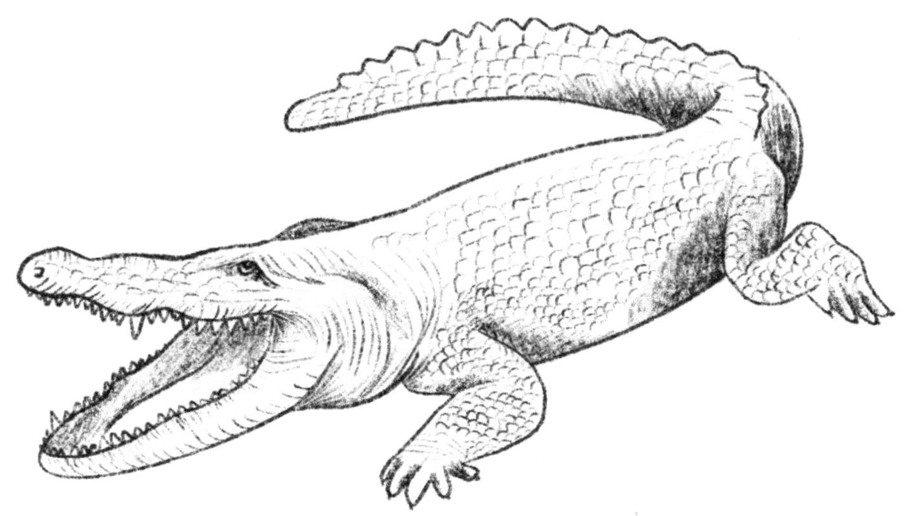

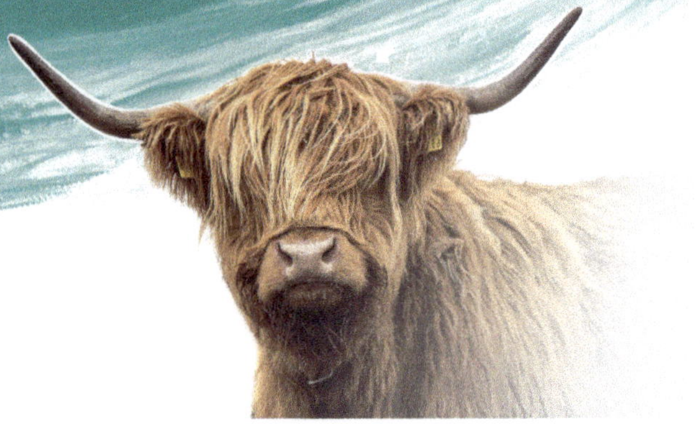

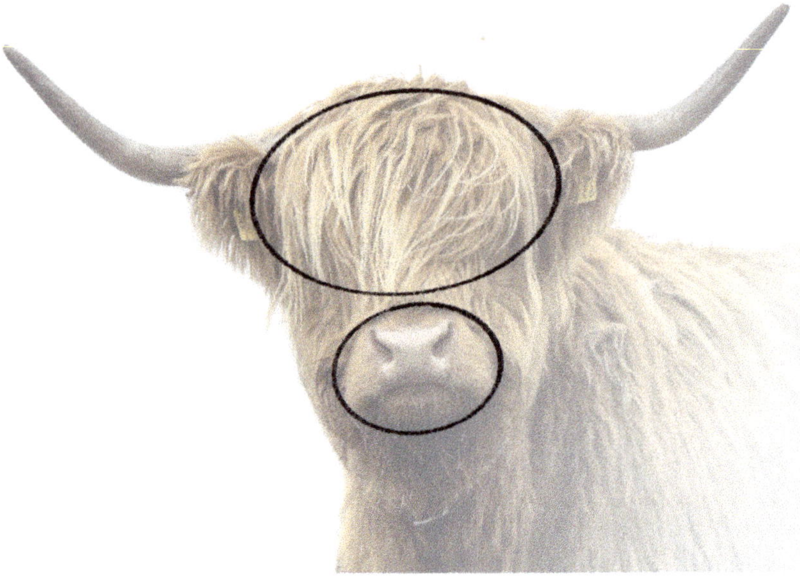

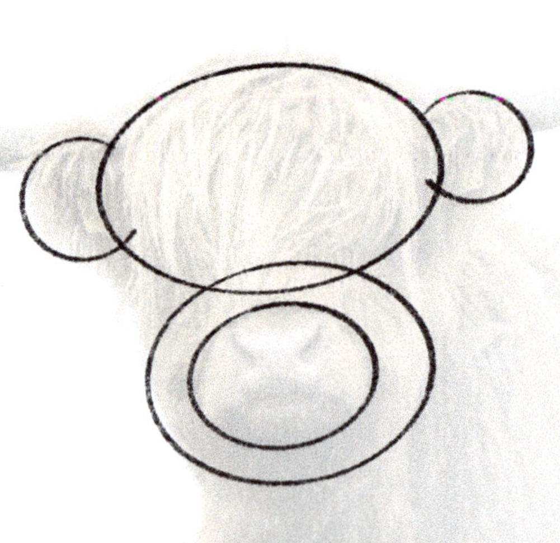

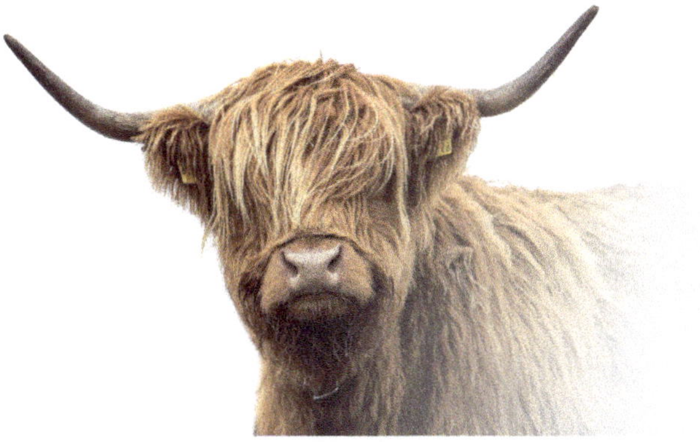

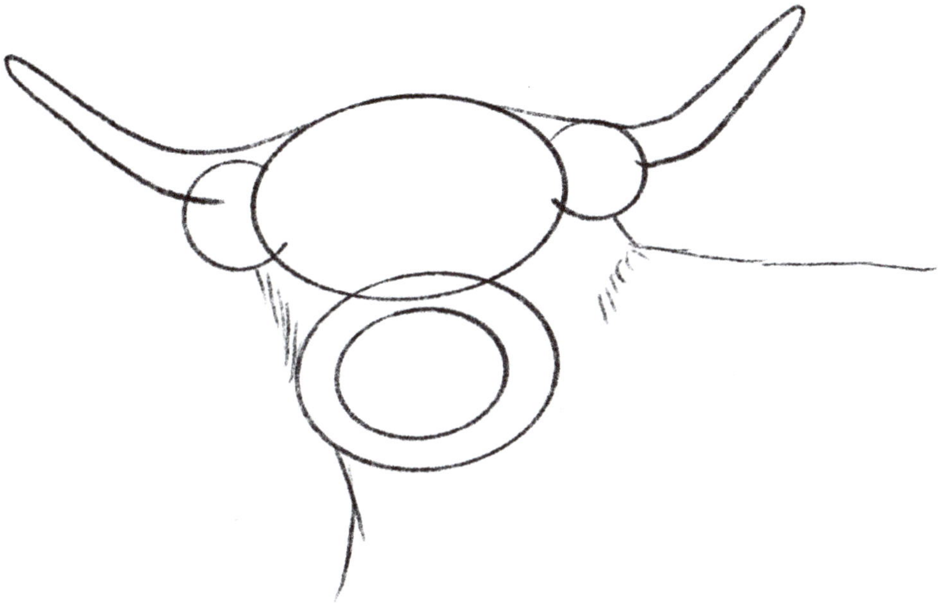

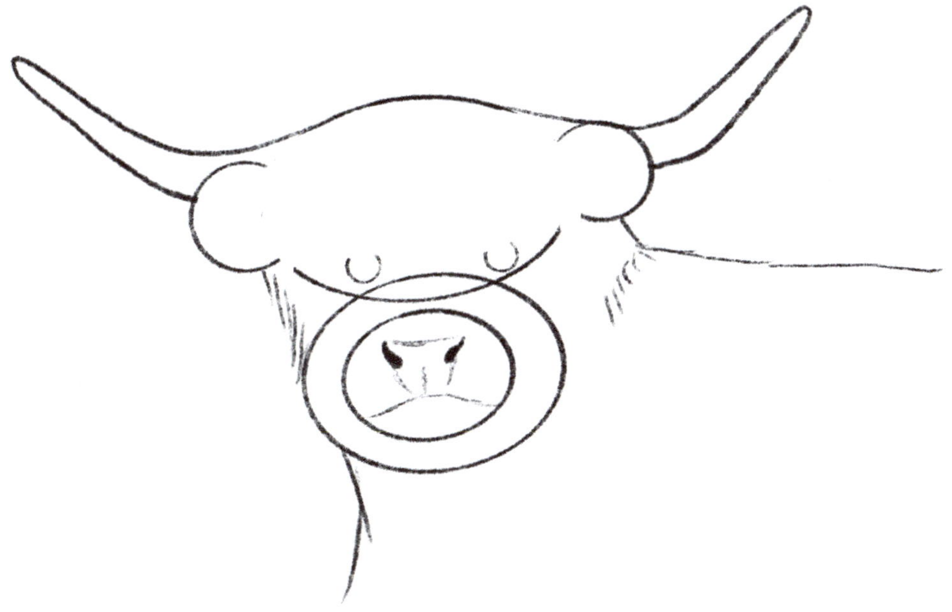

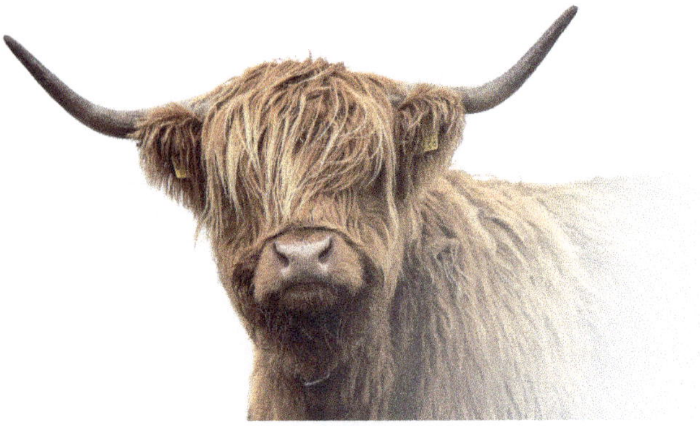

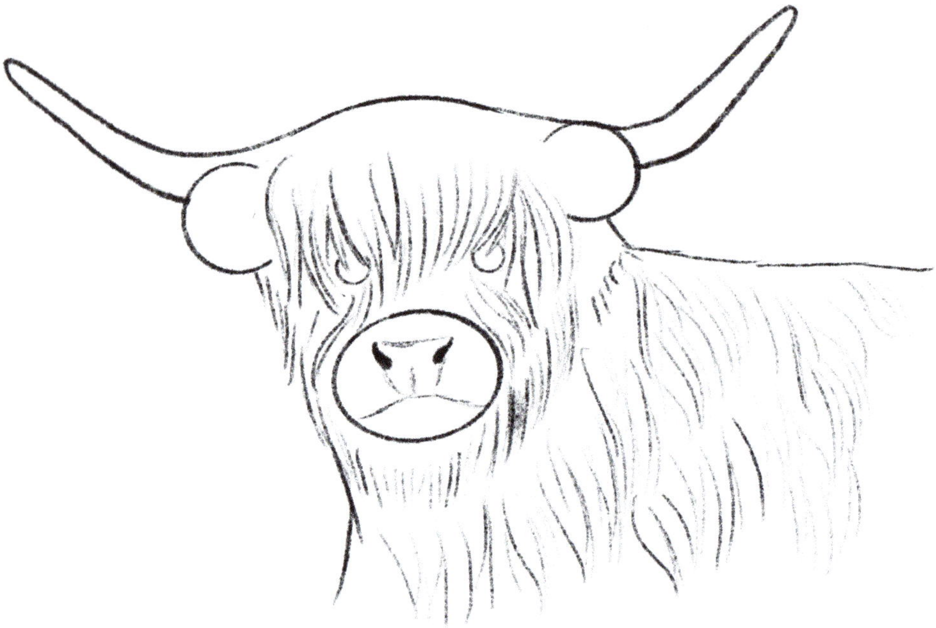

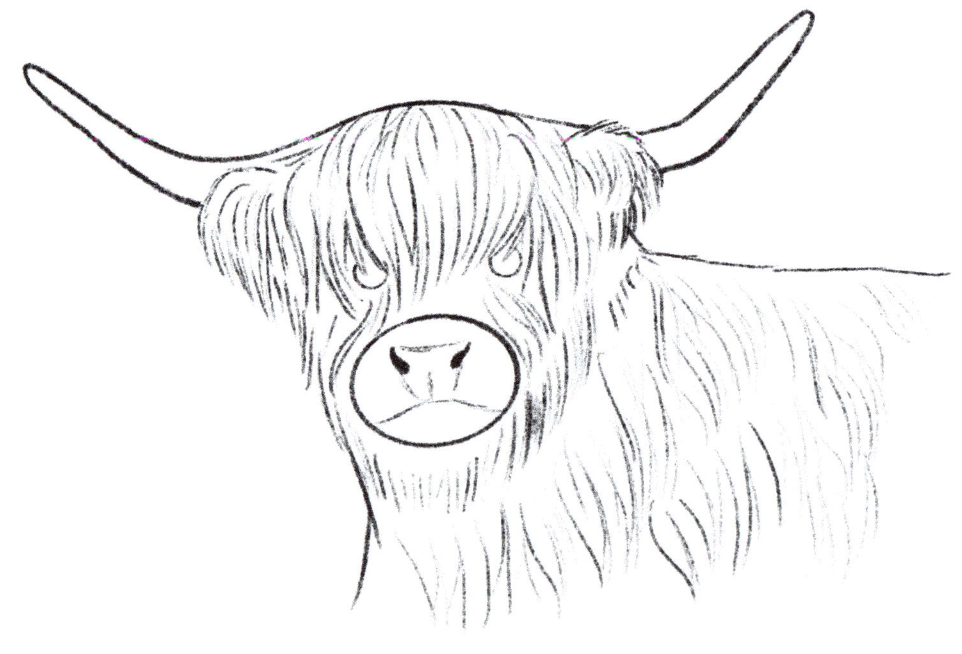

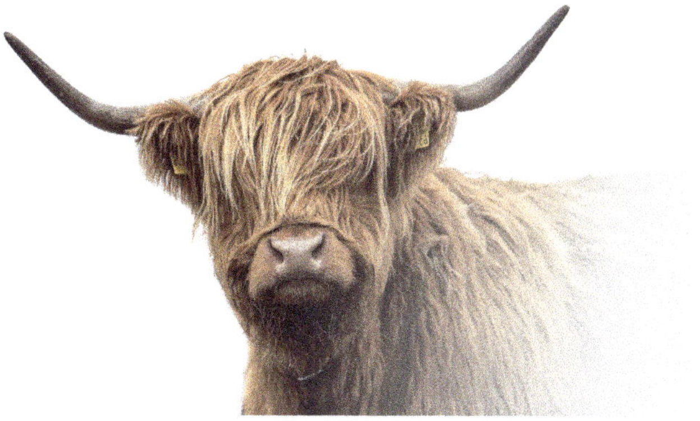

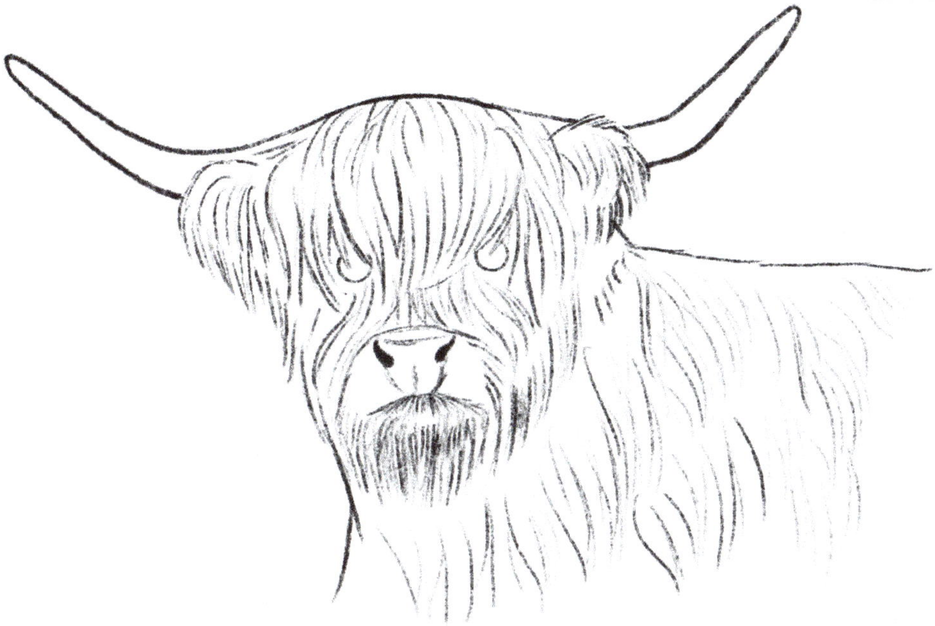

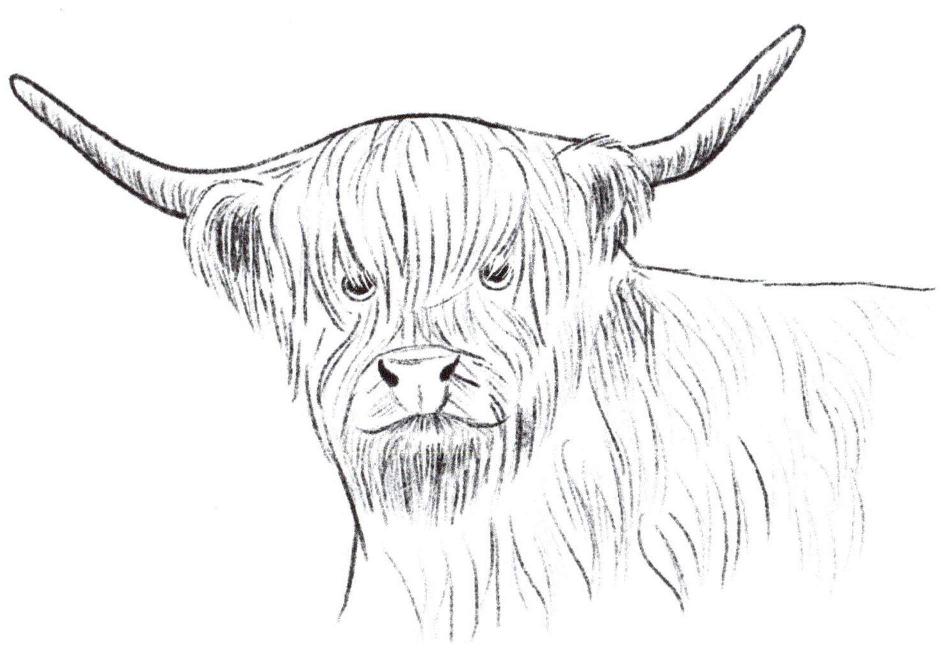

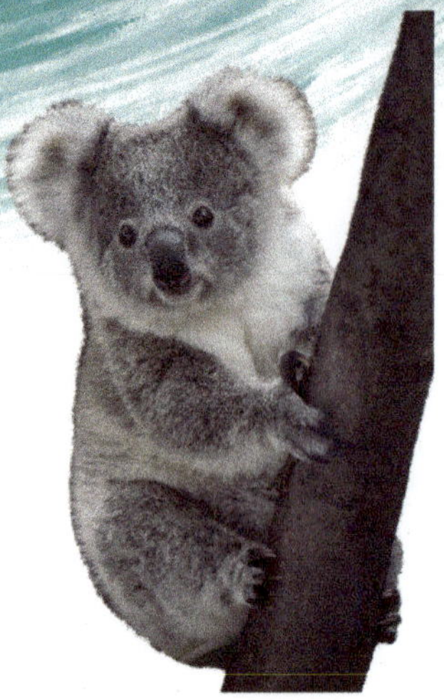

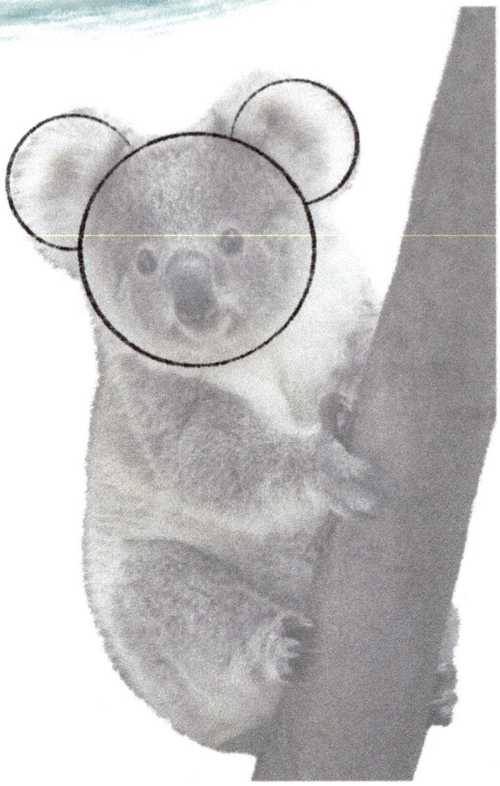

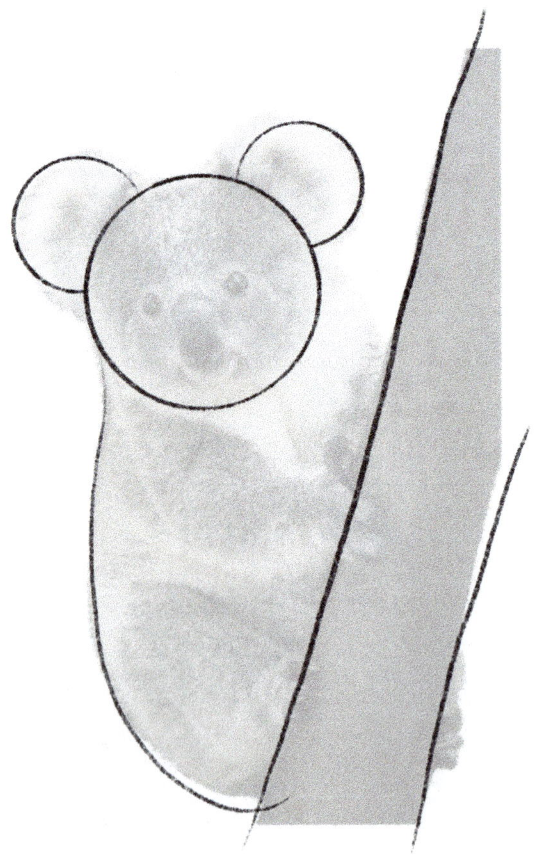

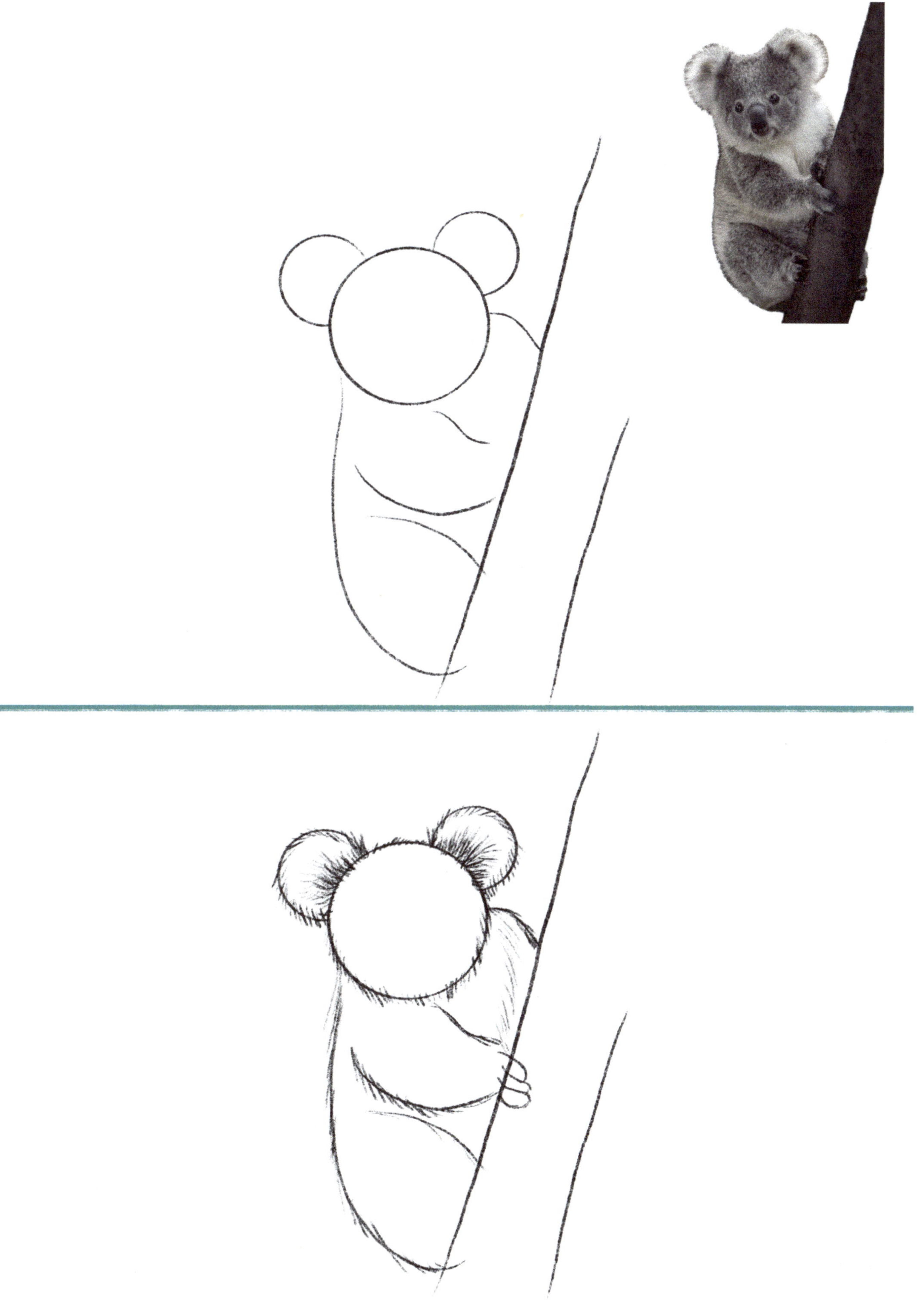

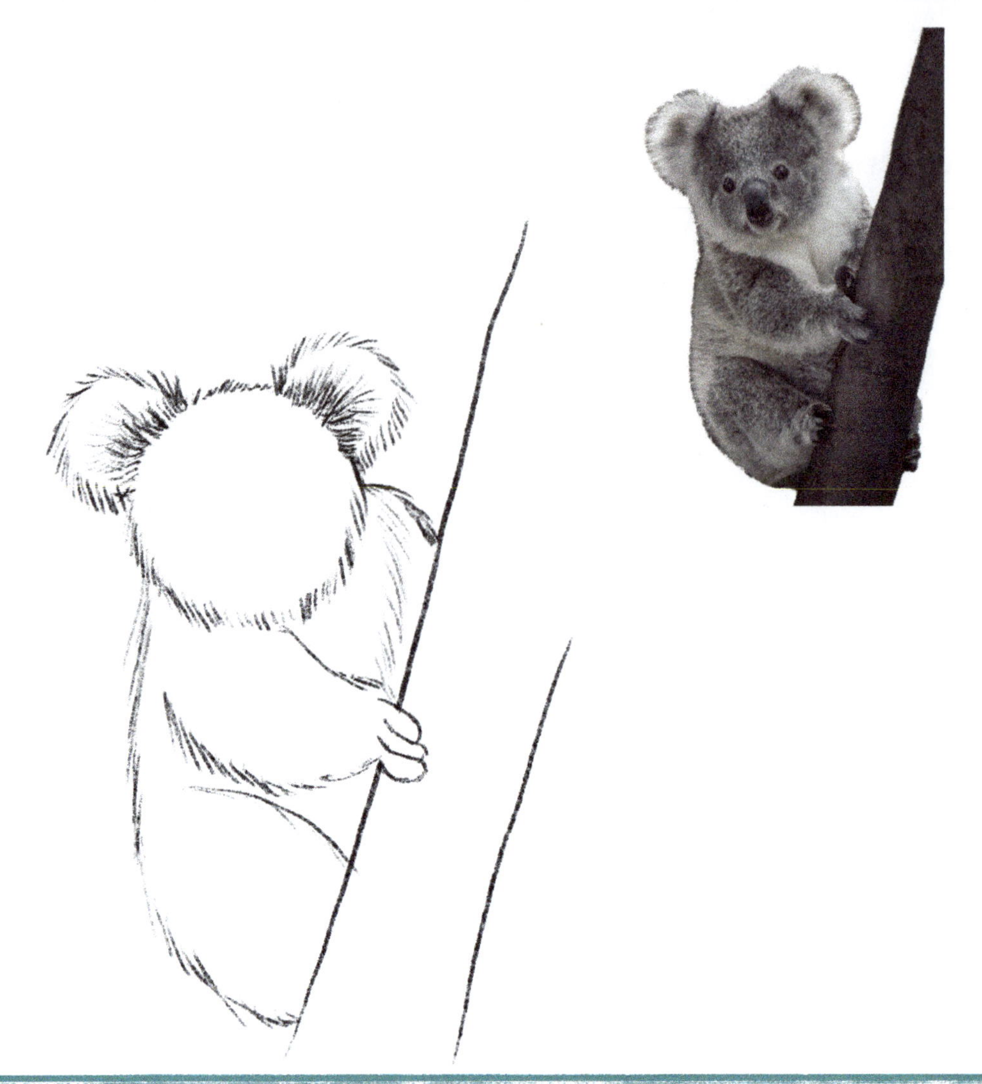

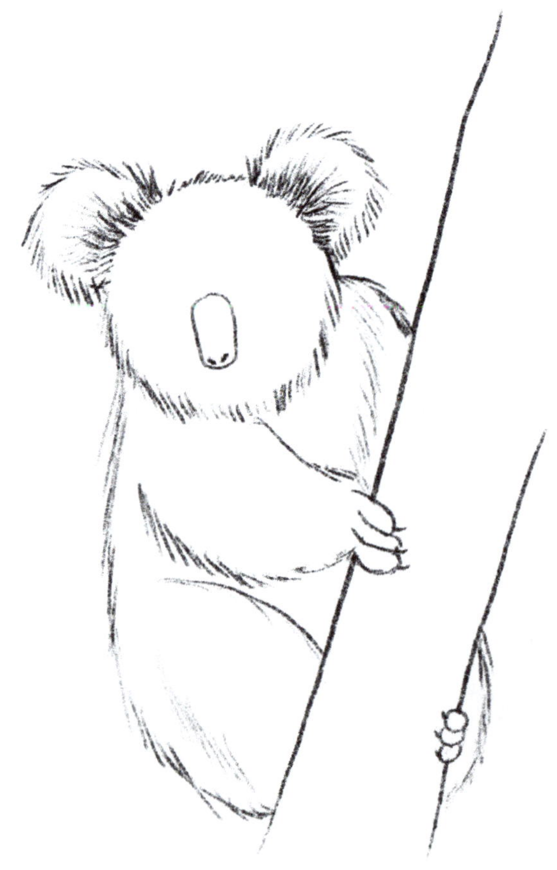

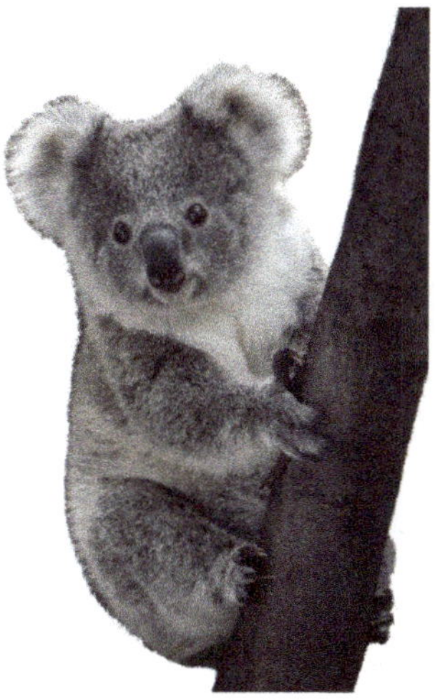

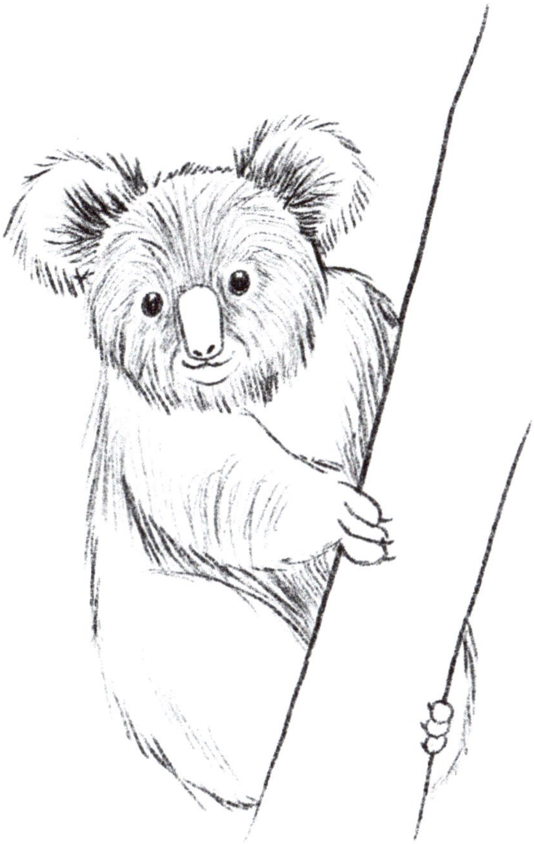

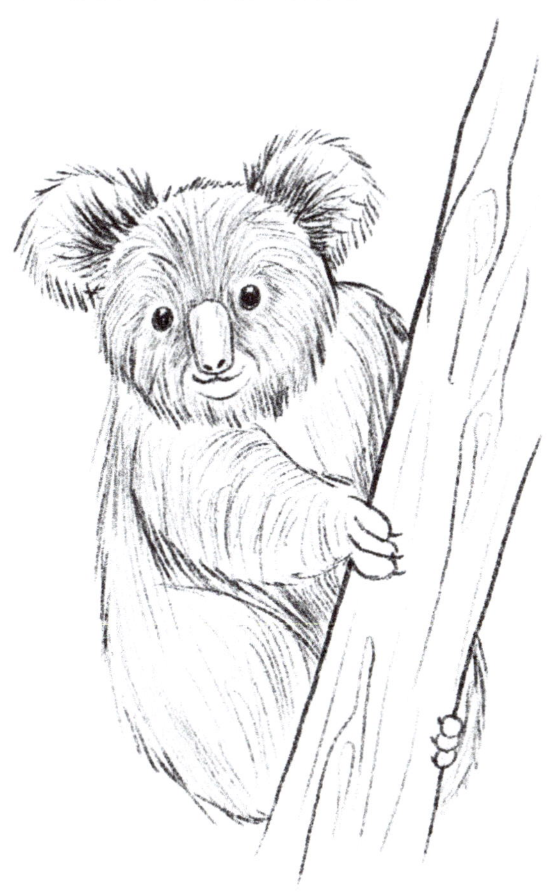

# Kookaburra

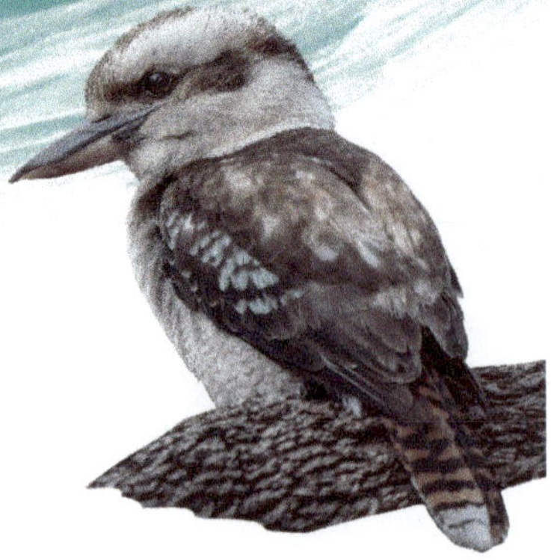

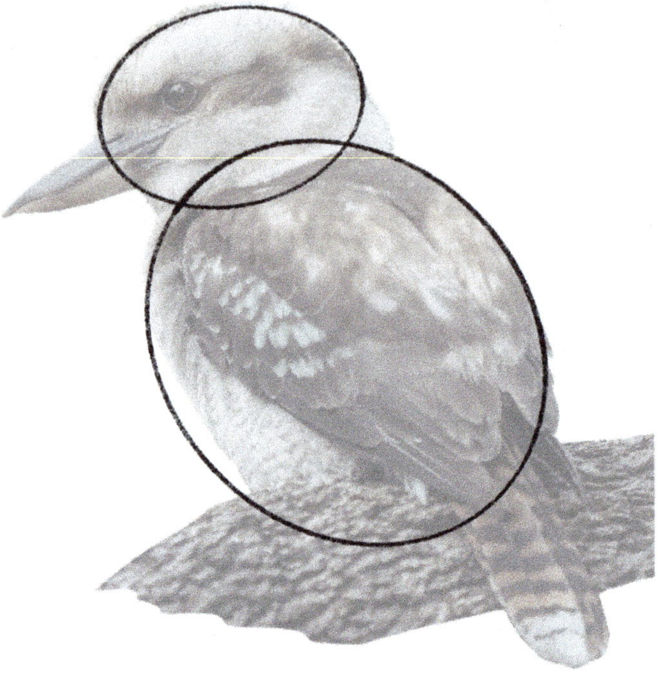

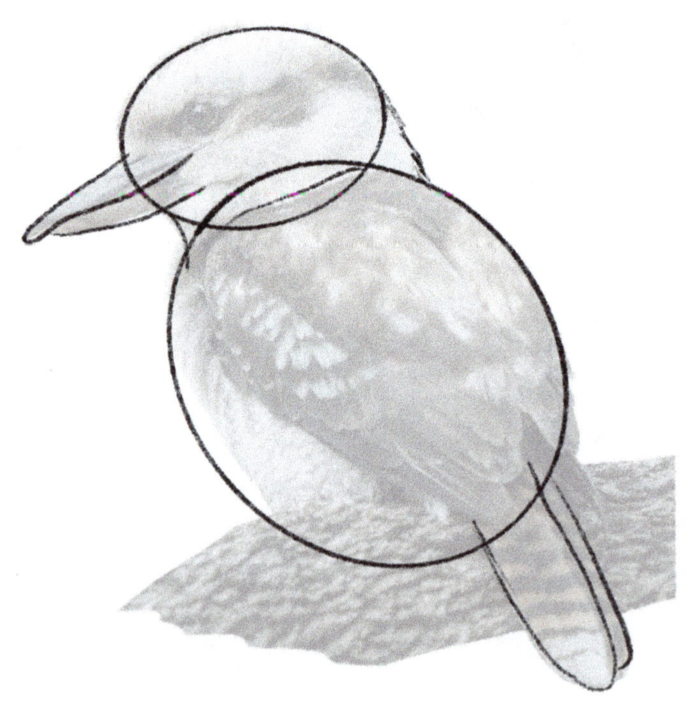

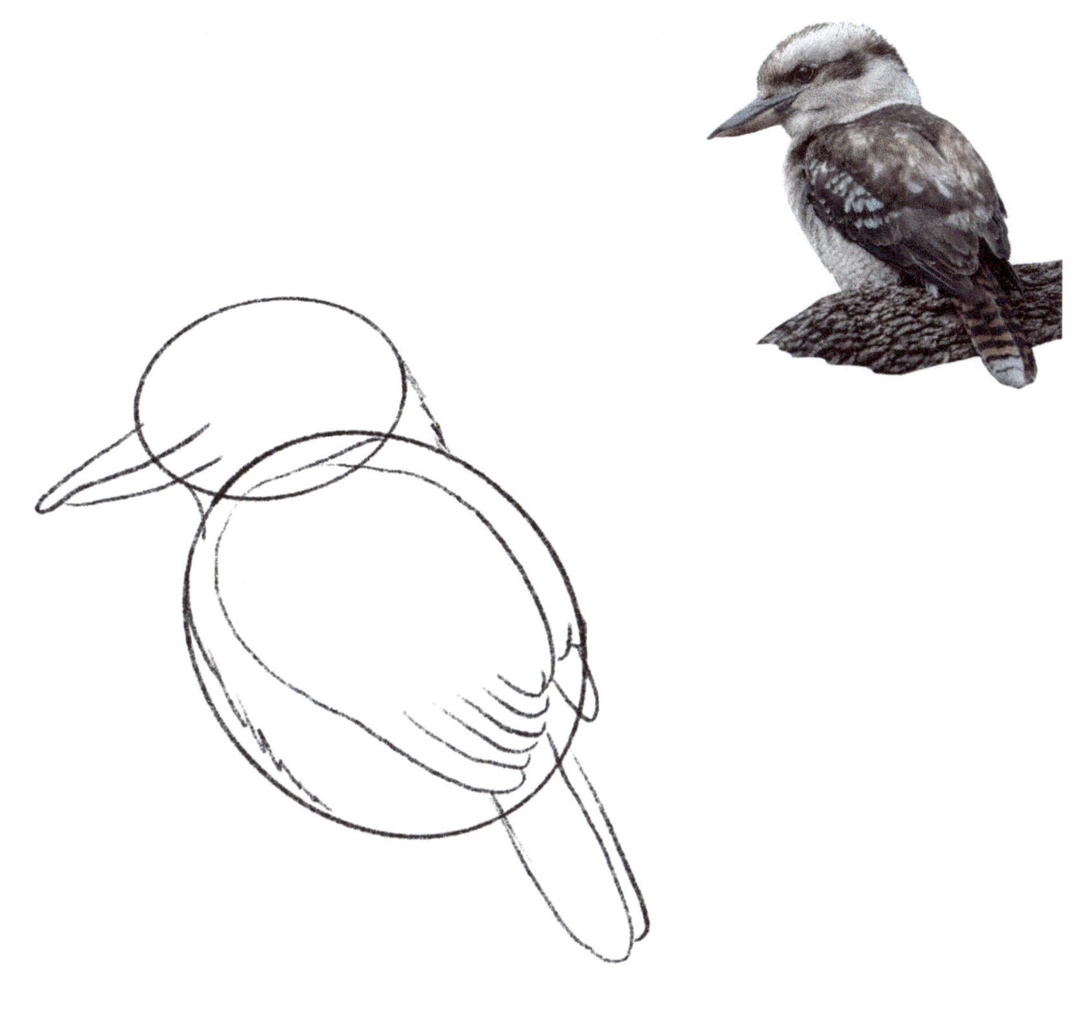

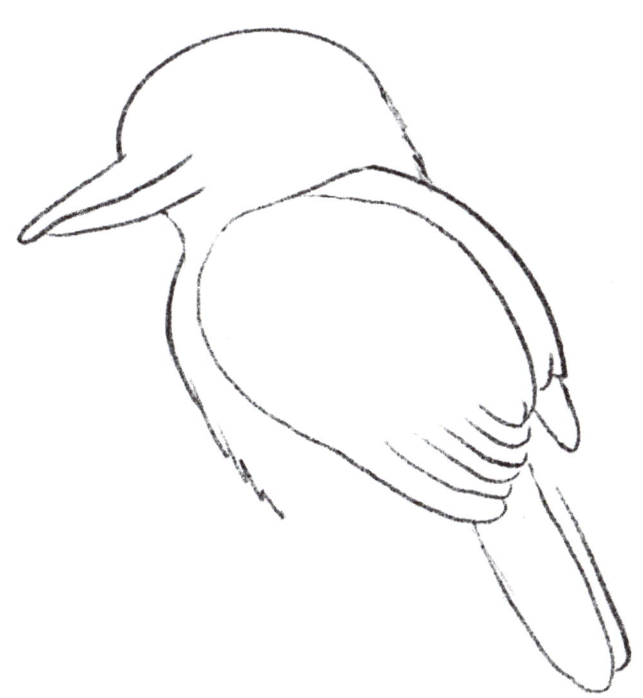

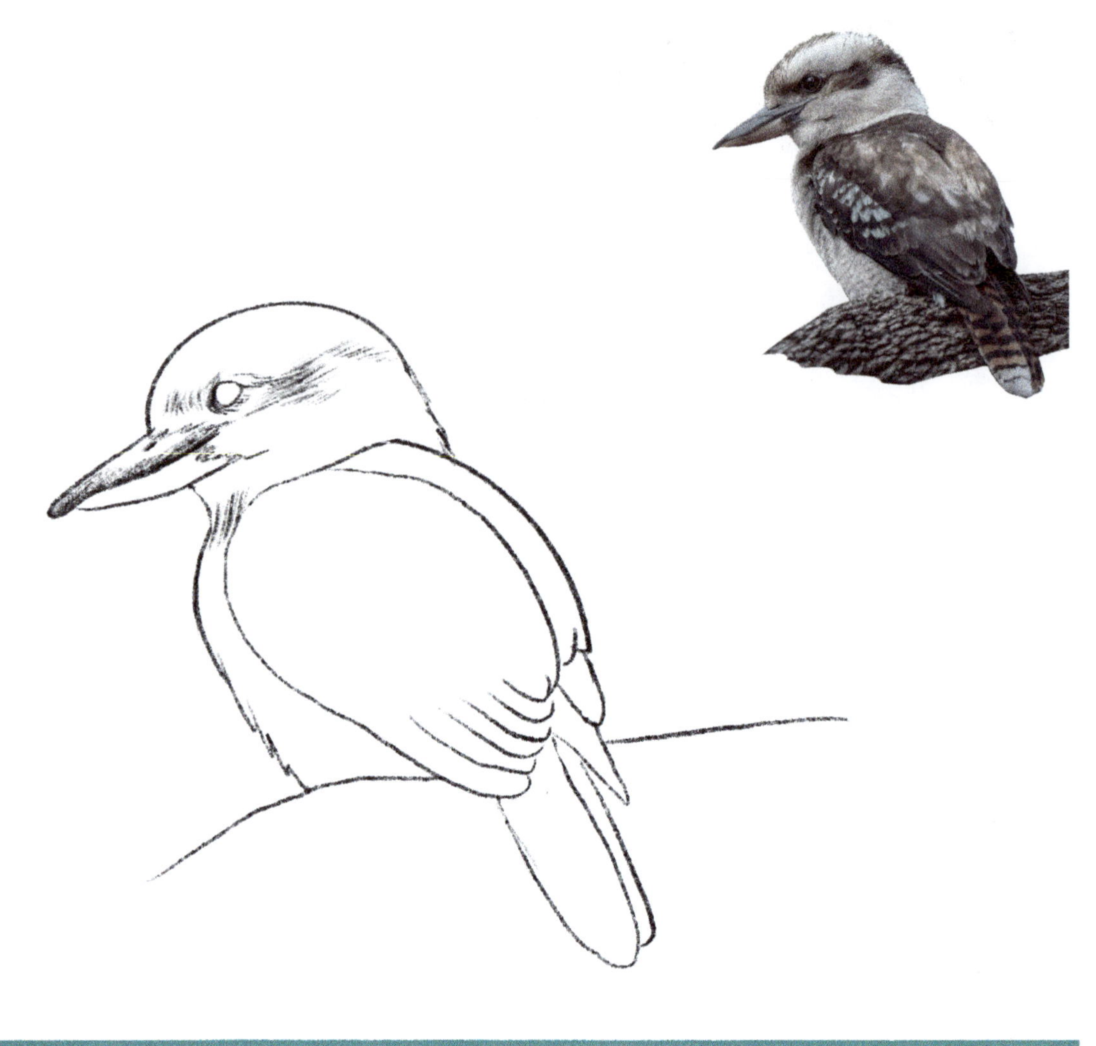

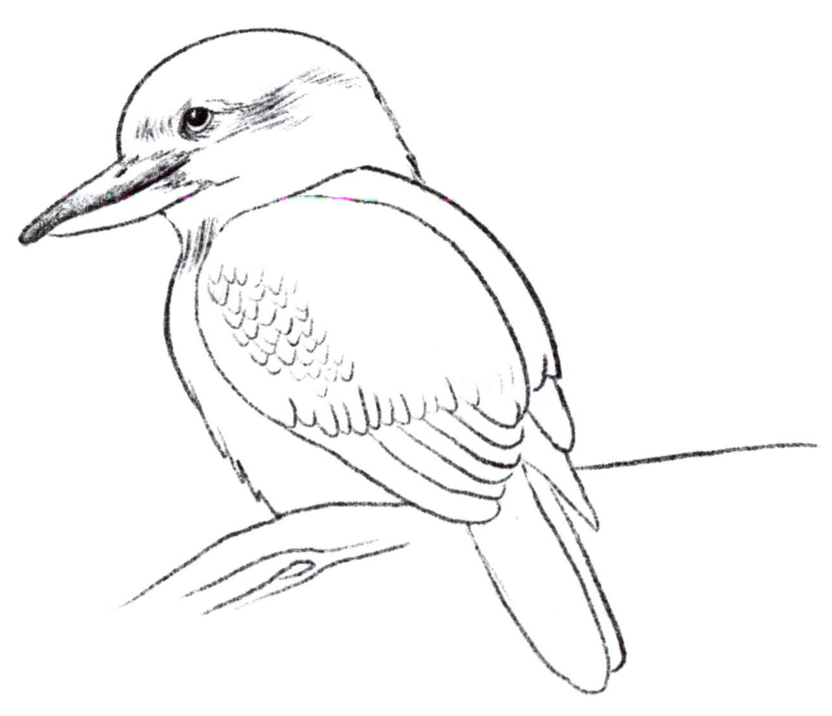

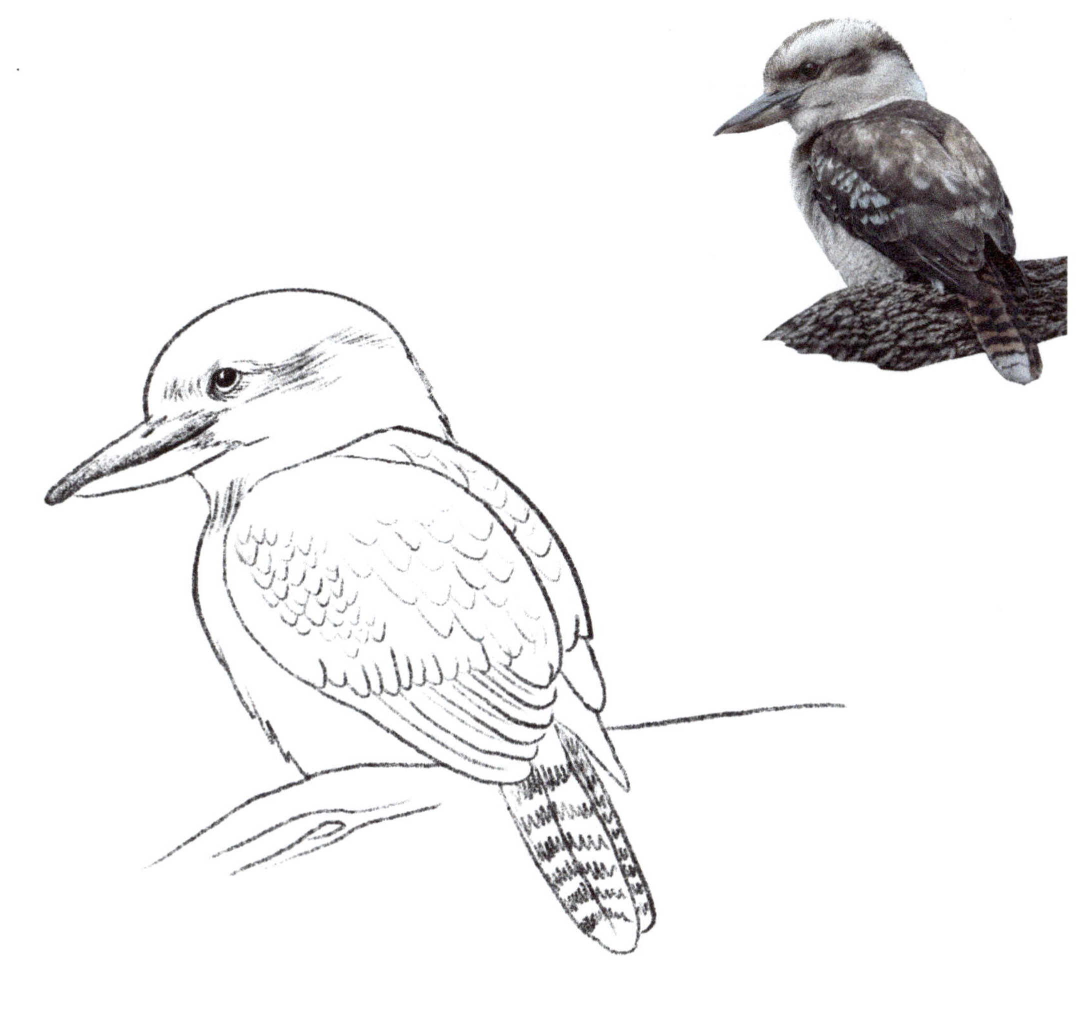

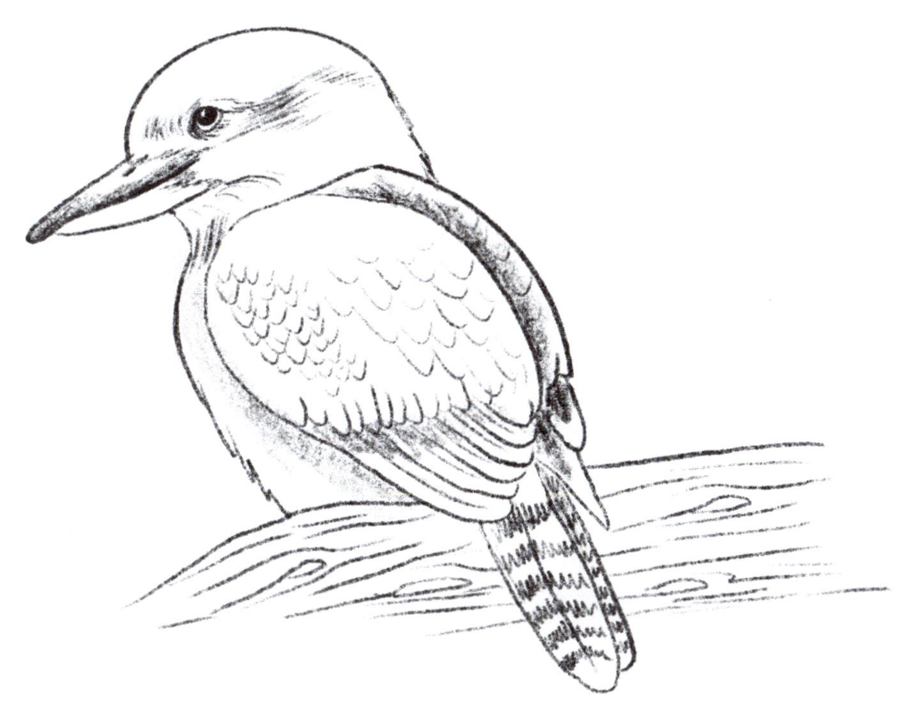

# Cockatoo

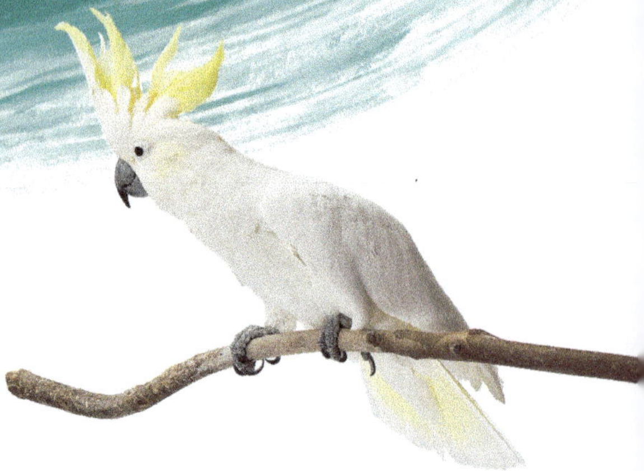

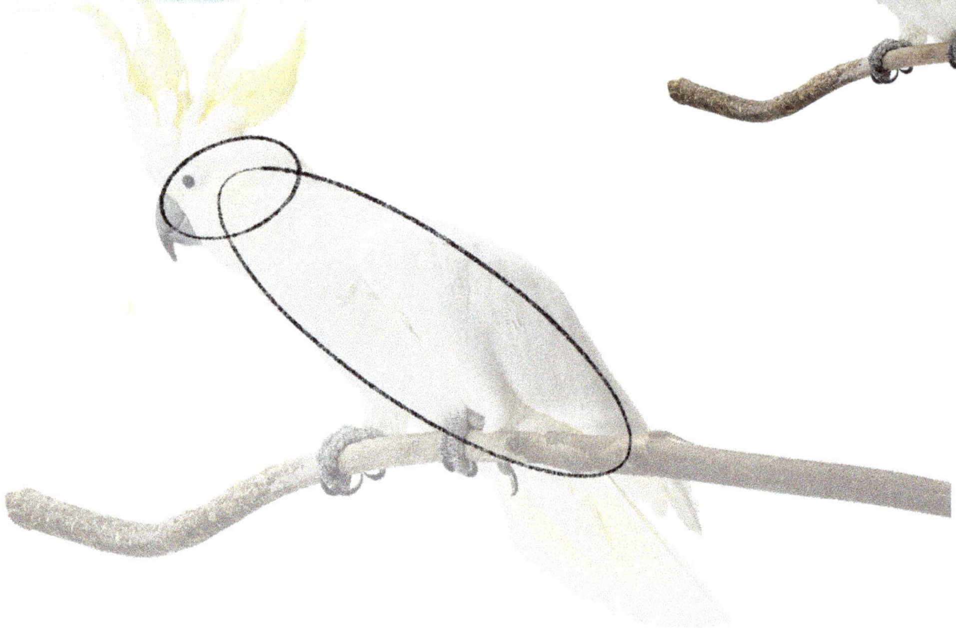

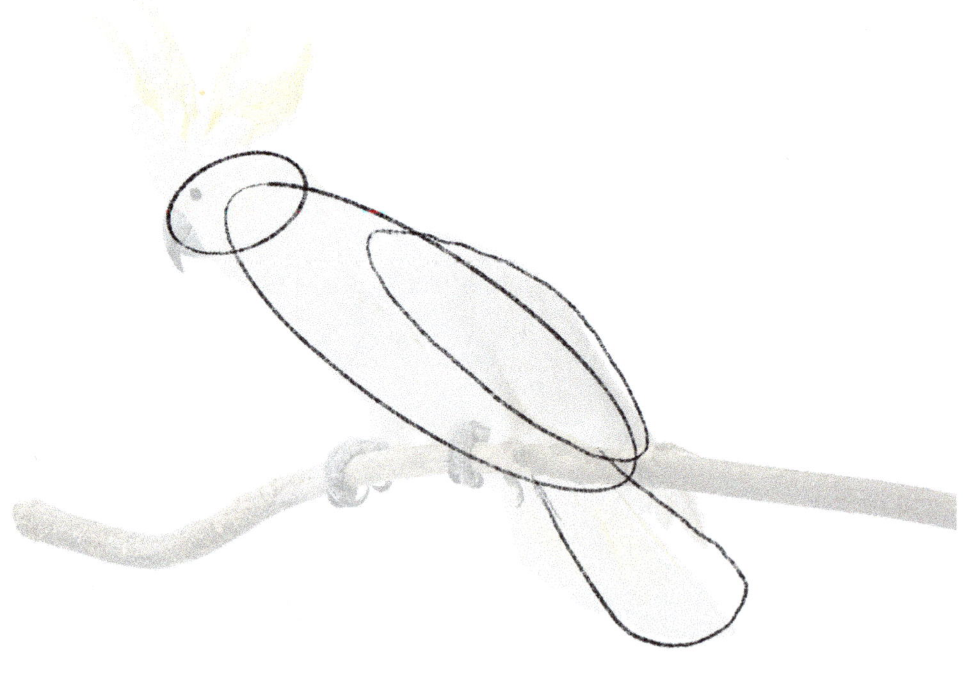

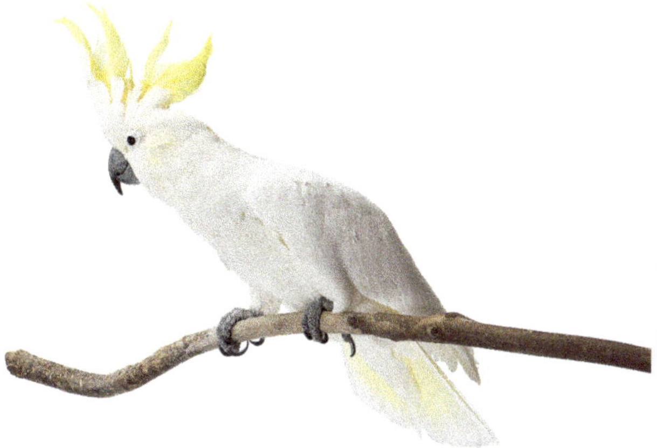

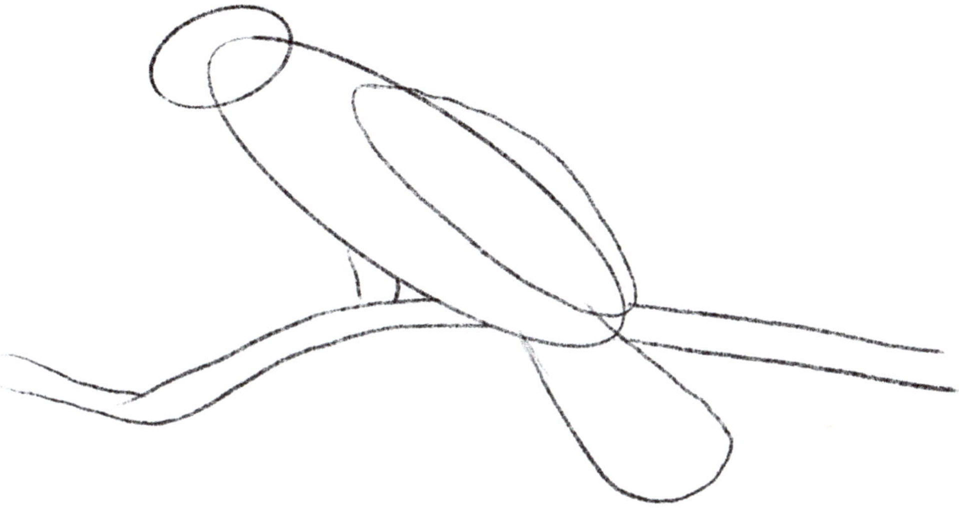

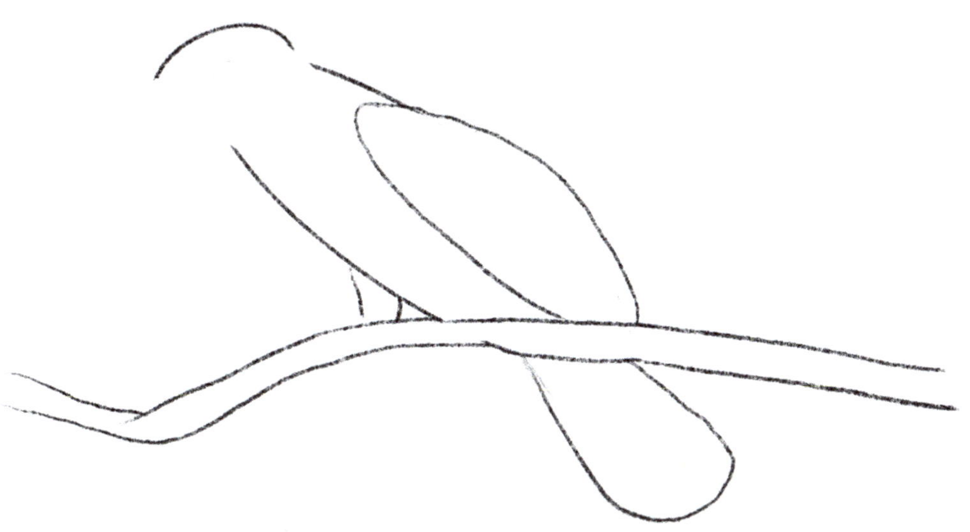

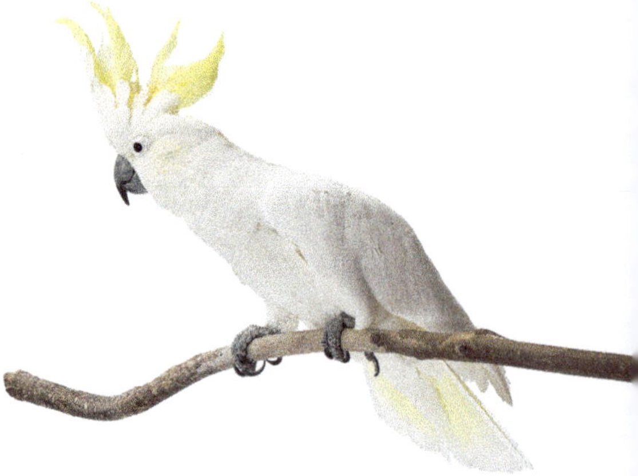

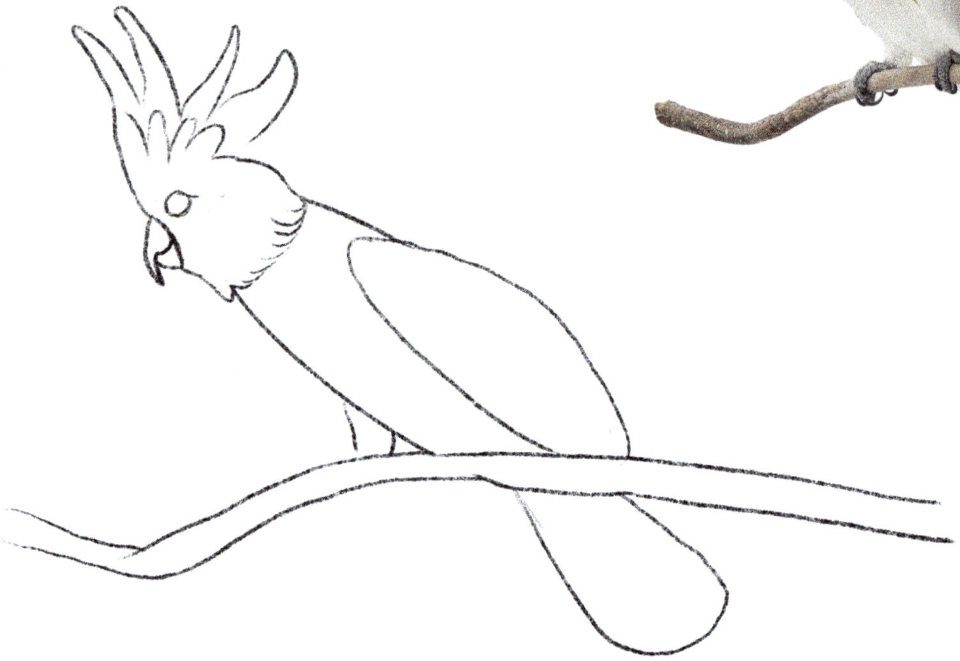

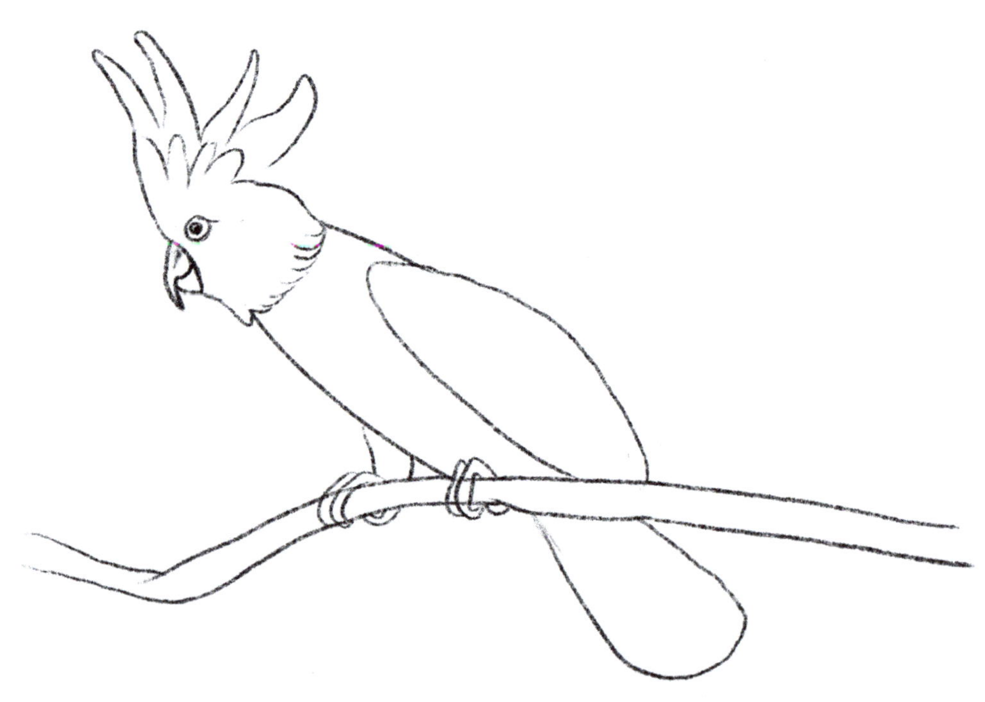

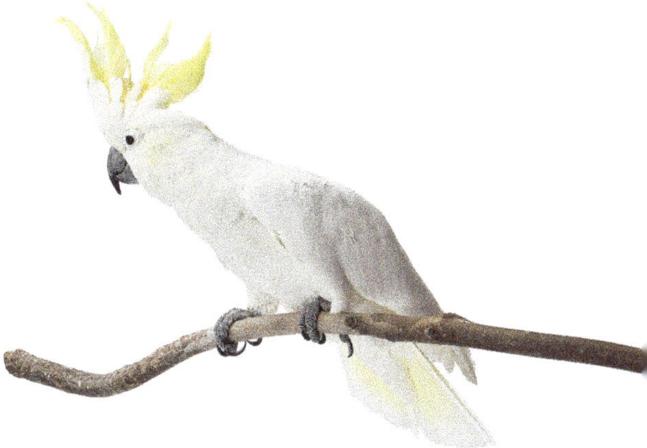

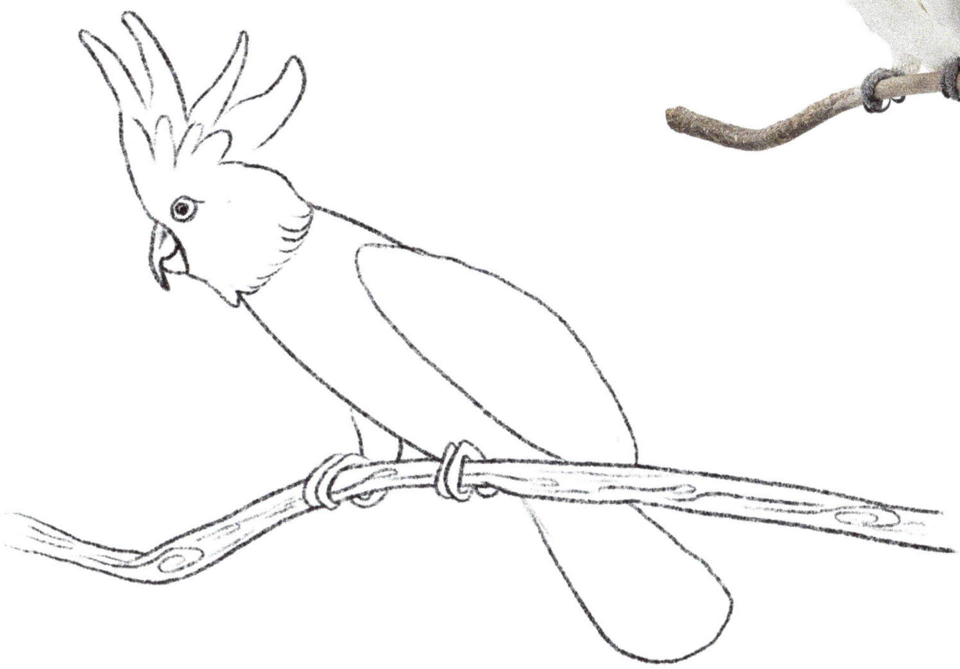

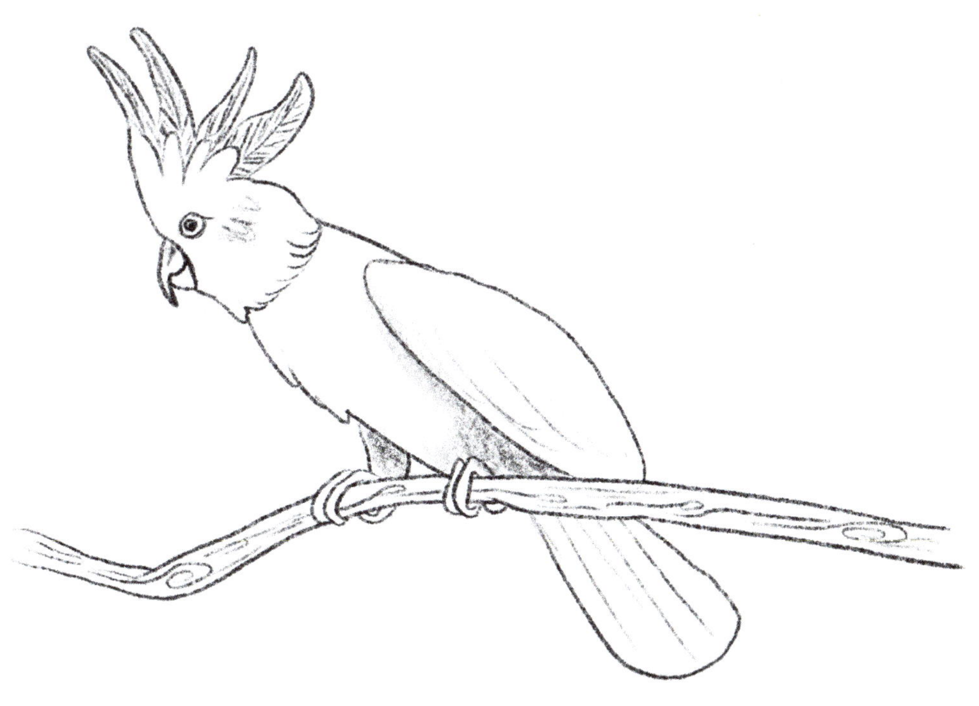

# Budgie

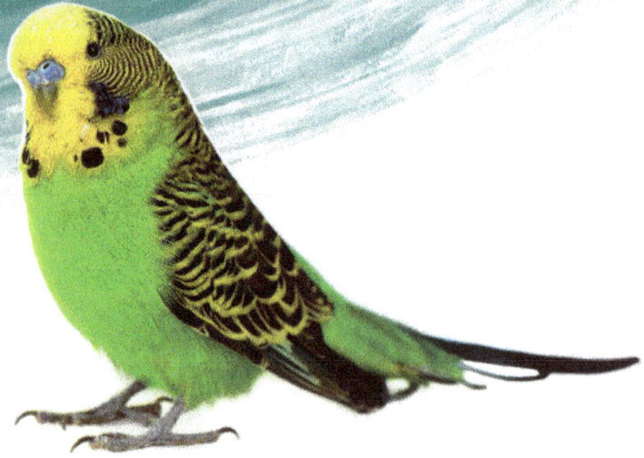

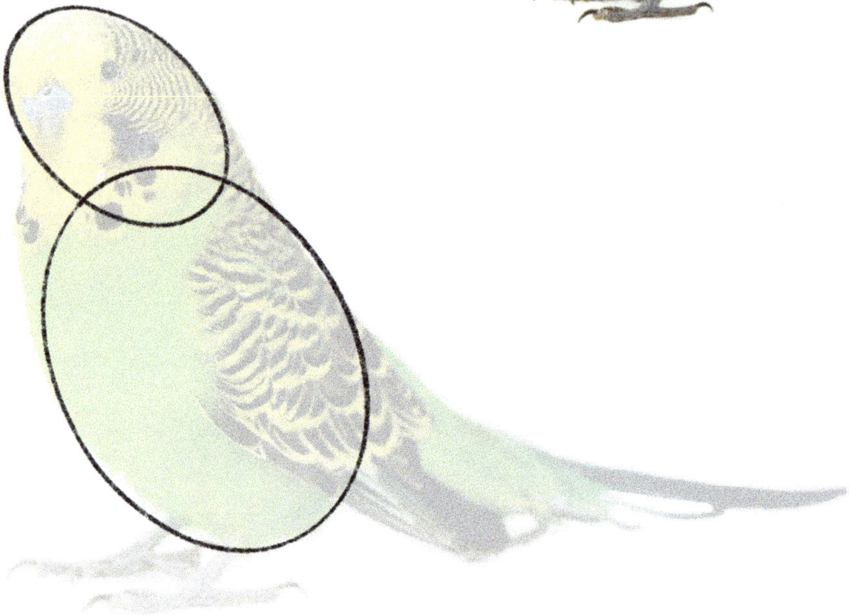

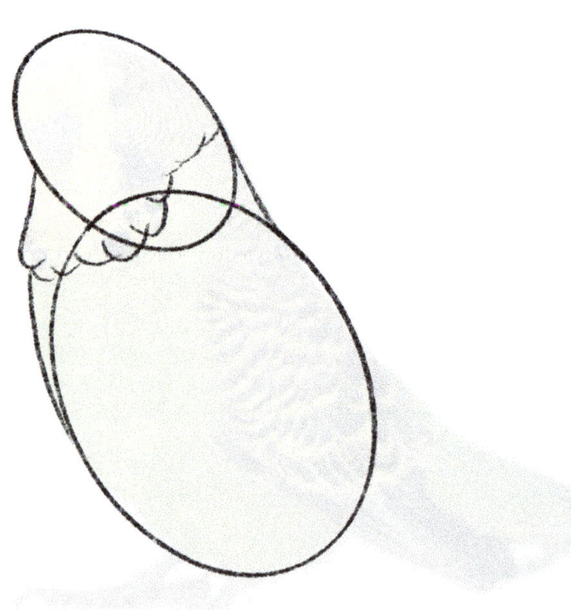

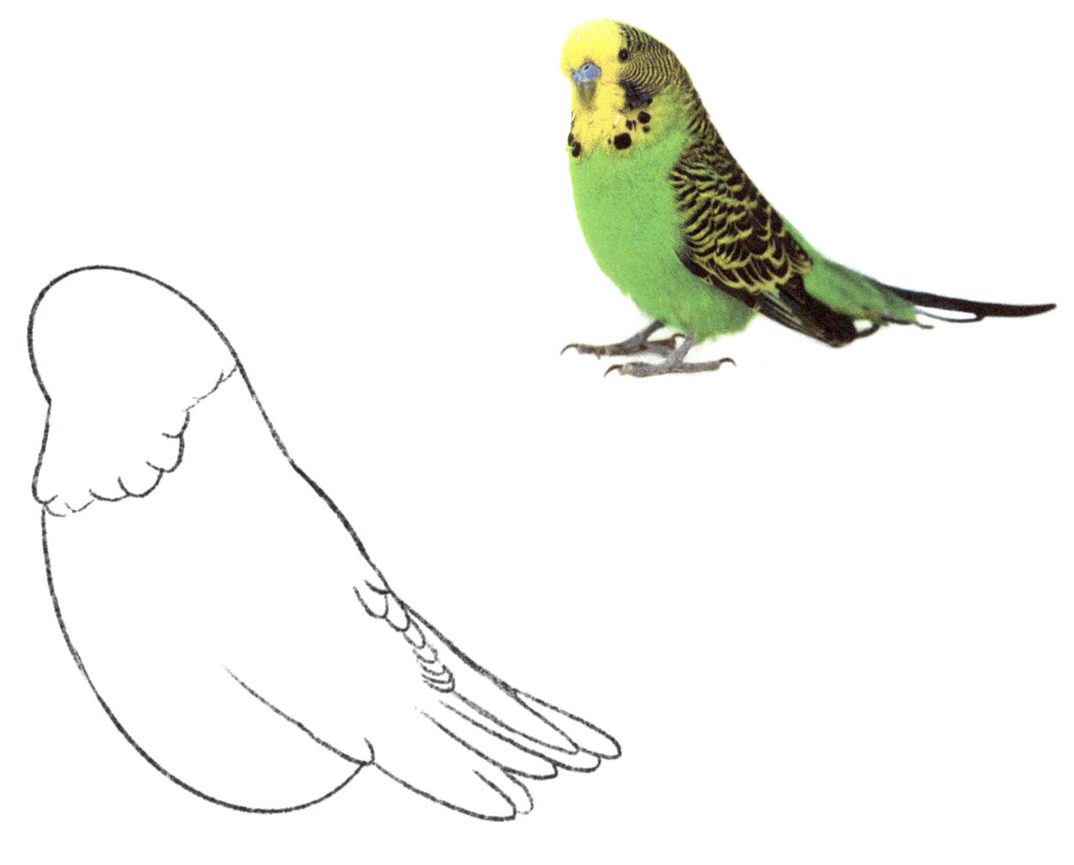

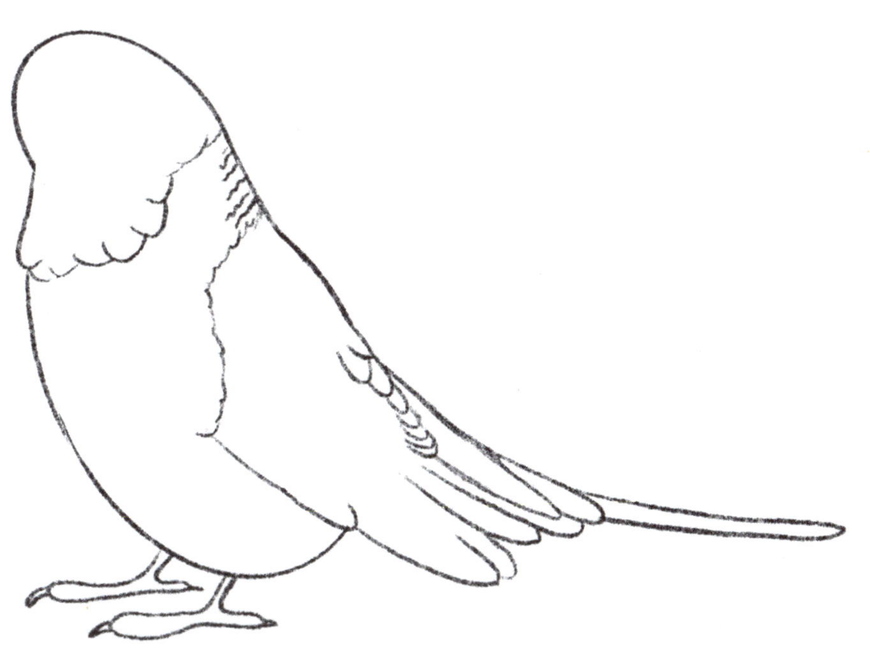

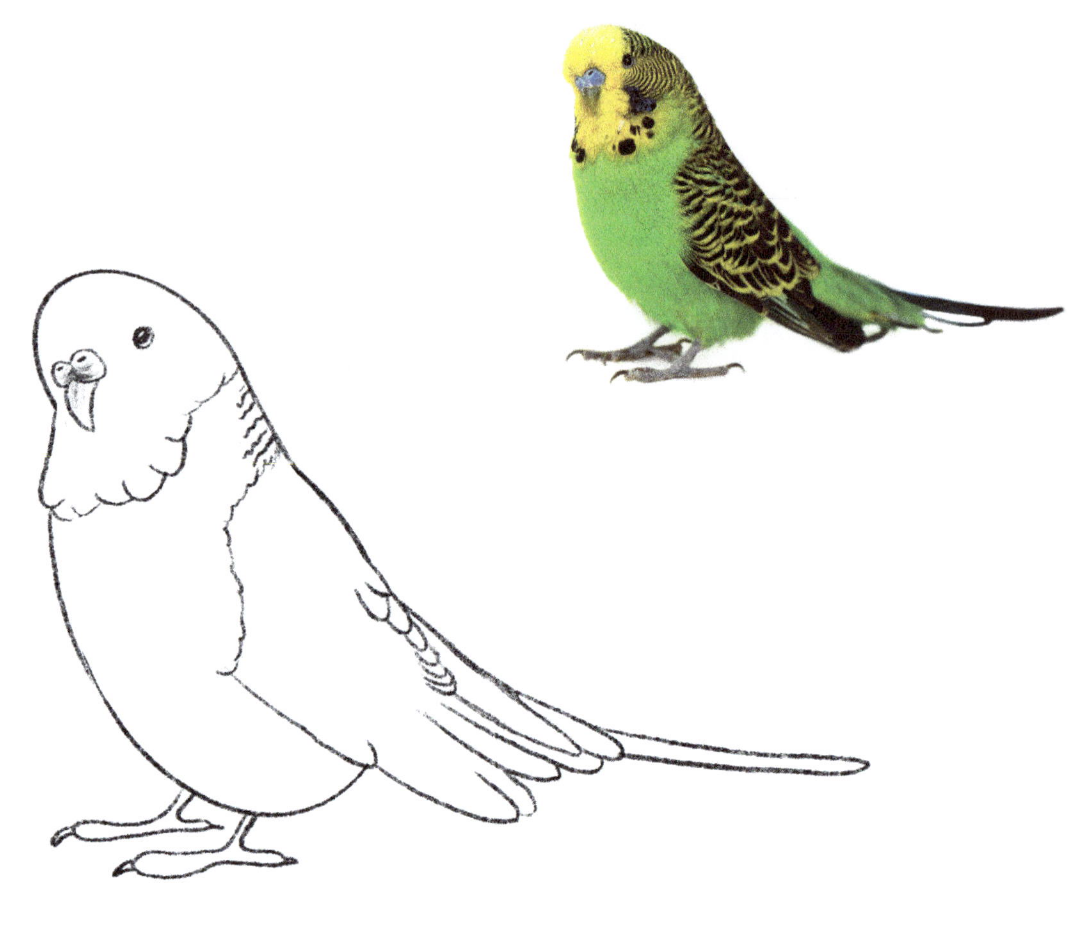

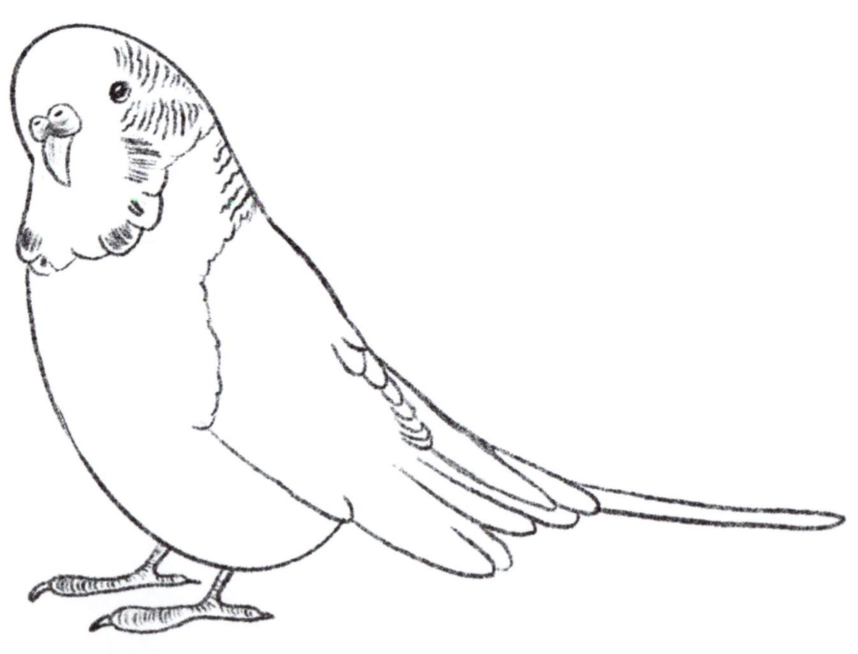

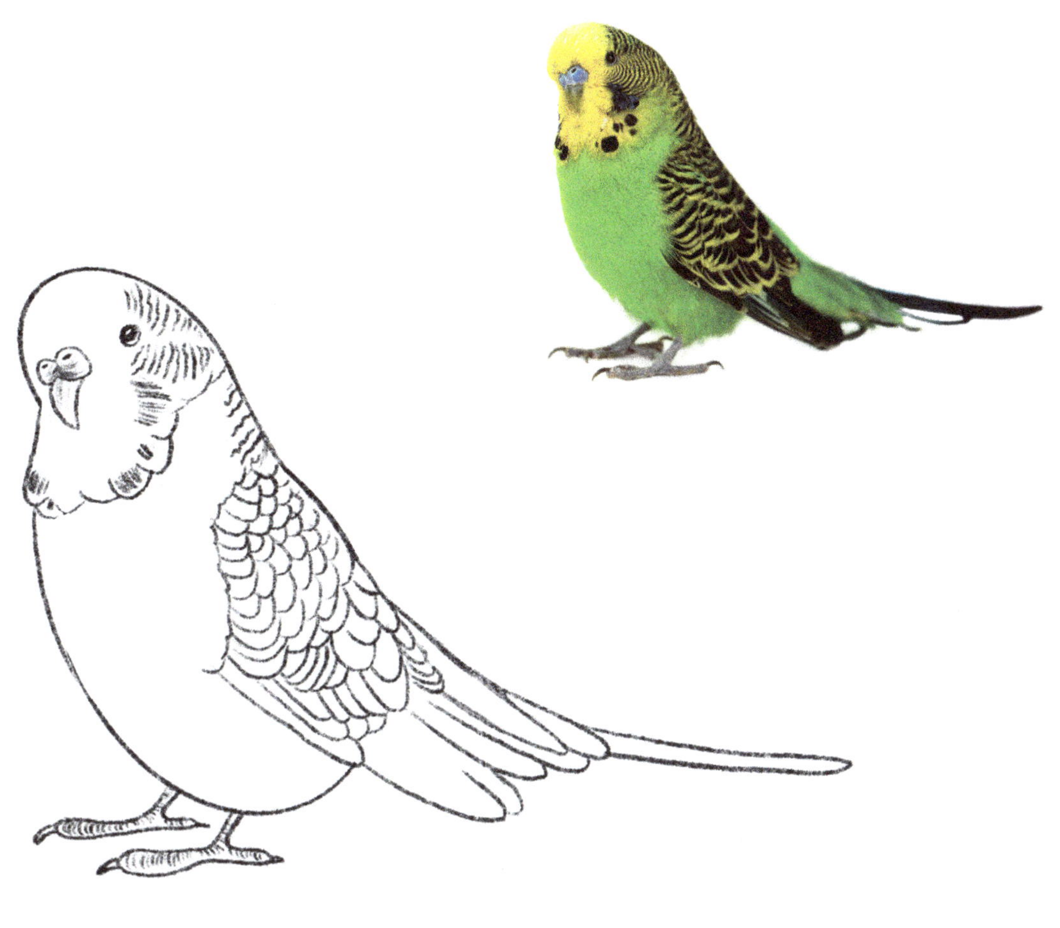

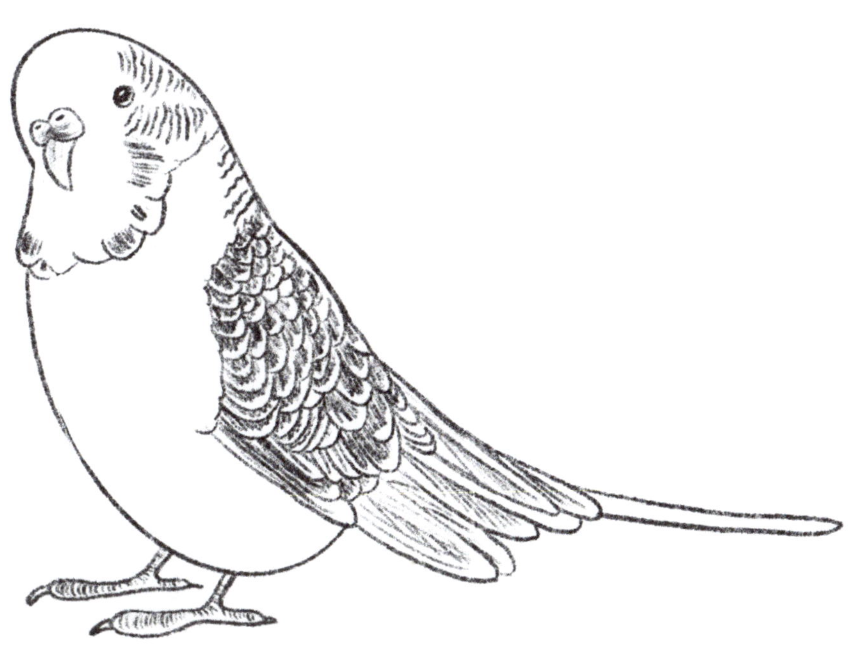

# Lion

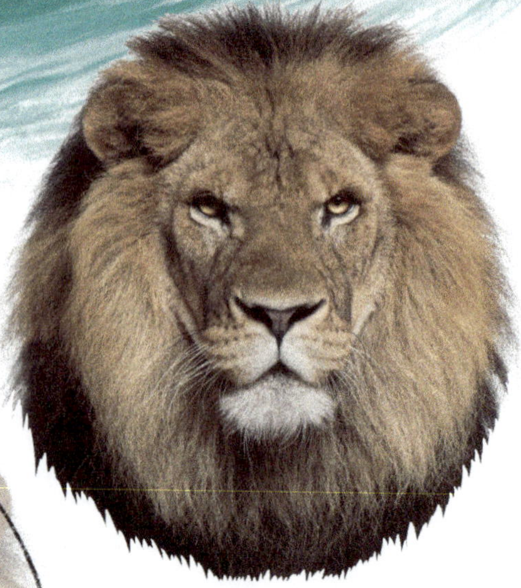

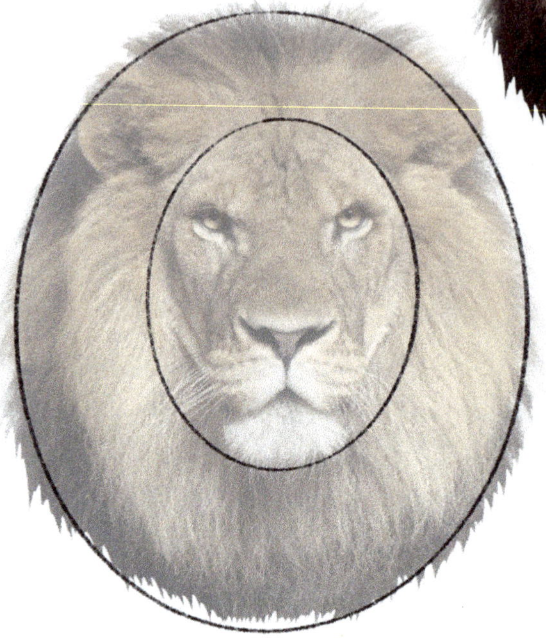

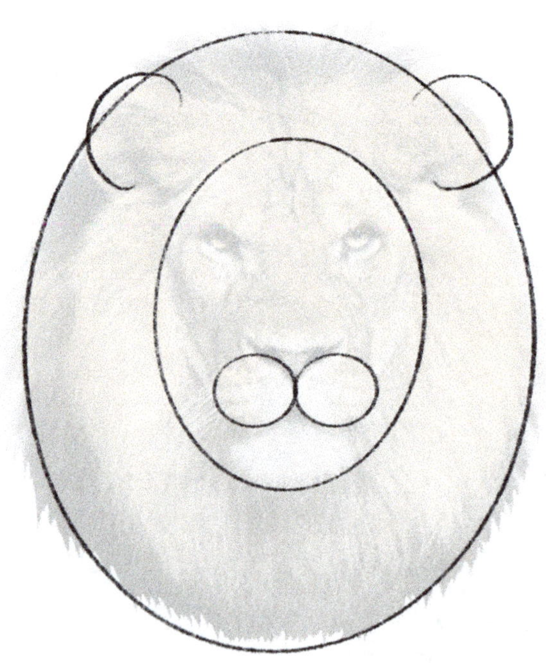

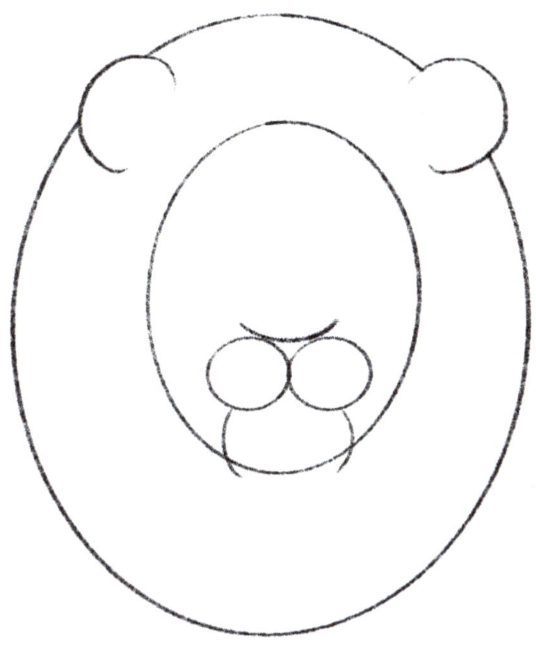

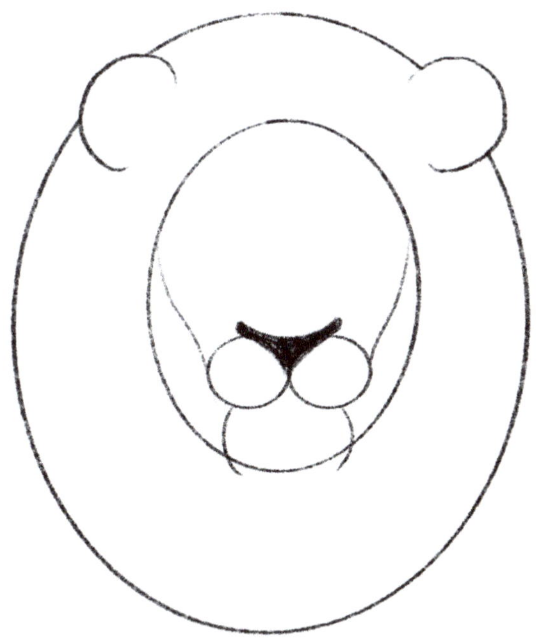

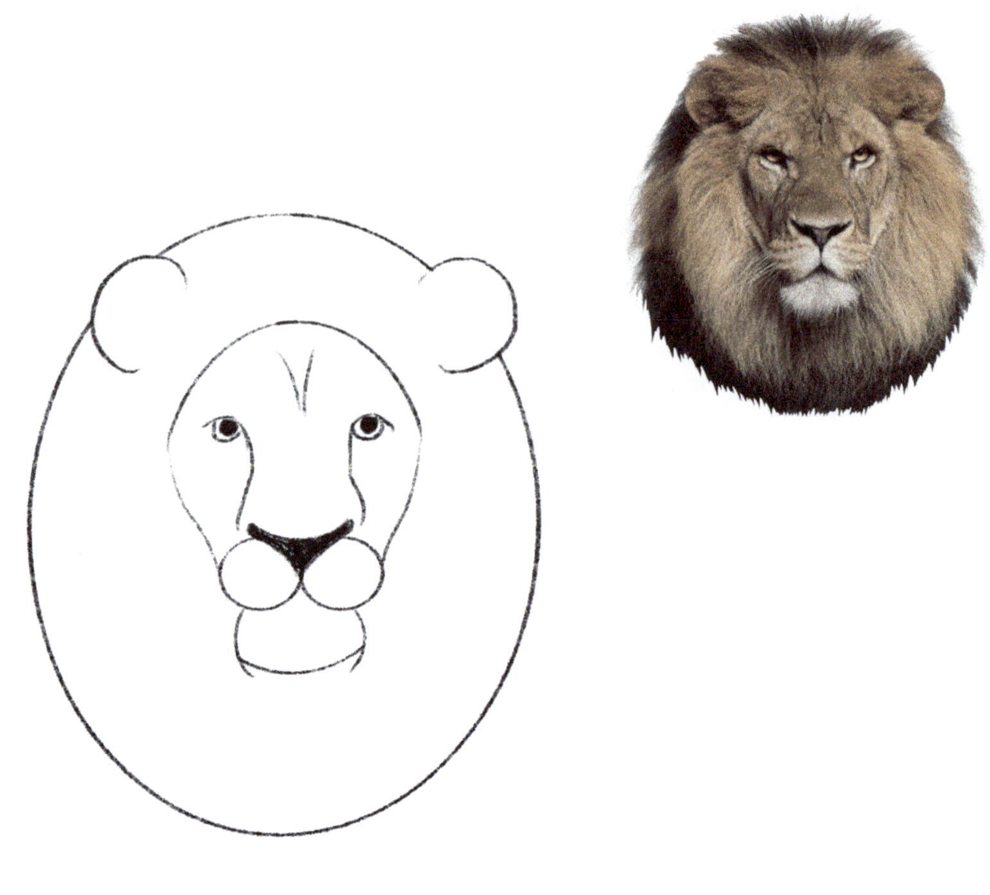

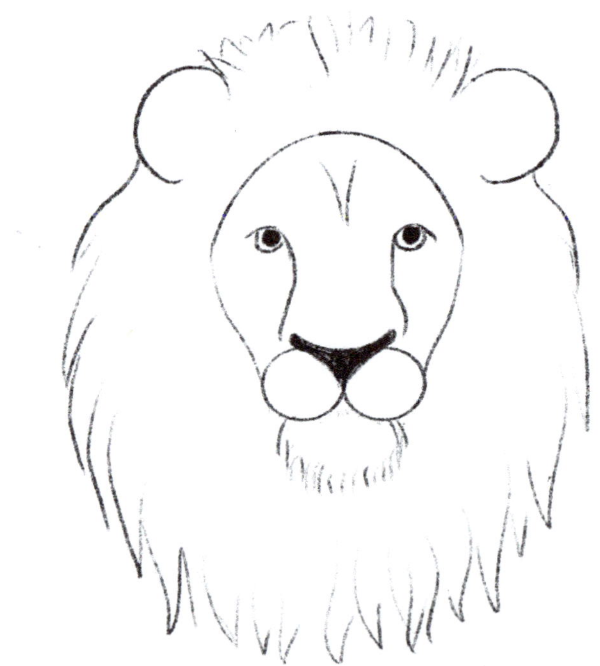

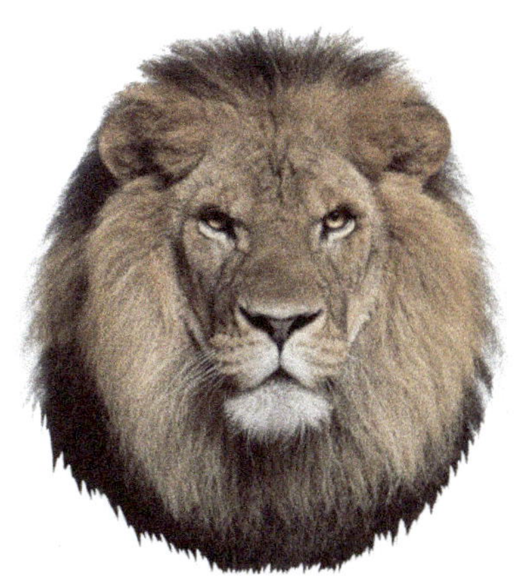

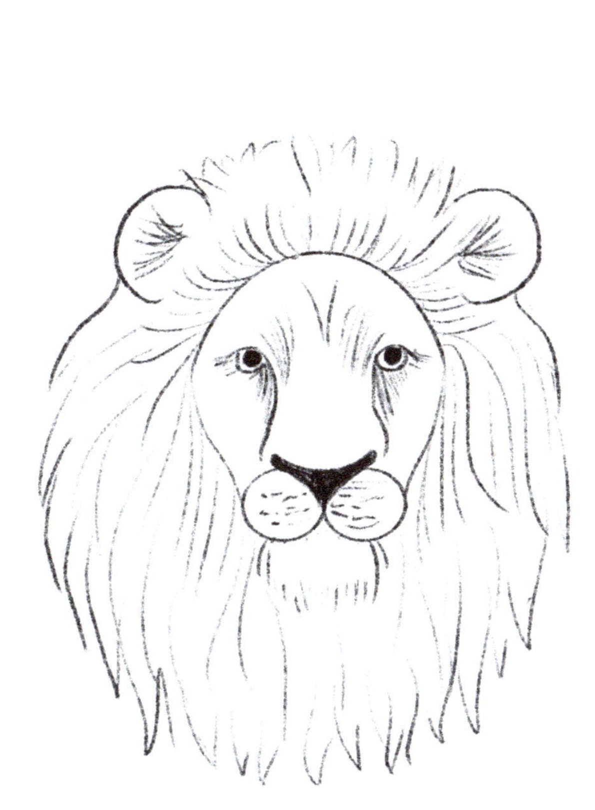

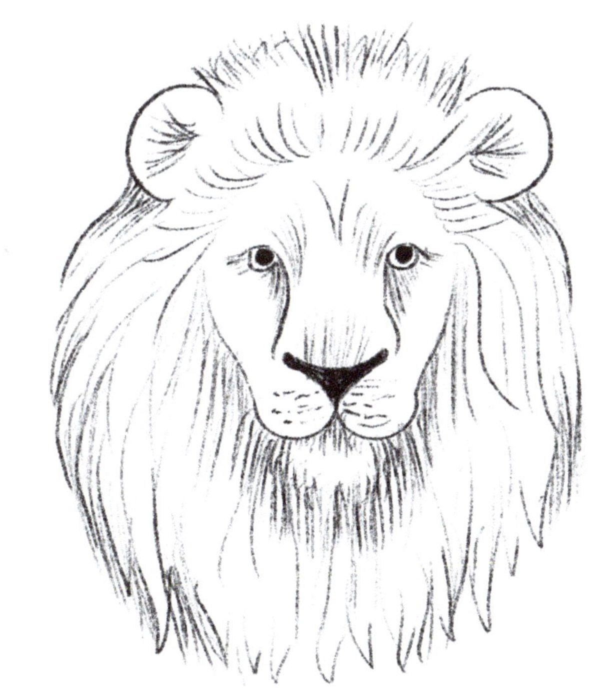

# Jaguar

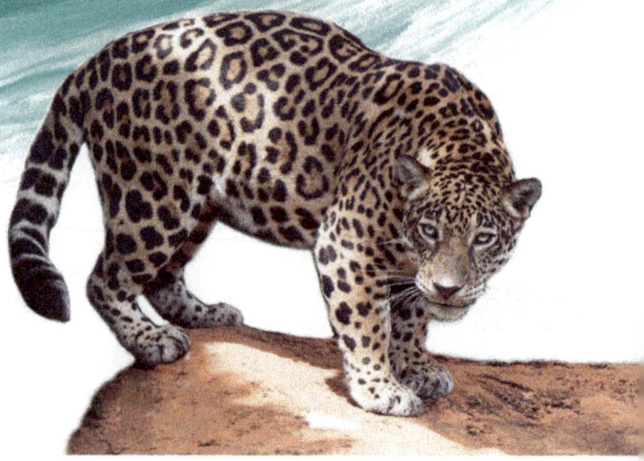

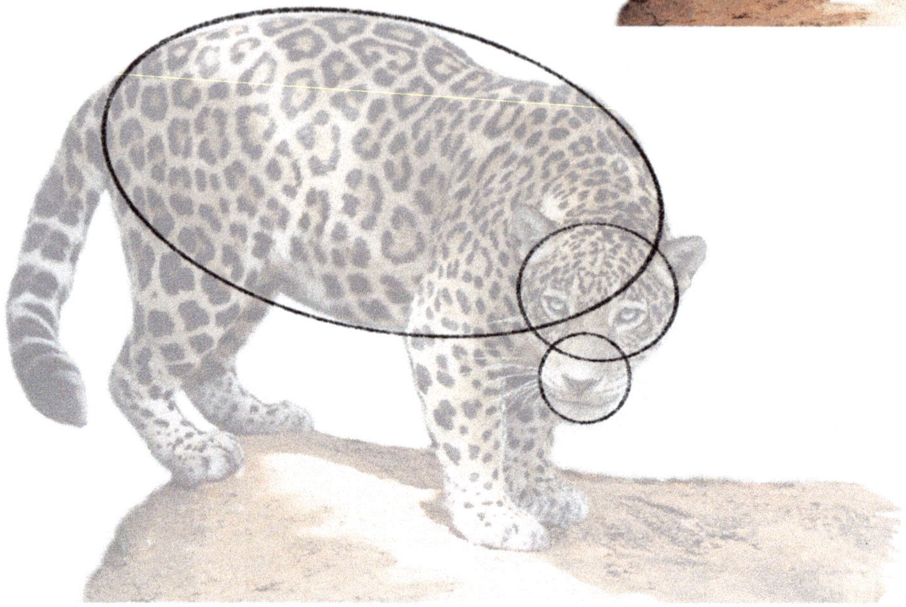

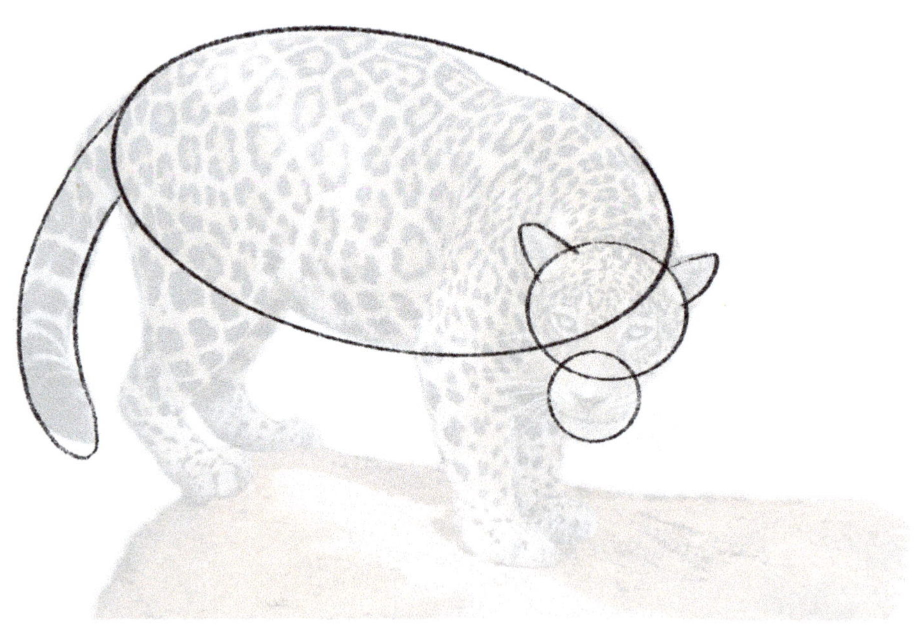

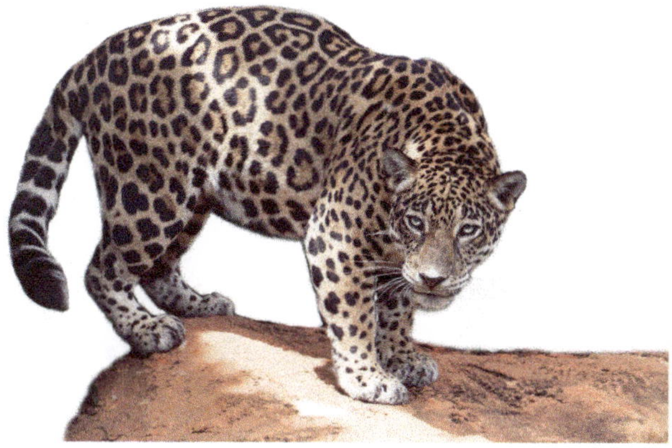

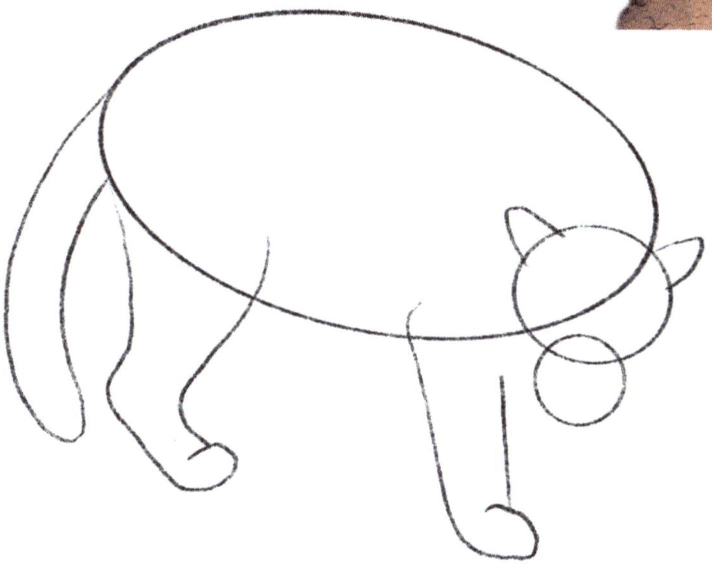

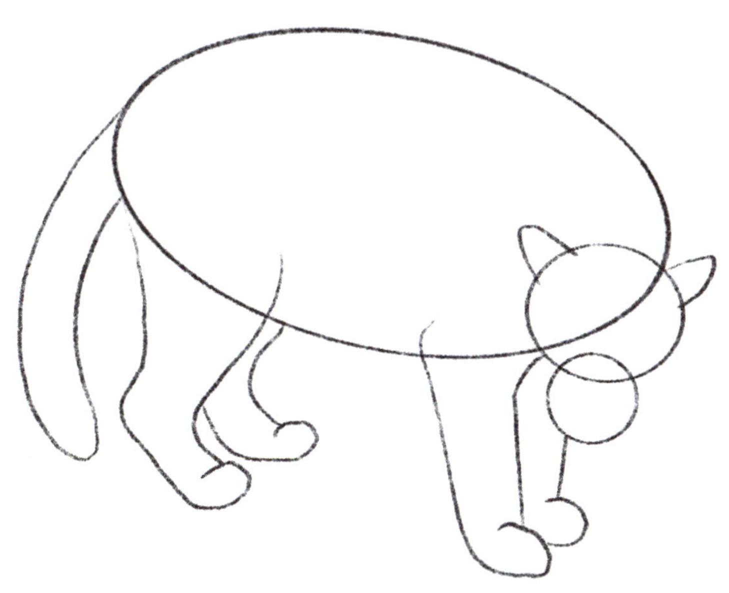

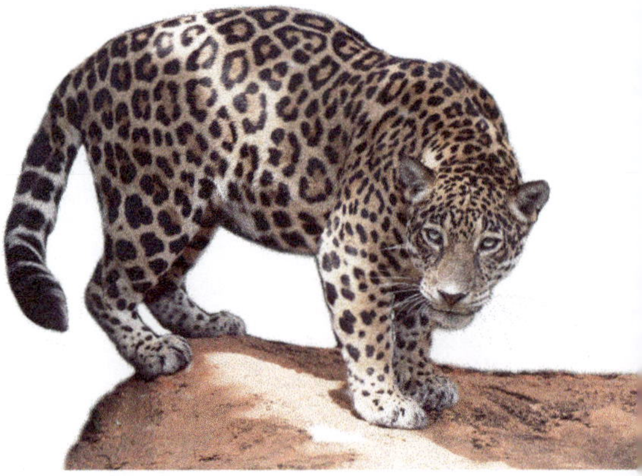

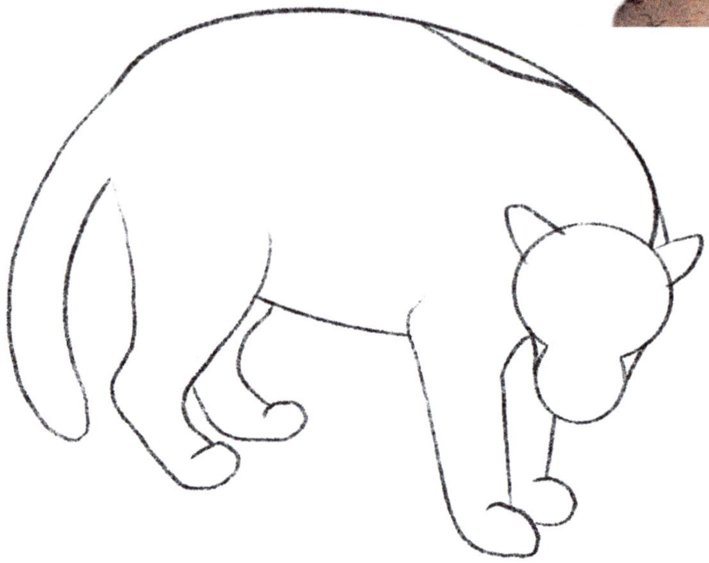

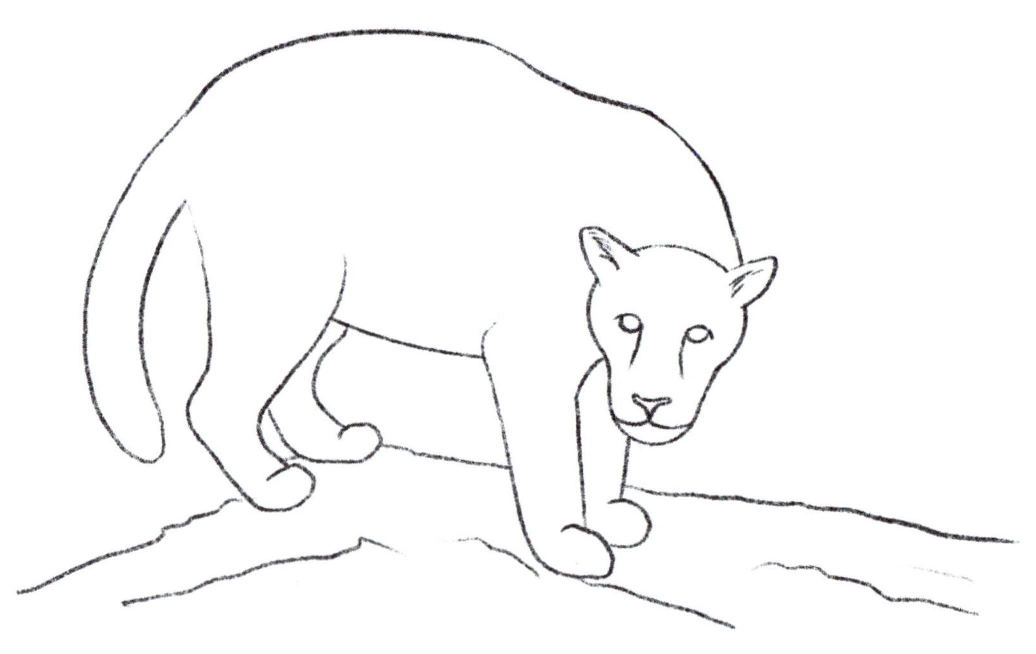

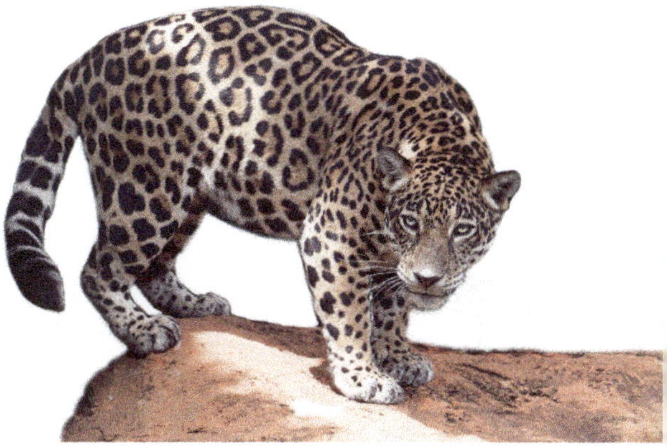

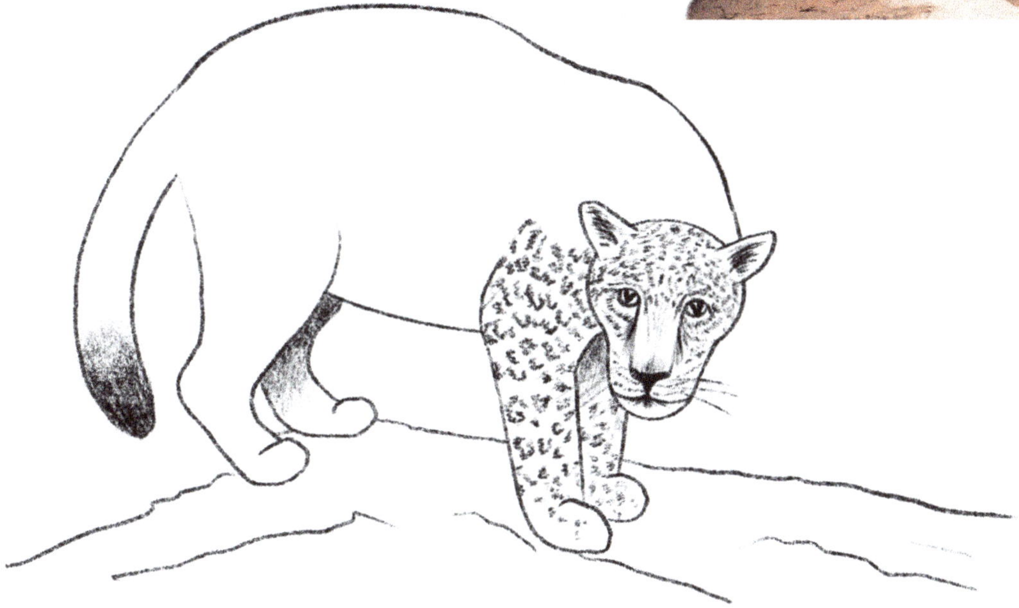

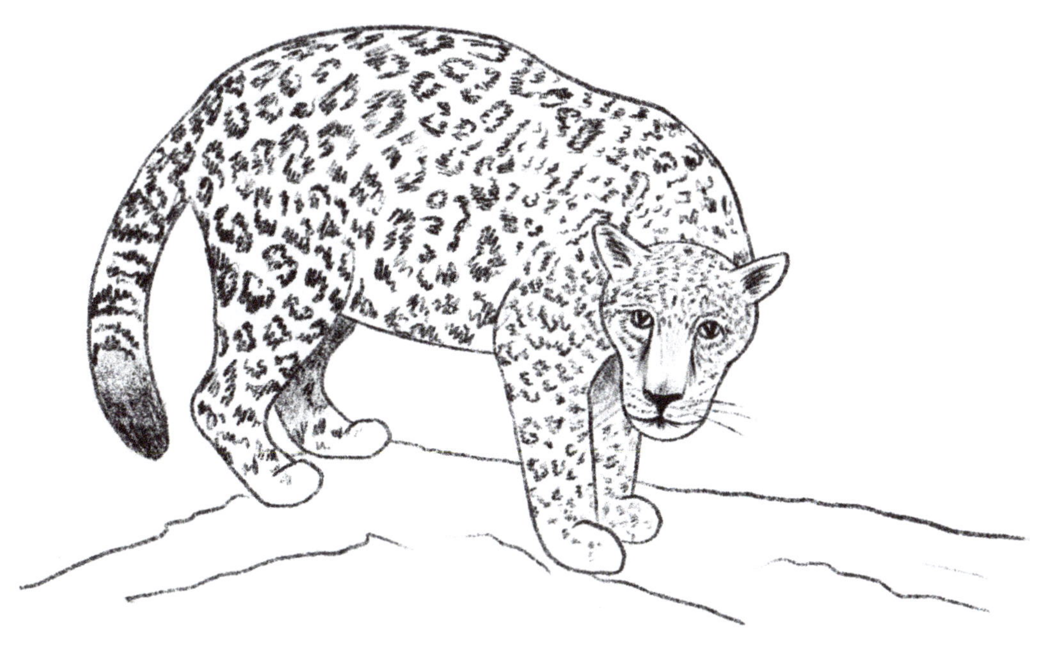

# Wolf

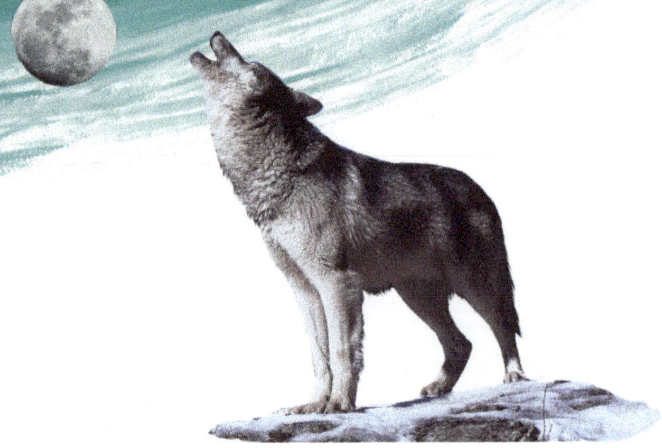

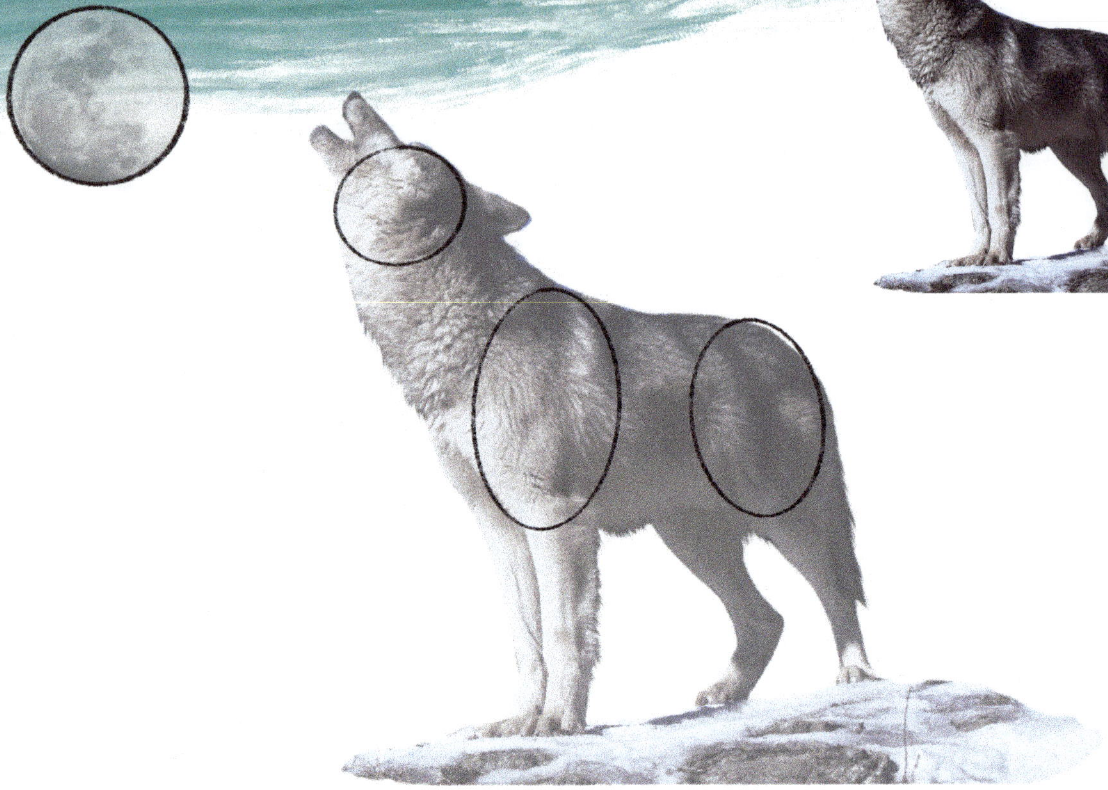

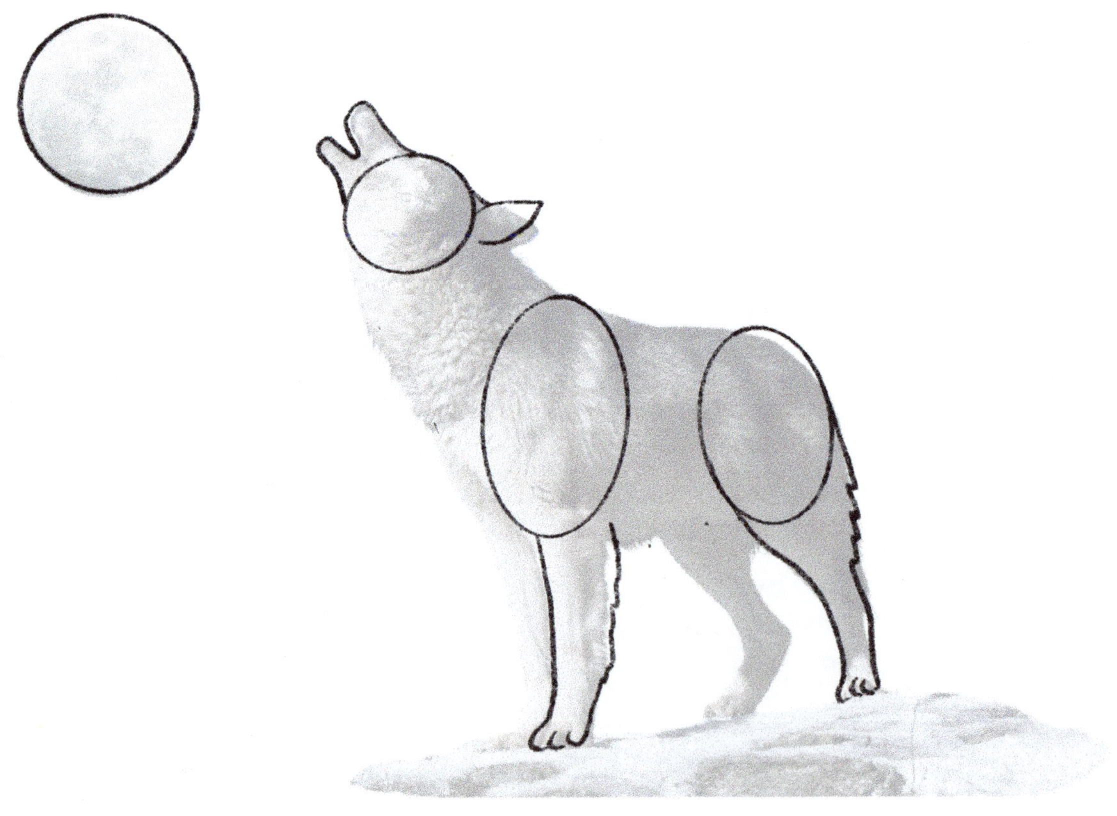

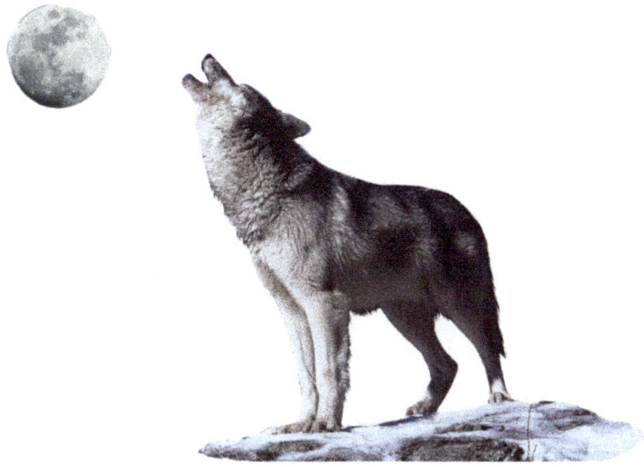

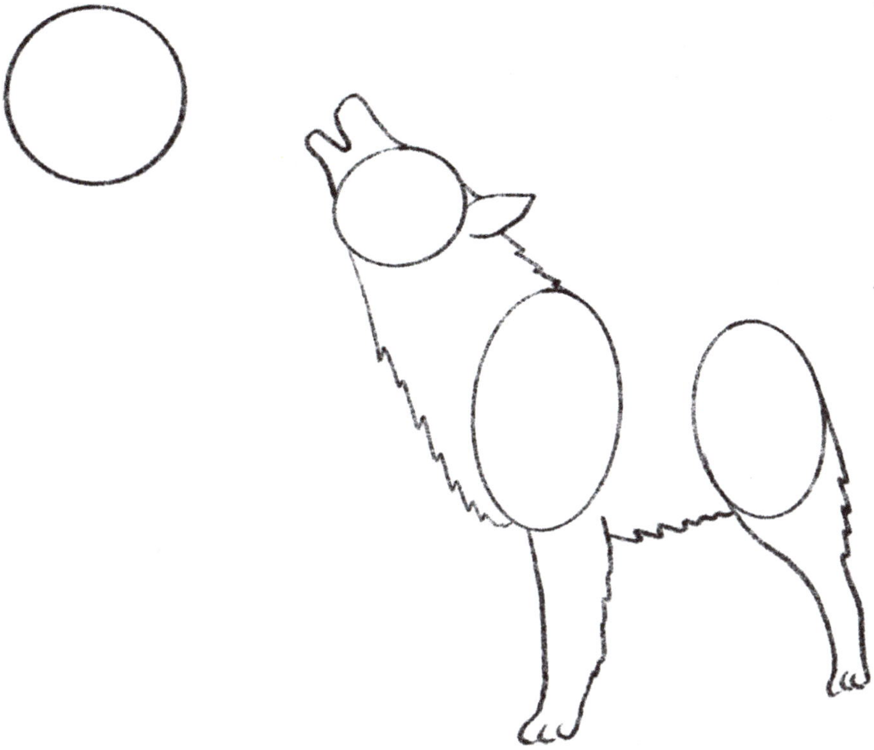

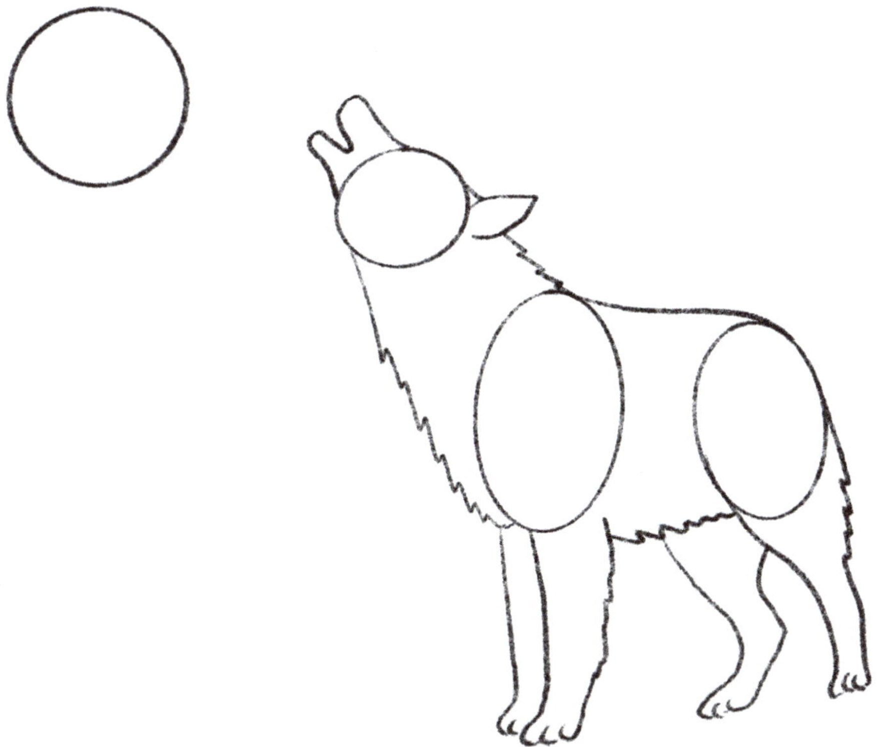

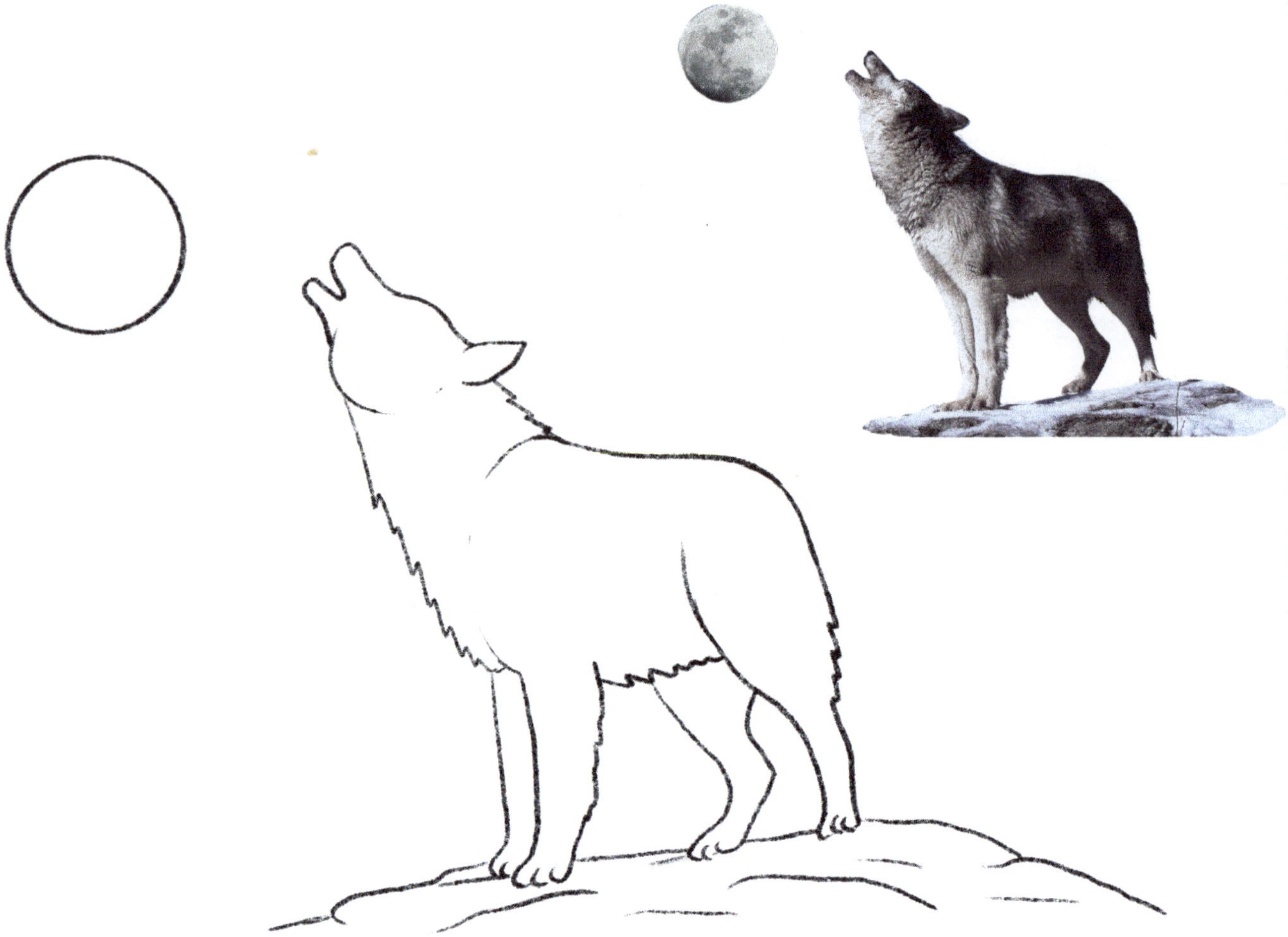

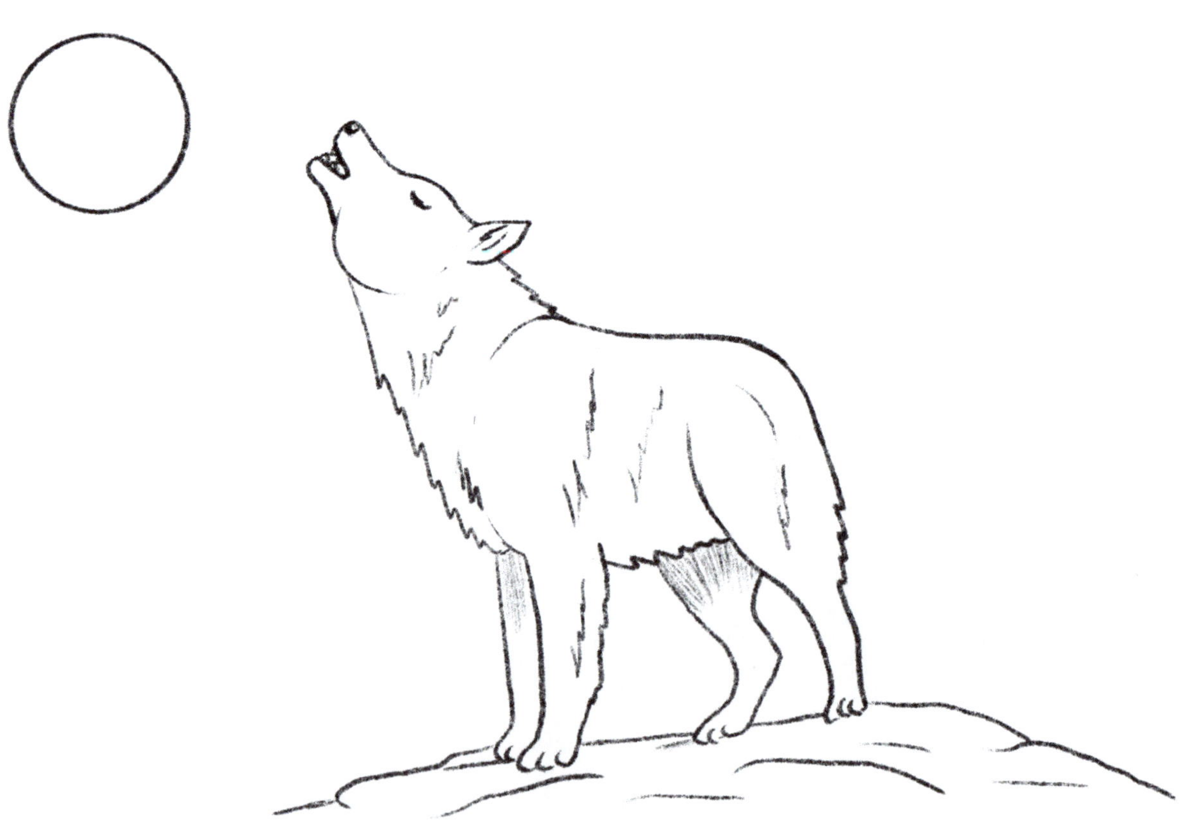

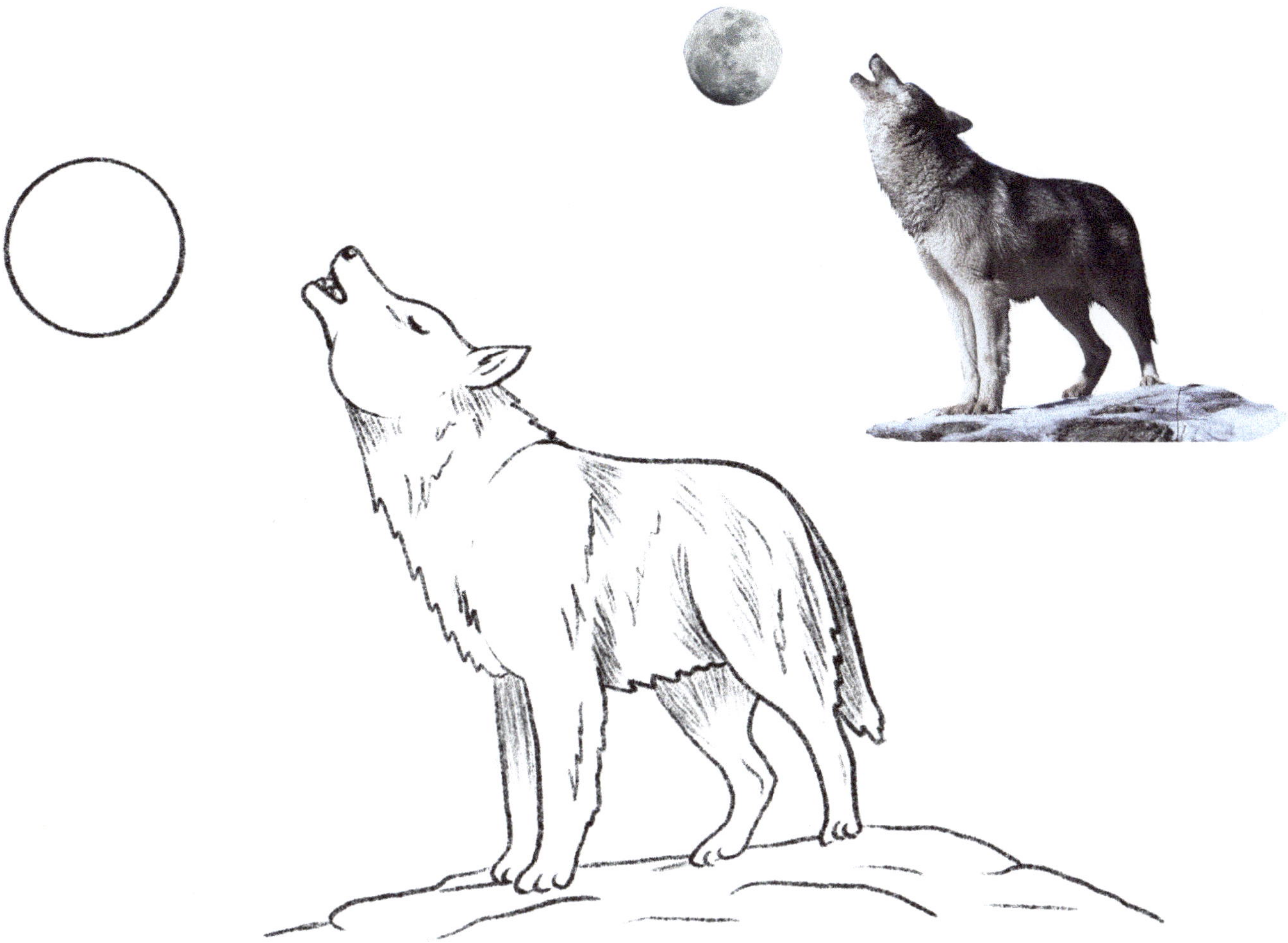

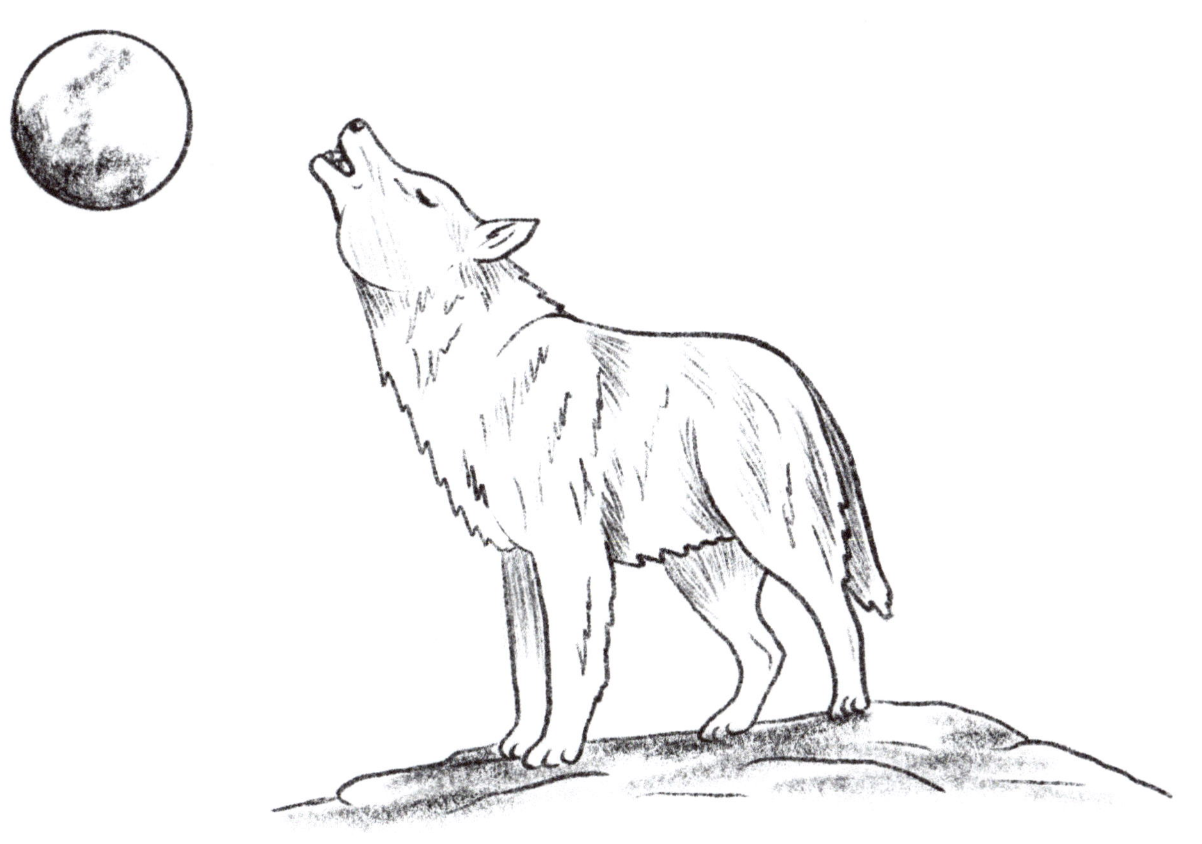

# Tiger

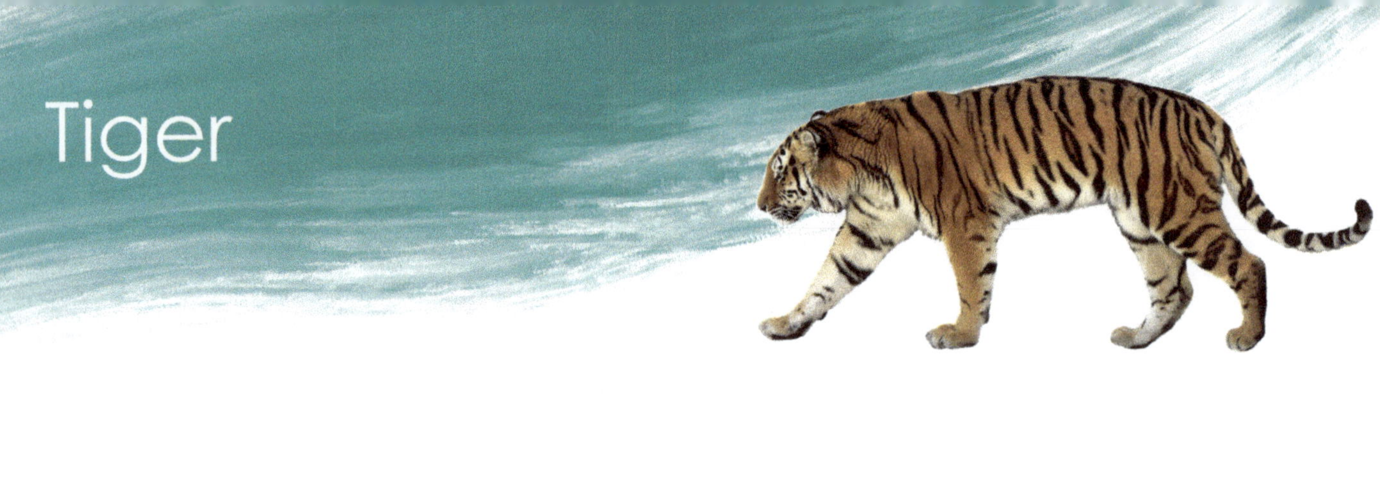

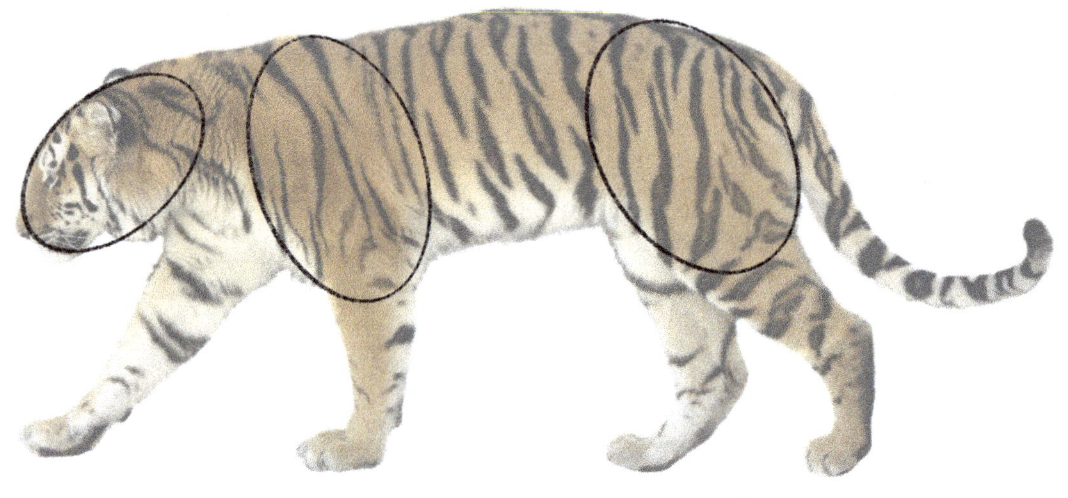

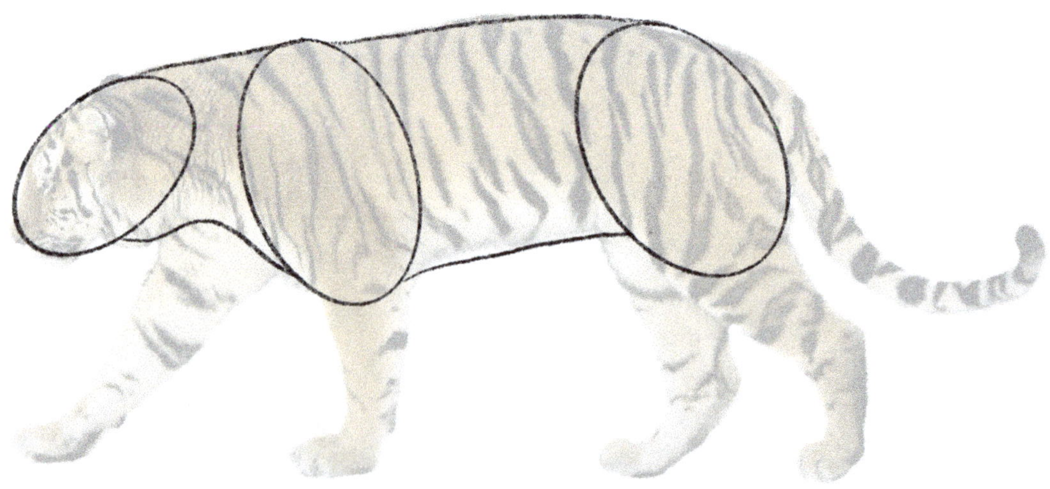

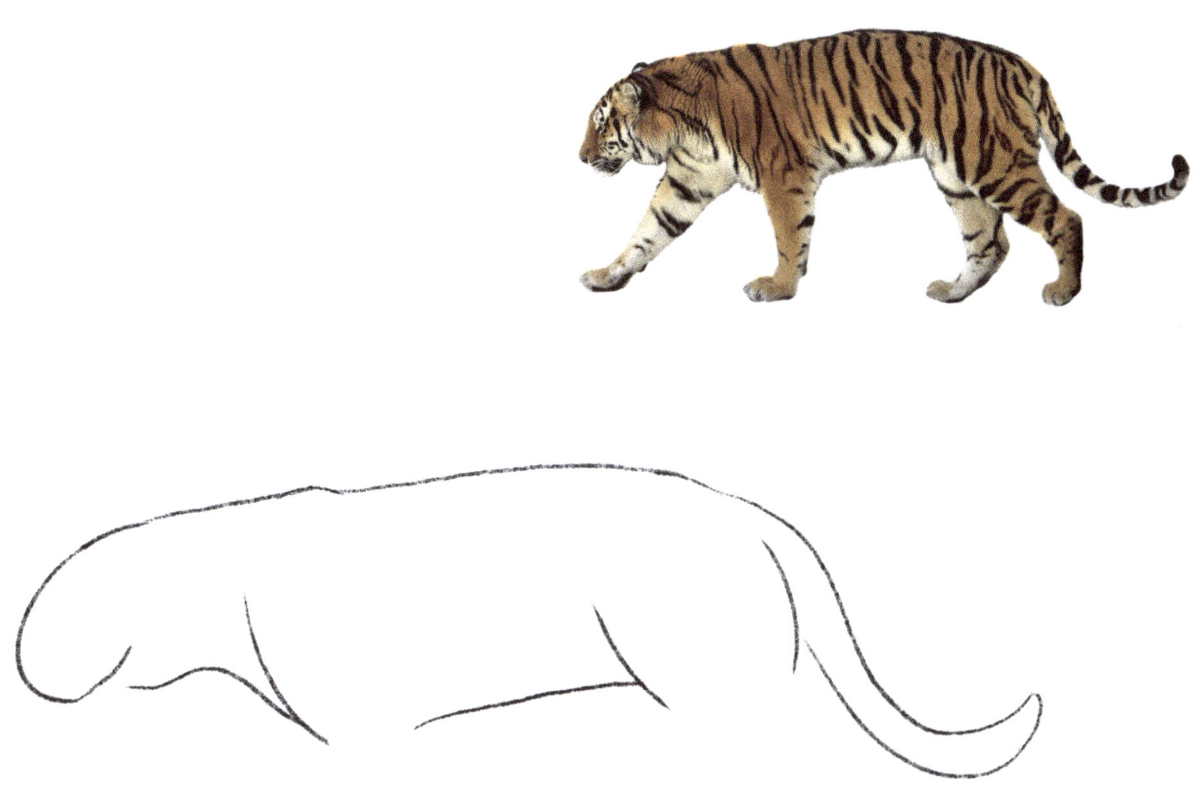

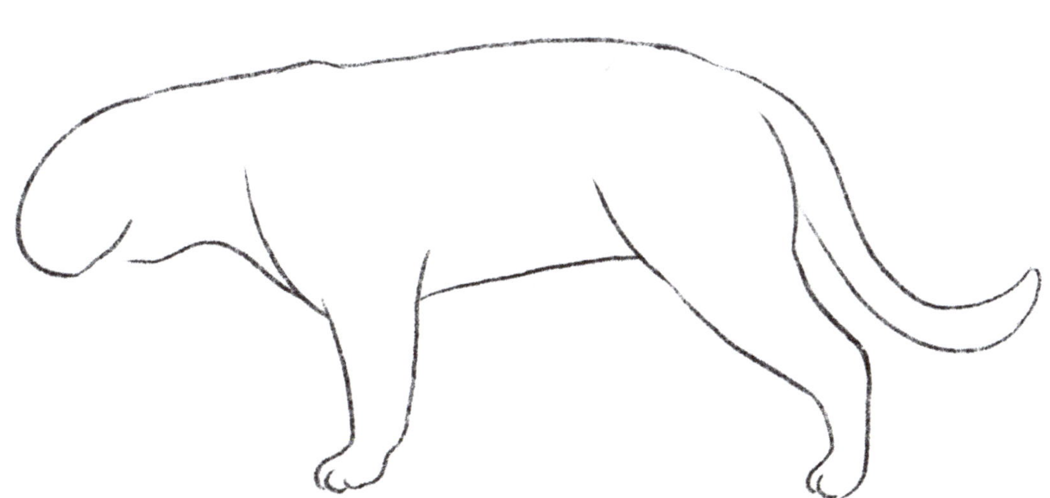

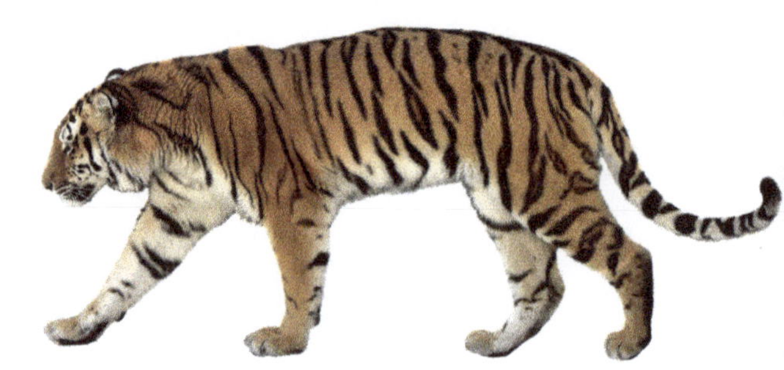

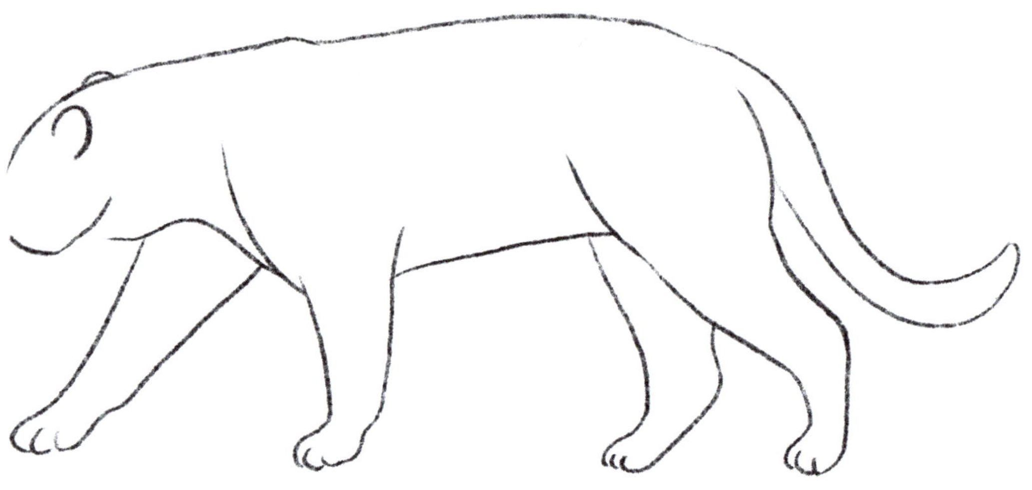

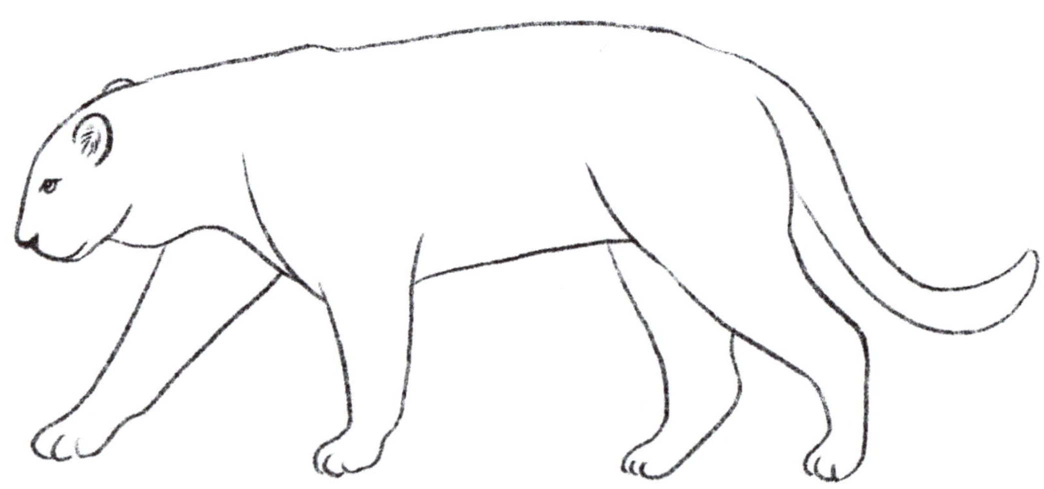

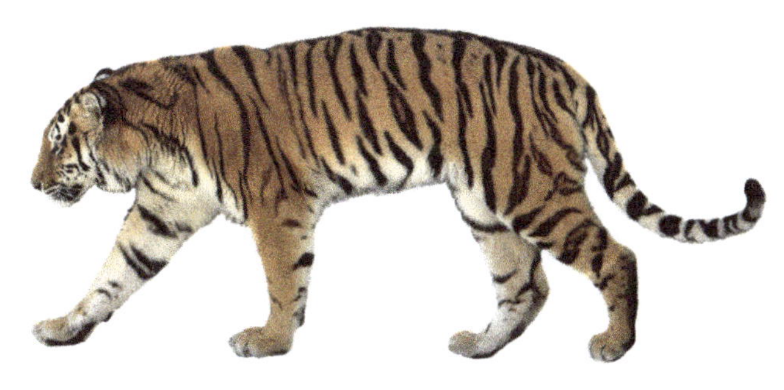

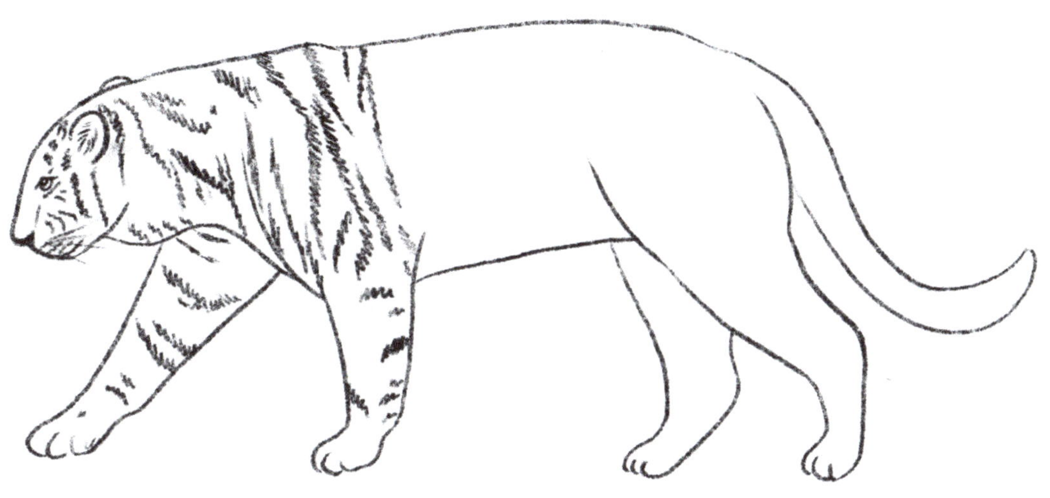

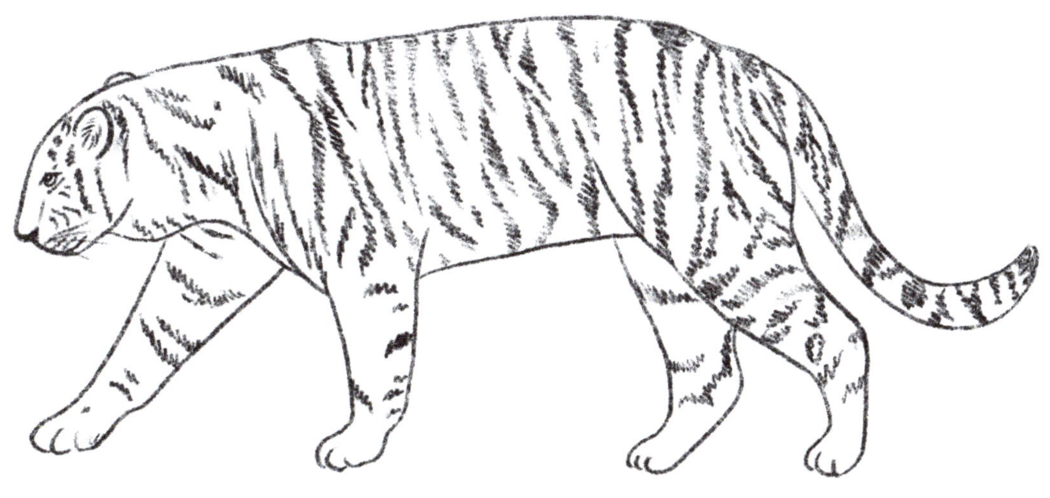

# Crocodile

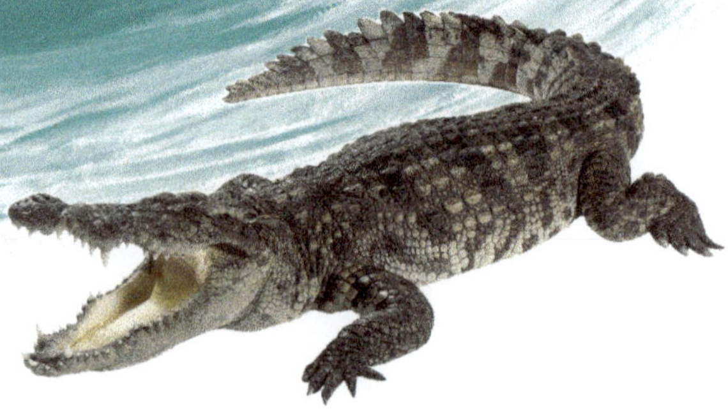

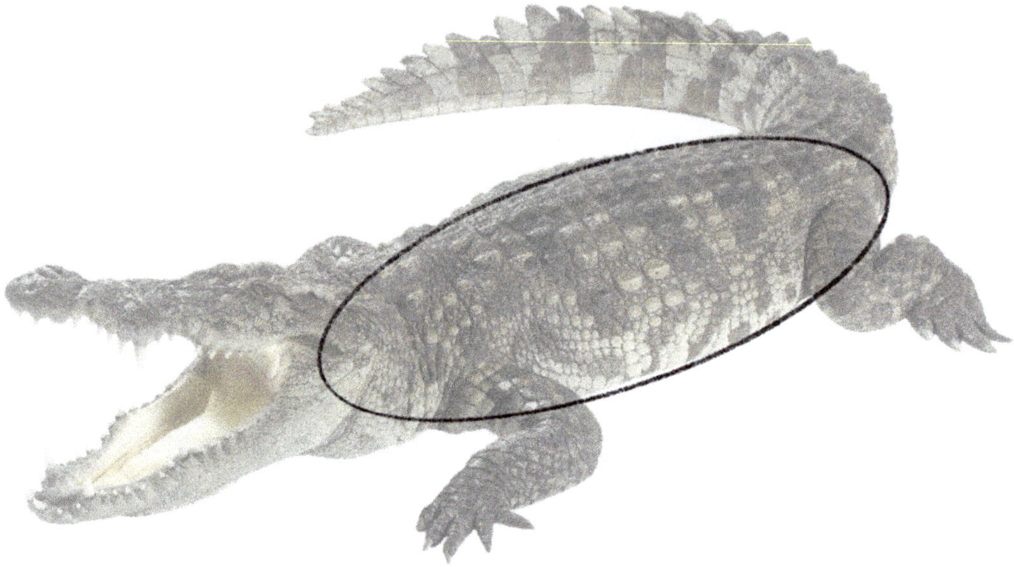

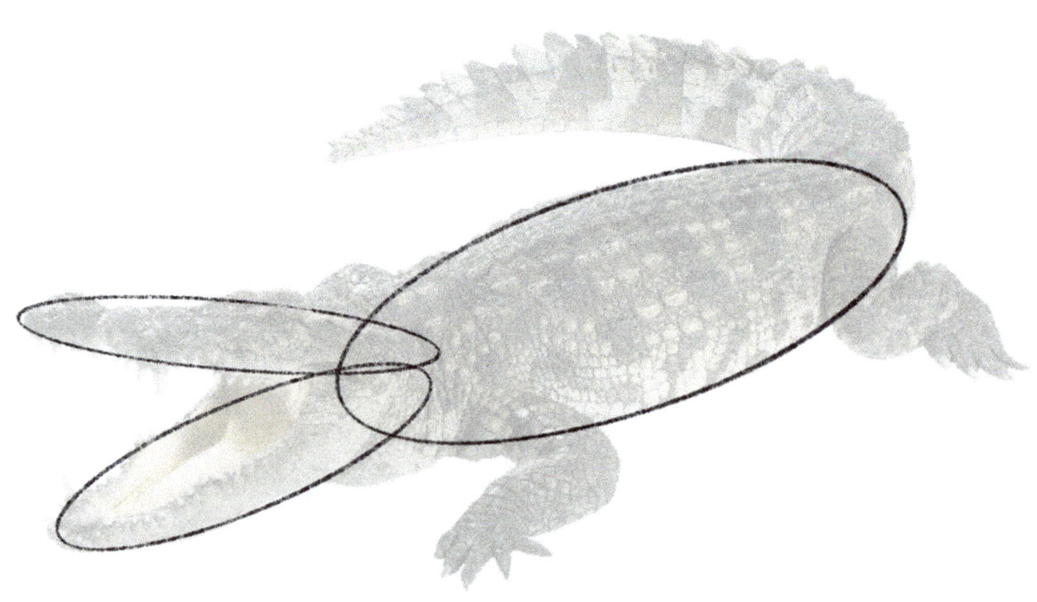

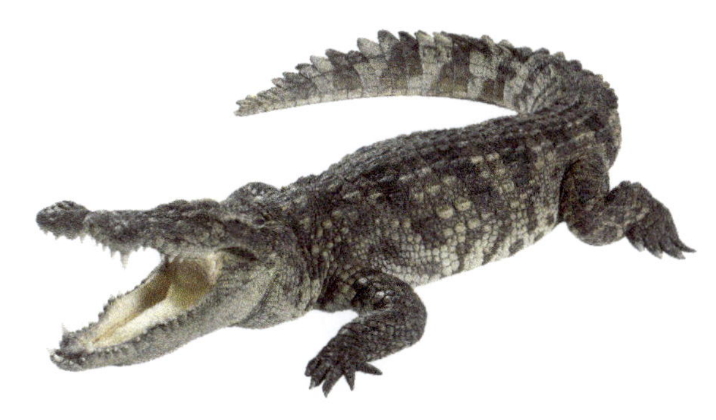

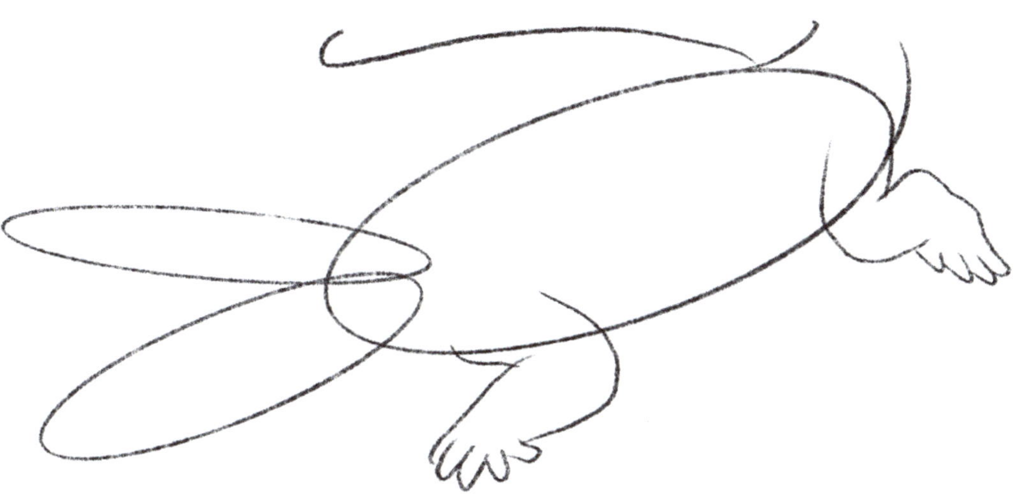

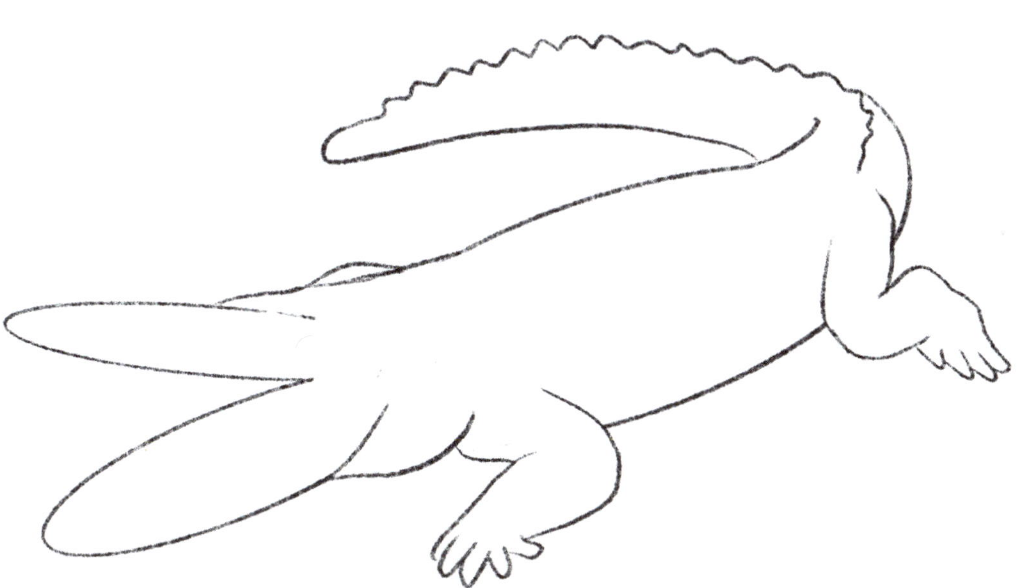

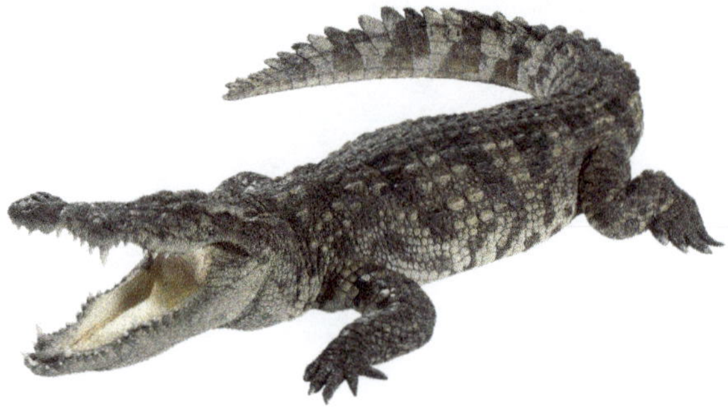

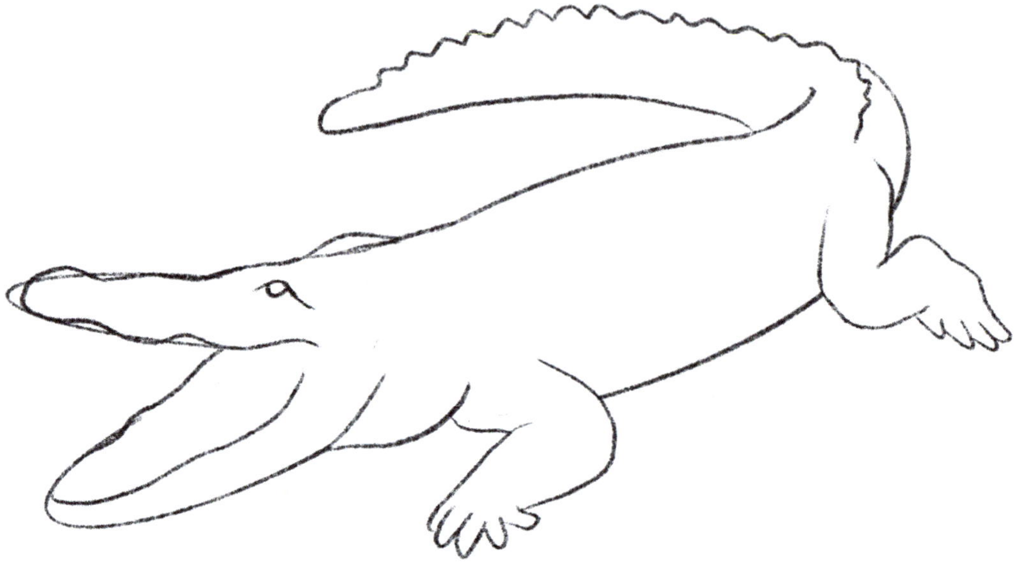

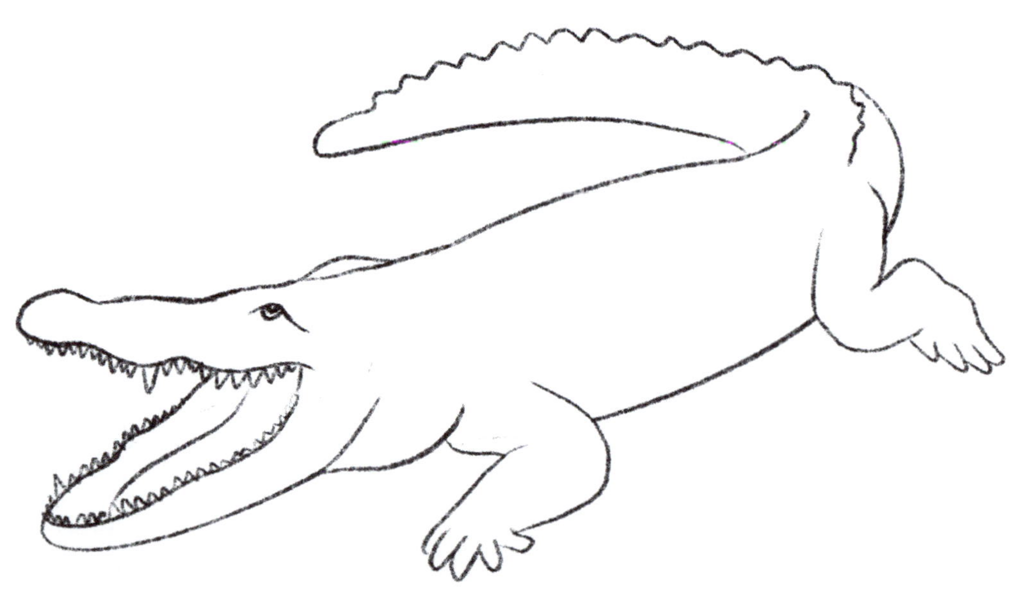

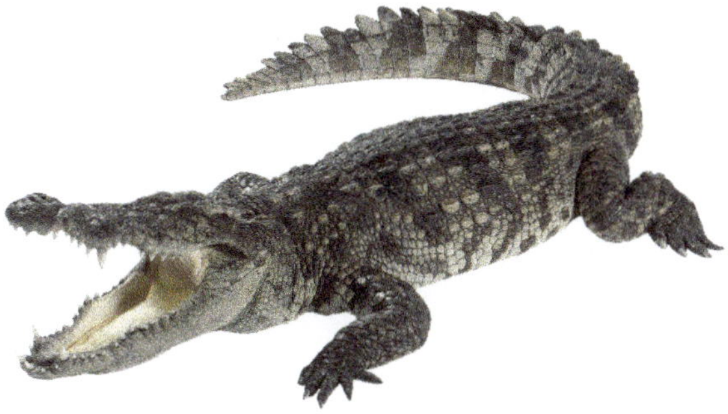

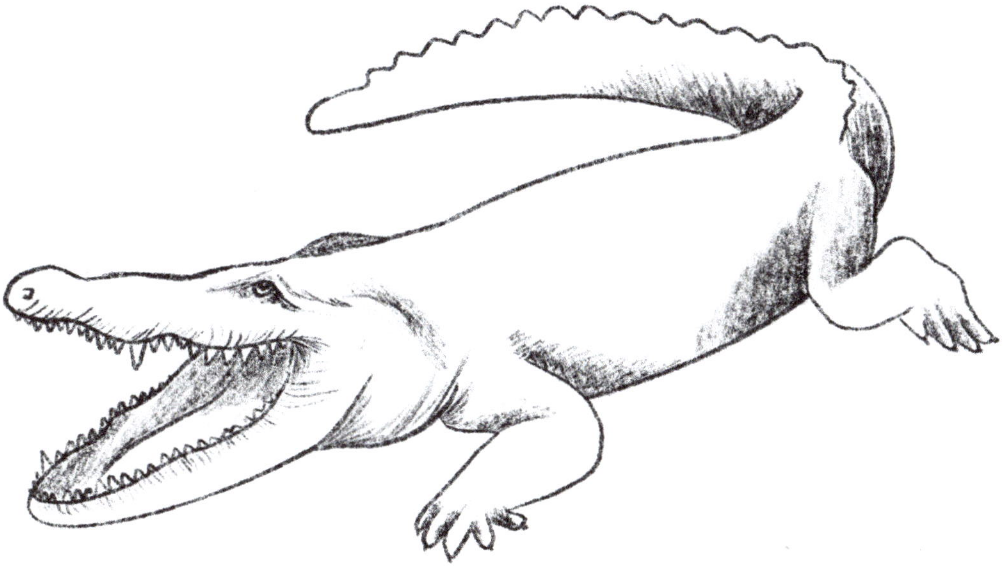

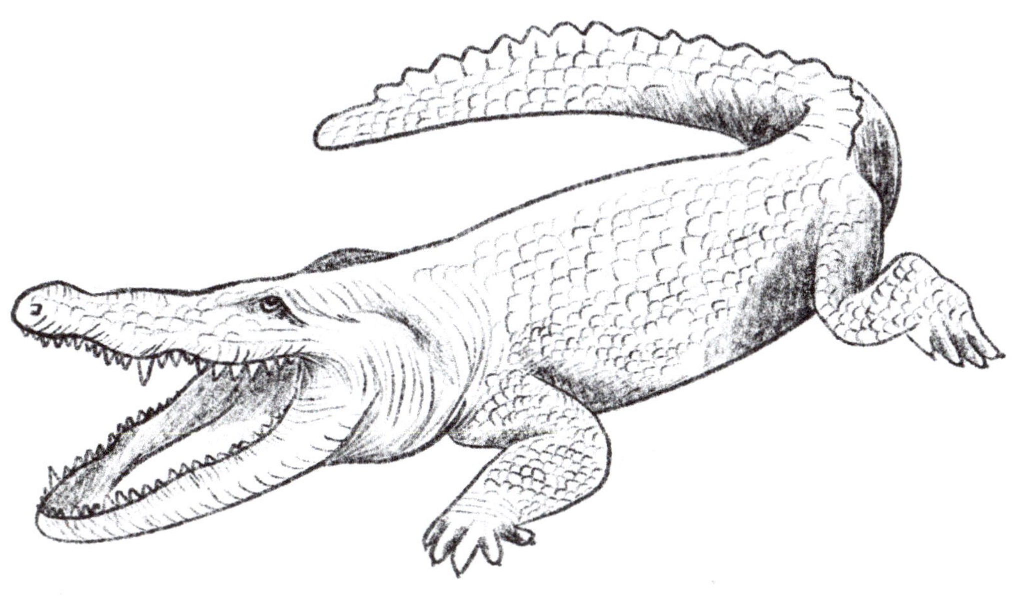

# Eagle

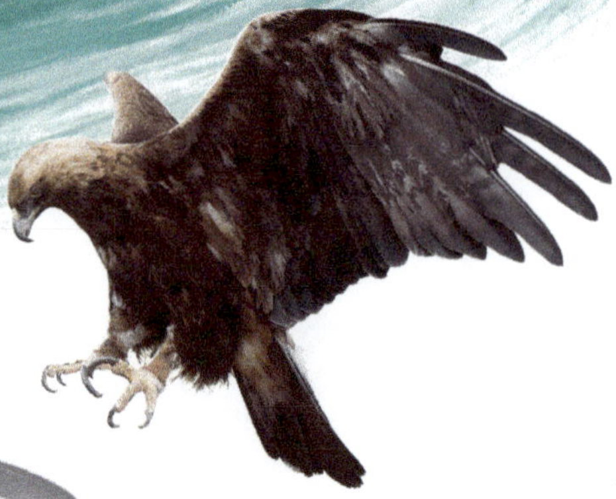

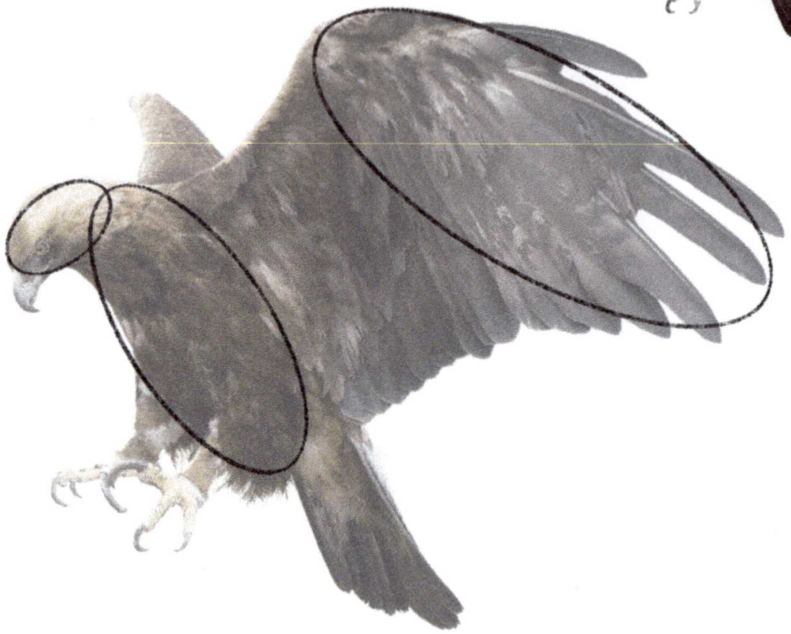

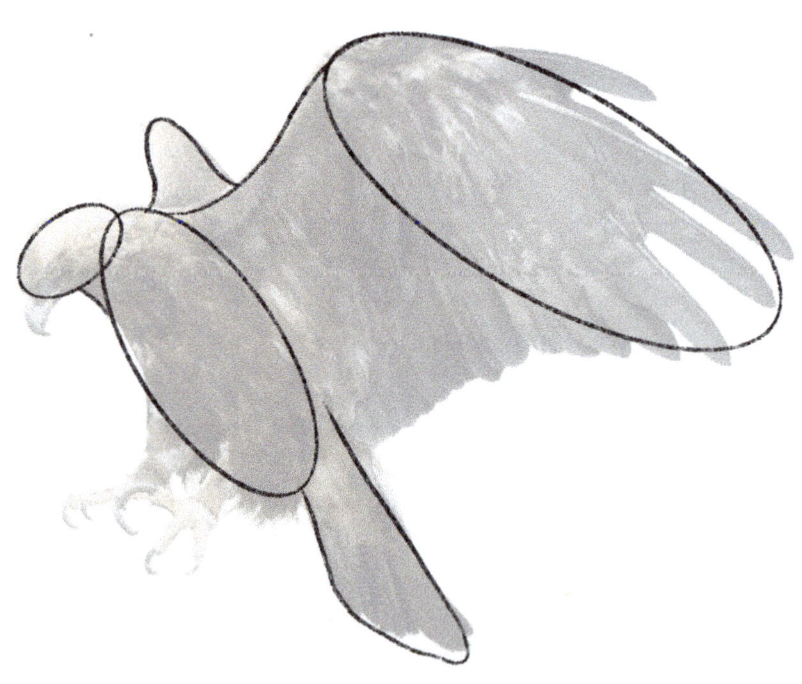

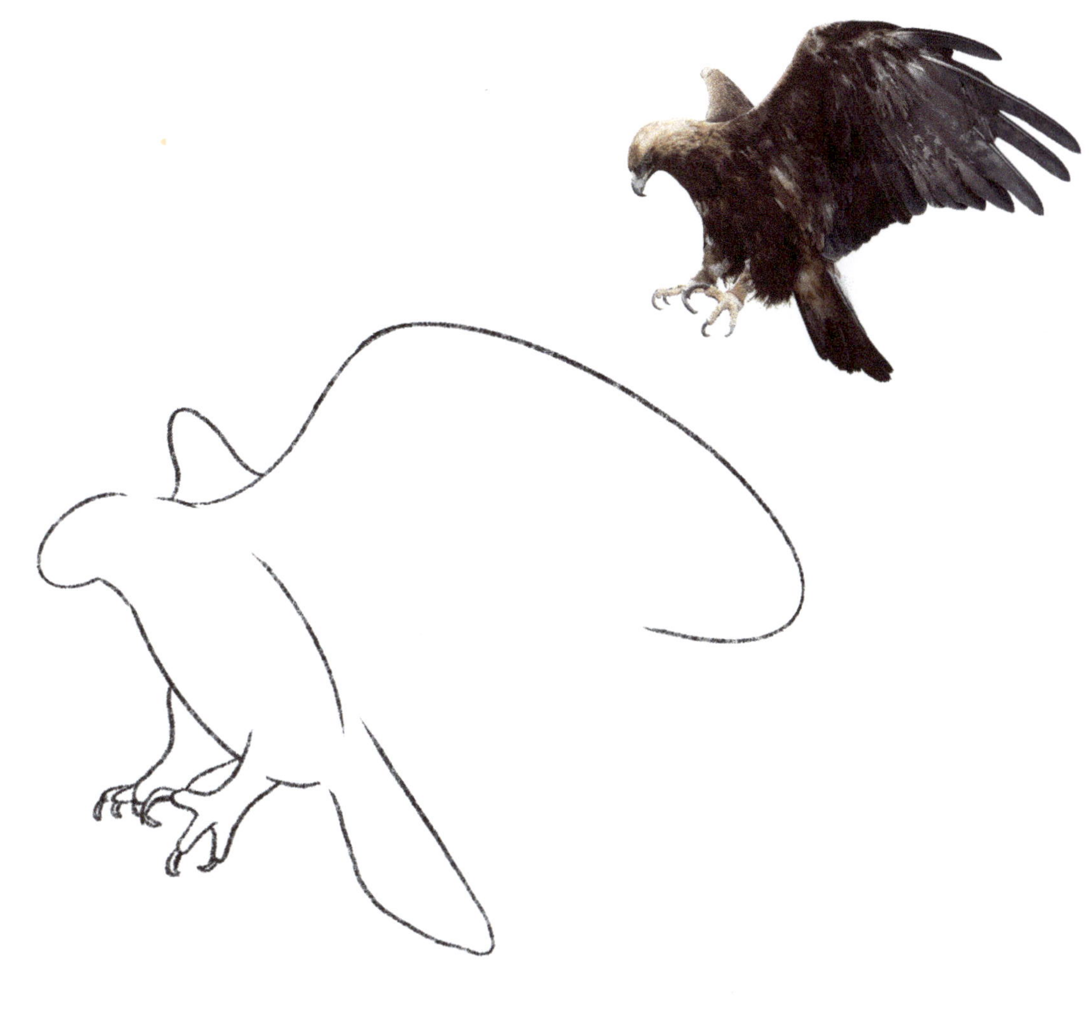

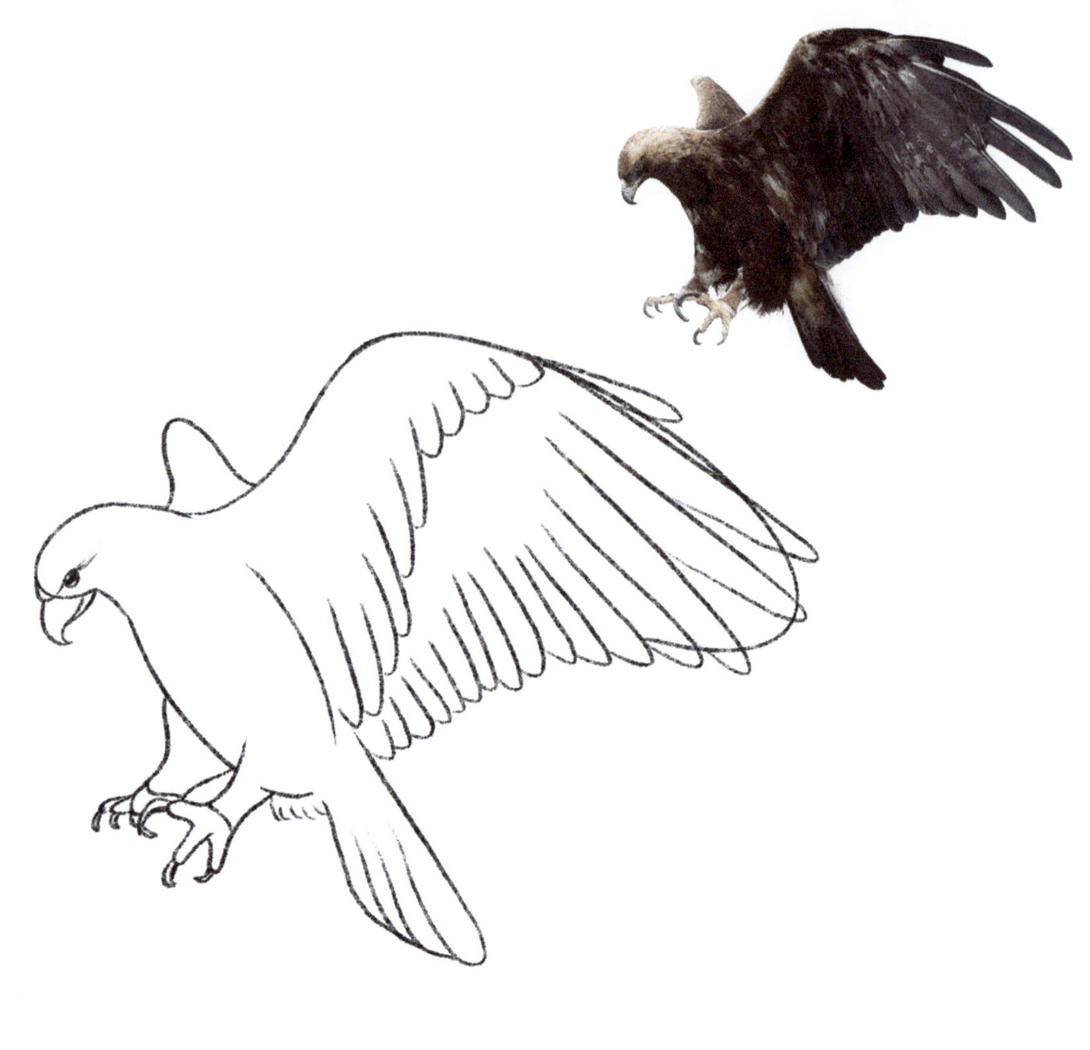

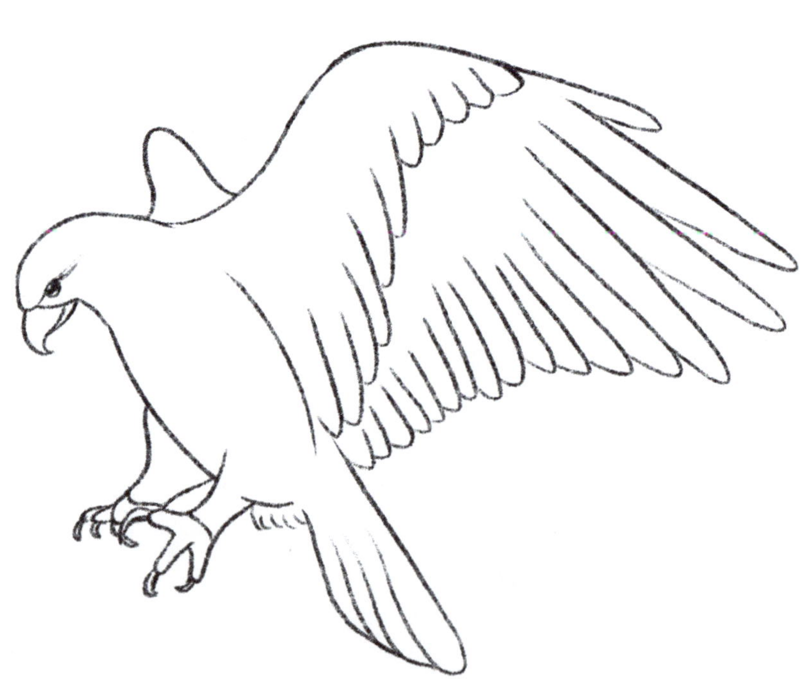

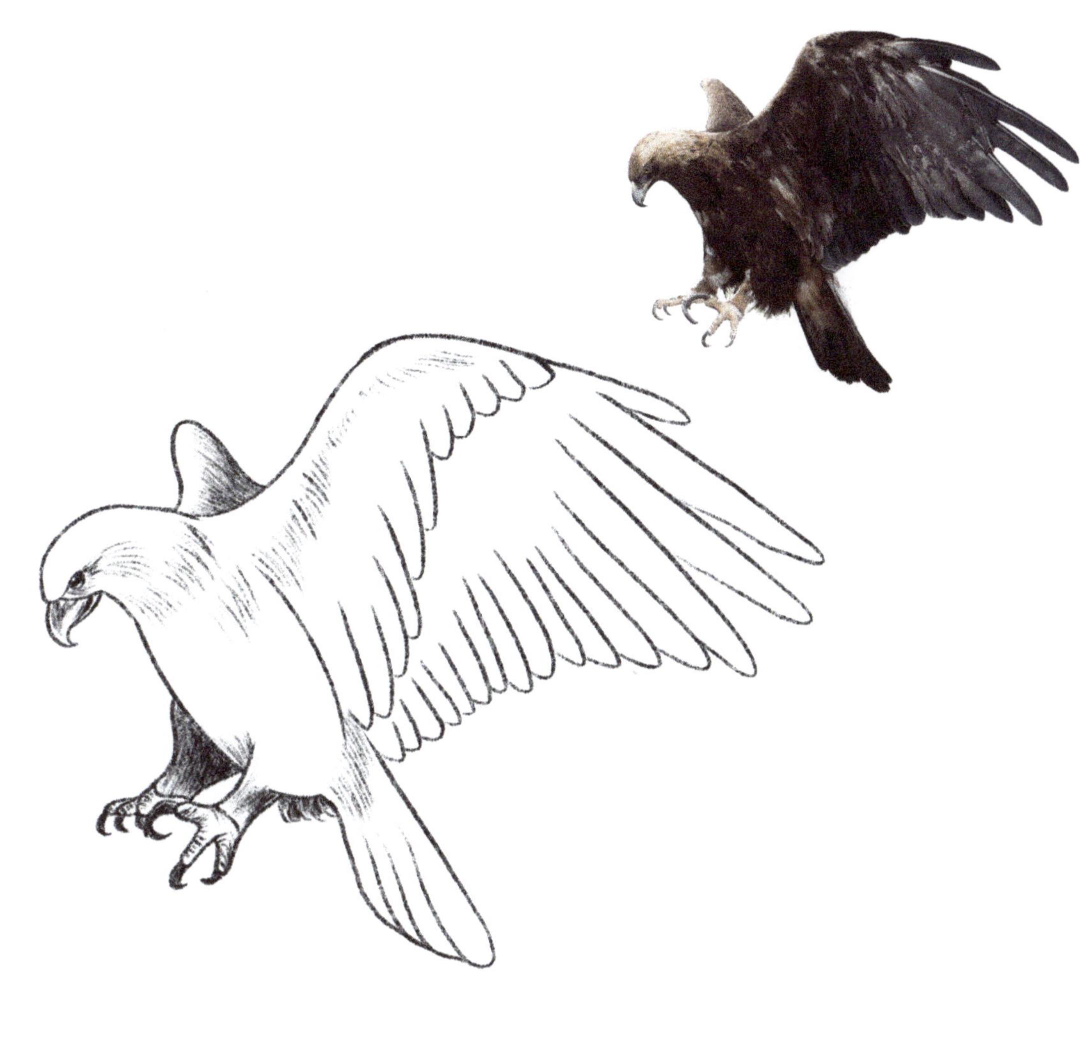

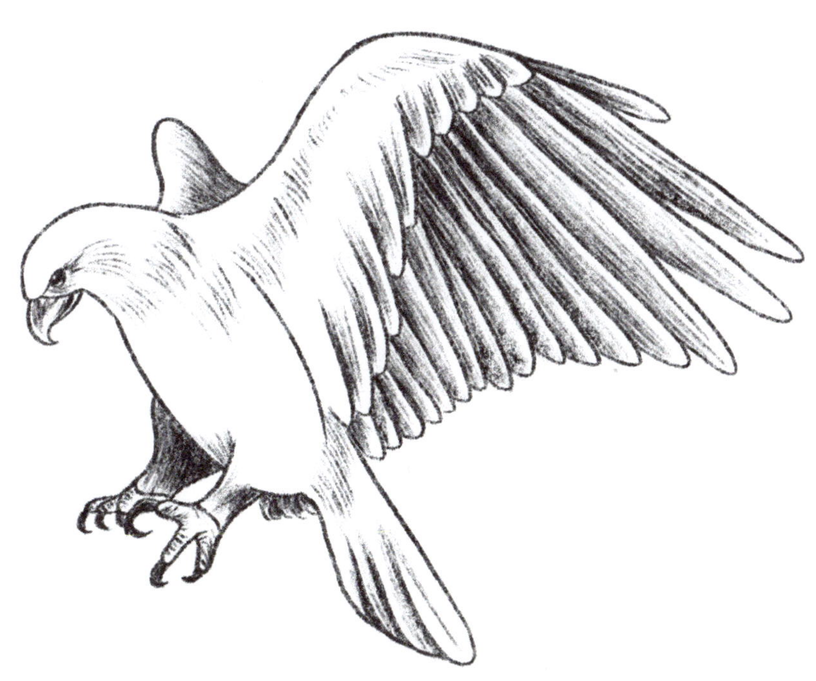

# Sloth

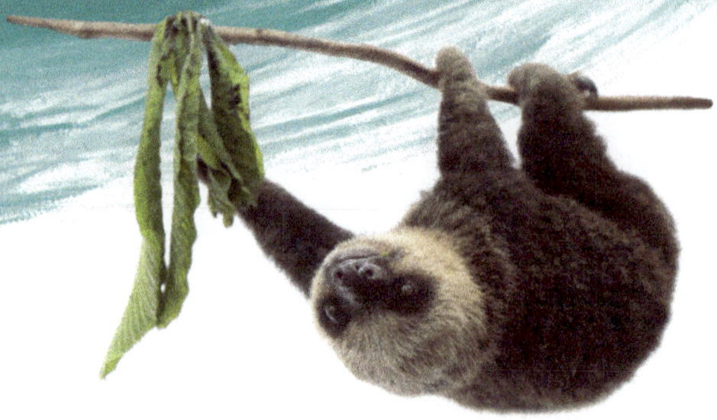

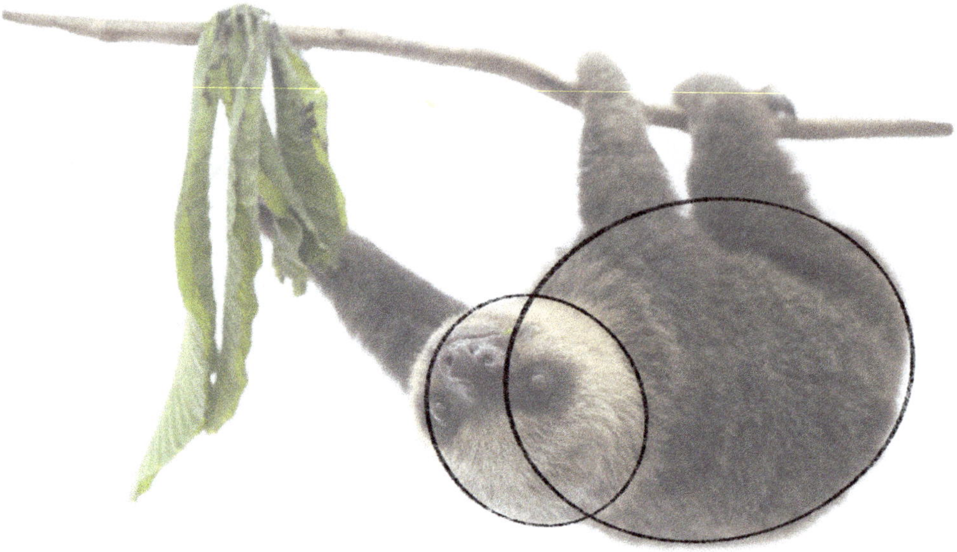

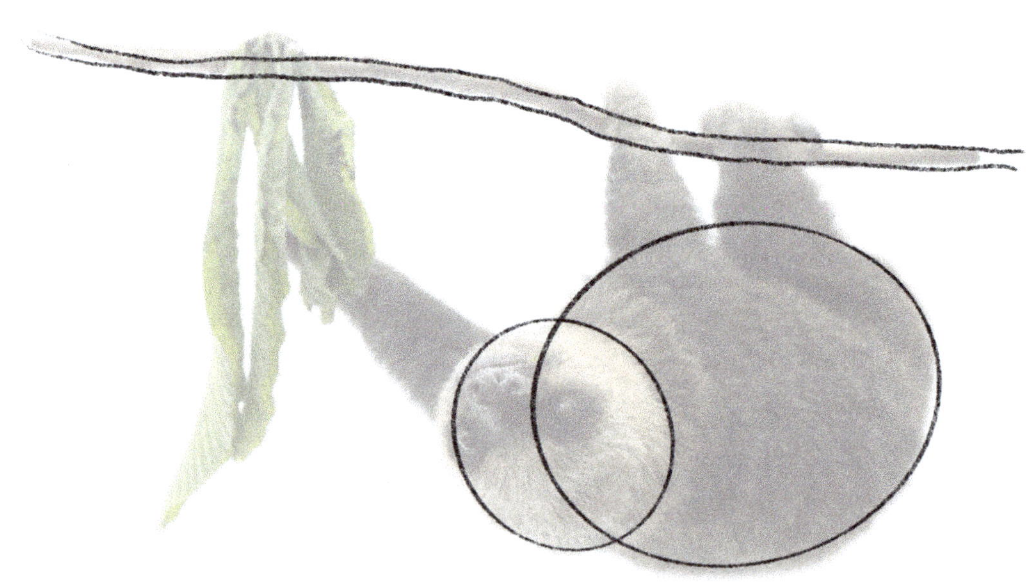

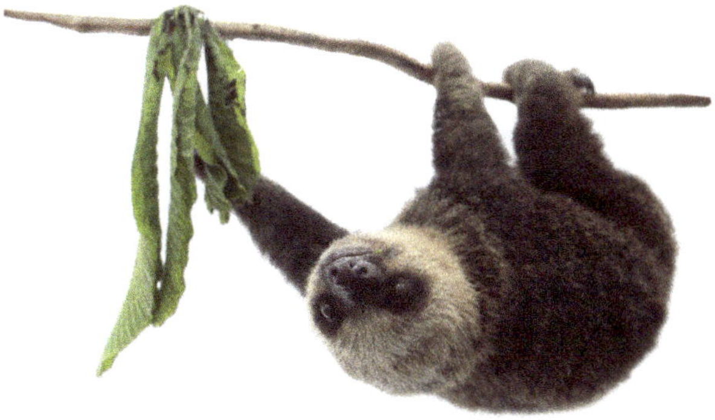

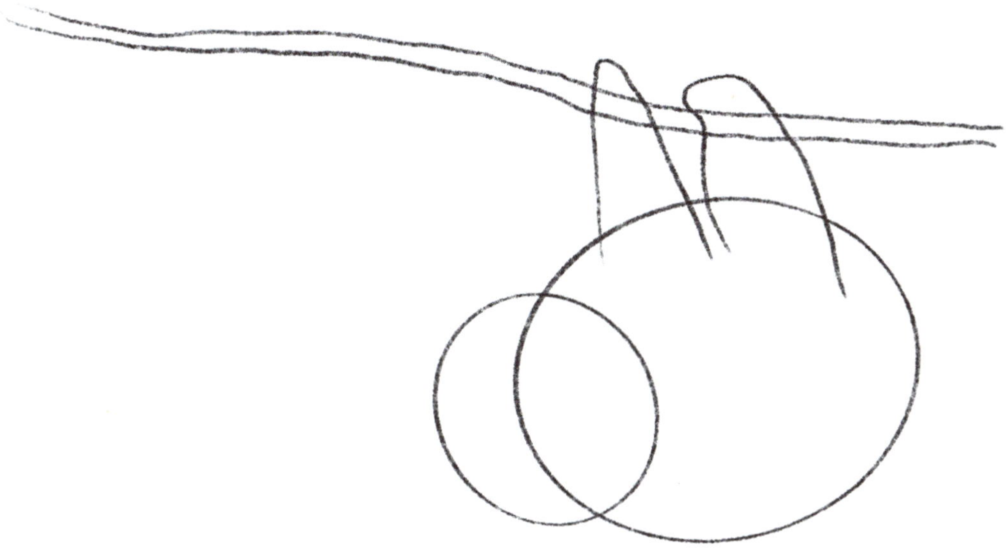

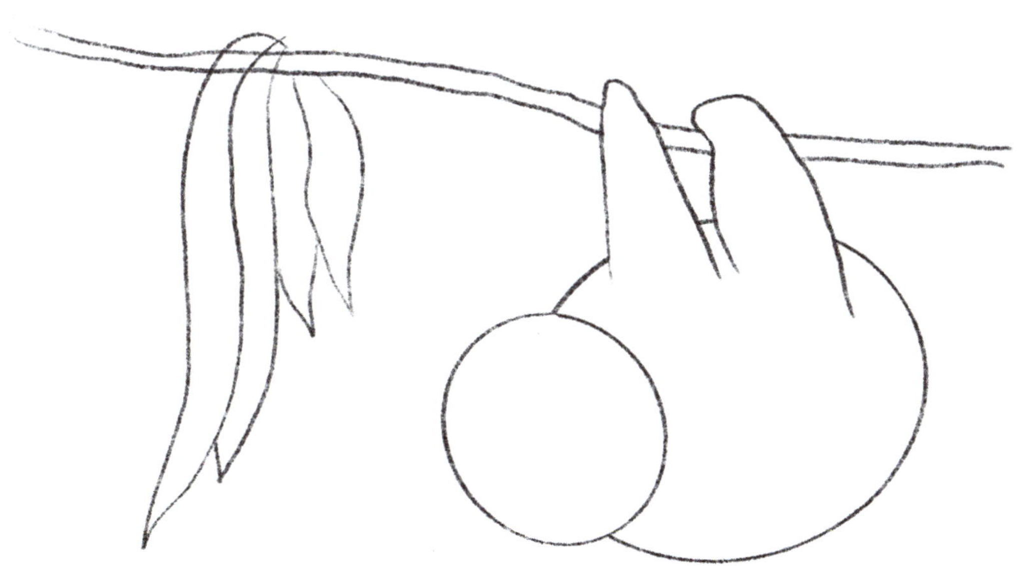

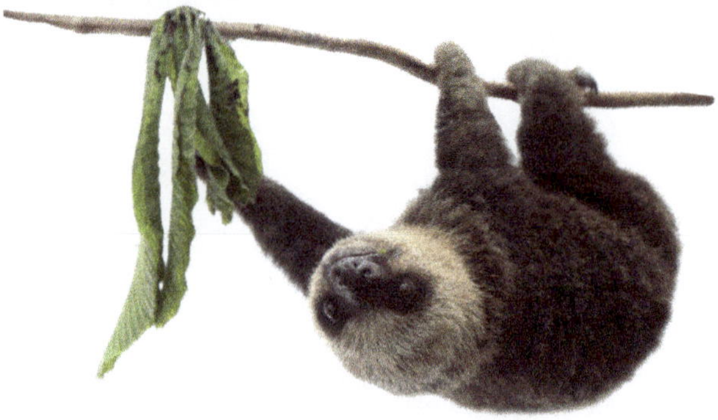

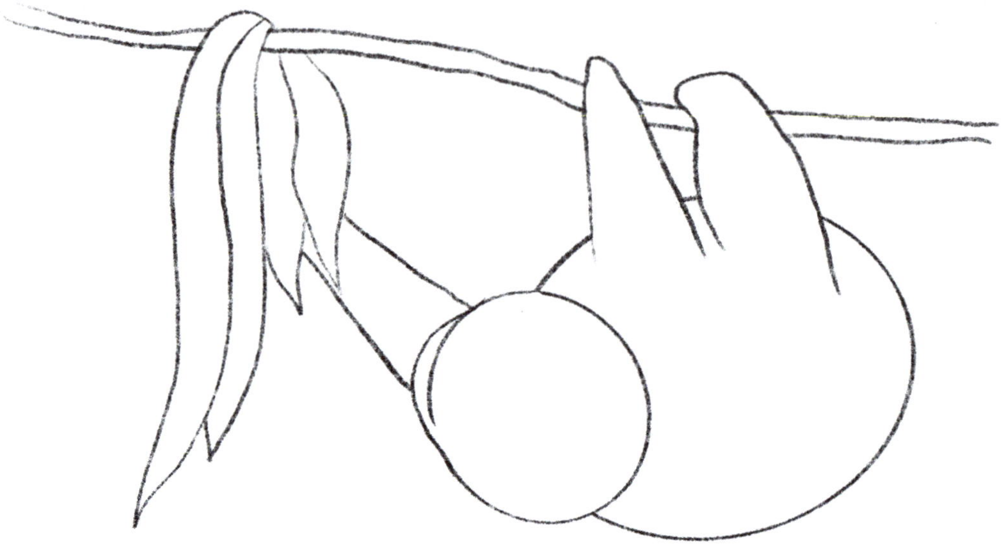

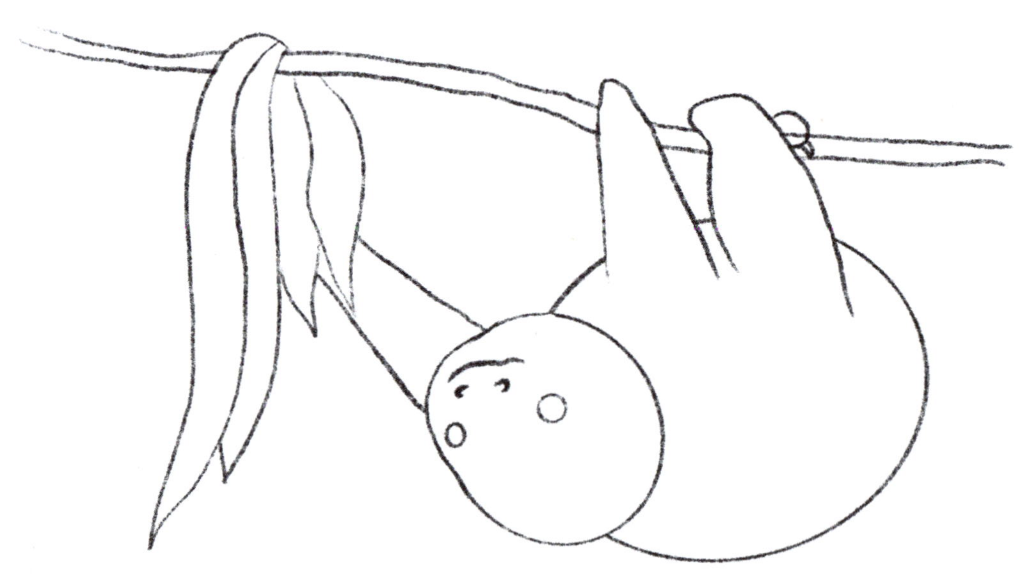

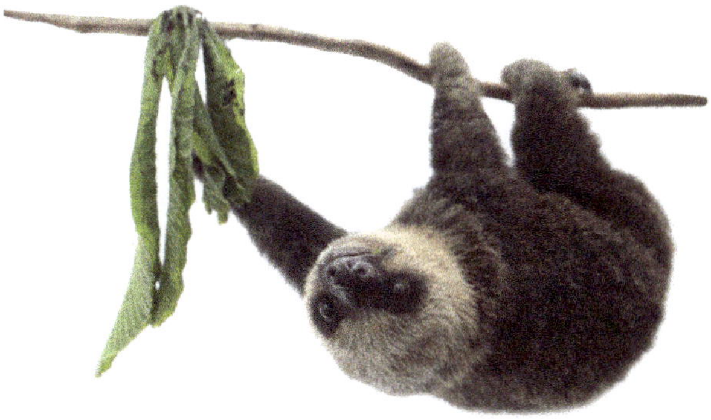

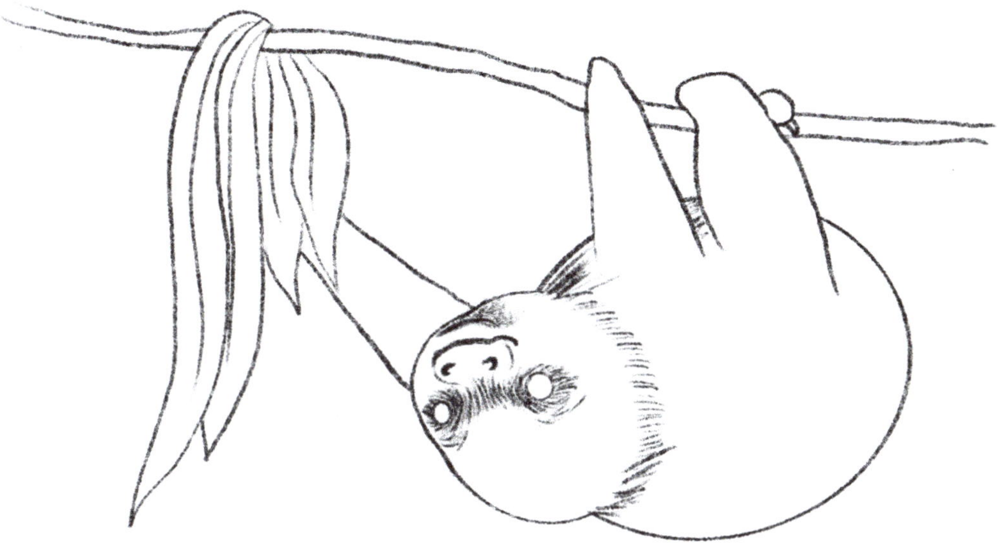

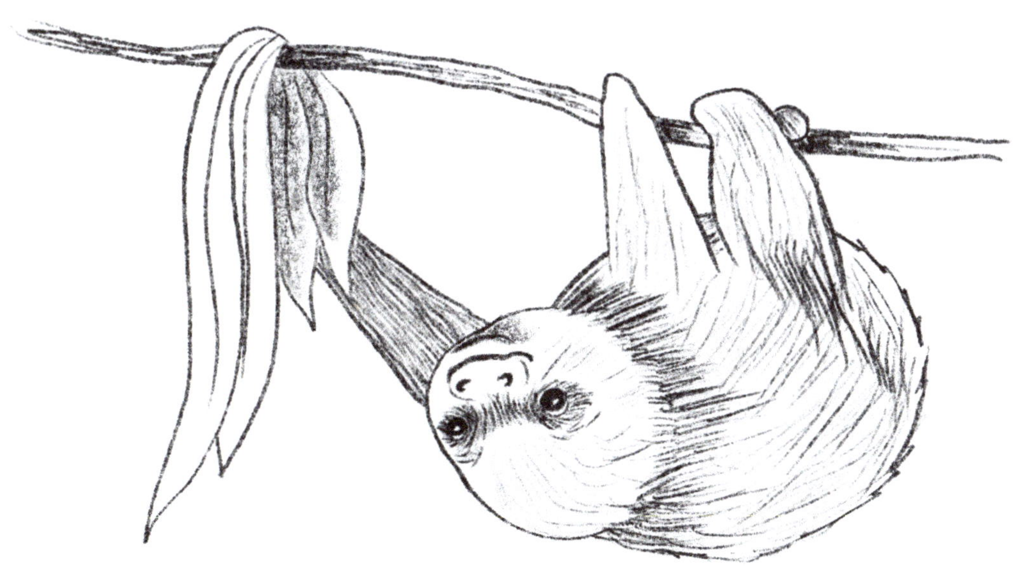

# People - Eyes

Eyes can be tricky to draw, but once you master them the rest of the face will be easy.

Some general rules;
  1. eyes are in the middle of the face (the pupils on the midline)
  2. eyes are one eye width apart from each other
  3. looking straight on, each eye is one eye width from the edge of the face, so
4. the middle of a face is five eye widths wide.

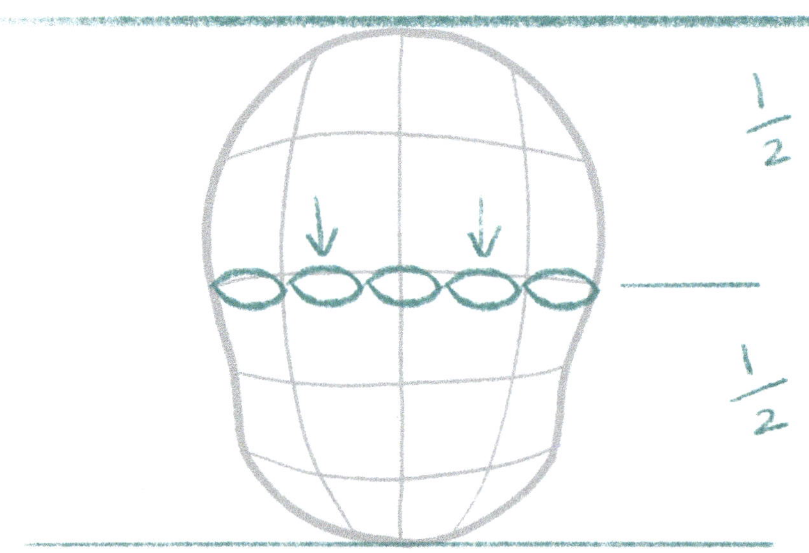

Eyes come in different shapes and colors. They are complex, but we don't be intimidated by them. With a little practice, anyone can learn to draw realistic eyes.

Let's begin. Remember,  between the two eyes is an equal
eye space between them.

Within the two outer circles we now draw the corners of the
eyes and eyelids. Both the inner and outer corners of the eyes
should always be slightly rounded, as the skin does not run
together. The inner corners of the eyes should be given a small
curved shape.

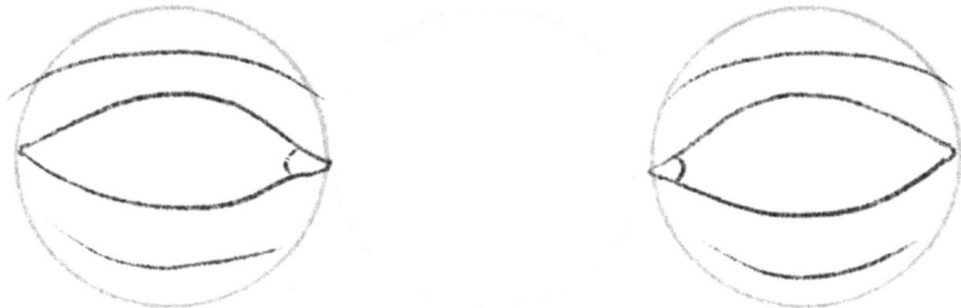

The drawing won't look at us if we just centre her pupil, as the
closer an object is that we are looking at, the more we squint.
The further away the object is, the more the pupils move to
the centre. So how do you draw eyes so that they look at
you? You should make them squint just slightly. Also, the edge
of the iris should touch the lower eyelid and be slightly
covered by the upper eyelid.

Don't forget to mark light reflections (catch lights) in the eyes
when you are drawing in the pupils.

Now for the details! I will demonstrate on one eye. Since the eyeball is round, we draw rounded strokes for the fine shadows in both corners of the eye, running gently from the outside to the inside. In the outer corners of the eye we can get a little darker. Along the lower edge we can set a fine accent in the form of white lines.

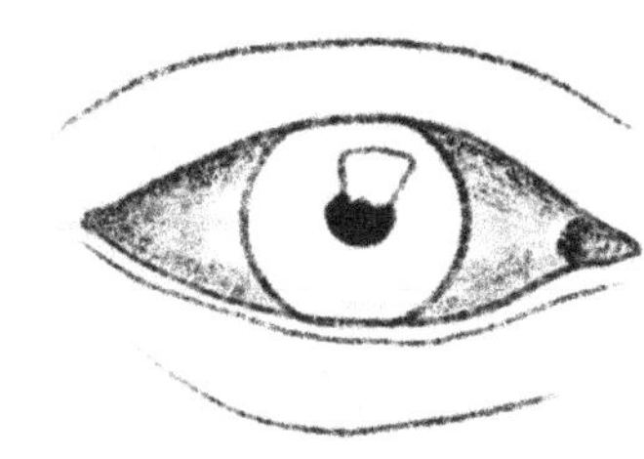

Next, shade the inner edge of the lower eyelid, it should blend into the rest of the eyelid by soft shading. Just like the eyeball, the eyelids are also slightly rounded, as they wrap around it. Therefore, we should draw the shadows more strongly on both ends.

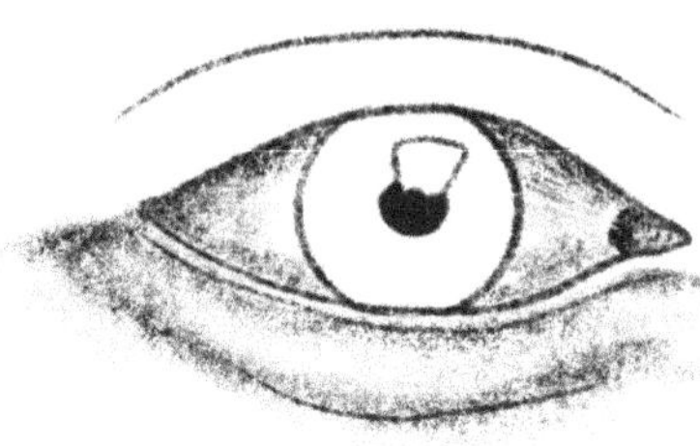

For the upper eyelid we draw dark shadows along the crease of the eyelid. In the outer area I would always draw laugh lines. Depending on the age of the person we draw, we can draw them fine or pronounced, they contribute to making the eye look more realistic. In the inner area, near the nose, we set shadows that indicate the transition to the bridge of the nose.

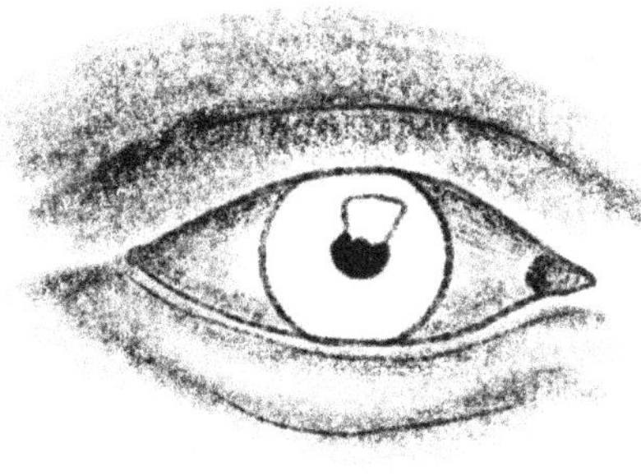

The iris gives life to the drawing. The upper eyelid usually throws a shadow on the iris. We blend this shadow a little more towards the sides. The iris does not lie flat on the eyeball, but is surrounded by the cornea. You have to think of it as another round shape that protrudes slightly from the eyeball.

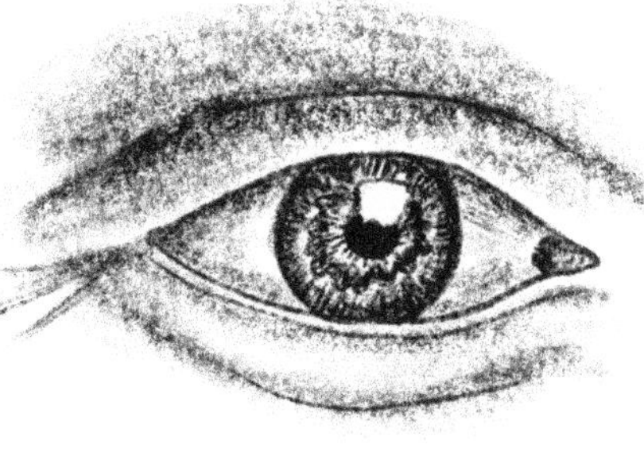

Finally we draw the lashes and their shadows.

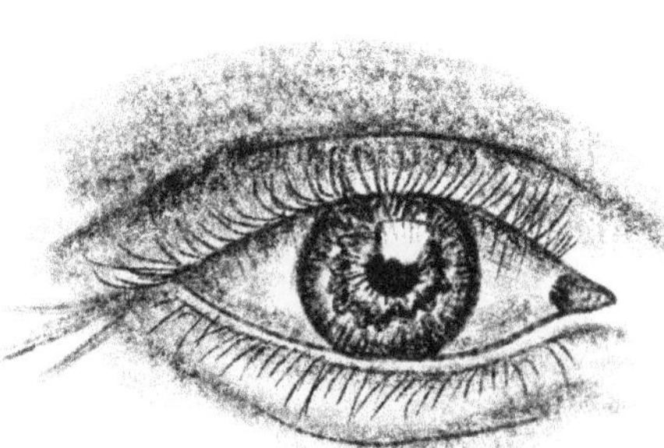

Practise your eye details.

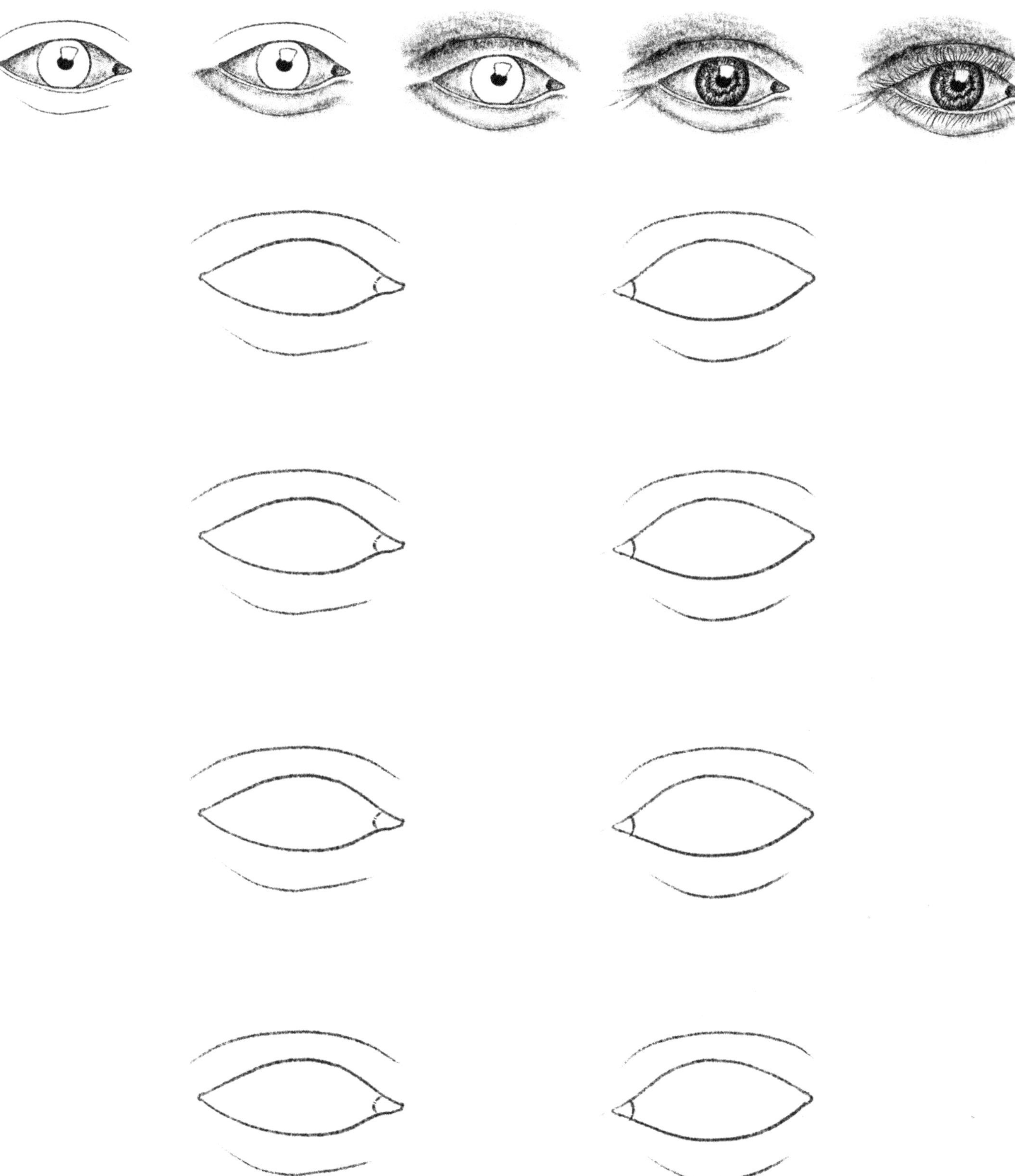

# People - Faces

When starting a face, think of the basic shape as a sphere, not a circle. A sphere is three dimensional, a circle is only two. Then, picture a line half way around this sphere.

The line around the middle of the sphere represents the eye line. The chin will fall at the bottom of the oval. The bottom of the nose is halfway in between the eye and the chin. The mouth is halfway between the nose line and the chin.

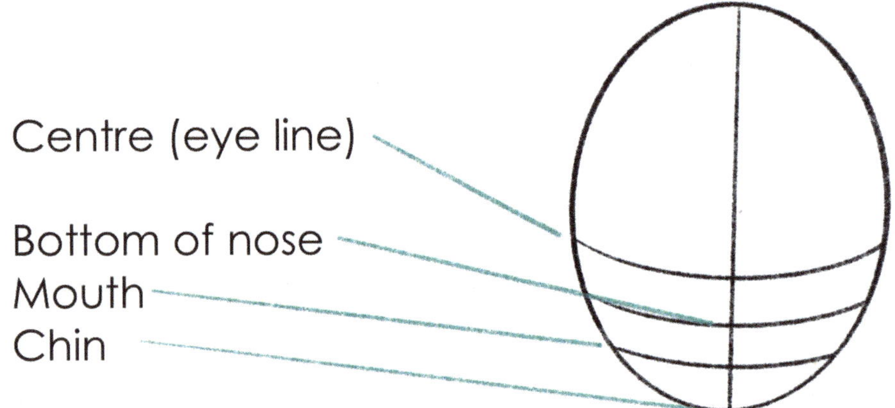


You can use these guidelines when sketching out, just remember to use light strokes so you can erase them later. As you progress, add a curved line for the neck. The neck always has a curve.

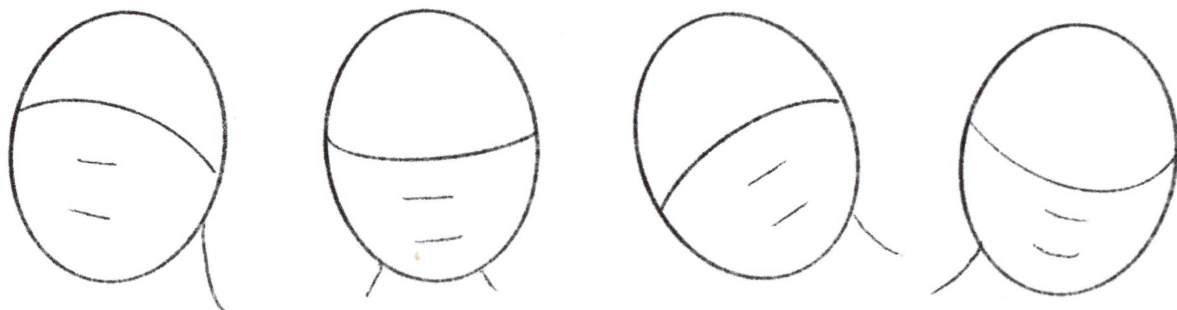

# Practise your faces

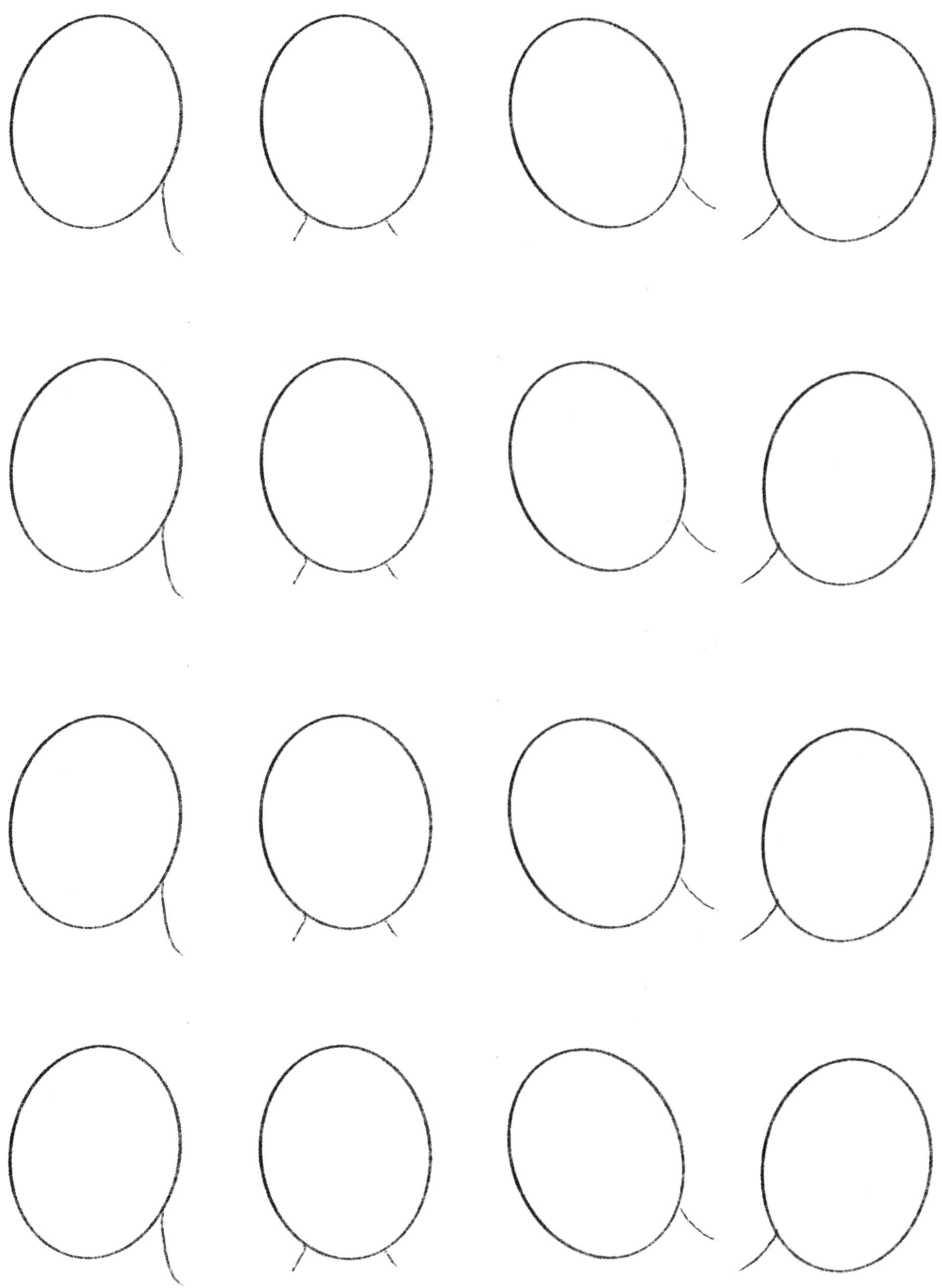

# Bodies

When it comes to learning how to draw bodies, start simple to ensure success. And what is simpler than drawing armatures? They are almost like glorified stick figures! When you stop worrying about getting the proportions of the torso and legs just right, you can focus more on the basic idea of the body — where things go, how they work together, how they move. In starting this way, you can take your time, slowly working to then refine your skills.

Torso - Start by drawing a line to represent the torso. Like the neck, this line follows the general motion of the spine.

Hips are represented by a straight line that is at a 90-degree angle from the base of the spine. This makes it easy to figure out how to draw the hip line. Once you've drawn the torso line, the hip line will be perpendicular to it. Facing forward, the hips are wider than the head. But, as the body turns to the side, this line shortens and could be as small as a single point.

Legs should be about as long as the head, neck and torso combined (assuming the body isn't foreshortened), bending at the middle for the knee. Add a simple line to indicate the direction of the feet and to anchor your figure on the ground.

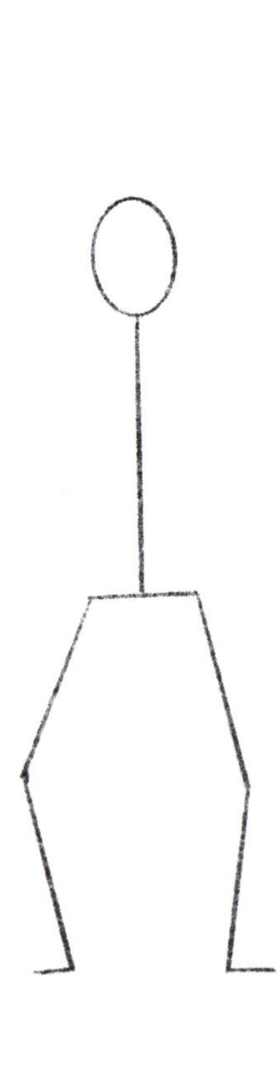

Shoulders - Each shoulder moves independently, so they aren't represented by a straight line like the hips are. When the shoulders are shrugged or rotated forward, the shoulder line should reflect this with a curved line. The shoulder line connects to the torso at a right angle, similar to the hips, but it curves up, down, forward or back as it moves away from the body, according to the pose.

Add the arms and hand in a similar fashion to the legs and feet, only a little shorter.

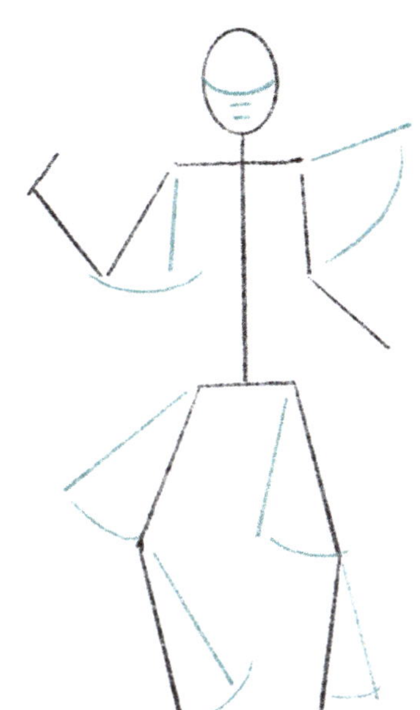

## Proportions

Once you're comfortable posing an armature, you'll need to start paying attention to getting the proportion correct. Every person is a little bit different. Some people have long legs and a short torso. Other people might have long arms or wide shoulders or a squat head, so you have a lot of leeway in drawing these things.

That said, the classical proportion of an adult is roughly eight heads tall. The top of the head to the pubic area is four heads high, and the legs are about four heads tall.

The classic proportion of a child is 4-5 head lengths.

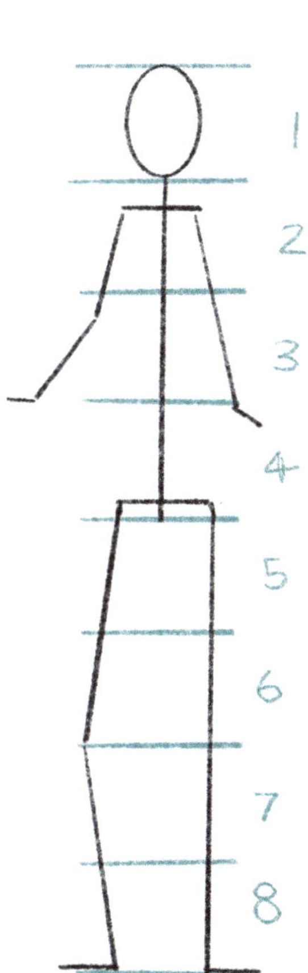

# Adult Male

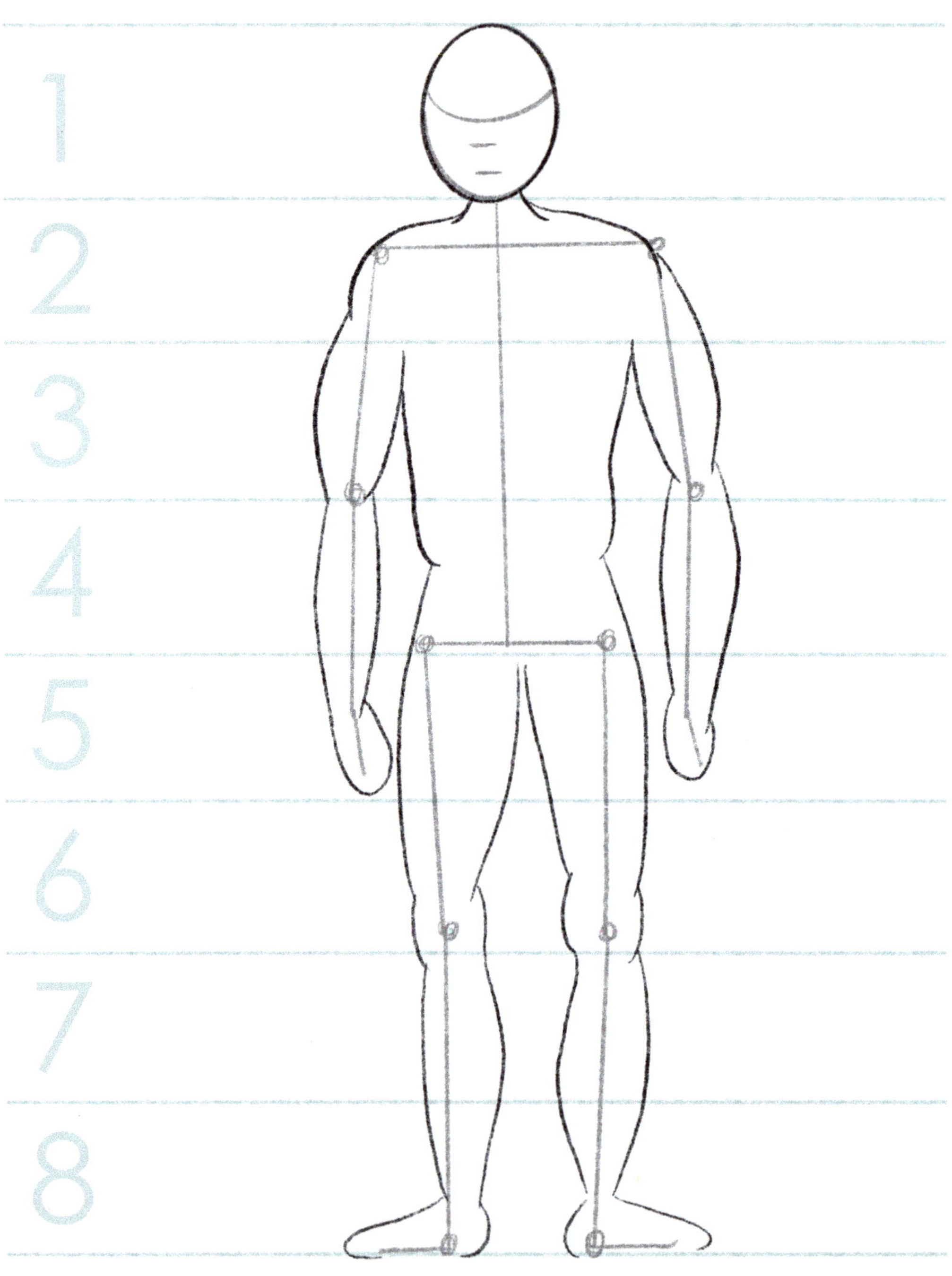

# Adult Female

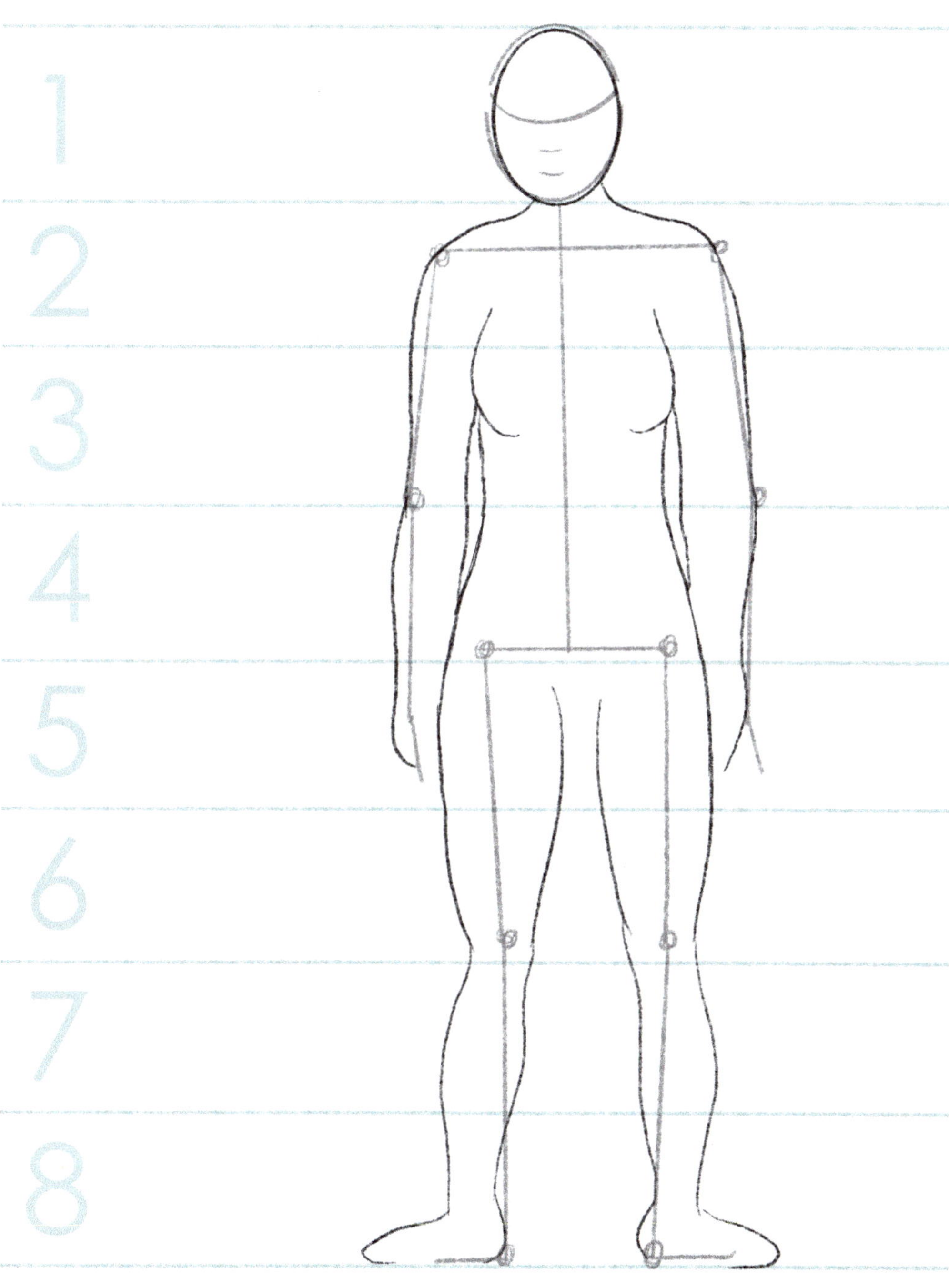

# Children

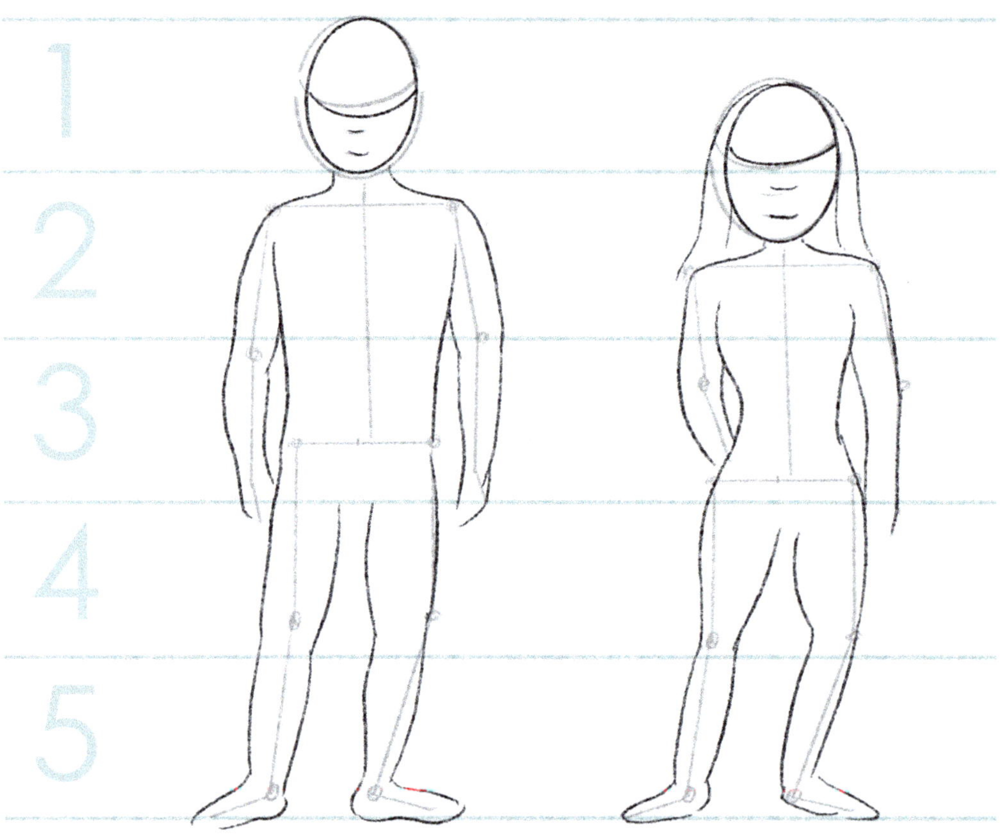

Practise your body proportions.

# Car

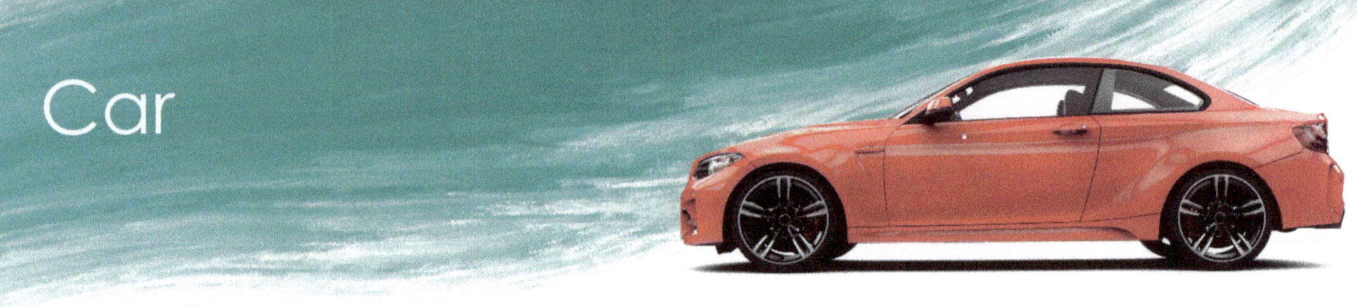

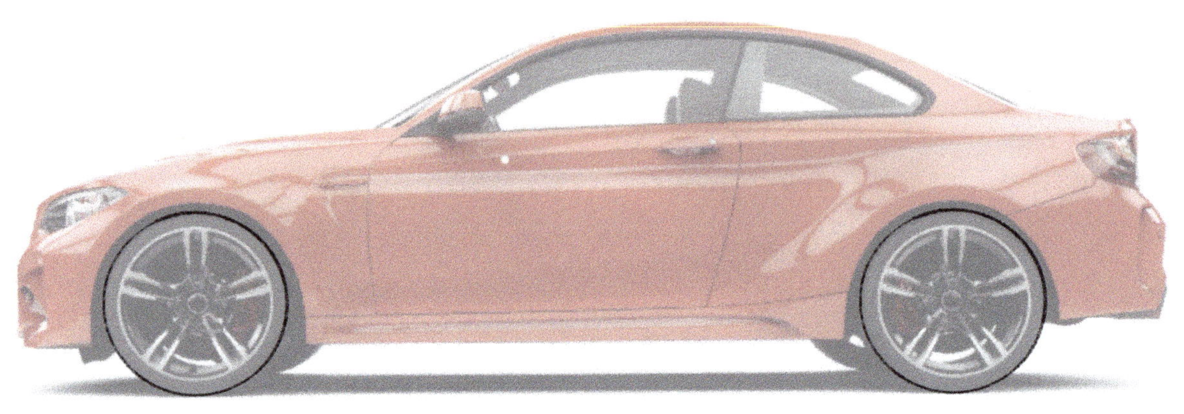

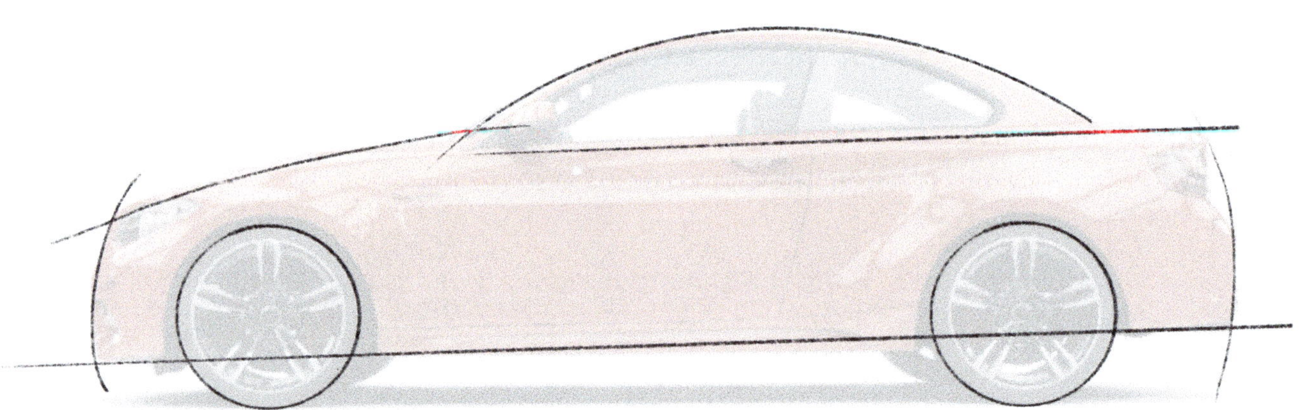

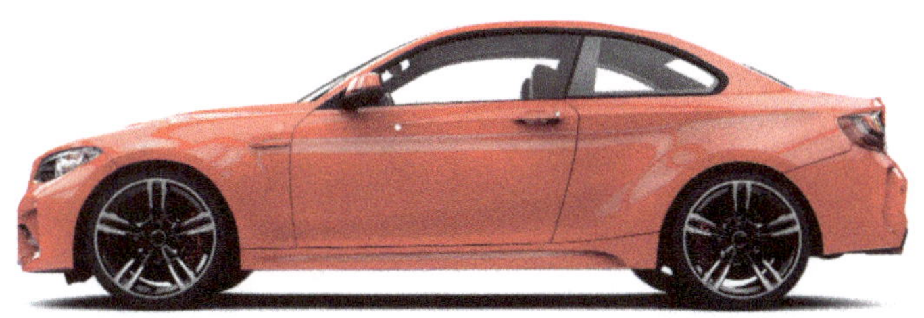

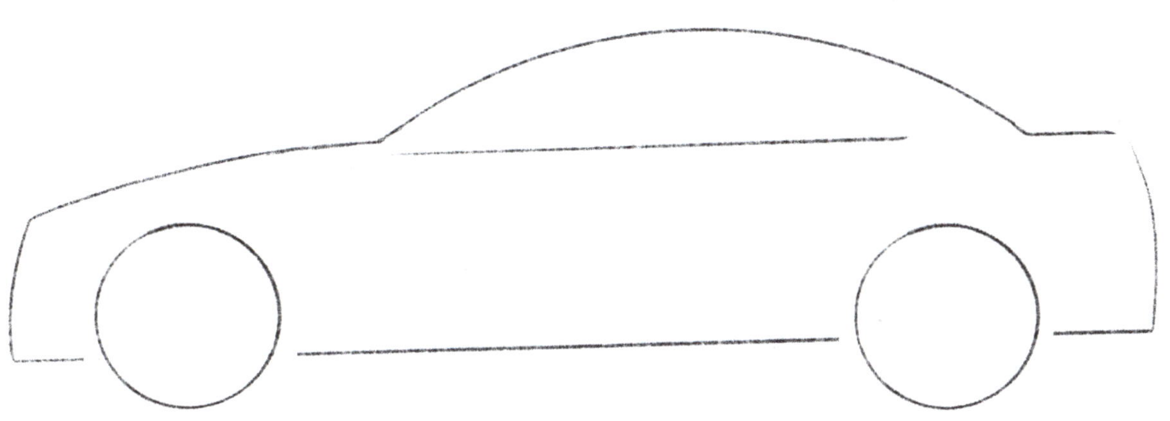

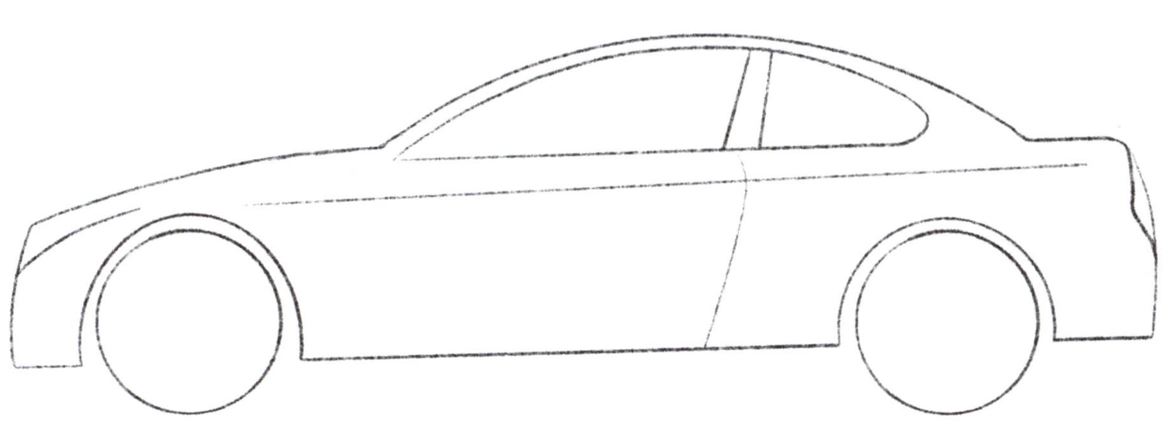

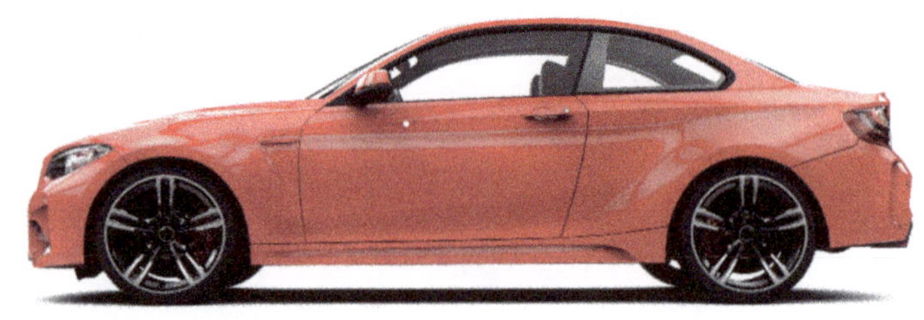

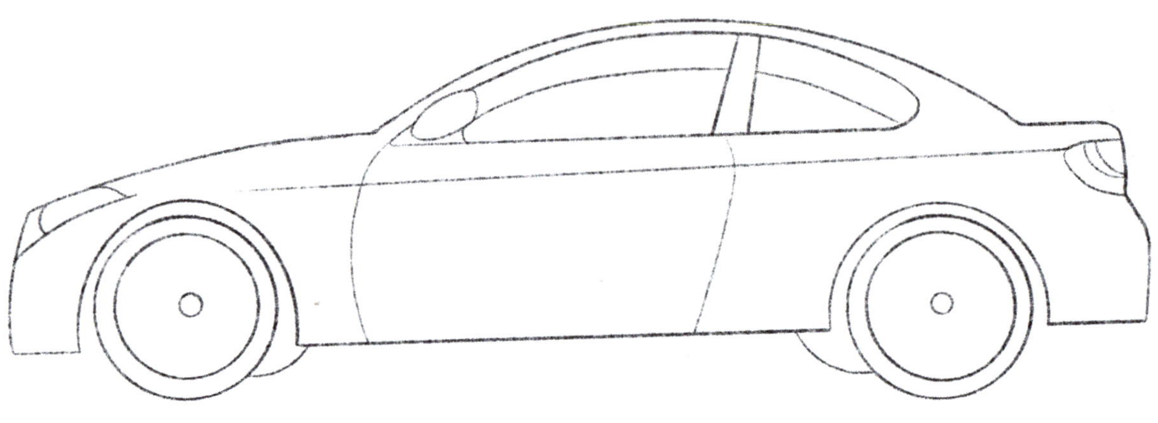

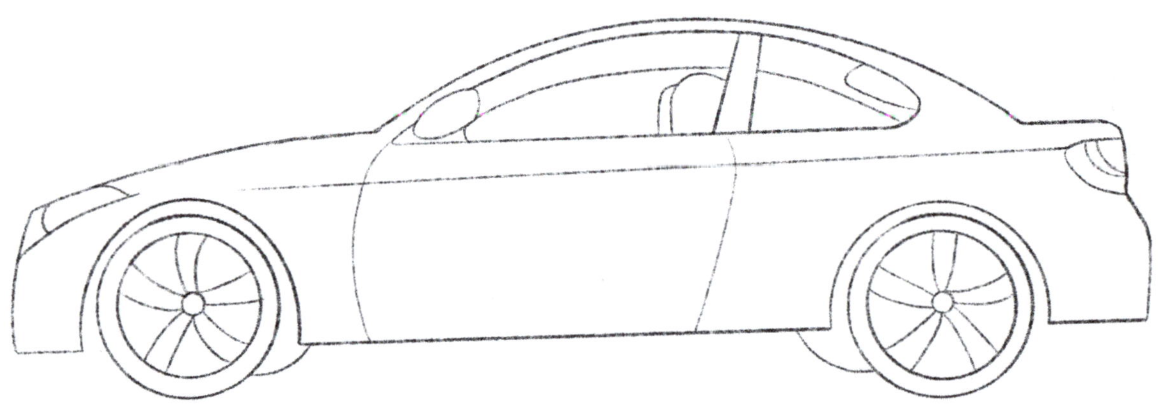

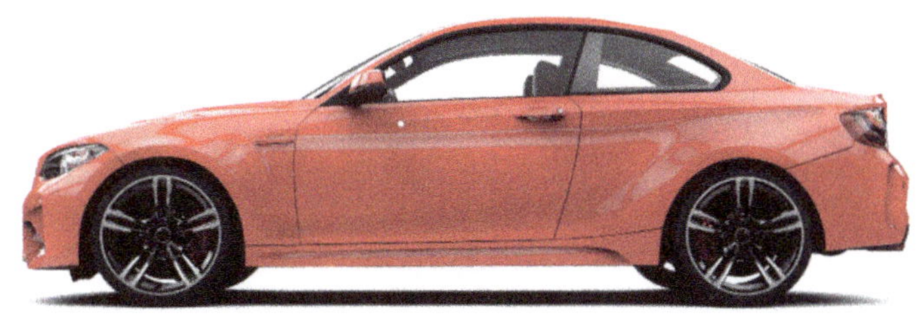

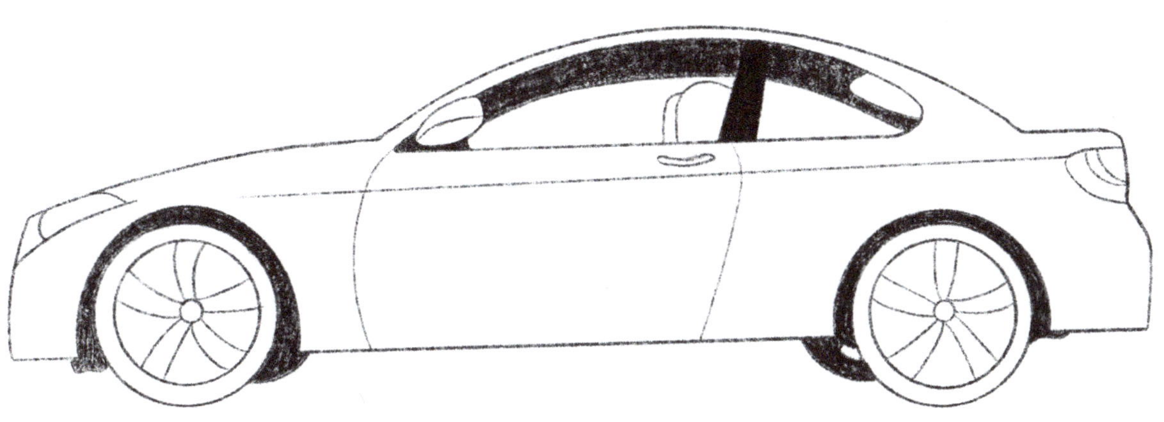

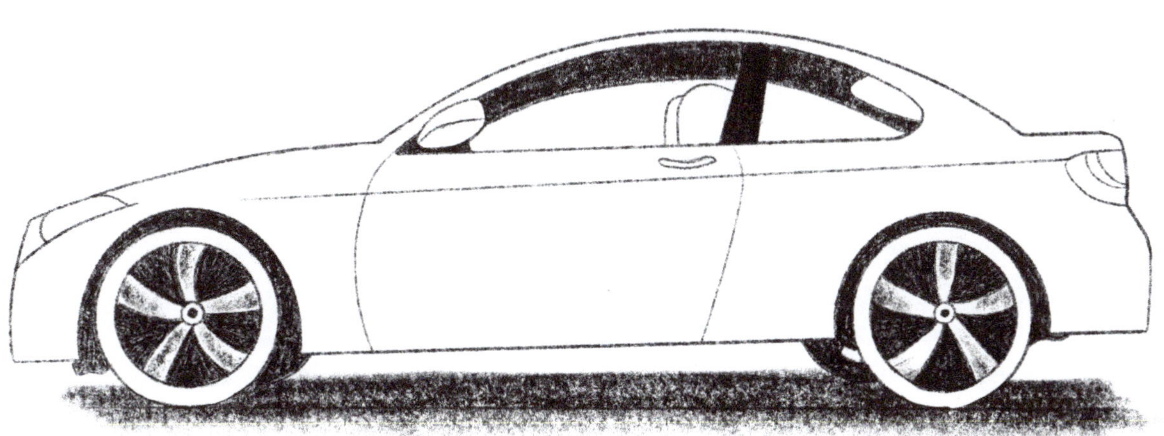

# Dirt Bike

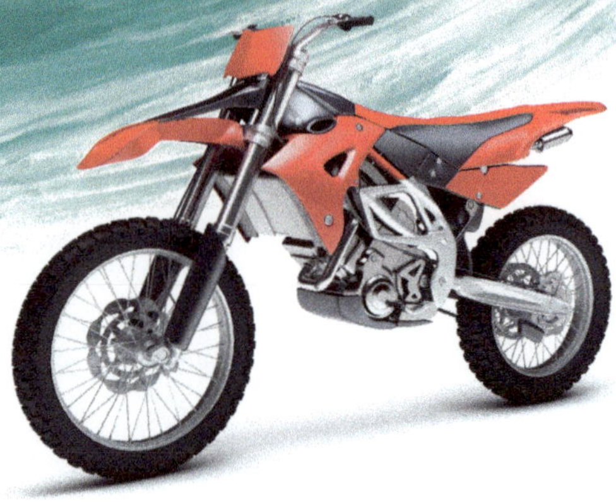

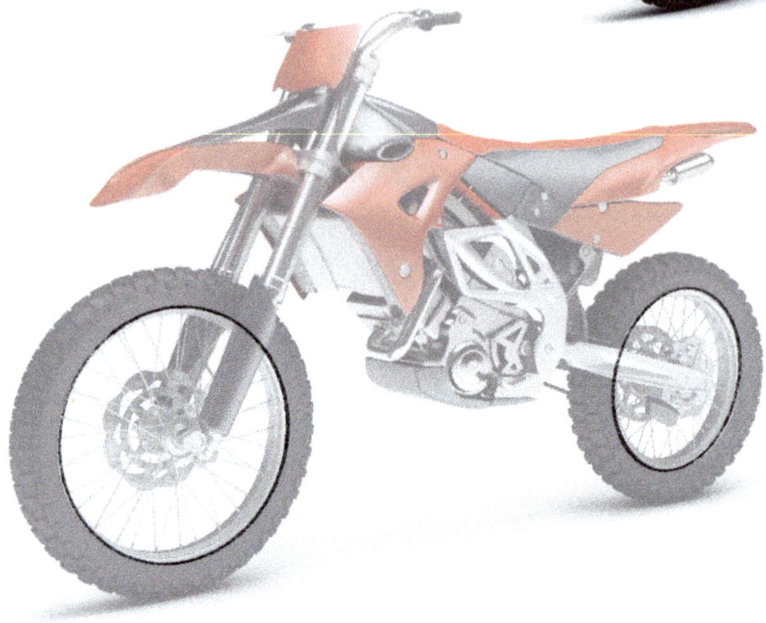

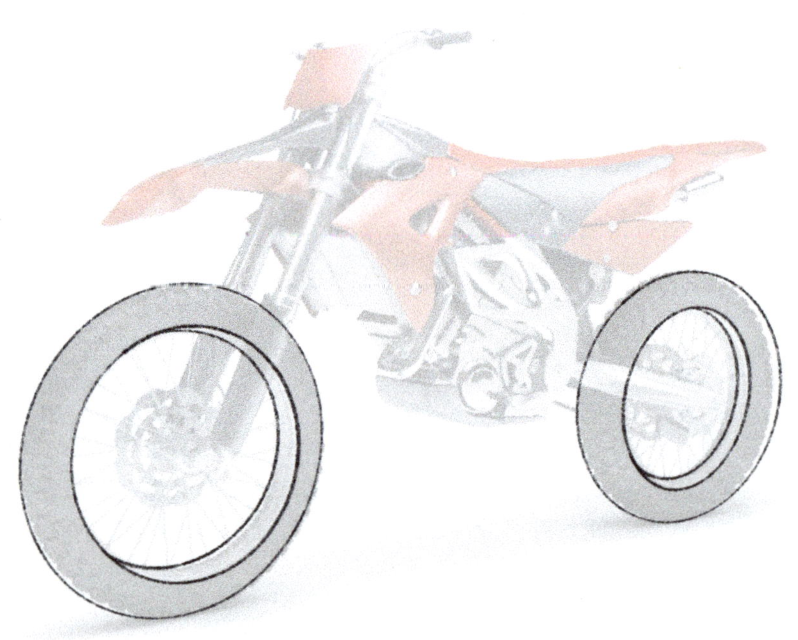

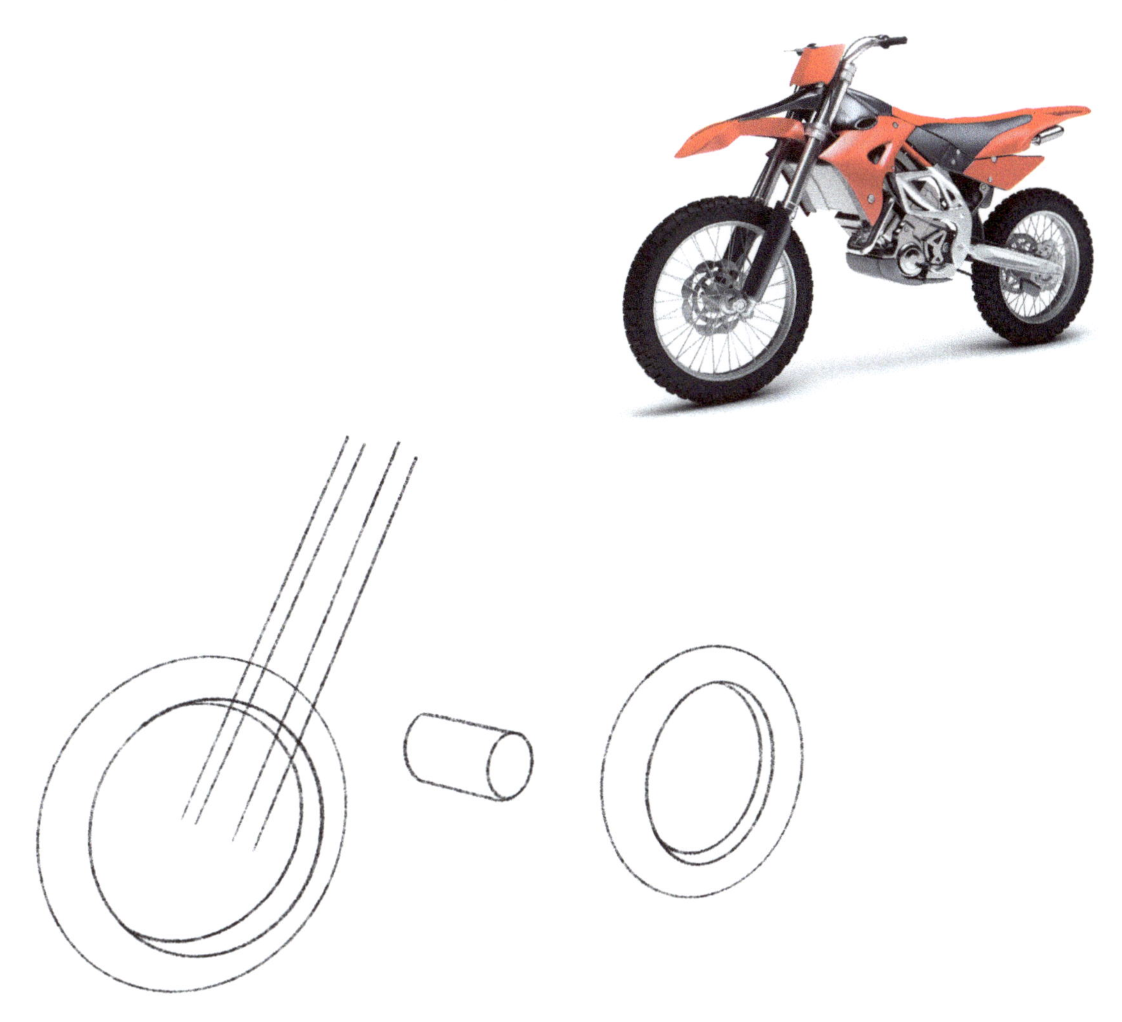

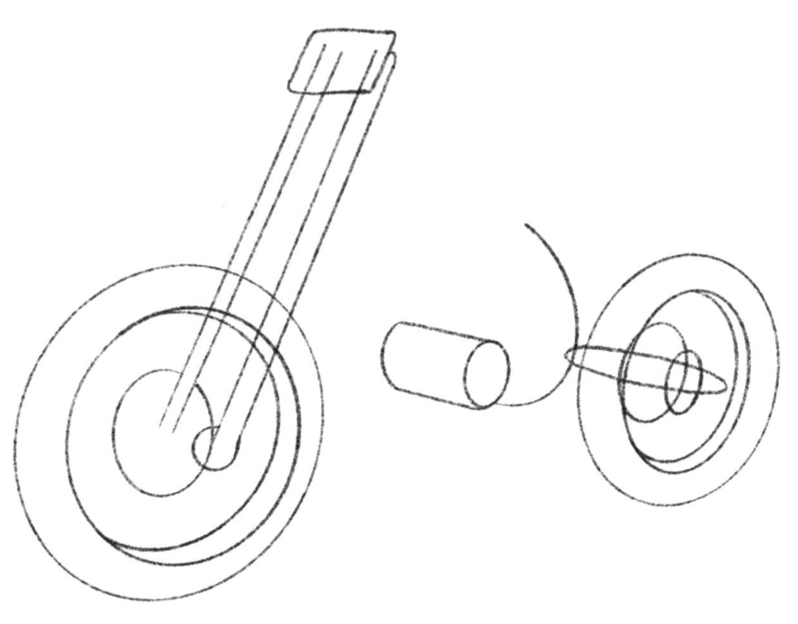

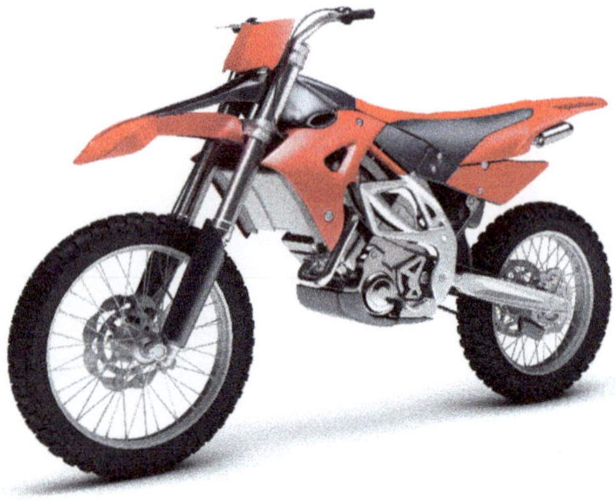

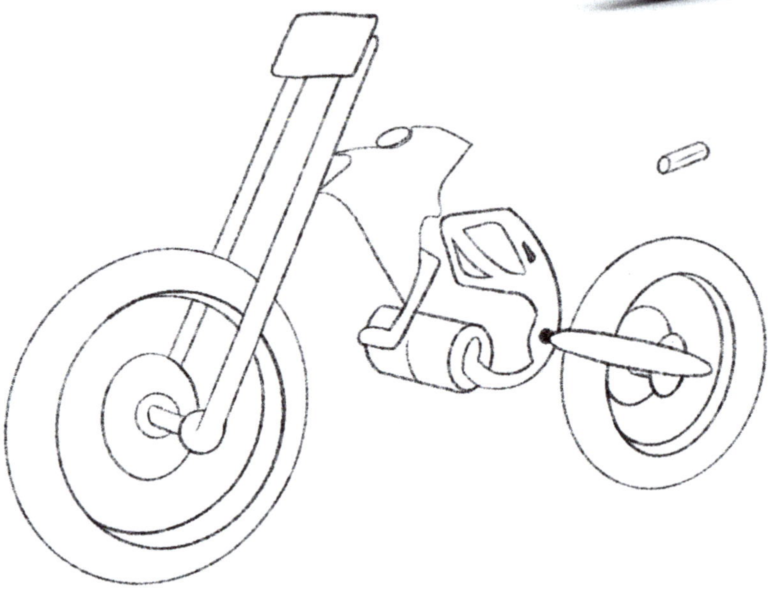

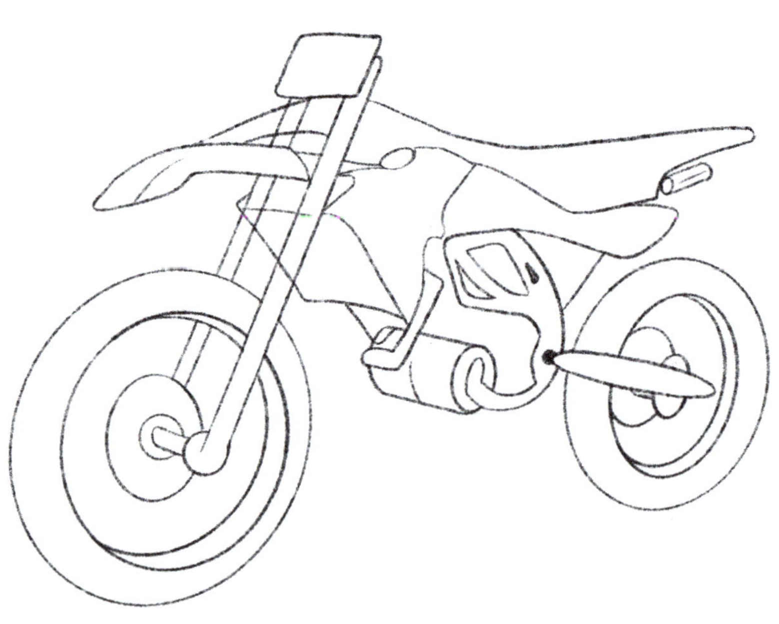

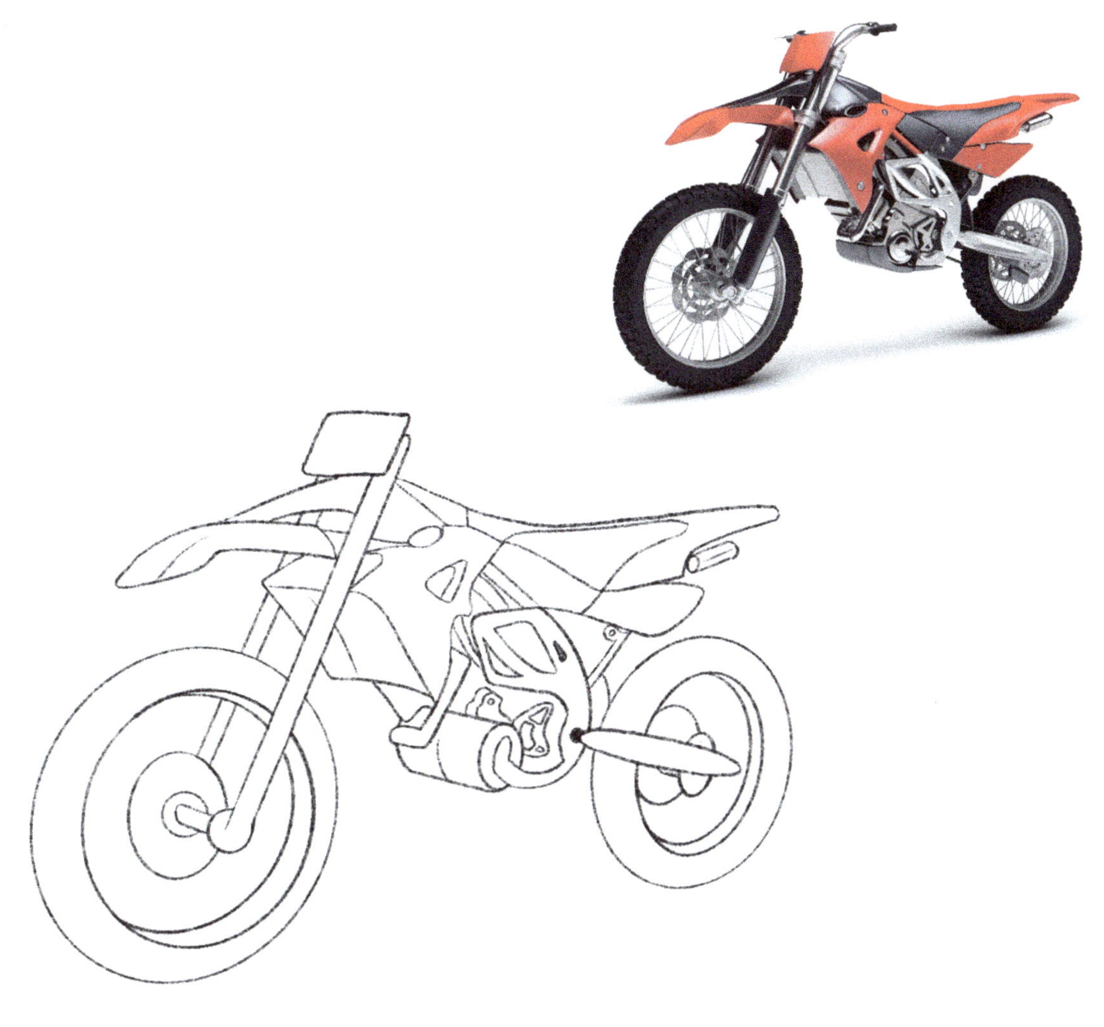

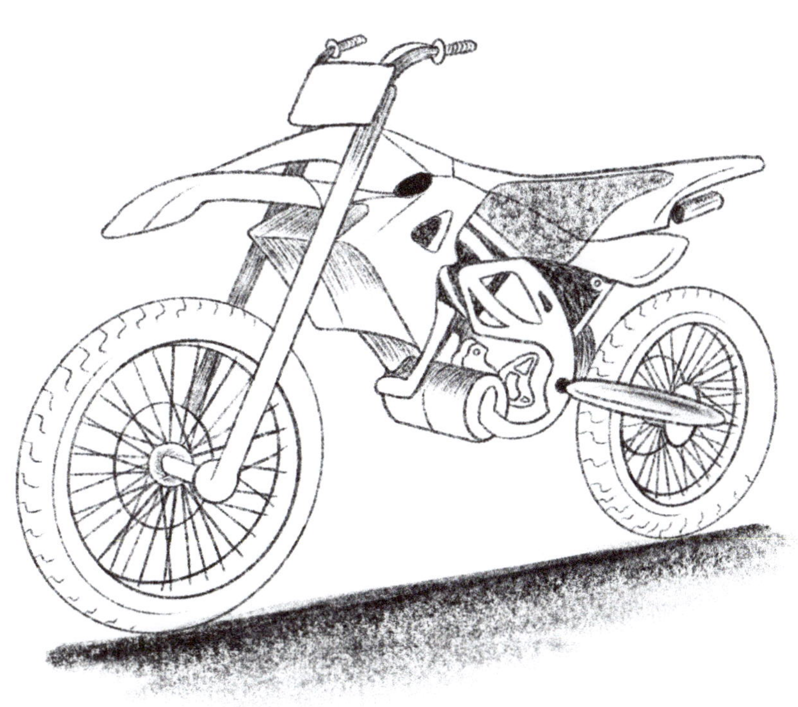

# Tractor

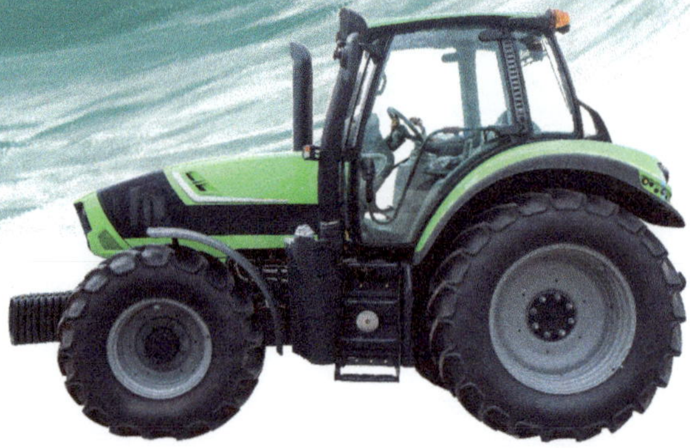

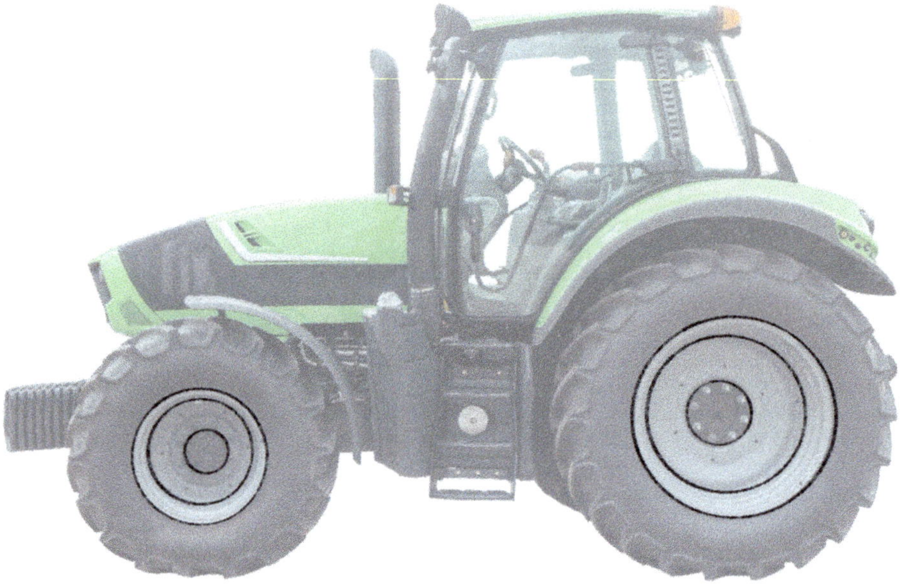

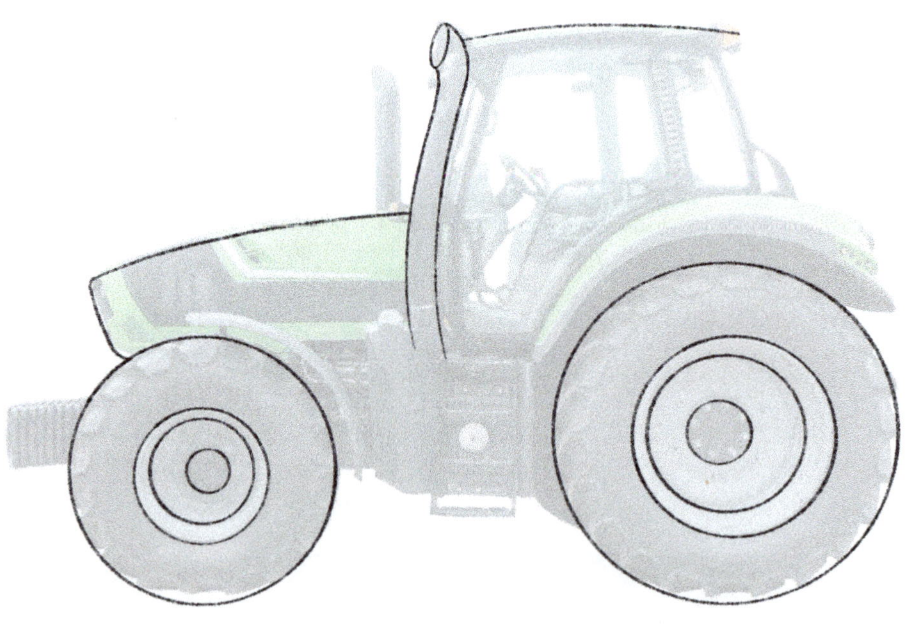

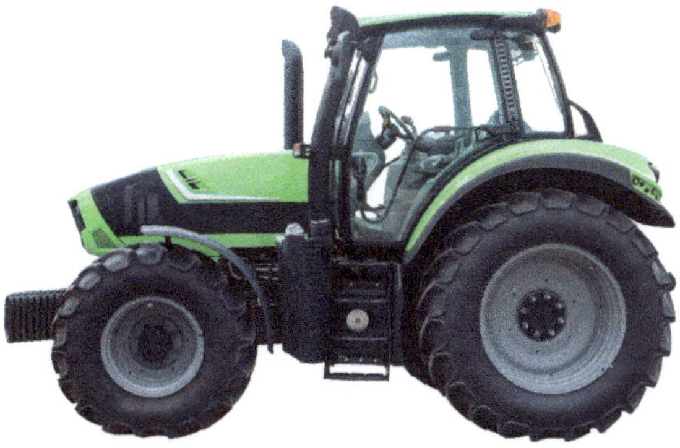

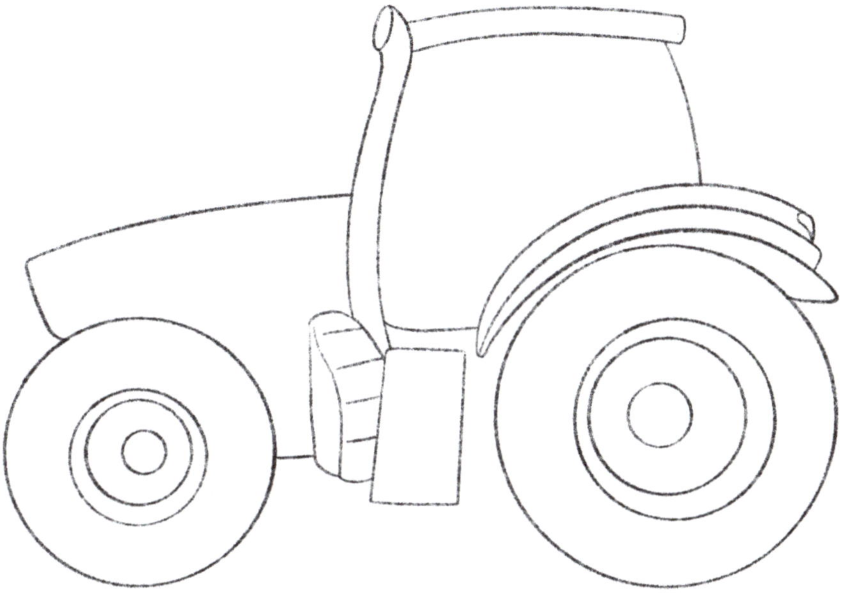

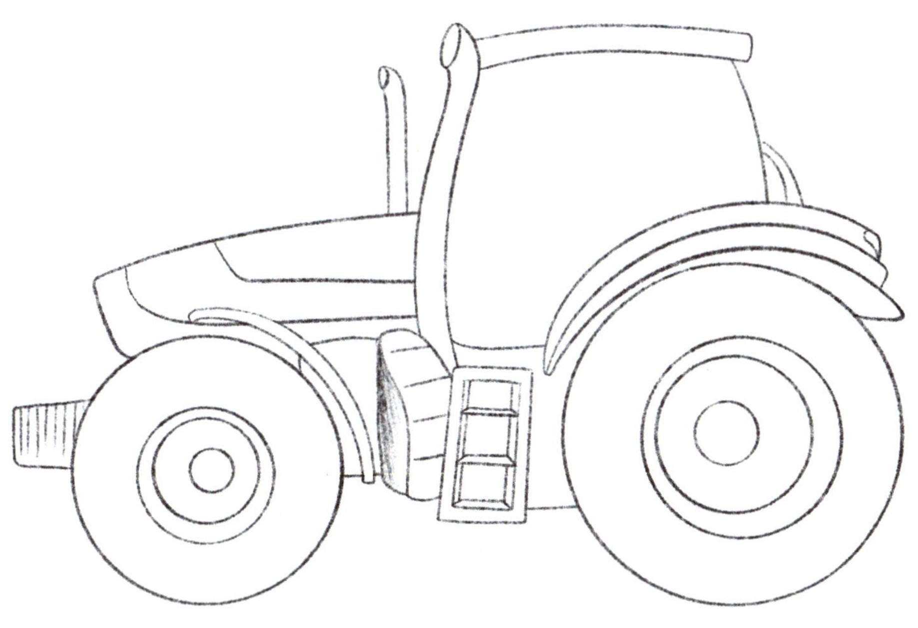

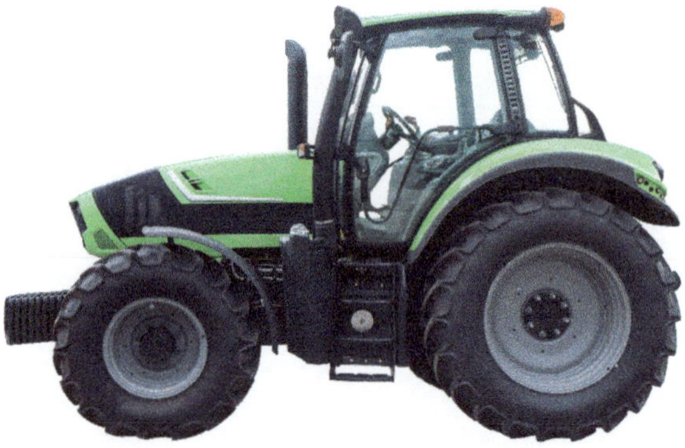

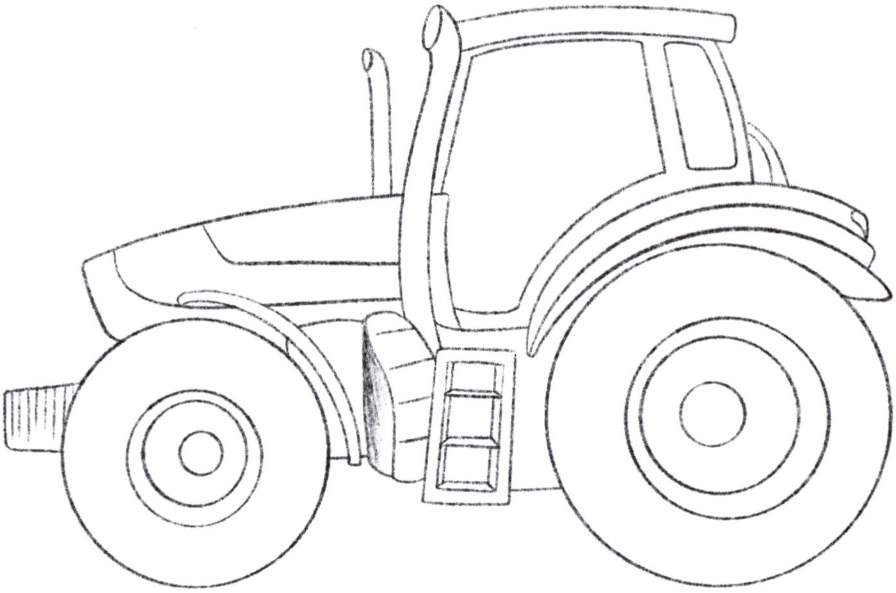

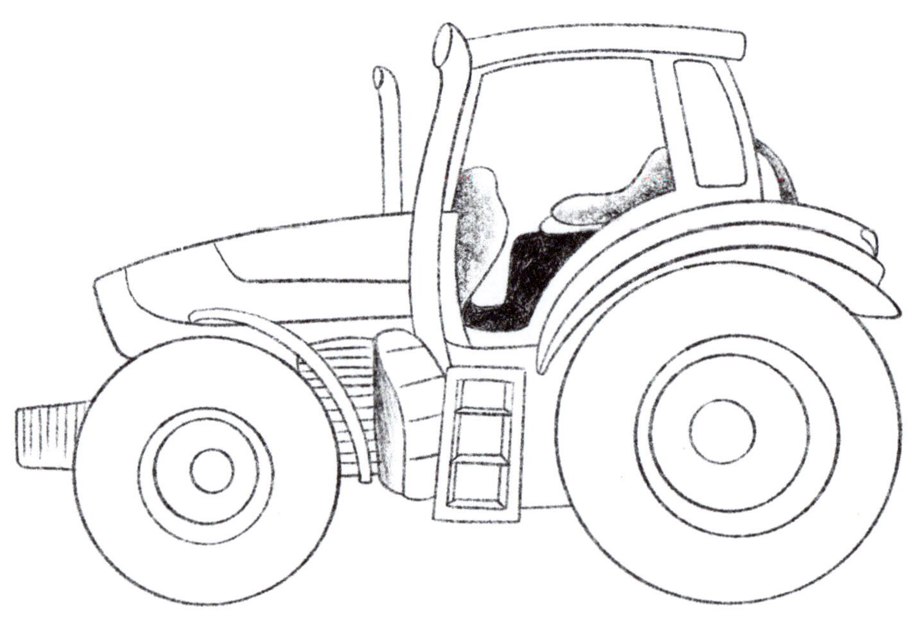

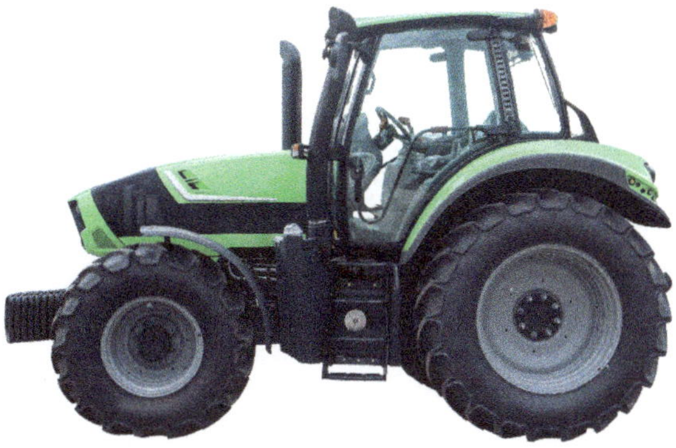

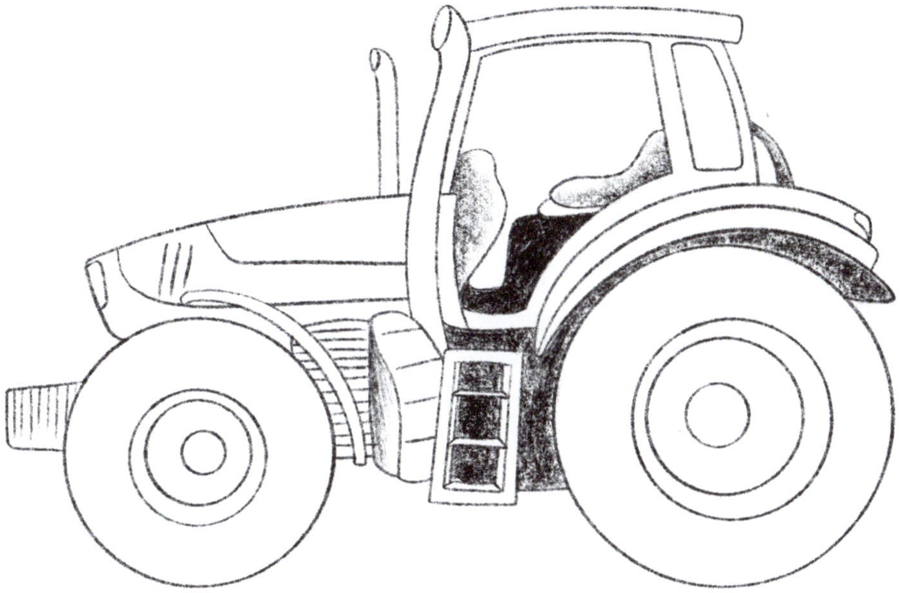

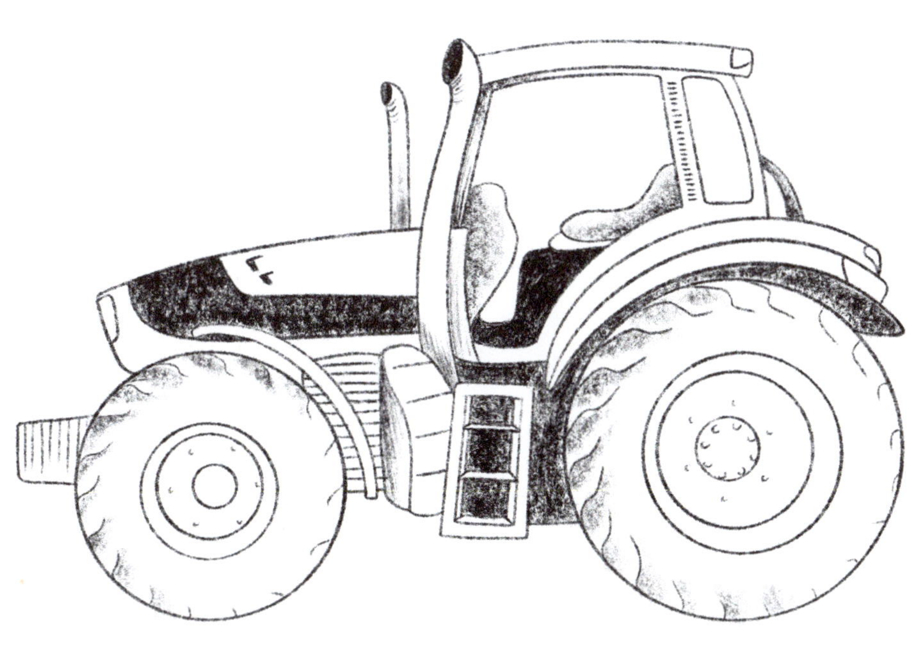

# Monster Truck

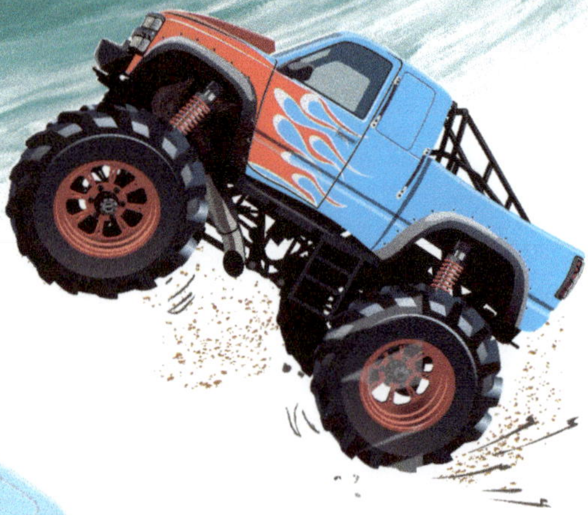

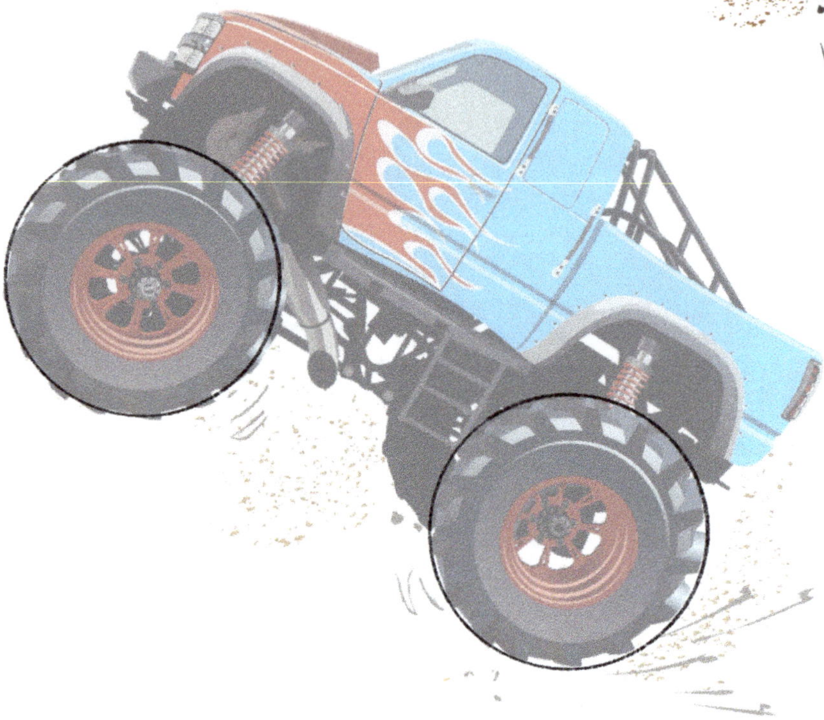

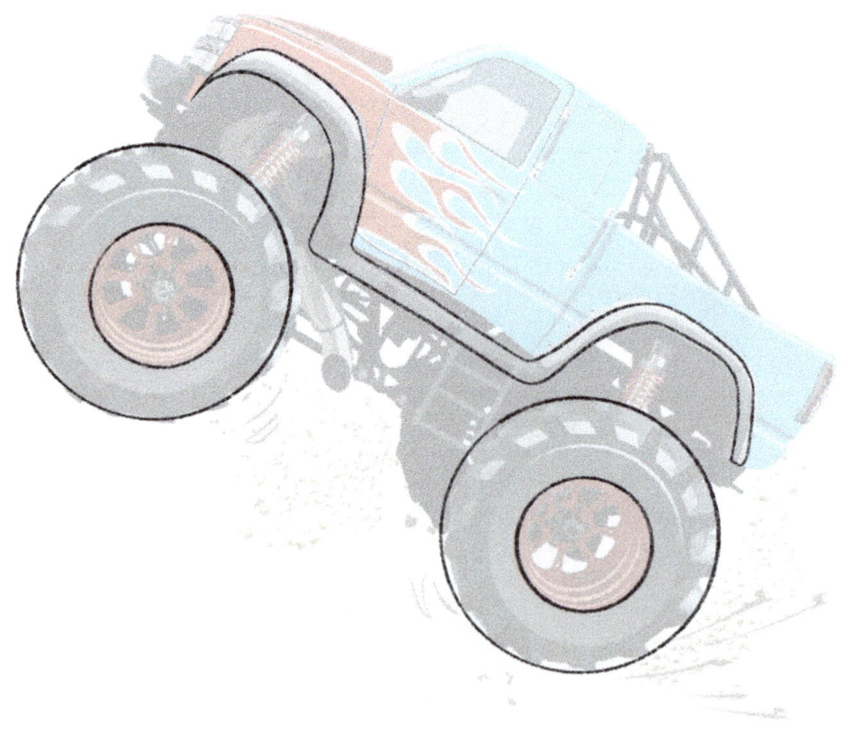

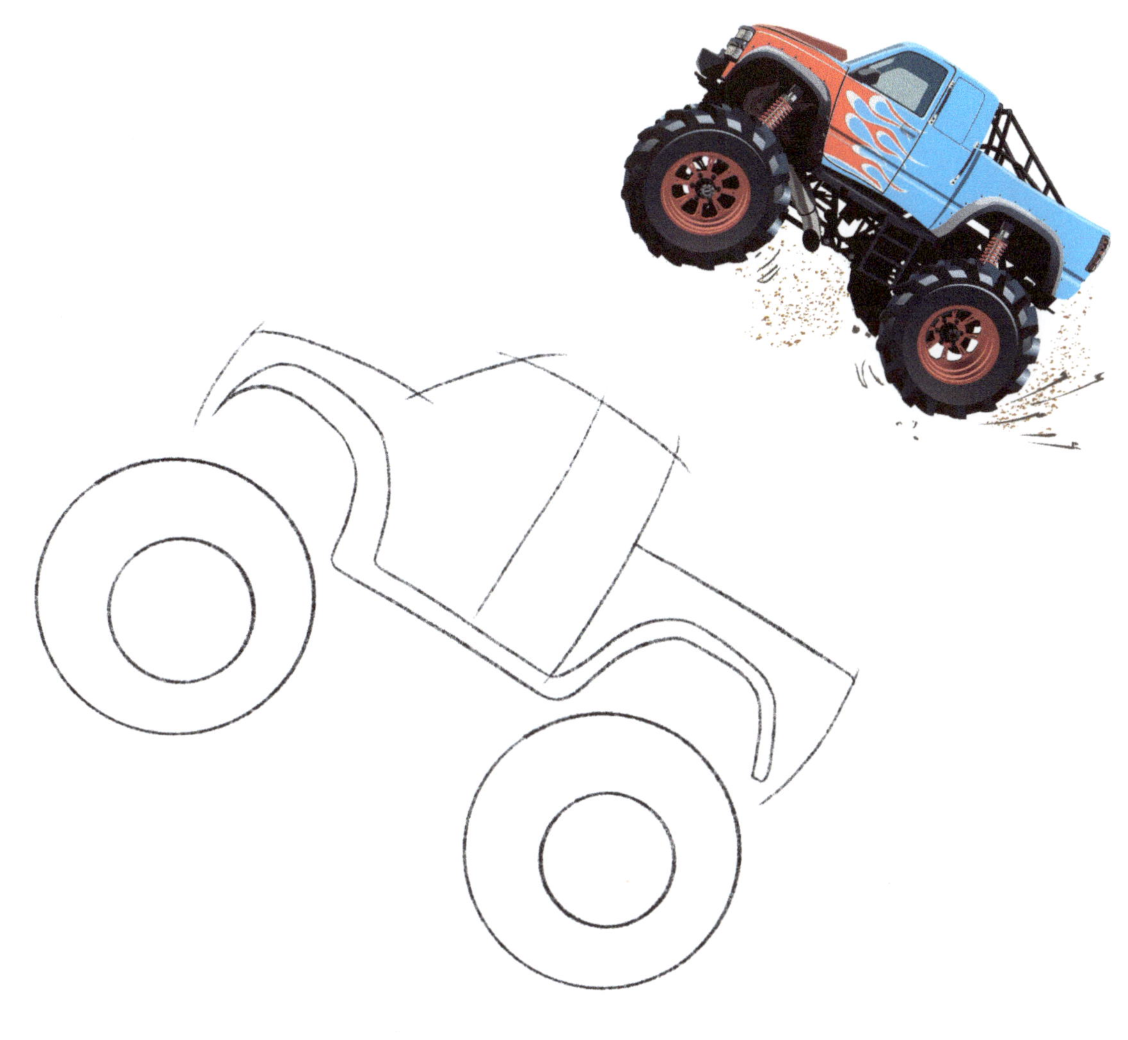

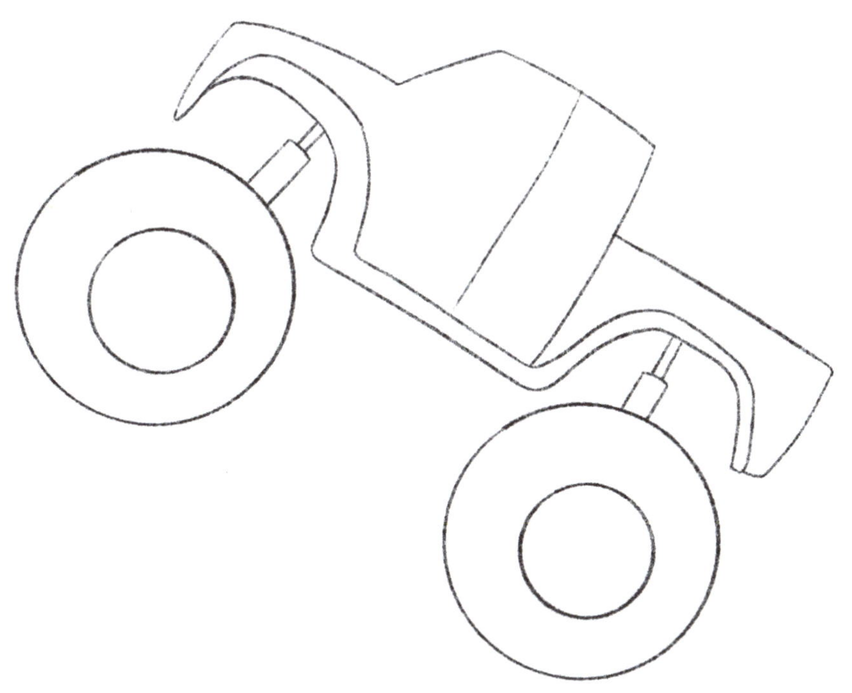

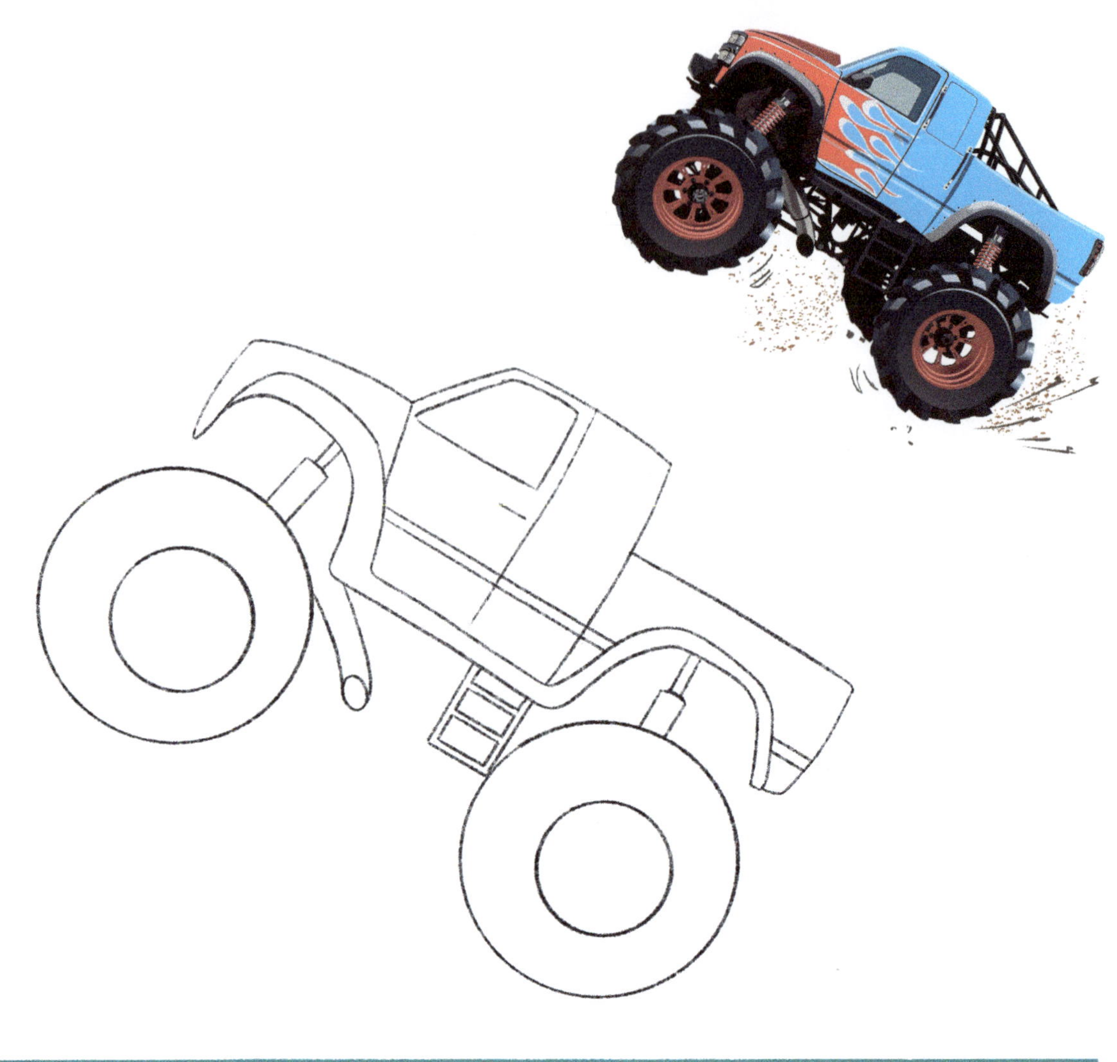

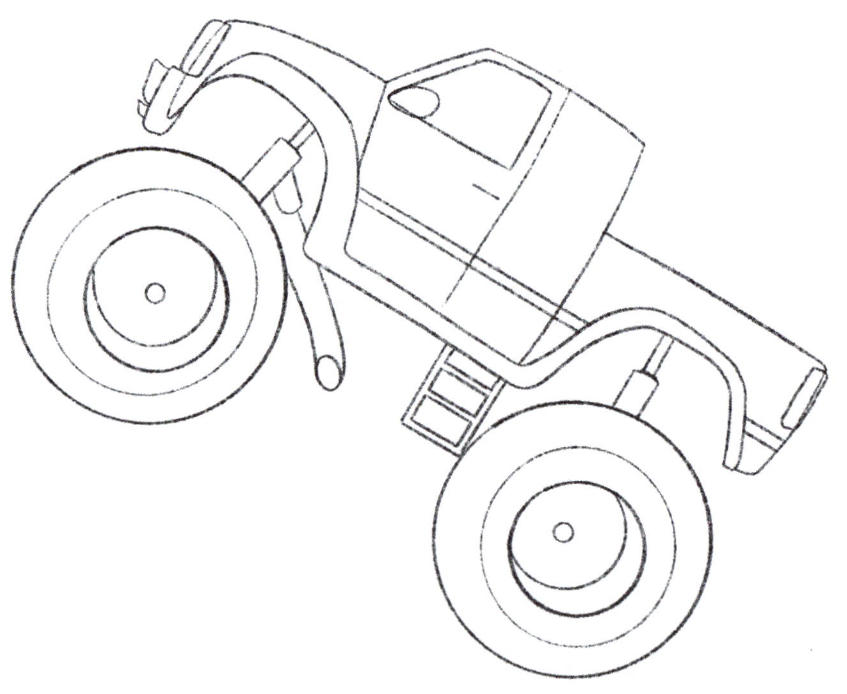

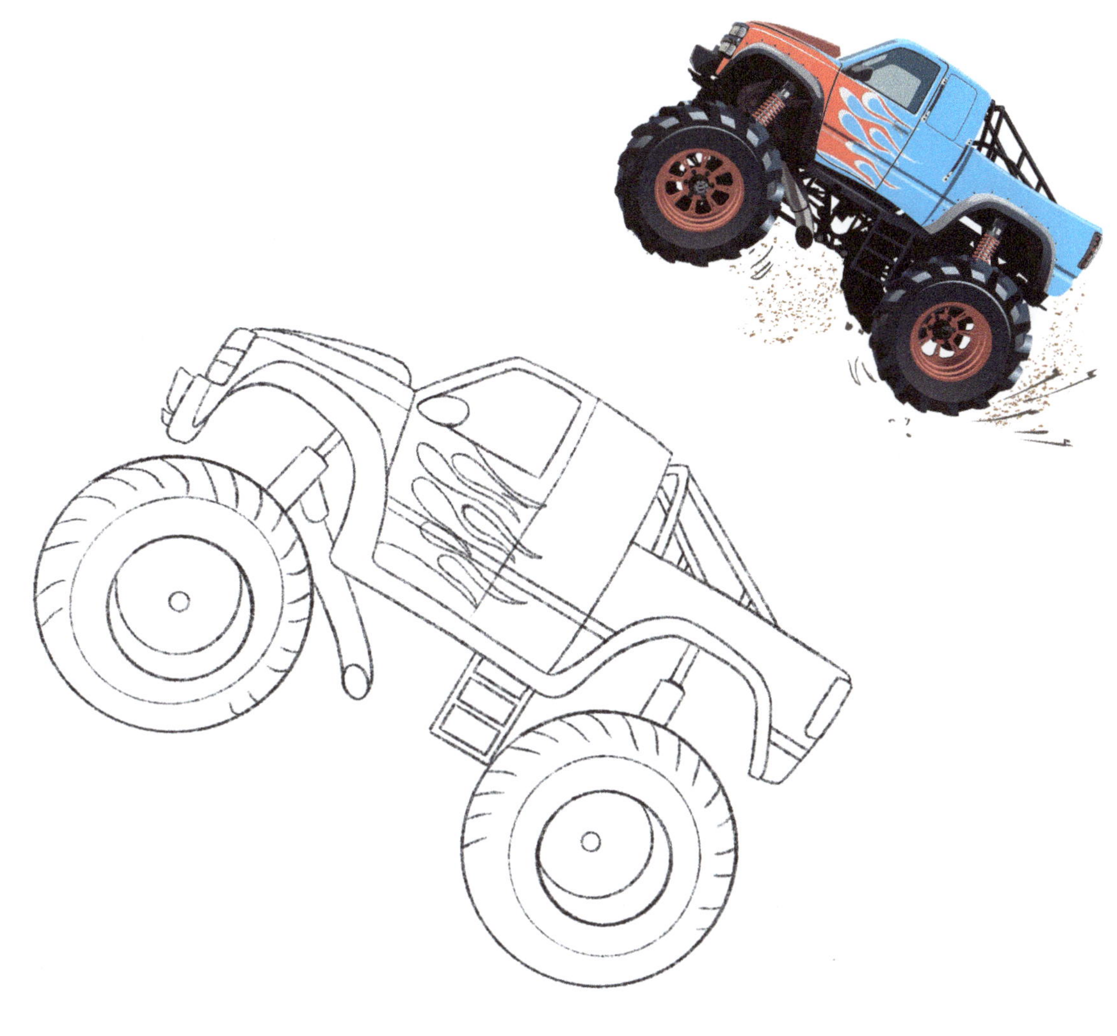

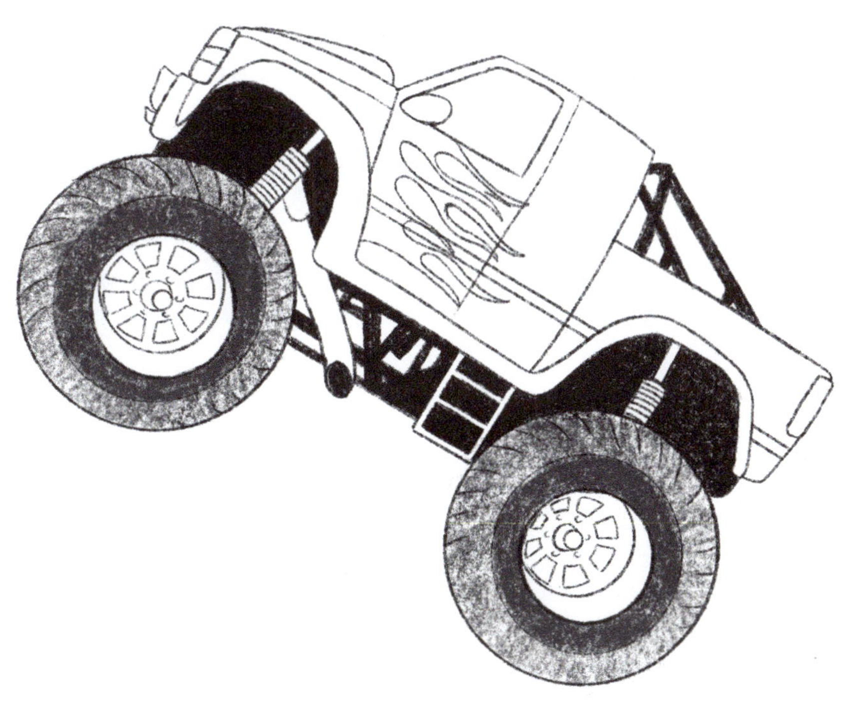

# Semi Trailer

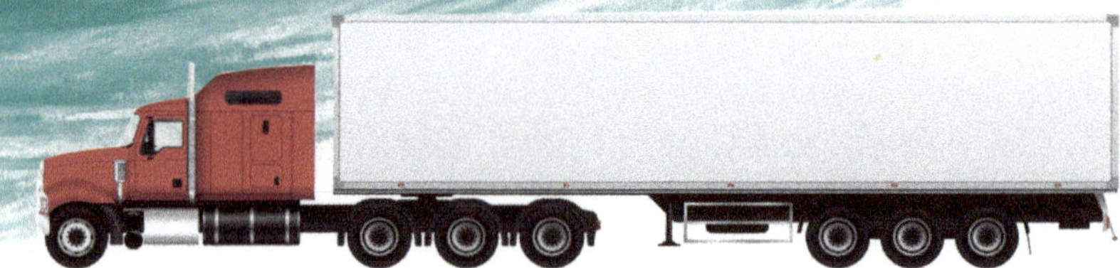

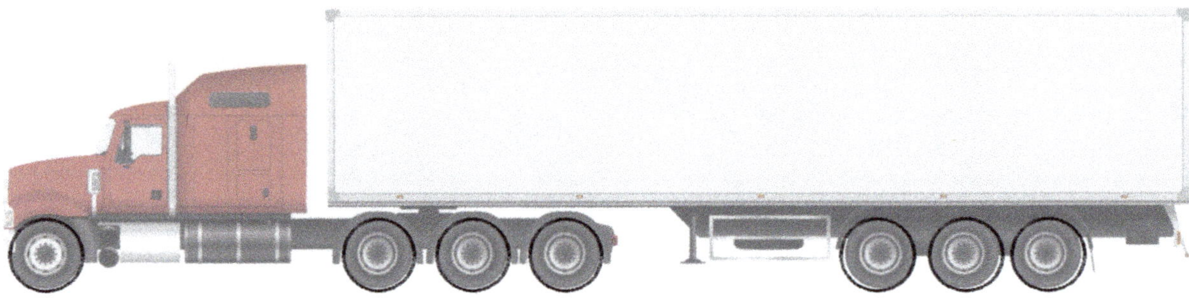

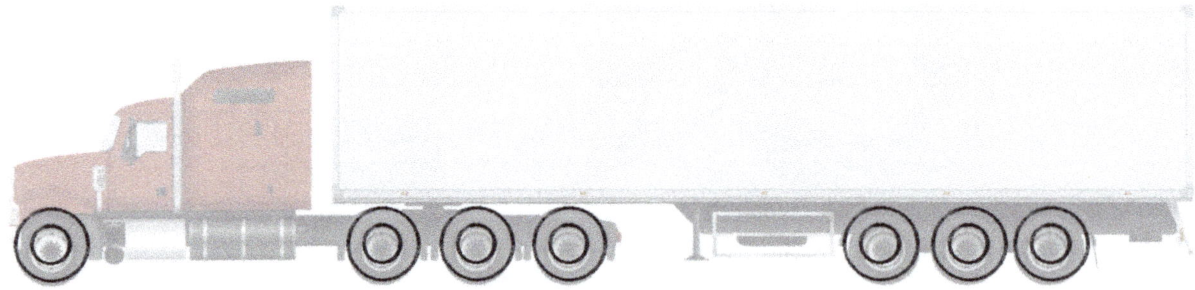

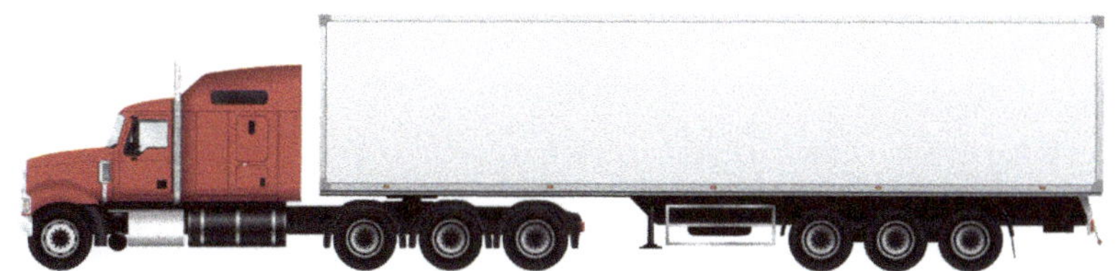

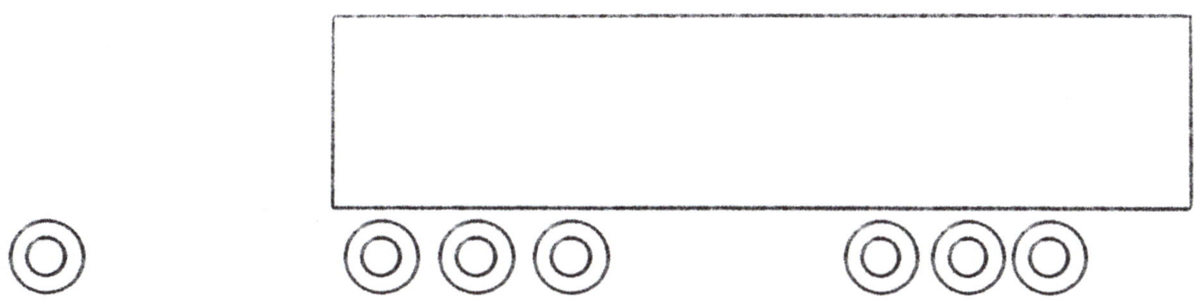

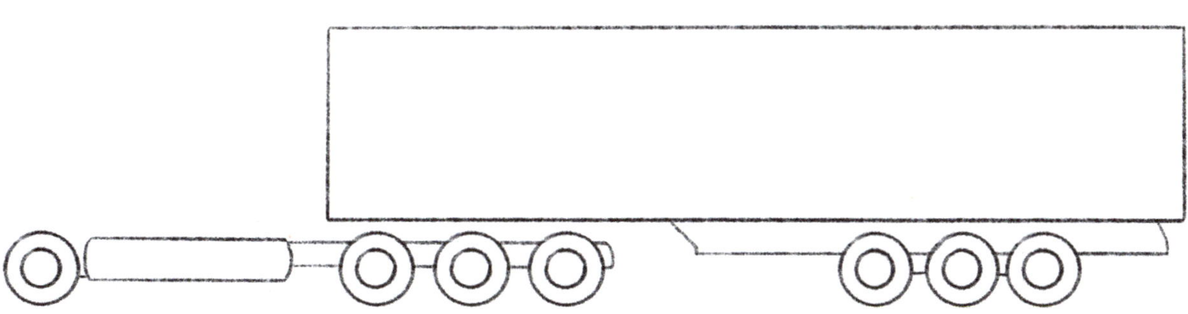

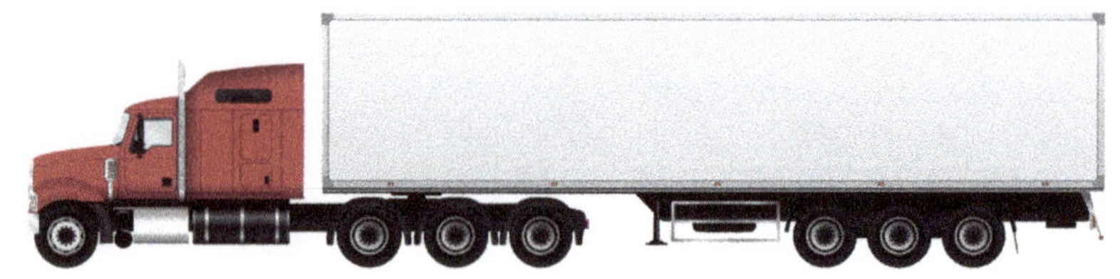

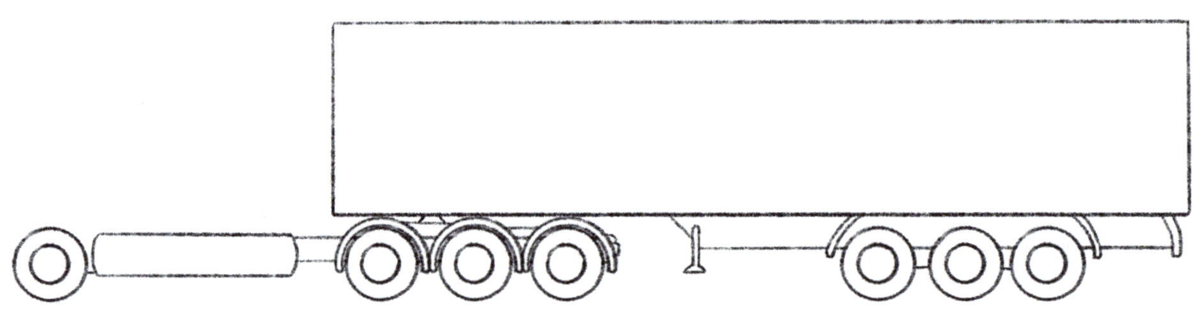

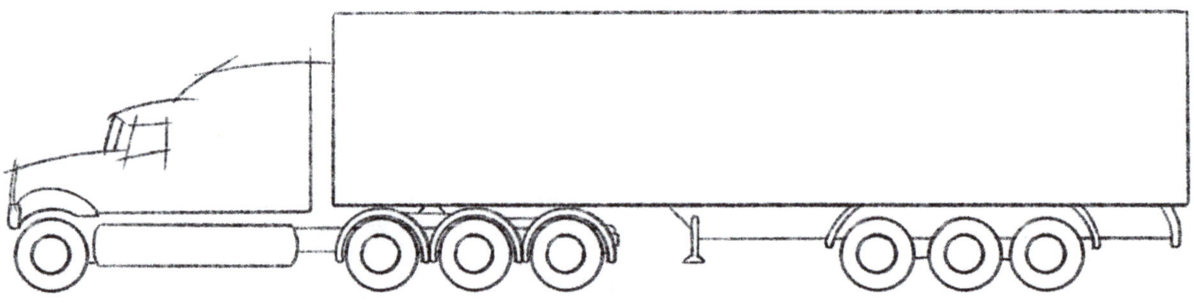

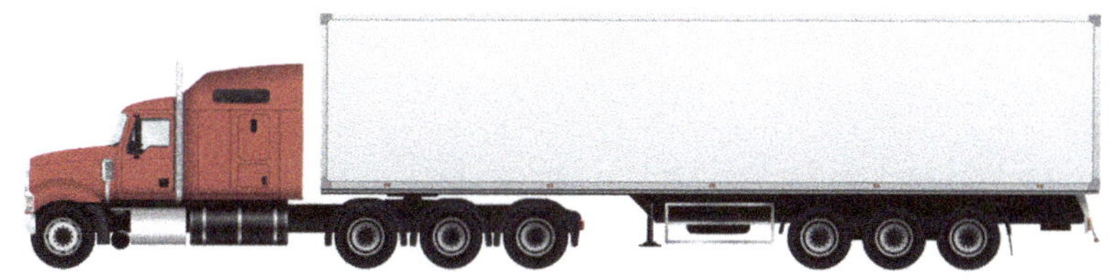

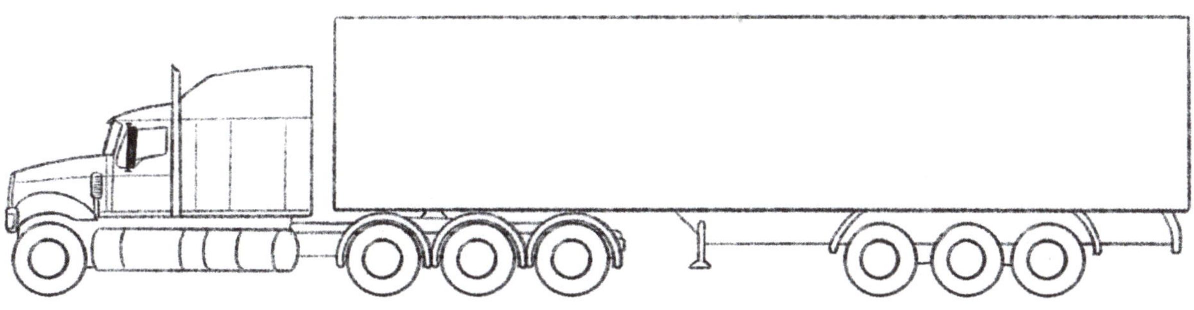

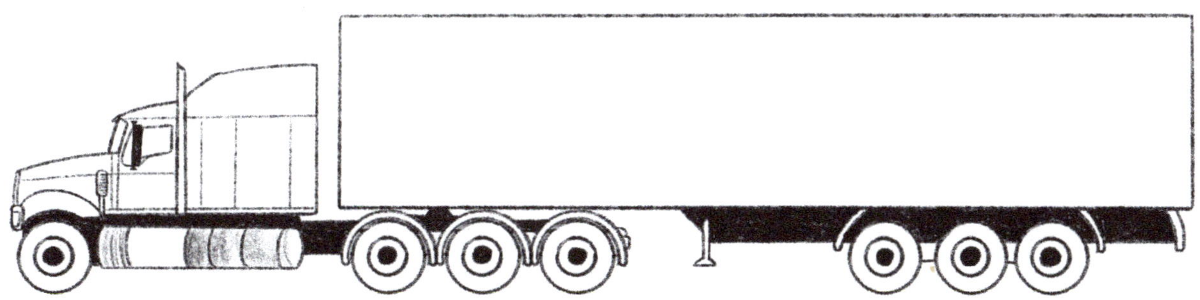

Congratulations on completing all three levels
of drawings in this book.

Remember to practice and practice some
more. Find your own reference photos and use
the techniques you have learned to create
amazing drawings from them.

The next part of this book covers advanced
techniques such as perspective and shading.

Let's go!

# Perspective and Shading

# Perspective

Perspectives can be difficult to grasp when first starting and require a lot of practice. There are numerous books that are dedicated JUST to perspective drawing so this is not a stand-alone guide by any means at all. In this chapter, I'll be helping you to understand the basic rules of perspective and how to use them to create drawings with depth and dimension.

There are six different types of perspective, but for this book we will concentrate on the two most popular, starting perspectives. One point perspective, and two point perspective. One point perspective has one vanishing point on the horizon, two point perspective has two vanishing points on the horizon.

Before we start drawing there are few terms to know:

Horizon line: the horizon line is found in the break between two parts of the picture… commonly land and sky. Imagining this line in different scenes will allow you to establish your perspective.

Vanishing point: This is the point on the horizon line where the objects disappear. Objects become smaller the further they are away and the vanishing point is the point where these things vanish.

Perspective lines: These are lines that can be drawn from the outside of a picture to the vanishing point. All lines should converge at the vanishing point and are used to help create guidelines for drawing in other details of the picture. You can use these lines to guide yourself when drawing in details of the picture.

There are three tips on perspective drawing:
 1 - Overlapping.
Draw some trees, but overlap them to create a sense of depth. Don't
worry if you don't know how to draw trees yet! Just draw simple ones.
 2 - Sizing and spaces.
The trees closest to the viewer-should be the largest, while the ones
furthest from the viewer will be smaller. Draw in perspective lines if
you need to help you with the proportions.
 3 - Details.
Details are going to be more prominent on objects closest to the
viewer. On the trees that are closest, draw more pronounced leaves.
On the trees that are the furthest, your leaves should be less detailed.
You can also use lighter values and softer strokes to create this sense
of depth in your drawing.

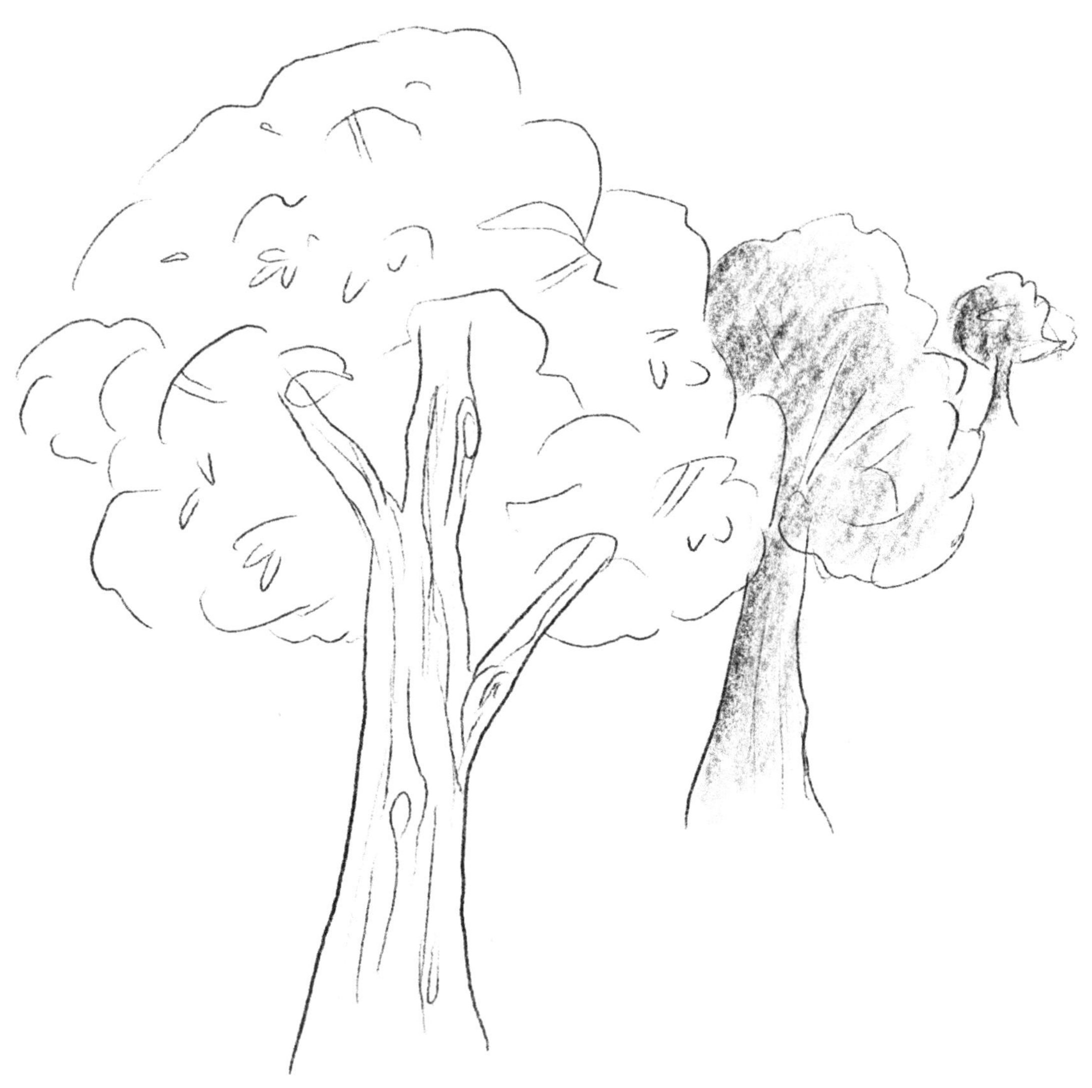

# One point perspective

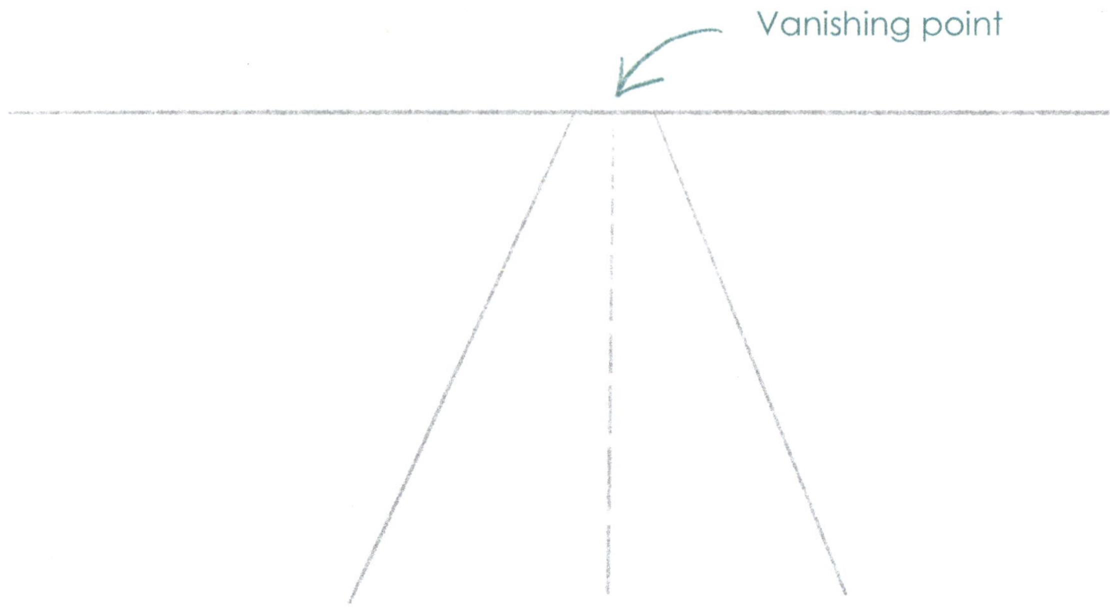



One point perspective has one vanishing point on the horizon.
The vanishing point can be anywhere on the horizon.

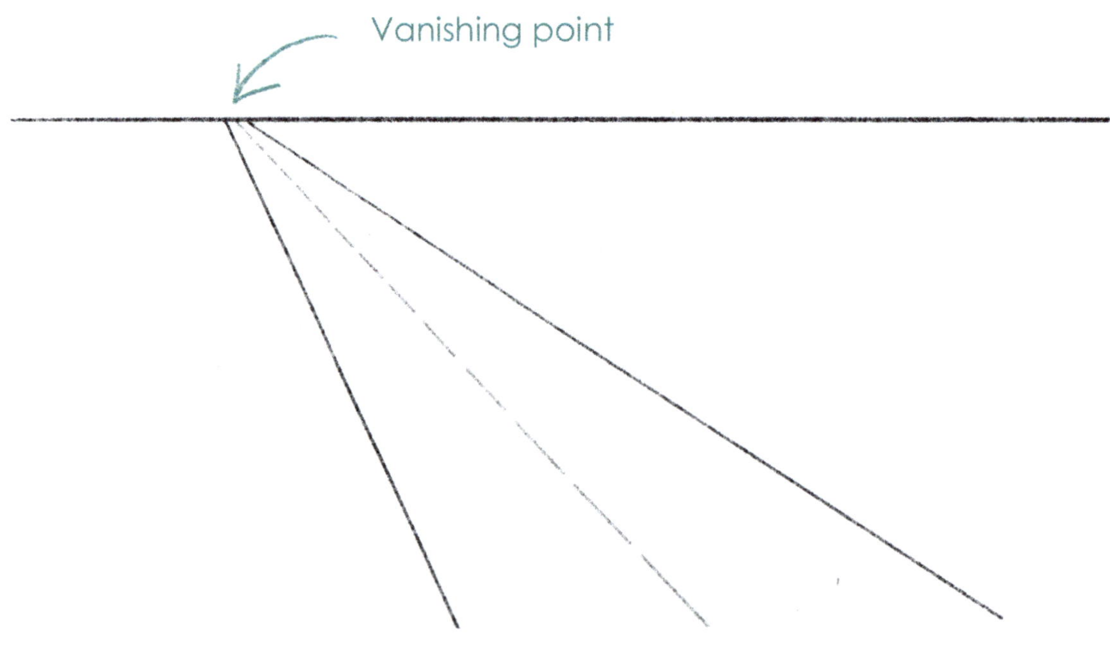

<h1 style="text-align:center">Two point perspective</h1>

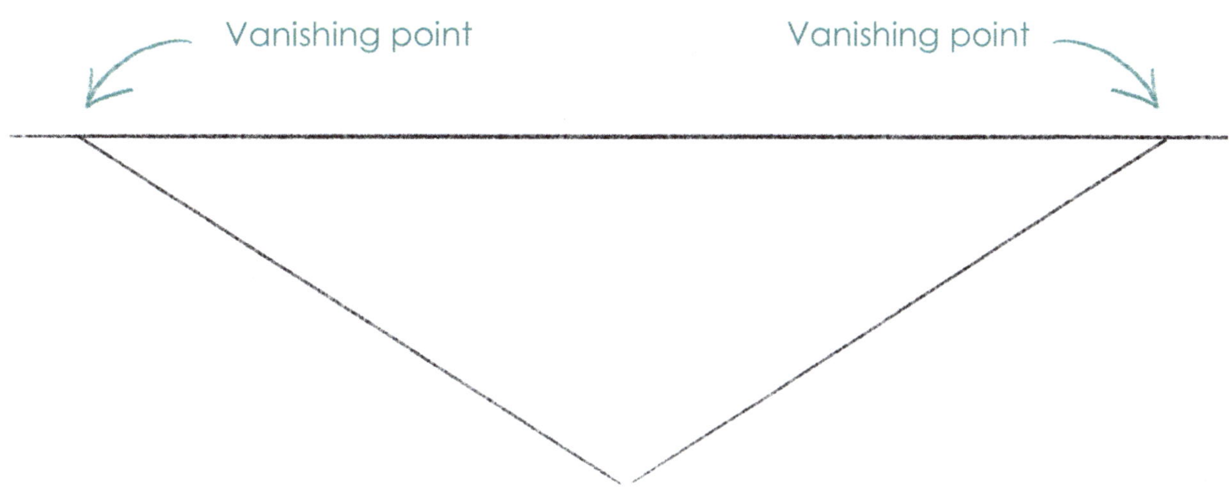


Two point perspective has two vanishing points on the horizon.
The vanishing points can run off the paper and still keep the effect.

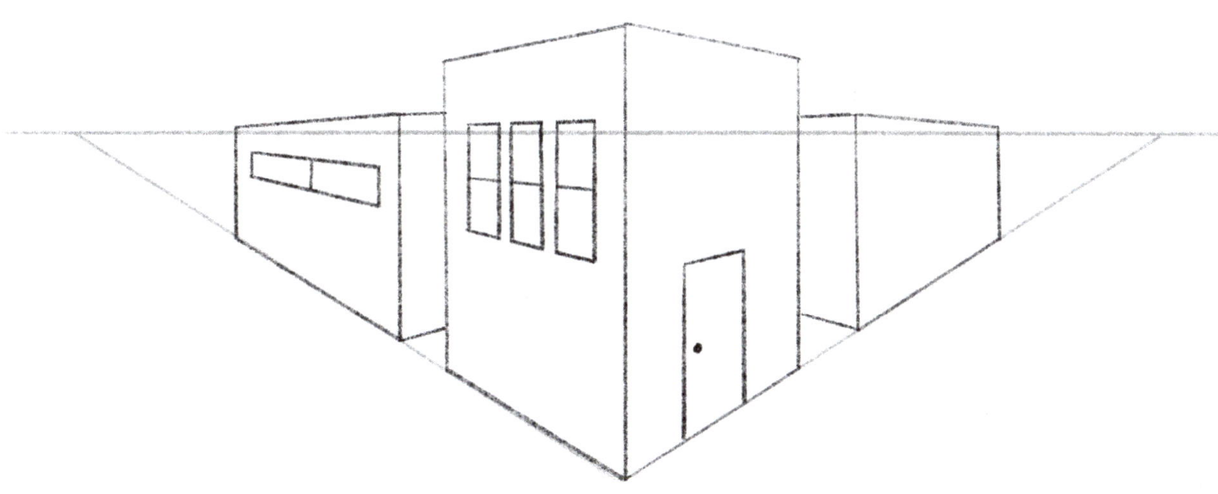

# Perspective practice

Draw your own landscape or street scenes using these horizon lines.
Add trees and other elements, practicing making them smaller as
they are further away.

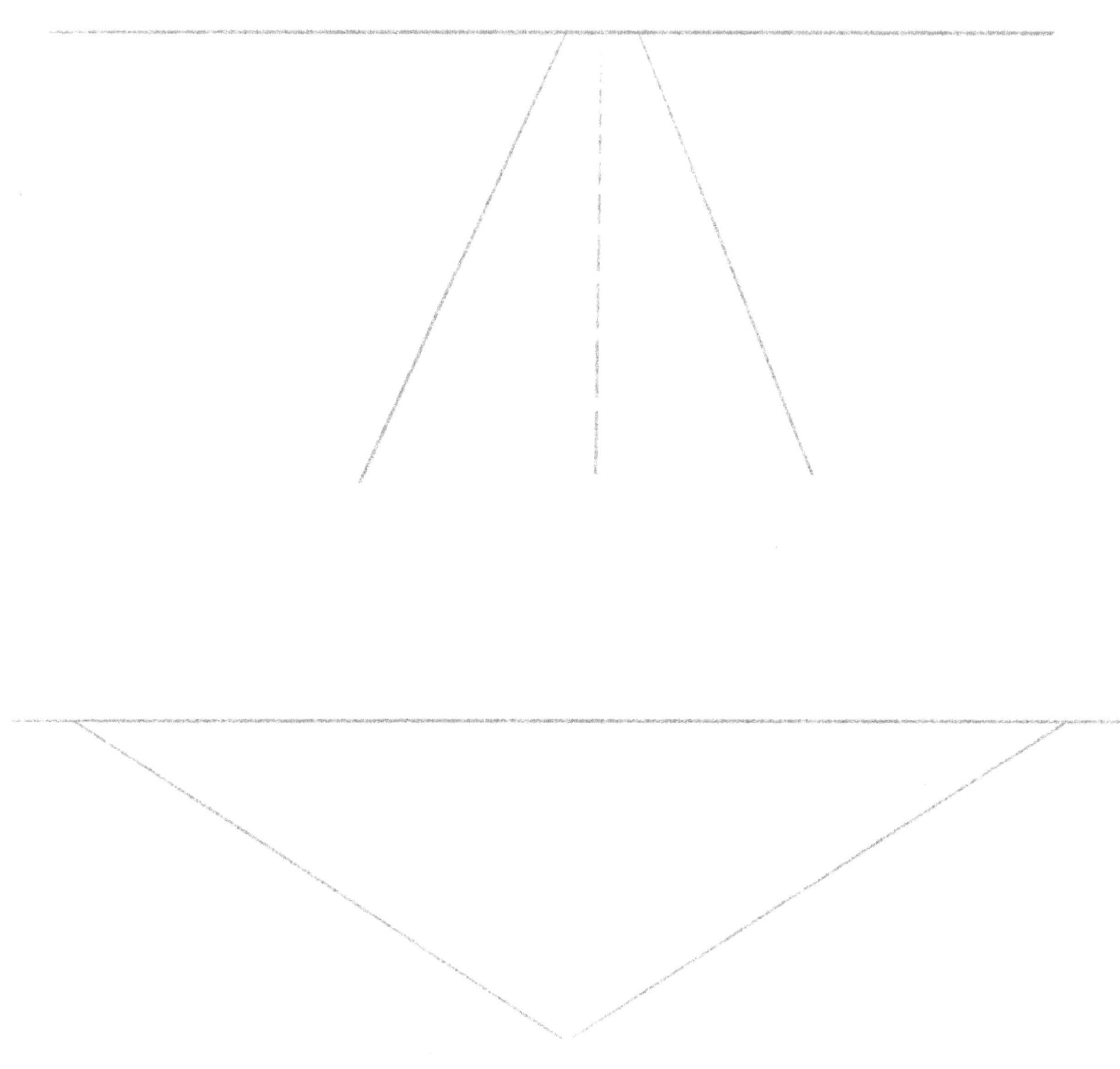

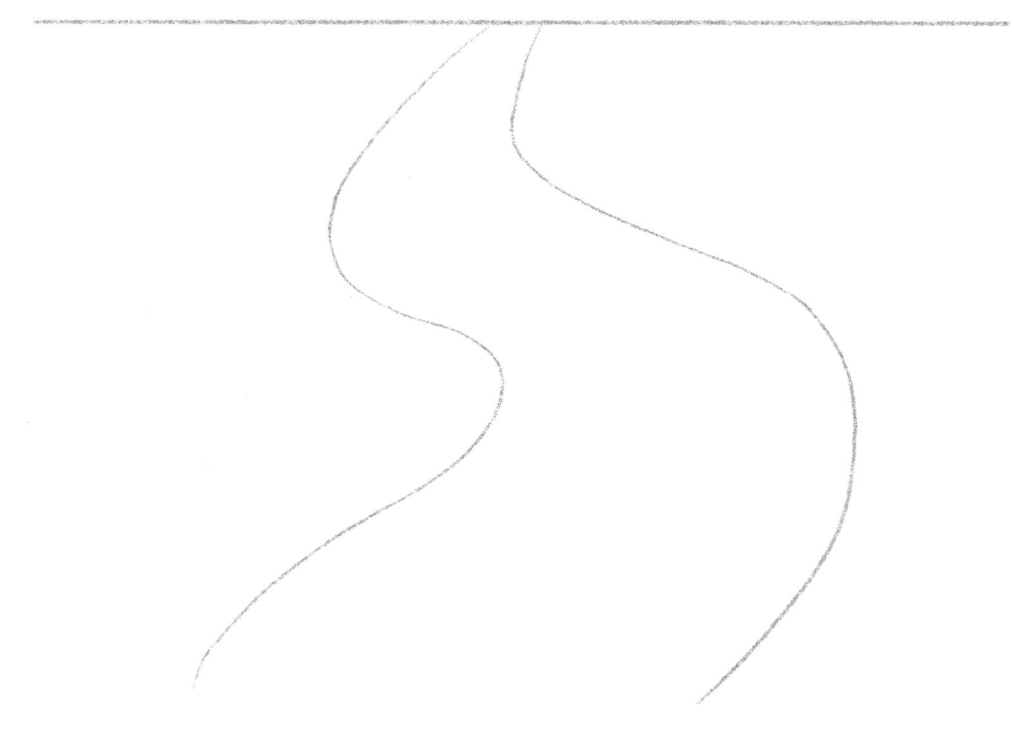

# Shading techniques

There are many different grades of pencils, but once you learn what the letters and numbers mean, you'll be able to choose the right pencil quickly. There are hard pencils and soft pencils.

HB is the most commonly used pencil, as it is right in the middle of the grades. As you go through the B's, the pencil lead becomes softer, and darker. This is because more graphite is released due to the pencil being softer.

If you go the other way, through the H's, the pencil lead is harder, and lighter, because less graphite is released.

You can remember it like this... H is for HARD, and B is for BLACK. Hard lead = lighter marks, and Black lead = soft, darker marks.

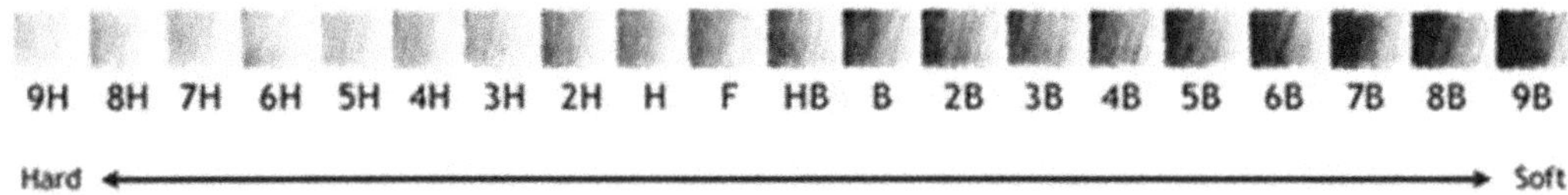


Hard pencils (H) produce sharp lines which are great for sketching out your picture, but are difficult to shade with and blend. Be careful how hard you press because they can easily indent paper.

Soft pencils (B) produce dark lines with less effort, making them ideal for smudging and blending. Be careful where your hand goes, as these pencils easily smudge and may leave marks on your paper (or your hands!) where you don't want them.

In this chapter we will be using HB, 2B, 4B and 6B. These are the easiest for younger students to learn with, as you don't need to press very hard to see their different effects.

Now we can move on to techniques. Shading makes a drawing go from a flat image to a 3 dimensional illusion.

There are three types of shading that you should know to commence your drawing journey.

HATCHING
CONTOUR
SCUMBLING

In the following examples note the direction of the light (coming from the right side).

## HATCHING

With hatching you are drawing parallel lines, varying the direction of the lines and layering them to obtain different levels of light and dark. Hatching includes 'cross hatching' like the image, or just parallel lines all going in the same direction.

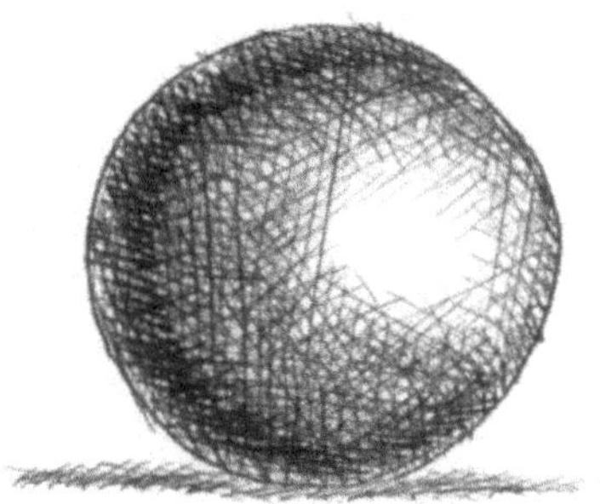

## CONTOUR

Contour lines follow the shape of what you are drawing.

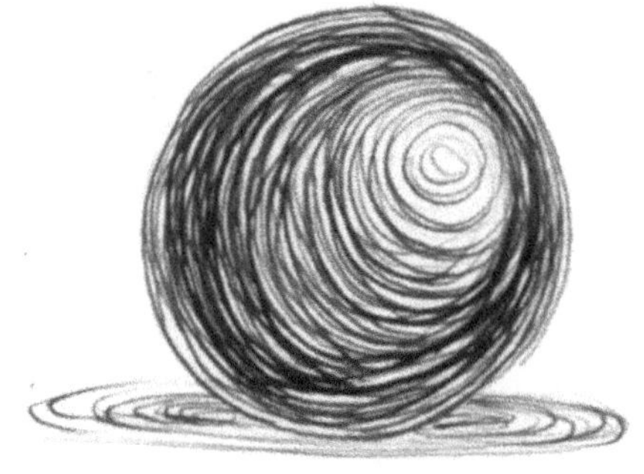

## SCUMBLING

Scumbling (or scribbling) is a fast way to shade a drawing, using smaller darker scribbles with bigger lighter scribbles.

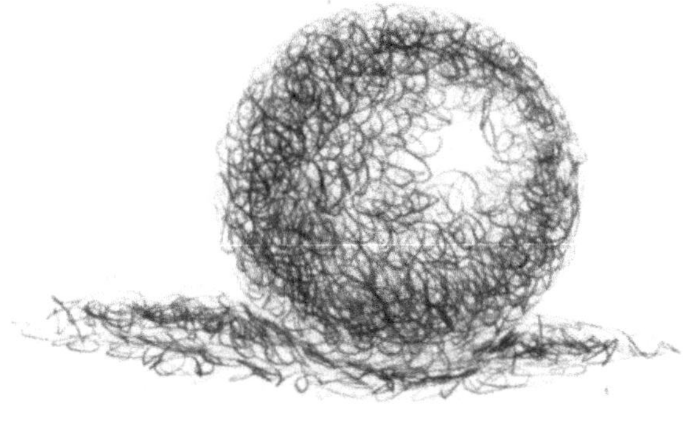

Another technique for shading is pressure control. Pressure control simply refers to how hard (or softly) you press down on your pencil.

For this exercise, implement the shading techniques in the previous lesson. Choose whether to use hatching, contour or scumbling, or practise the exercise with all three.

Exercise 1
Without lifting your pencil, or taking any breaks... draw lines back and forth from one side of your sketchbook to the other. Gradually increase the pressure as you go. The goal is a smooth gradient (transition from light to dark).

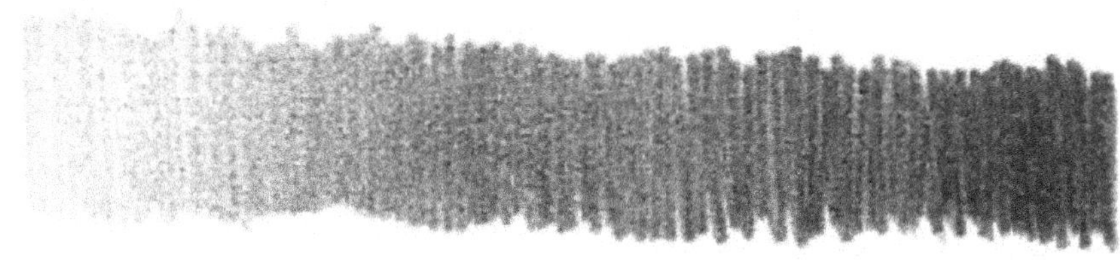

Exercise 2
Using a HB, 2B, 4B and 6B, shade in order from the hardest pencil to the softest. Your goal is to blend as seamlessly as possible, making it look like your pencils never left the page.

Shading practice

Here you can practice the techniques in this chapter.

# Be inspired!

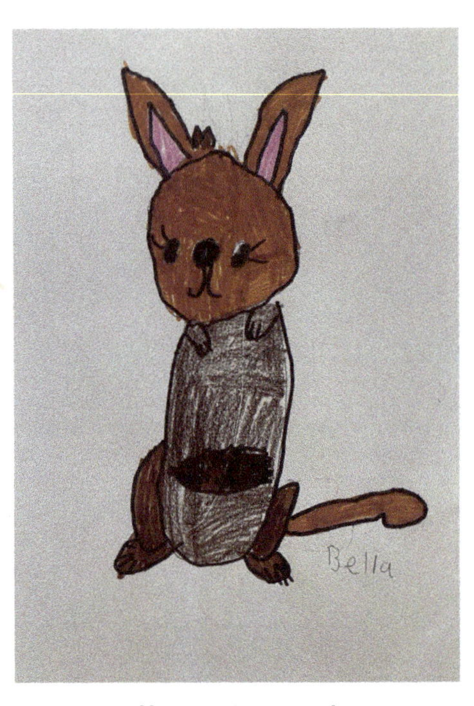

Bella Hayden

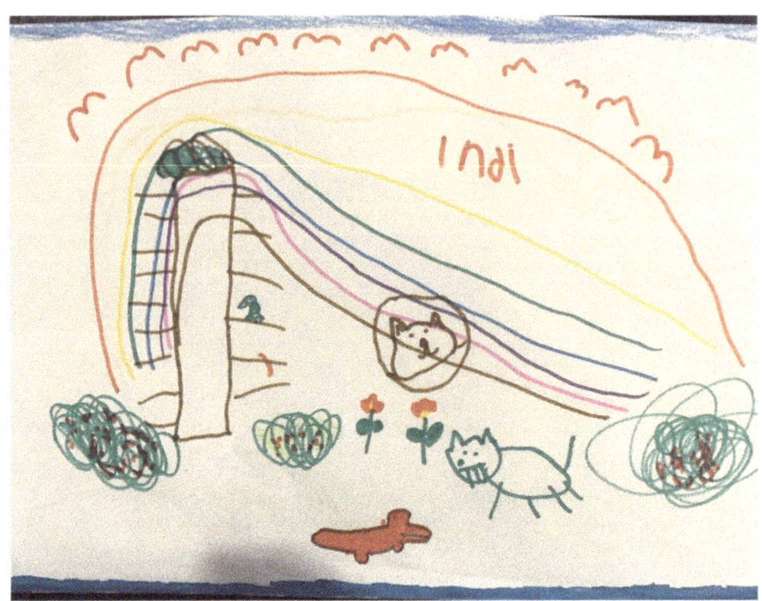

Indi Campagna

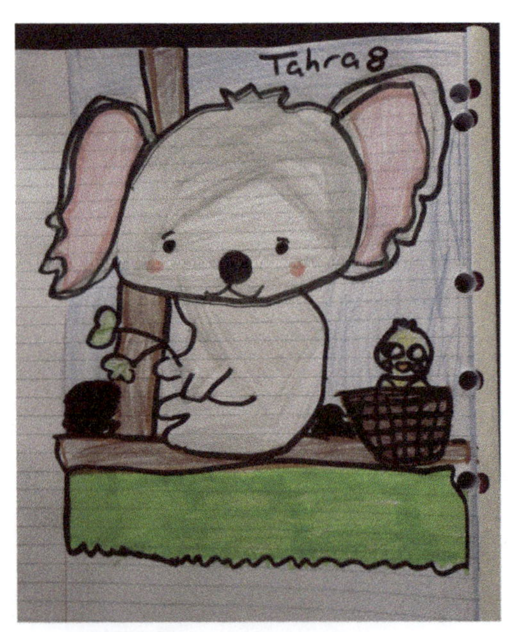

Tahra Gibbons

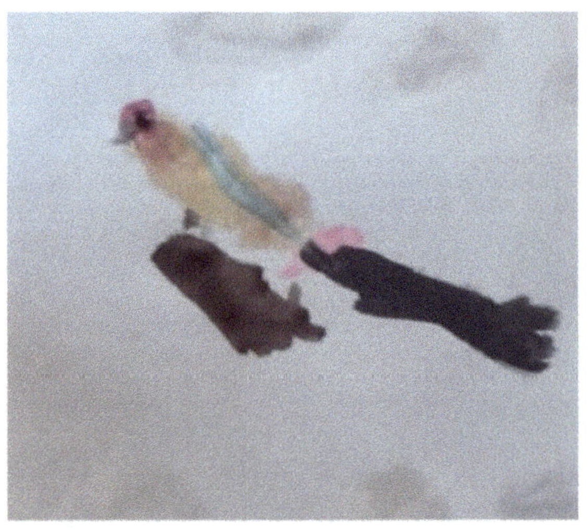

Mackenzie Greer

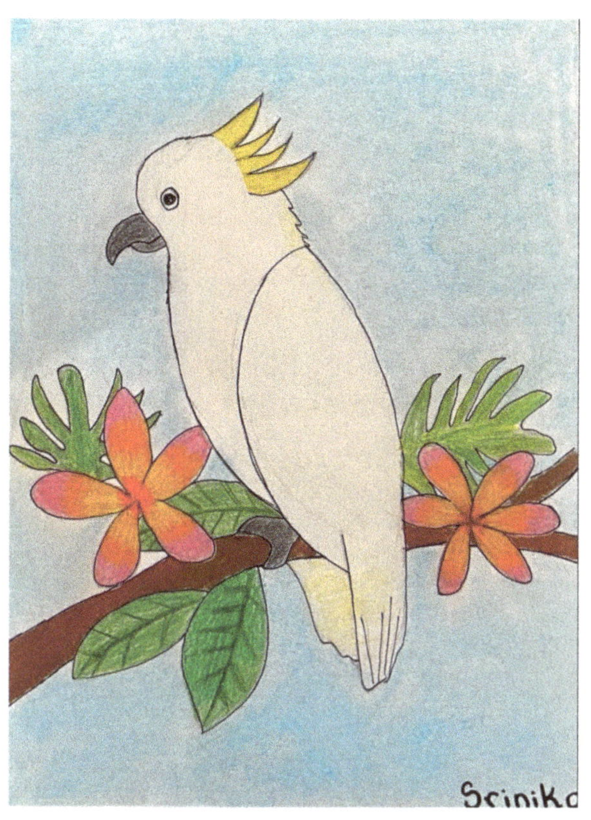

Srinka Karthik

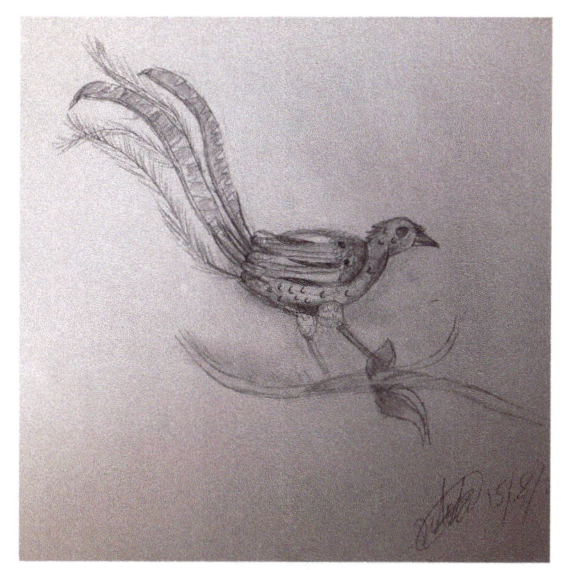

Dakota Tyson

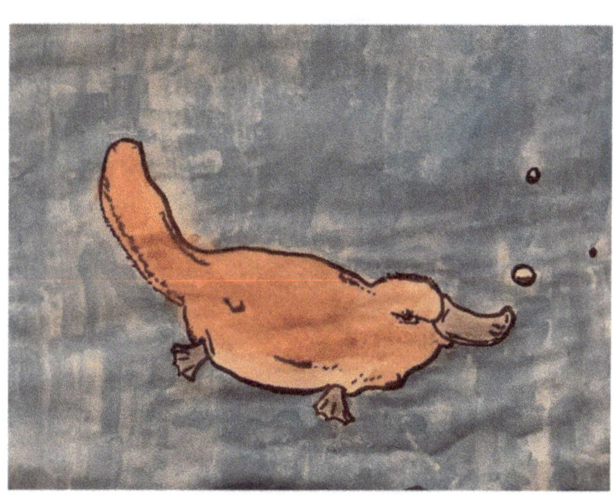

Mia Reynolds

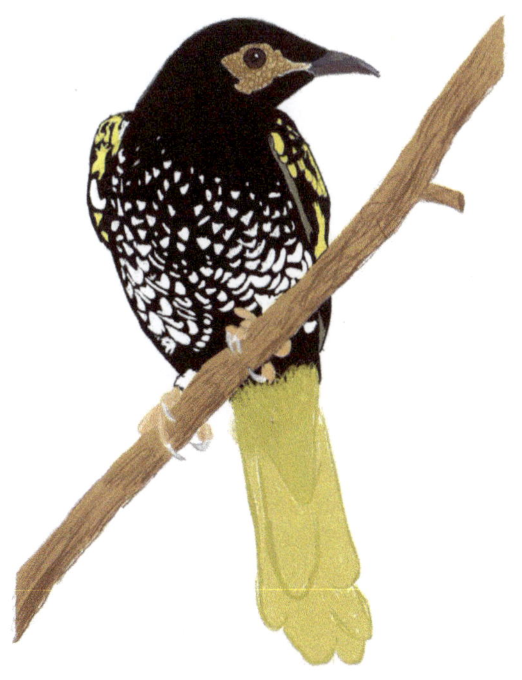

Hannah Gorman

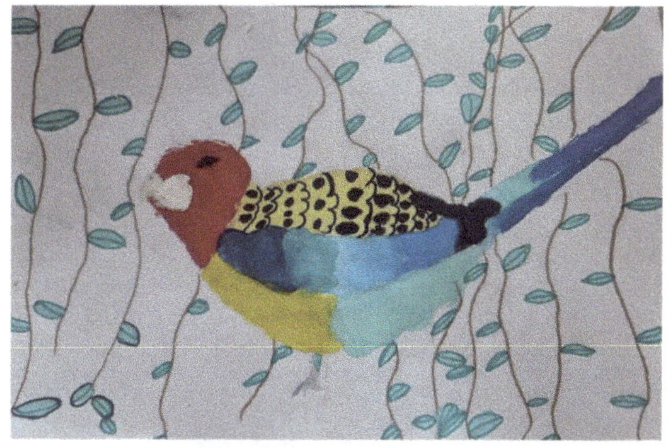

Bella Greer

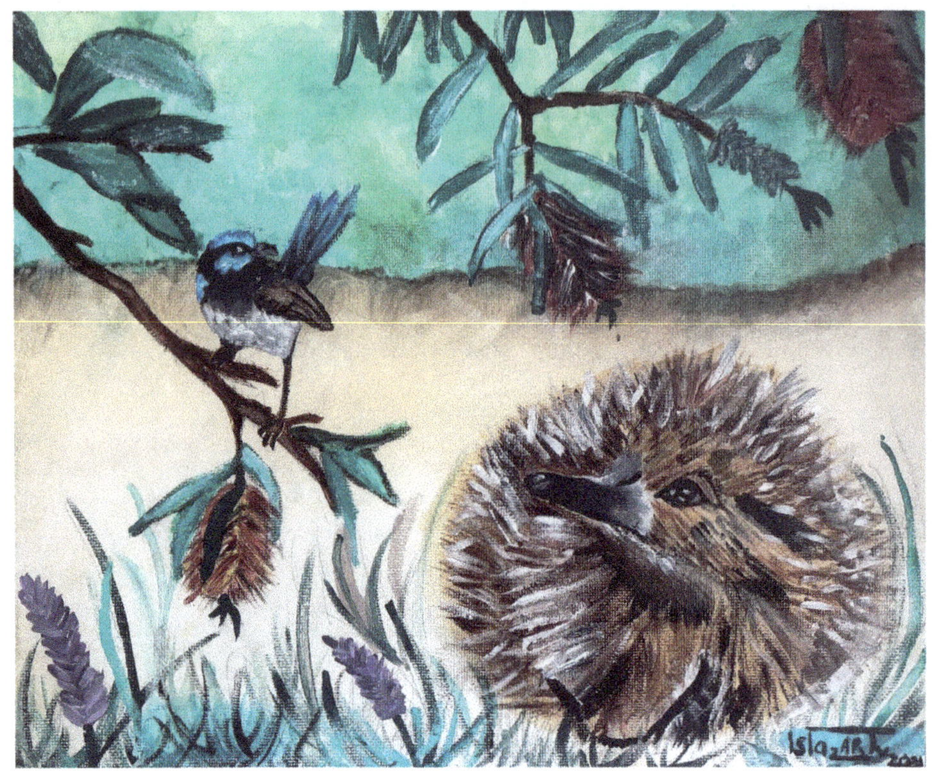

Isla Mondon

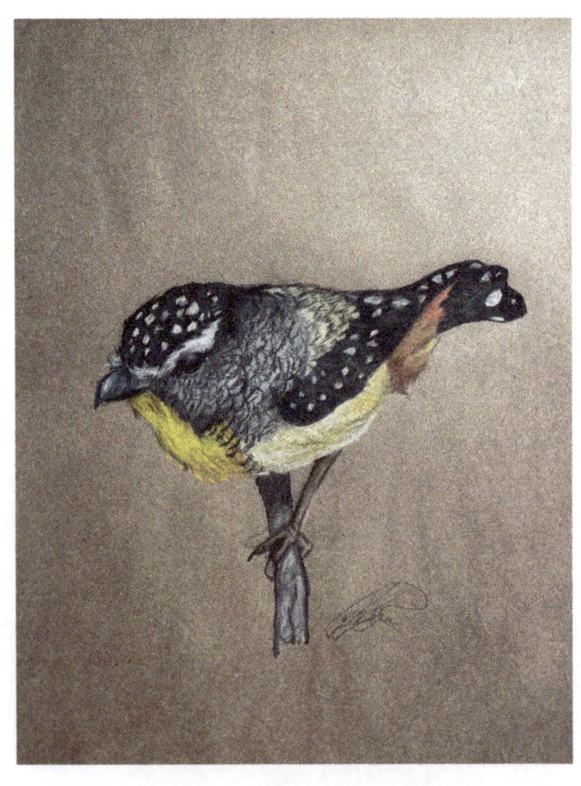

Ayla Johnston

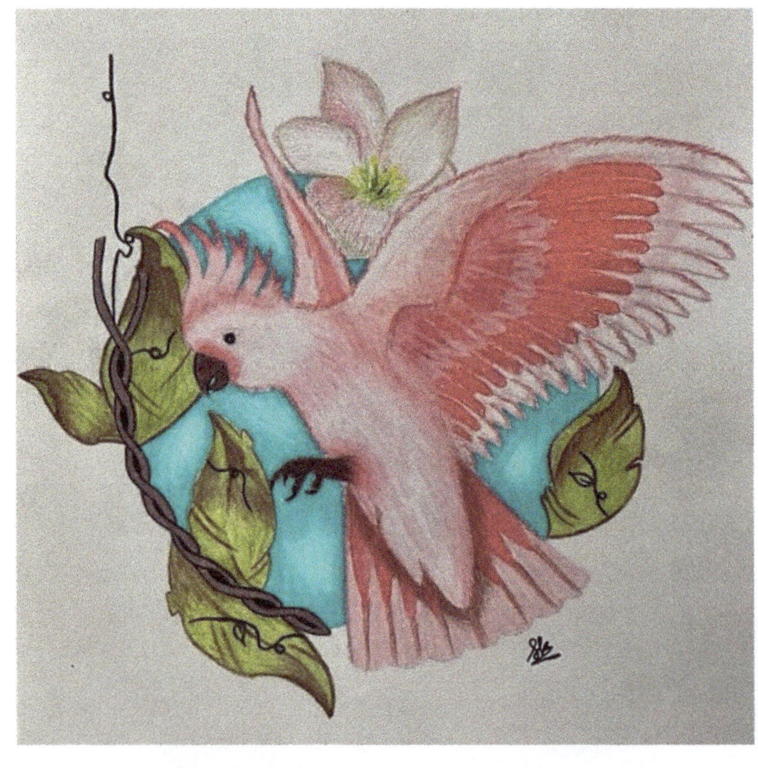

Sudhiksha Karthik

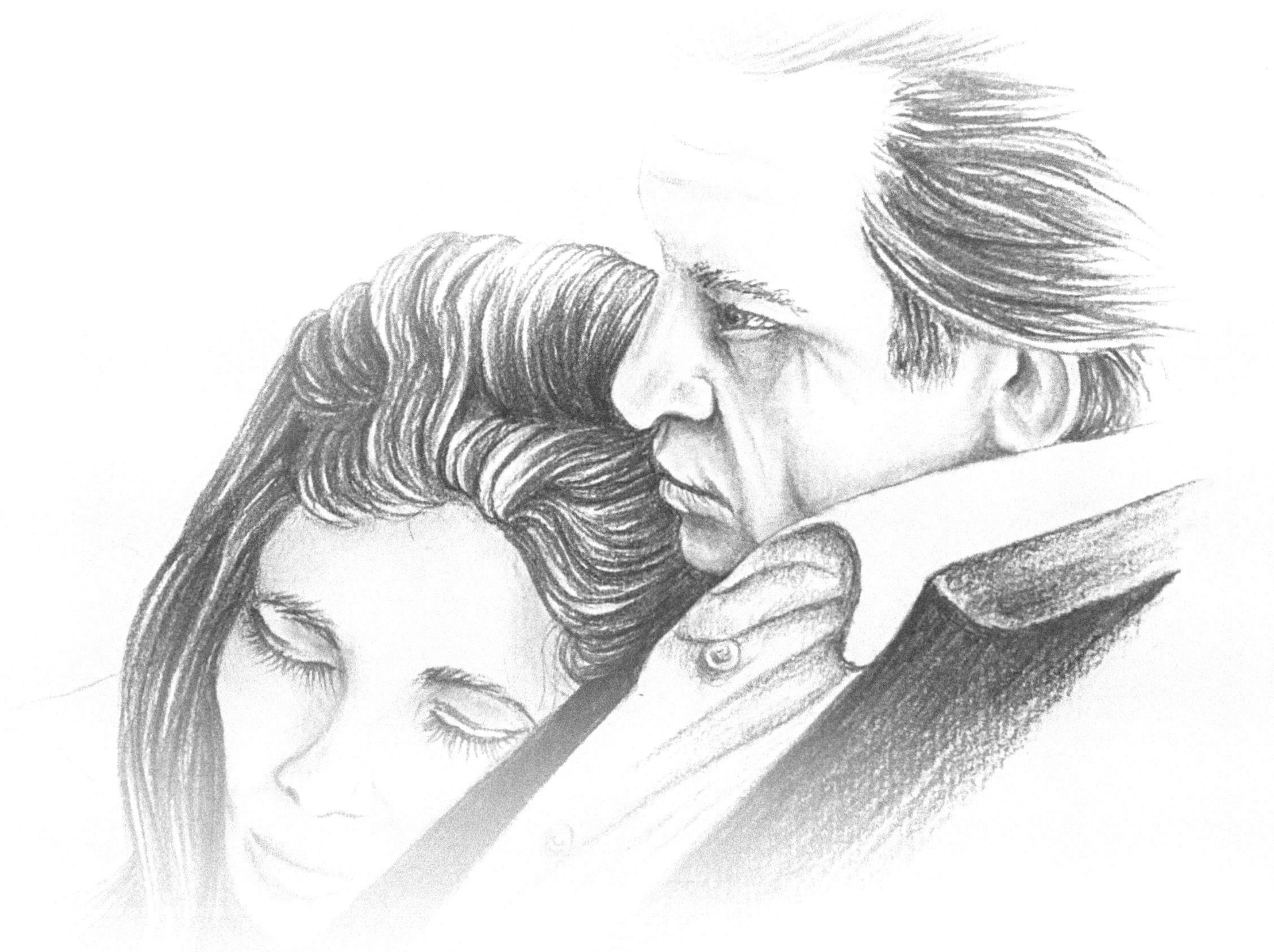

# Thank you

Thank you, and congratulations on reaching the end of the book! I hope you've enjoyed the tutorials, learnt a lot and had loads of fun.

I'd also like to thank the hundreds of you that check my Facebook page and website to see what I am up to all the time, your likes and kind words go a long way.

*Amy*

www.AmyCurran.com.au

*Image: Johnny Cash and June Carter Cash
by Amy Curran*